THE SIX-DAY WAR

THE SIX-DAY WAR

THE BREAKING OF THE MIDDLE EAST

GUY LARON

YALE UNIVERSITY PRESS
NEW HAVEN AND LONDON

For information about this and other Yale University Press publications, please contact:

U.S. Office: sales.press@yale.edu   yalebooks.com
Europe Office: sales@yaleup.co.uk   yalebooks.co.uk

Typeset in Minion Pro by IDSUK (DataConnection) Ltd
Printed in Great Britain by Gomer Press, Llandysul, Ceredigion, Wales

Library of Congress Control Number: 2016957143

ISBN 978-0-300-22270-8

A catalogue record for this book is available from the British Library.

10 9 8 7 6 5 4 3 2 1

CONTENTS

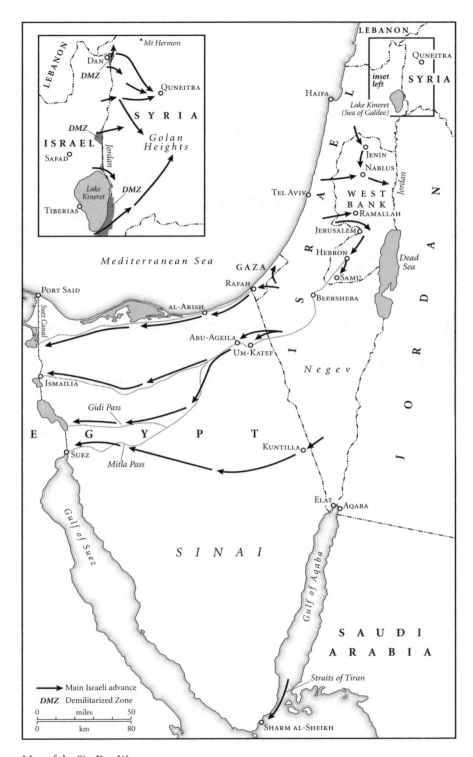

Map of the Six-Day War

PREFACE

I USED TO HATE books that started with the writer's admission that he wrote the book by accident. I could never understand how someone would complete "by accident" a project that demanded single-minded devotion and perseverance. Having said that, I wrote this book by accident; or rather as a result of several coincidences. The first happened in the summer of 2007 when I was in the last throes of writing my dissertation. Christian Ostermann, director of the Cold War International History Project (CWIHP) at the Wilson Center, invited me to participate in a book launch event that doubled as a conference on the 1967 Six-Day War. At the time, I was immersed in writing my dissertation on the 1956 Suez Crisis. Since a decade separated the two wars and I had only a short time to come up with something to say, I thought of refusing outright. But my wife, a far more practical person than I, politely pointed out that, as a jobless academic with cloudy prospects, it would be extremely foolish of me not to accept the invitation. In short, beggars can't be choosers. So, I sent back an e-mail confirming my participation and started to go over relevant documents in Czech and Arabic that were available to me.

The book I was supposed to comment on was titled *Foxbats over Dimona*. The authors, Gideon Remez and Isabella Ginor, claimed that the Soviet Union had planned the Six-Day War years in advance in order to stop the Israeli race toward a nuclear bomb by destroying the reactor at Dimona. The book's Soviet angle was the reason I was invited, together with other scholars, to comment on the book. Two years earlier I had written an article on the 1955 Czech–Egyptian arms deal that used East European archives to overcome the relative inaccessibility of Russian archives and the complete inaccessibility of relevant Arab archives. Since at the time very few people made use of East European archives to explore Middle Eastern history, I was sort of an expert.

I did not know what to make of *Foxbats over Dimona*. But the documents I had read before I left Israel painted a different picture. Soviet officials seemed rather surprised by the rapid turn of events in the Middle East. If there were signs of Soviet design, I could not find them. On the designated day I found myself seated on a panel that also included the authors and another Israeli professor, Yaacov Ro'i. In short, most of the people on the stage were Israelis who now had the chance to rehash an old internal Israeli debate in a foreign setting. If Remez and Ginor were right, then Israel did the right thing when it decided to attack its neighbors in June 1967. If they were wrong, the question of whether Israel was the aggressor was still in play.

After the event ended, several scholars approached me to ask about the documents I presented a few minutes earlier. They wondered if they could get a copy or a translation. It was at that moment that I realized there was something new in the documents I had unearthed a year earlier in the archives in Prague and in Egyptian memoirs I had found at the Library of Congress. In journalistic terms, I had a scoop. I decided then and there to produce an article of my own.

When I came back to Israel, things started to fall into place. Ehud Toledano, then director of the Graduate School of History, and Vice Rector Eyal Zisser, both at Tel Aviv University, helped me secure funding for a post-doctoral fellowship. The following months took me to archives in Prague, Berlin, Boston, and Washington. These research trips were generously funded by the Minerva Foundation, CWIHP, and, later on, the history department at Northwestern University. Mark Kramer of the Davis Center at Harvard, who is one of the leading scholars of the Communist bloc, was particularly helpful in guiding me through the RGANI holdings at the Lamont Library.

One of the more curious moments in my journey occurred in the Czech national archives, when I discovered that the document I was reading was a KGB memo. Those were still pretty rare. I had to look over my shoulder (twice!), but no commissar was there to protect the deceased empire's secrets. Certainly the proudest moment was when I raided the basement of the humanities building at Tel Aviv University, where Syrian materials captured by the IDF during the war had been kept, untouched, for thirty years. The yellow pages had gathered an extraordinary amount of dust. By the time I boarded the bus home, I looked like a coal miner.

I am grateful to the editors of *Cold War History* and the *Journal of Cold War Studies* who kindly enabled me to publish my first findings in 2010. The grants I received in the following years from the Israel Science Foundation, the German-Israeli Foundation, the Leonard Davis Institute for International Relations, and the Harry S. Truman Research Institute for the Advancement of Peace enabled me to further my interest in the Six-Day War. Thanks to that funding I was able to hire excellent research assistants such as Shiri Shapira, Olga Alekseev-Semerdjiev, Anat Vatouri, Emily Neilson, and Dina Skin. Avner De-Shalit, former dean of the social sciences at the Hebrew University, and Aharon Shai, then rector of Tel Aviv University, were especially helpful in facilitating the funds needed to take a sabbatical, which I spent in 2014–15 at St. Antony's College, University of Oxford, as a visiting fellow.

St. Antony's was the right place to start the writing process. Eugene Rogan, the director of the Middle East Center, was a wonderful host. Two eminent scholars at Oxford – Avi Shlaim and Avner Offer – worked closely with me and helped me produce a well-crafted book proposal. I am very grateful to them for their good advice. During that year I also received excellent feedback from Walter Armbrust, Oscar Sanchez-Sibony, Nathan Citino, Robert Vitalis, Arne Westad, Oren Barak, and participants of the LSE's international history seminar and the Middle East Centre's seminar. I should also thank Lorenz Lüthi for pushing me in the past few years to internationalize the story of the war. The two workshops he organized at McGill in 2010 and 2013 were congenial venues to try out new ideas.

If it weren't for Heather McCallum and Rachael Lonsdale from Yale University Press, it might have taken me another six years to write the book about the Six-Day War. But once a deadline was firmly set and the awesome opportunity to publish with Yale presented itself, I threw myself into full writing mode. I want to thank them both for expertly shepherding the editing and publication process. Safra Nimrod and Beth Humphries have also helped to improve the text.

I owe the deepest debt of gratitude to those close and near. Thank you, Sharon, for being there for me every step of the way, emotionally and intellectually. It meant the world to me. We made this book together and hopefully there will be more adventures to share. Tal, as we both know, the Six-Day War has accompanied you for too many years. As a baby I tried to make you laugh by blurting out the name of the Egyptian minister of war (never worked) and as a toddler I cured your bouts of insomnia by telling you about the 1966 Baath coup (worked like magic). I am putting this project to bed now, but I hope to develop a new set of obsessions pretty soon.

Tel Aviv, October 2016

FROM THE LOCAL TO THE GLOBAL

FOLLOWING THE WAR for Palestine in 1948 and the Suez War in 1956, the third round of Arab–Israeli conflict was a rather brief affair. It lasted just six days, but its fate had been decided in an even shorter time. During the first three hours of June 5, the opening day of the Six-Day War, Israeli aircraft wiped out the entire air forces of Egypt, Syria, Jordan, and Iraq. From that point on, Arab armies had to operate without air cover, totally exposed to incessant bombardment by the Israeli Air Force. That made the war as consequential as it was short. Over six days, the Israel Defense Forces transformed the map of the modern Middle East by capturing the Sinai Peninsula, the West Bank, and the Golan Heights. As a result, after June 1967 Israel tripled in size, controlling a regional empire stretching from the banks of the Suez Canal in the west to the Jordan River in the east, and from Sharm al-Sheikh, jutting deep into the Red Sea, to the snowy peaks of Mount Hermon, within sight of the suburbs of Damascus. The Middle East would never be the same again.

War is one of the most destructive things that humans can do to one another. Beyond the ruined cities, the graveyards, the blood-soaked gurneys, the invalids, the orphans, the widows, and the refugees, there is the emotional sediment of trauma and fear that passes from generation to generation. It's no wonder, then, that scholars throughout the ages have tried to understand why and how wars occur. Looking for answers to this question by studying the June 1967 Six-Day War is, however, a somewhat novel approach. Most histories of this conflict attempt to understand how this brief but significant clash grew out of specific Middle Eastern circumstances. To a lesser extent, the international or Cold War context might be referred to. Historians seem to be in agreement that the prelude to and eruption of the Six-Day War was at root inadvertent – the result of a series of miscalculations and misunderstandings.[1] This assumption explains why all the books about the Six-Day War seek to understand its origins and consequences by exploring the short period between May 15, when a regional crisis started, and June 10, when the war ended.

This study takes a different approach, arguing that the process that led to the war was not only much deeper, much longer, and influenced by global trends, but also that it was designed and even desired by prominent military figures in the warring countries. It emerged out of a global crisis, which engulfed the developing world in the 1960s and shifted the balance of power between civilians and generals in Israel, Egypt, and Syria. This crisis also caused the Soviet Union and the US to increase their arms sales and their military presence in the Middle East. In turn, these changes exacerbated existing tensions in the region and made war more probable. The Six-Day War's crucible of weak civilian leaderships, trigger-happy generals, and intrusive great powers provides a salient example of how a regional conflict may start.

These processes had been going on for years before the Six-Day War actually occurred. It is for this reason that this book is devoted to a long-term inquiry into the roots of the war. In some cases it traces the story back as far as the post-World War II period to explore the rise of domestic politics and the creation of international entanglements that made the region a ticking bomb. In this book, the war is not seen as a historical accident but rather as the meeting point of various historical trends, some regional, some global, each wending its own meandering way but, once coalescing, causing the drums of war to beat louder and faster.

Patterns

In presenting a comprehensive explanation of the Six-Day War's origins, two features in the story must be emphasized. The first is the antagonistic relationship between the civilians and the generals. The conflict between the Israeli cabinet and the IDF's General Staff was mirrored on the other side of border in Egypt, where as early as 1962 President Gamal Abd al-Nasser felt he had lost control over the army.[2] During 1965–67 he found it hard to withstand the pressure applied by Abd al-Hakim Amer – his vice president and supreme commander of the Egyptian Armed Forces – to remilitarize Sinai. And in Syria, the army actually took matters into its own hands by launching two military coups in 1963 and in 1966.

From that point onward, Syria's policy toward Israel became much more confrontational.

In short, the three major combatants of the Six-Day War saw their generals leaning on civilians to take belligerent action. That in itself is not entirely surprising. The copious literature on civilian–military relations predicts some degree of friction between the two parties due to their different roles and life experiences. As a rule of thumb, generals hold a conflict-centered worldview and are quicker to resort to force in response to international crises. They tend to support an offensive doctrine that enhances the army's prestige, autonomy, and resources. Civilian leaders, however, are prone to seek international cooperation and practice diplomacy to resolve conflicts. They also strive to limit the resources allocated to military use to enable spending on social services, which helps to buy electoral support. The theory of civilian–military relations also assumes that this inherent tension is better managed in developed democracies than in developing dictatorships. In North America and Western Europe, civilians may rely on a robust civil society and strong state agencies (the police, secret services, education, and so on) to tame the military. In contrast, Third World countries possess weak institutions and strong armies. Many armed forces in Africa and the Middle East originate in the pre-independence era, when they engaged in struggles against colonial governments; this granted them prestige and strengthened the military tendency to disobey civilians, who were, traditionally, part of the colonial administration. In addition, civil society tends to be weaker in post-colonial countries, which accept the rule of the gun indifferently.[3]

To some degree this explains the different patterns of civil–military relations in Israel, Egypt, and Syria. In Israel, the most developed of the three, the government had to respond to strong pressures exerted by the military during the 1960s but it was not, nor had it ever been, in real danger of being removed from power. In Egypt, the most industrially developed Arab country, Nasser's fear of a coup made him take risks he would not have taken otherwise: the decision to defy Israel in May 1967, which Nasser tried earlier to avoid, is a prime example. In Syria, the least developed of the three countries, a coup had occurred and the country had been effectively under military rule since 1966. As we shall see, civil–military relations in Syria, Egypt, and Israel were fraught with tension ever since the late 1940s. Nevertheless, confrontation between politicians and officers became more acute in all of these countries during the 1960s. The fact that these internal processes happened almost simultaneously in the three countries suggests that domestic politics alone cannot explain the turn of events that translated into the Six-Day War.

This should draw our attention to the second factor: the pervasive issue of balance of payments crises. From 1962 onward, Egypt had been buying from the world more than it was selling to it. Israel had the same problem, and for that reason both Nasser and Prime Minister Levi Eshkol implemented recessionary measures in 1965, triggering an economic slump that eroded their popularity. But while Israel's unemployed brandished placards with the slogan "Bread! Jobs!" as they marched in the streets, Egyptian workers and farmers, whose wages were constantly being eroded, could not risk the same public defiance; behind closed doors, though, vicious jokes were told about the once-revered dictator. Weakened politically, both Nasser and Eshkol found it hard in May 1967 to withstand their militaries' pressure. Similarly, the measures that the Syrian government took in 1962 to deal with the large deficit in the balance of payments created a popular backlash that ended with a military coup in March 1963. The coup did away with the long reign of Syria's traditional elite of large landowners, merchants, and industrialists, and set Syria on its path to confrontation with its Jewish neighbor.[4]

A Global Debt Crisis

These balance of payments crises had a single source: what economists refer to as the "collapse" of the Bretton Woods system in the 1960s; although what actually happened was its transformation.

The economic conference convened in 1944 in Bretton Woods, a town in New Hampshire, was intended to devise measures to restart the flow of international trade after the end of World War II, the most important being a scheme that would decide how national currencies would be exchanged. The result was a new gold–dollar standard. All national currencies were to be pegged to the dollar within fixed exchange ratios, while the dollar itself was convertible to gold at $35 to an ounce. Governments were allowed to depreciate or appreciate their currencies only after receiving permission from the International Monetary Fund (IMF). In practice, during the first decade of Bretton Woods, governments acted more autonomously in their affairs and did not consult much with the IMF before raising or lowering interest rates. But in any case, the system seemed to be working. Western governments were busy building welfare states and implementing full employment policies. The American economy was prospering and no one thought that the Federal Reserve would have trouble honoring its gold obligation. The dollar was as good as gold and served as an anchor for the whole monetary system.[5]

The US had a small deficit in its balance of payments throughout the 1950s but the problem became more acute toward the end of the decade and during the 1960s. The main reasons for that change were growing competition from West German and Japanese manufacturers, increased investment by American multinationals abroad rather than at home, and the ballooning costs of the involvement in Vietnam. The more the American deficit grew, the more insecure the position of the dollar seemed. By the late 1960s it was no secret that the Federal Reserve could no longer honor its $35 per ounce of gold obligation. Nevertheless, the US refused to devalue the dollar for fear that this would undermine the stability of the world economy and end its own financial hegemony. But currency speculators kept trying to convert dollars to gold, anticipating devaluation. And it was not just the dollar that was under attack. Any government that ran a current account deficit could expect to be punished by global financial markets. That was a sign that the rules of the game were changing. Gradually, the Bretton Woods system lost its elasticity and governments could no longer depreciate or appreciate their currencies at will. If the value of the currency was artificially inflated, as was often the case, governments could expect speculators to sell large quantities of it. If governments tried to intervene, they found that nothing could allay the wrath of the markets.[6]

The currency crises of the second Bretton Woods decade were a problem for both developed and developing countries. Britain, for instance, suffered recurrent currency crises throughout the 1960s. This was the case also in the US, especially from 1968. But Third World countries were hit particularly hard during the 1960s. Striving to accelerate the growth of their industry, underdeveloped states were importing large quantities of industrial equipment. Almost all of them were raw-materials exporters and, since the price of raw materials was always lower than that of finished goods, they quickly went deep into debt. Their governments made an already bad situation worse by misallocating the foreign aid they received from developed countries. Dependent on the support of a rising and assertive urban middle class, many Third World elites invested in the industries that could employ university graduates. These choices were not always the most economically viable (overinvestment in heavy industry was a case in point). Those selected to head state-owned companies were appointed according to their political or tribal affiliation rather than their skills. Beyond that, there was a severe shortage of the professional staff needed to run government departments or manage factories. Theoretically, the new factories could become a source of income if they were able to export their way out of debt. But in reality, developing countries' industries were unable to produce goods of the quality or at the price sought by global consumers. In other words, Third World factories were never capable of covering the costs incurred in building them.[7]

Large external debts often led to currency crises – a situation where international speculation in a currency threatens to considerably lower its value in relation to other currencies, thereby abruptly eroding its purchasing power. A related phenomenon was a balance of payments crisis – where the debt of a certain country is so large that it can no longer borrow from banks or states in order to pay its day-to-day expenses. When these happened (usually in tandem), the only way to regain the trust of the markets was to lower the debt drastically. This meant that Third World governments had to raise interest rates, limit imports, devalue their currencies, cut subsidies, and shrink their budgets. The result was popular discontent among workers and the middle class. In the eyes of the latter, the state had broken its promise that the post-independence era would be much better than the colonial past, a promise that seemed to hold during the 1950s when many developing countries posted high growth rates, sometimes in the double digits. But the good times ended in the 1960s. The public tended to blame government rather than contemplate the abstract and nameless forces of the global economy.

The military stepped into the resulting political mayhem. The only viable means of forcing the population into accepting a severe reduction in the standard of living, the army became indispensable. In some cases, generals decided that, since they were running the show anyway, they might as well take over from the government. Indeed, the balance of payments crises of the 1960s were accompanied by a host of military coups in the underdeveloped world: Turkey in 1960, Ecuador in 1961, Argentina in 1962, Syria and Uruguay in 1963, Brazil in 1964, Indonesia and Colombia in 1965, and Ghana in 1966.[8]

These balance of payments crises influenced not only domestic politics, but foreign policies as well. Third World governments searched abroad for the success that had eluded them at home. The result was an arc of instability that stretched across the Afro-Asian world. In India, for instance, the economy was showing signs of strain by the late 1950s: the value of the rupee had deteriorated and external debt was increasing. In response, the government curbed imports and froze wages and prices. This policy brought about the rise of conservative and nationalist parties, which challenged the leadership of Nehru and the Indian National Congress. The fear of losing votes to the opposition in the 1962 election caused Nehru to escalate his rhetoric regarding the Chinese encroachment on a barren and

mountainous terrain along the Indo–Chinese border. At that time, the
Chinese exaggerated their territorial demands for tactical reasons: they
assumed that India would agree to negotiate this dispute. Yet, Nehru passed
up several opportunities to negotiate away the crisis with China, and
ordered his troops to advance into Chinese-held territory. The outcome of
Nehru's hawkish turn was the Sino-Indian War of 1962.[9]

Indonesia was facing similar problems at that time. To get further loans
from the US and the IMF, the government was required to sharply cut its
budget and devalue the rupiah. Both demands threatened to destabilize
President Sukarno's regime. He had been able to hold on to power for so
long (serving in office since 1945) by leaning on the Indonesian Communist
Party and the army. The military resented the demands imposed by the US
and the IMF as they threatened to shrink its budget, and the Communists
were suspicious of any arrangement that would create financial dependence
on the US. In 1963, when several British colonies were about to unite and
create a new neighboring country, Malaysia, Sukarno was quick to recognize it as providing a useful distraction. In several trenchant speeches he
railed against Malaysia, depicting it as a puppet of British imperialism. The
Communist Party and the military welcomed the conflict, the former in
order to forge an alliance with China, and the latter in being spared the loss
of resources. While the war with Malaysia seemingly strengthened Sukarno's
regime, it also weakened the economy: the US and the IMF withdrew their
offer of a loan, inflation and the external debt grew apace, infrastructure
crumbled, and hunger became widespread. When in 1965 the Communists
(with Sukarno's silent assent) staged a coup to purge the military of right-
wing officers, the army responded with a counter-coup and the massacre of
hundreds of thousands of Communists. After eliminating the Communists,
the military proceeded to gradually strip Sukarno of his powers, until the
president was forced to resign in 1967. The new military dictatorship, led by
General Suharto, also ended the conflict with Malaysia and severed ties
with China. A host of measures was adopted in order to resuscitate the
economy: subsidies were cut, and foreign investment was encouraged (it
was frowned upon under Sukarno). The moderate foreign policy of the
Suharto regime helped to secure aid from the US and from other Western
countries. Inflation went down from 660 percent in 1966 to 19 percent in
1969.[10]

In both the Indian and the Indonesian cases, the military had been used
as a political tool to shore up the popularity of a government that found
itself under pressure to implement austerity measures. The story of the
1965 coup in Indonesia also demonstrates the ability of the military to

resolve a balance of payments crisis by the application of brute force. While Sukarno, who relied on popular support, felt cornered when pressed to implement unpopular measures, the military, using its firepower and hier- archical organization, was able to enforce them. Both stories demonstrate how balance of payments crises in developing countries during the 1960s strengthened generals and humbled civilians. Indeed, the currency crises of the late 1960s offer the best explanations as to why civil–military relations were changing at the same time in Israel, Syria, and Egypt.

The Superpowers and the Foreign Aid Crisis of the 1960s

During the 1950s, Khrushchev, Eisenhower, and Kennedy pumped billions of dollars of aid money into Third World countries, in order to promote development, open African and Asian markets to Soviet and American goods, and acquire the loyalty of underdeveloped nations. In hindsight, the policies of both superpowers were tainted by naiveté. Development experts in Moscow and Washington believed that Third World industrialization could be easily jump-started by the injection of capital, technology, and know-how.[11] The results of these policies were disappointing. It was not only that money was spent on ill-devised economic schemes (not to mention some abysmal failures); it was also that many aid recipients were not as loyal, democratic, or politically stable as the superpowers had expected. In addition, Afro-Asian countries disappointed both superpowers by playing the Soviet Union off against the US in order to increase the amount of aid they were getting from each side.[12]

The ascent to power of new leaderships both in Moscow and in Washington between 1963 and 1964 created a new opportunity for a recon- sideration of aid policy. Soviet Premier Alexei Kosygin, Party Chairman Leonid Brezhnev, and US President Lyndon Johnson were unwilling to maintain business as usual. In contrast to his predecessor, President Johnson's approach to foreign aid was to demand complete fealty from recipients, and he cut the flow of money mercilessly when they disobeyed. Johnson was fond of calling it the "short-tether" policy. Likewise, Moscow, judging that Khrushchev's generosity had brought few tangible benefits, decided to cut its foreign aid budget and focus on "mutually beneficial" trade with developing countries.[13] One can see a pattern here: stalled economic progress in developing countries translated into a general feeling among aid donors that foreign aid was broken; it was doing no good either by the donors or the recipients. And so it happened that just when devel- oping countries needed foreign aid the most – to tackle their balance of payments issues – it became scarce. As will be demonstrated later, that had a real effect on Middle Eastern politics.

In any event, modernization theory was cast aside in Moscow and Washington in favor of more hard-nosed policies. Both the US and the Soviet Union now viewed the Third World as an arena for military jockeying. The US increased its arms sales to the Middle East, and the Soviet Union sought to augment its naval presence in the Mediterranean by way of promising more arms sales to Egypt. Both the current American deals and the Soviet promises of future trade created the impression among Israeli and Egyptian generals that they would have superpower support in confronting their enemies. One conclusion that emerges is that superpower involvement in the region between 1958 and 1964, in the form of aid, helped mitigate the severity of the Arab–Israeli conflict; superpower intervention after 1964, consisting of curtailing aid and selling weapons, destabilized the region.

It is clear that generals were at the helm in a host of Middle Eastern countries during the 1960s because a global crisis had changed the balance of power between civilian structures and the military. The tendency of the superpowers to militarize their relations with regional parties further empowered the generals. However, this was not an entirely new phenomenon in world history. There was a historical precedent to all of this and the American ambassador to Amman, Findley Burns, was perhaps the first to identify it. "In sum," he wrote at the height of the May 1967 crisis in the Middle East, "the developments of yesterday are alarmingly reminiscent of August 1914."[14]

The Precedent

Born of discussions about the relationship between military doctrine and international stability, the theory of "defensive realism" has been used to link global trends, civil–military relations, and war initiation. The theory's main case study was the outbreak of World War I. According to a defensive-realist interpretation, continental Europe was in the throes of accelerated modernization in the years leading to 1914. Urbanization and industrialization created new classes and pressure groups – mainly industrial workers, a salaried middle class, and industrialists – which threatened the hegemonic position of the landed aristocracy. Neither the old elite nor the new social groups were strong enough to secure the apex of power. Resulting domestic instability allowed General Staffs to develop their war strategies without much civilian supervision. Left to their own devices, generals preferred to adopt offensive doctrines. These stipulated that the army that mobilized and attacked first would emerge as the victor. This development in and of itself did not cause World War I, but it created an incendiary strategic situation in Europe. Anything that might give one country reason to mobilize would trigger similar responses from other countries. And indeed, once the conflict between Austria-Hungary and Serbia caused Russia to mobilize, a wild chain reaction followed. Within days, all of Europe's armies were on tenterhooks, their commanders eager to attack. Politicians and diplomats were left with little time to negotiate the crisis away. Within a month of the first mobilization, Europe had sunk into a carnage that changed the course of world history.[15]

Several analogies can be drawn. Syria in the 1960s was very much like Serbia in 1914 – a terrorist haven that was a source of regional instability, and which provided the spark that ignited the crisis.[16] The Austro-Hungarian Empire's fear of the Pan-Slav movement seems to foreshadow Israel's apprehension regarding Pan-Arab encirclement. As in Wilhelmine Germany, there were many in Israel who were displeased with the regional status quo and thought that the country's military prowess should enable it to carve off some more of its neighbors' territory. Egypt in 1967 brings to mind Russia in 1914: the mobilization of its large and inefficient army pushed events beyond the point of no return. An interlocking set of regional alliances had driven Europe to the brink in 1914. Similarly, the alliance between Syria and Egypt in 1967 had triggered Egypt's mobilization, which in turn caused an Israeli countermove. Jordan's decision to join the Egyptian–Syrian alliance strengthened the hand of those Israeli generals who wanted to launch a preventive war because, like their 1914 predecessors, they adopted an offensive doctrine without much consultation with their nominal civilian superiors. Even the end results of these crises were not that different. The 1914 crisis ended with a protracted, bloody war. The Six-Day War seemingly ended in one of the swiftest victories in modern history; in reality, the new post-1967 lines created new war zones, especially along the Suez Canal, where the warring sides were conducting a six-year trench warfare, which ended only with a bold assault by the Syrians and the Egyptians in 1973.

The similarities between the two conflicts – the regional context, the month-long crisis that led up to the war, the primacy of offensive doctrine in the decision-making process – have already led several political scientists to make the comparison.[17] These scholars have had in the back of their minds the saying that history does not repeat itself, but it does rhyme. Indeed, I share many social scientists' hope that history might teach us lessons. This book will show that the lessons from the 1914 crisis hold true also for the Six-Day War: when global shifts cause domestic and social upheavals, civilian supervision over the military in contiguous countries weakens. As a result, the regional situation becomes enflamed and ignitable. General Staffs push for belligerent foreign policies and offensive doctrines. As each state adopts these measures it reinforces the tendency of other countries to do the same. The victory of hawkish generals in one country strengthens the hand of hawkish generals in other countries and a spiral of violence starts to unfold. The simultaneous rise of offensive doctrines in a regional system is both a sign of its emerging instability and a facilitator of even greater instability.[18]

Outliers

One outlier to the patterns I have described was Jordan, which participated in the Six-Day War despite the fact that it did not suffer from a balance of payments crisis. Hussein, king of Jordan, did everything he could to avoid clashing with Israel, and even secretly met with Israeli officials from 1963 onward. However, Hussein's generals informed him in May 1967 that they could not guarantee the loyalty of the army if Jordan sat out the coming confrontation with Israel. As a result, Jordan was sucked into the conflict. The same outcome – the ability of generals to twist the arms of civilian leaders – resulted from different causes: the military in Jordan was strong not because the economy was weak, but because the monarchy had been unpopular.

Placing civilian–military relations at the center of my analysis is also not without its problems. For instance, it is not always easy to draw the line between civilians and military men. Israeli Defense Minister Moshe Dayan and Nasser were former officers. King Hussein liked to wear uniforms from time to time. And not all generals were gung-ho. Yitzhak Rabin, the Israeli chief of staff, initially did not want to conquer Sinai or the West Bank. Egyptian generals, for example, thought the attempts of their supreme commander, Abd al-Hakim Amer, to plan attacks against Israel were foolhardy. It is also true that there were civilians who had sought confrontation, such as Dayan.

To complicate things further, while civilian–military relations are the axis around which this book's argument revolves, another important undercurrent is intergenerational conflict. For instance, it was crucial that ministers in the Israeli government were not only civilians with little military background, but also on average twenty years older than the generals. The Fatah guerrilla fighters, who performed the acts of sabotage that precipitated the war, were young, educated men rebelling against the authority of older Palestinian notables. The glib, trigger-happy Syrian leadership was a decade younger than that jaded revolutionary Nasser, whose moderate policy they defied. Young people in the Middle East were generally more militant and they were purposefully using their militancy to reach the top. Finally, not all generals were cut from the same cloth; there were rivalries concerning strategy and tactics between different groups of generals in all of the armies I survey.

As with any attempt to generalize in the social sciences, this one has to bear the burden of exceptions to the rule. Nevertheless, most of those who sought to promote belligerent foreign policies in those years wore uniforms and were unequivocally part of the military. My argument does not contradict other explanations of the war's outbreak. The civilian–military perspective is an addition to a list of contributing factors. The fact that military officers had more say in the years leading up to the Six-Day War made a Middle Eastern war more probable, but not inevitable. Certainly, regional tensions had helped the crisis slide down the slippery slope that led to violence.

Finally, if we accept a model that illustrates the causal link between global economic shifts and the rise of the military as an institution, what room is left for human agency? Does this not lift from the shoulders of the historical protagonists the responsibility for the choices they made? There is no dearth of historians who try to explain the unfolding of history through the personal foibles of leaders. Thus, various developments in the process that led to the outbreak of the Six-Day War are explained by Nasser's impulsiveness, King Hussein's inexperience, or Eshkol's weak character. But the fact that all of these leaders, who wanted to avoid war, were pushed in the same direction suggests that the choices they made were not of their own choosing. Their freedom of action was limited by circumstances beyond their control. Call it the human condition. At any rate, since my protagonists have stumbled into this war and fought it, it is high time to begin to tell the tale.

1

THE ARTICLE

THE DEMONSTRATIONS IN Damascus started on Friday, May 5, 1967. The cause of the ensuing mayhem was an article that was published on April 25 in the official journal of the Syrian army, *Jaysh al-Shaab* (The People's Army). The author, Ibrahim Khlas, a junior Alawite officer and a member of the ruling Baath Party, wrote:

> all [religious] values made the Arab man a miserable one, resigned, fatalistic and dependent. We don't need a man who prays and kneels . . . the only way to establish the culture of the Arabs and build an Arab society is to create the new Socialist Arab man who believes that God, the religions . . . are nothing but mummies embalmed in the museums of history.[1]

At the time, Syria was a military dictatorship led by officers who were members of the Baath Party. The article was the quintessential expression of its ideology, but in view of the growing tensions between the government and the Muslim Brotherhood, its publication was less than circumspect.

On Thursday, May 4, religious leaders (*ulema*) met in Damascus to discuss the ways in which they would vent their outrage. The government knew that the Muslim Brotherhood would use Friday prayers to bring the masses out into the streets and they took no chances. On May 5, in front of a mosque in the lower-class Muhajarin quarter, which was unusually crowded that Friday, five armed police cars were parked at the main entrance. Another car with more police officers and yet another with plain-clothes were not far behind. Police jeeps and riot wagons patrolled the road in front of the mosque. Similar scenes played out in mosques all over Damascus. Public radio suddenly began to include in its broadcasts the phrase "Greetings citizens, peace upon you and the blessing of God." The police confiscated copies of the journal containing the article.[2]

Defying the government's heavy-handed measures, Shaykh Hasan Habanaka, aged 59, the unofficial leader of Damascene *ulema*, gave a fiery sermon attacking the regime in the Manjak Mosque. The Lebanese daily, *al-Hayat*, which was known to have excellent sources inside this secretive police state, reported that on that day a crowd of 20,000 people filled the streets chanting "No to Communism and no to Baathism – Quranic Islam!" The demonstrations soon spread to the northern cities of Aleppo, Homs, and Hama where Christians and Muslims were protesting side by side. Initially the government's response was mild: security forces were ordered to disperse the demonstrators without using force. But at night, the arrests of at least forty senior religious figures were made. Among them was Habanaka, who was also the mufti of the drab al-Maydan neighborhood in Damascus.[3]

By the next day the situation had grown worse. Butchers, bakers, and shop owners announced a strike to protest the arrest of the well-liked Habanka who was a shopkeeper himself. The market in Damascus closed down and in the following days customers were hard-pressed to find meat, bread, and basic staples.[4] Demonstrations turned into riots as protesters clashed with security forces. Gunshots were heard in the streets. Some demonstrators were killed, others injured. Denizens of Damascus heard sounds of explosions near Baath Party headquarters, in the main streets, and in the squares. The government lost control over what was happening in the cities of Homs, Hama, and Aleppo where, during Sunday and Monday, unrest continued to simmer. The military commander of the Homs region, Mustafa Tlass, ignored commands from Damascus to bring law and order into the streets. In response, forces loyal to the regime laid siege to Homs; one could not leave or enter by car. Political commentators believed that this was the most serious political crisis in Syria since the bloody 1963 coup that brought the Baath Party to power.[5]

The government, now clearly alarmed, decided to take tougher measures. Shop owners who closed down their businesses were arrested. Truckloads of steel-helmeted riot police patrolled the main streets of Damascus to deter people from congregating. Army units replete with tanks took positions near politically sensitive sites such as radio and television stations, military headquarters, and the Ministry of Defense.[6] Cars with loudspeakers roamed the streets of Damascus on Sunday and Monday calling on shop owners to end the strike. State media outlets did the same. Units from the

National Guard and groups of regime-sanctioned thugs known as the proletarian brigades poured into the streets armed with machine pistols, automatics, sledgehammers, and crowbars. Their aim was to intimidate shop owners and force them to open their businesses. They smashed shop windows in Damascus and Aleppo and distributed the merchandise free of charge to passers-by. At the same time the government attempted damage control. The minister of the interior published a response in *Jaysh al-Shaab* denigrating the apostate article. The prime minister claimed that the article was arranged by the CIA and was part of an "American, Zionist [and] reactionary plot" to undermine the Baath regime.[7]

These measures failed to fix the problem. Tension between the government and opposition escalated during the following three days and the riots showed no sign of abating.

The Party and the Army

What seemed to be yet another chapter in a typical Middle Eastern tale of religious tensions fueling instability actually turned out to be a twist in a sordid plot that had been unfolding since Syria received its independence from France in 1944. The lines of division were well known to the *ulema*, their supporters, and the regime, each taking up its intended role in a well-rehearsed choreography of violence. The scenes on the Damascus streets were another battle in a slowly evolving and decades-old civil war between the haves and have-nots.

In Syria, religious and class identities overlapped in a way that created a deeply polarized society. Traditionally, the Sunni majority (about 57 percent of the population) resided in the cities where Sunnis were merchants, small-business owners, artisans, *ulema*, landowners, and industrialists. Around the cities lived religious minorities – the Alawites in the Latakia hills (11.5 percent of the population), the Druze in the southwestern mountainous area of Jabel al-Druze (3 percent), the Ismailis in the environs of Hama (1.5 percent) – in villages built mostly with mud and lacking piped water, sewerage, electricity, tarred roads, and modern medicine. Overcrowded and suffering from poor sanitation, the villages were ravaged by disease: malaria, tuberculosis, and diarrhea. In 1951–53, 36 percent of registered deaths occurred among children under five. The urban landowner was sole ruler of the people who inhabited his land and he demanded the utmost respect from them. He lived off the labor of the peasants and represented them to the authorities. No girl could marry without his approval. If the landlord desired a girl and her family resisted, they risked being turned off the land.[8]

These unequal relations could exist as long as farmers lived in isolated communities without knowledge of how to organize themselves to make demands. But from the end of World War II, Syria became more integrated into the world economy – especially through the export of cotton. Modernity brought with it better transportation and communication networks and wider access to education. The small world of the rural community was shattered, the authority of village and tribal elders undermined. The more educated were the villages' younger generations, the more politically aware they became. Ease of travel from the village to the city and between urban centers served to show the have-nots that many shared their plight. If the religious minorities could only come together, they would be formidable.[9]

The Baath Party was to play a key role in that process. Founded in 1947 by two Damascene intellectuals, Michel Aflaq (Christian) and Salah al-Bitar (Sunni), its ideology sought to transcend the various class loyalties and ethnic identities that threatened to tear independent Syria apart. The two loadstars of Baathism were Arabism and socialism (in that order of importance). Following romantic notions of nationalism, Aflaq envisaged Arabism as a living entity that would be able to grow naturally only within a united Pan-Arab state encompassing the entire Middle East. Thus, Syria's warring communities would be submerged in a larger political unit.

Baathism treated Islam as part of the rich heritage of Arabism but not necessarily its defining feature. According to that tenet, all Arabs, no matter what their religious affiliation was, were welcome to join the Baath and its mission to unite the Arab world. Moreover, the political order that the Baath would strive to establish would be secular, thus abolishing sectarian tensions. Socialism was to cure the deep chasm between rich and poor and between city dwellers and farmers. Baath ideology envisaged a major role for the state in promoting industrialization, building infrastructure, and enacting land reform. At the same time, Aflaq was careful to stress that his was an "Arab socialism" and not foreign-made Communism. Moreover, Aflaq explained that "[Arab] unity is higher in the hierarchy of values than socialism."[10]

The same could not be said about Aflaq's and Bitar's disciples, the country boys that came to the big city to acquire education and found themselves drawn into circles of discussion that Bitar and Aflaq conducted in Damascene cafés. When these students returned to their villages as schoolteachers they passed on the lore of Baathism to their eager pupils. Because it appealed foremost to educated Druse, Ismaili, and Alawite youth, the Baath was far more successful in rural areas than in the cities. This pattern was underlined when in 1953 Aflaq and Bitar struck an alliance with Akram

Hourani, a firebrand Sunni lawyer, who organized the farmers around Hama into a populist party.[11]

Nevertheless, the Baath was unable to win a majority in parliament in the elections that took place during the 1940s and 1950s. Despite the popularity of its message, it suffered from organizational weakness. Aflaq was a brooding intellectual, more accustomed to ideological debates in small forums. He shied away from taking formal posts and never served as a minister. Hourani was an energetic schemer and operator but proved too much of an opportunist to become a national leader. He zigged and zagged constantly to secure ultimate power for himself. Bitar served as a go-between for Aflaq and Hourani, but this awkward arrangement did not augur well for the Baath.[12] Yet the party that was unable to pave its way to power through the ballot box was finally able to establish itself there using bayonets.

When the French won a mandate from the League of Nations in 1920, they created a militia known as the Troupes spéciales du Levant (Special Troops of the Levant). The French preferred to recruit soldiers from religious or ethnic minorities who resided farther away from the capital, believing such recruits to be less amenable to nationalism. (This was a deliberate divide-and-rule policy employed by the French in other colonies.) The numerical strength of Alawites, Druze, and Ismailis among the troops thus outweighed their demographic footprint. Post-independence, the military academy at Homs opened its gates to all who were willing to register, without discrimination. Again, the minorities, seeing the army as their avenue to social mobility, seized the opportunity. Hourani, for his part, encouraged rural youths to join the military so that the Baath could build a base within the ranks.[13]

The sons of urban and affluent Sunni families refused to enlist. Under the French mandate they had led the nationalist struggle to independence and therefore would not agree to serve in an occupying army. But even after independence, landowning and commercial Sunni families considered serving in the army to be demeaning. They thus left one of the most important arenas in Syrian politics open to other groups. This did not mean that the army instantly became dominated by the impoverished religious minorities. Some Sunnis from well-to-do families did join the ranks. Encouraged by the military dictators who served between 1949 and 1954, many Sunnis from middle- or lower-class backgrounds also entered the military academies at Homs and Hama. Nevertheless, overall, the class composition of the army was different from that of the Syrian political and economic elite. This was a recipe for trouble. The army saw itself as representing the people's will against those of a corrupted ruling class, and used its power to intervene in politics.[14] It was also opposed to any attempt to make it answerable to civilian authority. Yet the Syrian army was not, so to speak, uniform. Various ideological currents were represented within the ranks – Communists, Baathists, Nasserites, Muslim Brothers, and independents. Struggles over authority and power therefore took place both within the military and between the military and the civilian politicians. Each time one military faction won, it took care to purge its opponents. Thus, unwittingly, Sunni officers purged each other to the point at which minority officers were able to prevail.

The Unruly Military, 1944–58

No sooner had Syria gained independence in 1944 than it found itself under military rule between 1949 and 1954. Syria participated in the 1948 war for Palestine in which Arab armies tried to prevent the establishment of a Jewish state. The Syrian army failed to conquer northern Palestine, although it was able to occupy a strip of land adjacent to the border. Following the war's conclusion, officers and civilians hurled the blame for the army's disappointing performance at each other. In March 1949, after several officers had been arrested for war-related corruption and the government added injury to insult by unilaterally cutting officers' salaries, the army launched a coup. The civilian government was reinstated, but it was toppled again in November 1951 via another military coup because it wanted to appoint a civilian rather than a general as minister of defense. A counter-coup in 1954 established democracy once more.[15]

The next four tumultuous years were typified by a return to parliamentary life and the ascendancy of parties representing the middle class, including the Baath. The power of the traditional elite declined. Those were also stormy years for the Middle East at large. In July 1956, Egyptian President Gamal Abd al-Nasser defied the West by nationalizing the Suez Canal Company, which was owned by British and French investors. A tripartite coalition, which included Israel, Britain, and France, launched a military operation in October to undo the nationalization and topple Nasser. Yet he emerged victorious from the 1956 Suez Crisis and became the hero of the Arab street. This affected Syrian politics as well. The Asali government that served between 1956 and 1958 and included Baathist Salah al-Bitar as foreign minister, adopted a Pan-Arab, pro-Egyptian, and Moscow-friendly foreign policy. In 1957 it had to withstand a regional crisis during which Iraq, Jordan, and Turkey, all of them US allies, concentrated their troops along Syria's borders and threatened to invade. That was their, and Washington's, response to the growing reliance of Syria on Soviet civil and military aid. Eventually the eagerness of Syria's neighbors to intervene cooled off, but growing Soviet influence in Syria was a source of concern to the Baathist officers and conservative parties. The Syrian Communist Party was enjoying mass support and could conceivably take over through free and fair elections.[16]

Unity and After, 1958–63

The feeling that Syria was under threat by both external and internal forces brought public calls for a merger with Egypt to fever pitch. That was true for the Syrian military as well. For many officers, Nasser seemed the perfect antidote to Syria's ills – a strongman who would put the Communists under the boot, scare "the imperialists" away, instill unity within the ranks of the Syrian army, and enforce land reform and government intervention from above as he did in Egypt. Deciding to ride the popular wave, on January 12, 1958, without consulting the government, a delegation of Syrian officers took a plane to Cairo to offer Gamal Abd al-Nasser a merger between the two countries. Syria's President Shukri al-Quwatli and Prime Minister Sabri al-Asali were stunned and enraged. But they decided not to buck the popular trend and refrained from criticizing the army's latest act of insubordination. As unity with Egypt seemed to offer an escape route from an election the Baath was bound to lose, the Baath leadership was especially enthusiastic about the coming merger. As Michel Aflaq later explained: "We hoped that the [Baath] party would have a basic and responsible share in the governing of the new nation which we helped to create."[17]

The years of the merger, though, proved to be a grave disappointment. Nasser made his acceptance of the Syrian offer conditional upon the agreement of all Syrian parties to dissolve. He also demanded that the Syrian army stop its interference in civilian affairs. Neither Syrian politicians nor officers were particularly keen to accept these demands, but back home in Syria, popular support for the coming union with Egypt, especially among the urban middle class, was overwhelming. In those years, Nasser personified the hope that Arabs would renew their past glory by coming together and forming one vast Arab state, equal in power and stature to the Soviet Union and the US. Whoever opposed Nasser's dictate would appear as a traitor to the Arab cause. Reluctantly, the Syrian government accepted Nasser's terms and in February 1958 Nasser and Quwatli, standing on a veranda in Damascus, announced the creation of a United Arab Republic (UAR) to an enthusiastic crowd. Within a few months Syrian politicians and officers realized that they had been duped and trapped.

The Syrian politicians involved in creating the union were relegated to second-tier positions in the new cabinet and hence grew resentful. Through various machinations Nasser also reduced Baath representation in the joint parliament. In December 1959 Nasser made a public speech in which he denounced the Baath so vehemently that al-Bitar and Hourani resigned in despair from the cabinet, realizing that Nasser would never accept them as equal partners. Nasser also forced 300 Syrian officers (62 of them Baath members) to relocate to Cairo where they were appointed to sinecures. Other officers were cashiered or elbowed into civilian positions. Syrian officers who remained in service found that their movements were monitored by Egyptian intelligence. A small army, 20,000 strong, of Egyptian bureaucrats, both civilian and military, moved to Syria to take over the day-to-day administration of the "northern province." In essence, Syria became an Egyptian colony.[18]

Eventually, the undoing of Nasser's rule over Syria came not because of his attempts to destroy the Communists and the Baathists. Rather, it was because he infuriated the Syrian business community by trying to regulate its activity. In the main, Nasser's decrees aimed at limiting the power of Syria's influential families and giving workers representation on companies' boards. Syrian capitalists reacted by trying to bypass the new regulations, moving their money abroad and putting all new investment in the Syrian economy on hold. Nasser tired of these cat-and-mouse games and responded by issuing the socialist decrees of July 1961 that mandated large-scale nationalization of industry, banks, and insurance companies. On September 28, 1961, it was the Syrian military's turn to issue a rebuttal: it launched a coup. This coup was the ironic outcome of Nasser's purge of the Communist and Baathist officers from the Syrian military. That created an army in which 50 percent of the officers were Damascene Sunnis with ties to Syria's businessmen. The two leaders of the coup were Colonel Abd al-Karim Nahlawi and Colonel Haidar al-Kuzbari. Kuzbari was a scion of a landowning family whose relative, Mamun al-Kuzbari (who later served briefly as the first post-coup prime minister), mediated between the plotters and the conglomerate, al-Sharika al-Khumasiya (the Company of Five), which expressed its readiness to place £1 million sterling at the officers' disposal. Nahlawi, meanwhile, was a member of the Muslim Brotherhood and invited Issam al-Attar, the Brotherhood's supreme guide, to take part in the coup. (Attar declined.) Nahlawi and Kuzbari therefore represented the two wings of Syria's emerging conservative coalition, one including the land- and factory-owning families, and the other comprising religious movements such as the Muslim Brotherhood. Linking these groups together were, first, the upper class's need for a grass-roots organization that would fight for it in the streets, and second, the dependence of religious leaders on large contributions from businessmen to fund their charitable activities.[19]

Following Nahlawi's coup, Egyptian forces left Syria and the union was dissolved. The elections in December 1961 sent an unprecedented number of business-friendly representatives to parliament. A new cabinet was duly sworn in, led by Maruf al-Dawalibi, a wealthy businessman who opposed the union with Egypt. The Dawalibi cabinet soon realized that the coffers of the state were empty. The years of union had nearly bankrupted the country. Two successive droughts, the dislocation caused by agrarian reforms, and the tension between the business community and the UAR authorities resulted in a sharp decline in agricultural and industrial production. Syria's balance of payments went from a $4 million surplus in 1957 to a $66 million deficit in 1958 and a $93 million deficit in 1960. The Dawalibi cabinet therefore sought loans from Western lending agencies such as the IMF, the World Bank, and the US government. These were to allow the government a breathing space to enact much-needed reforms. All in all, Syria was able to secure loans to the tune of $86 million. In return for these loans, the IMF demanded the enactment of several policy measures: the denationalization of industries nationalized by Nasser and the privatization of other state-owned industries, as well as export-promoting steps such as the devaluation of the Syrian pound by 6.3 percent. To ensure support from landowning representatives in the cabinet and parliament, the Dawalibi government added a revision of agrarian reform law, which Nasser legislated. While Nasser sought to break the power of the big landowners by splitting their estates among landless farmers, the Dawalibi cabinet wanted the law to preserve the unequal distribution of land.[20]

The package of measures adopted by the government proved to be extremely unpopular. While the union with Egypt was a controversial issue, the social reforms that Nasser enacted were much liked. Workers wanted to work in nationalized companies where job security was assured, and farmers wanted to have a plot of land of their own. Moreover, the Dawalibi government pushed the legislation through parliament despite stiff opposition from Baathists, Communists, and Nasserites, amid a wave of demonstrations and strikes. This proved to be a step too far. What seemed like a blatant attempt to benefit the rich created longing among workers, farmers, and the middle class for Nasser and the unionist period. In late March 1962 – only four months after it was inaugurated – the Dawalibi cabinet lost a vote of confidence in parliament and the government resigned. No sooner had negotiations over the creation of a new coalition started, than the army intervened.[21]

Abd al-Karim Nahlawi, the same officer who led the coup that dissolved the UAR, was also behind the March 28, 1962 coup. He justified his intervention by claiming that the Dawalibi government had deviated from the goals of the original September 1961 coup, which were, ostensibly, to create a new union with Egypt, albeit on more equal terms, and to maintain some of Nasser's reforms. Nahlawi's second coup did not work out according to plan. Other factions in the army were preparing to launch counter-coups of their own against Nahlawi who was now perceived as a supporter of the unpopular policies of the Dawalibi government. To prevent internecine fighting, it was decided to take the unorthodox step of calling a military conclave at Homs on April 1. Forty-one senior officers from all military regions and major units met there to decide the fate of Syria, thereby emphasizing the weakness of the parliamentary order. The emerging consensus was that Nahlawi and eleven other officers, all of them Sunnis, should be expelled from the army and sent into exile. That step marked the rise of minority officers to higher ranks as they stepped in to fill the vacated positions. Another agreement reached during the meeting was that a new and more progressive government should be formed.[22]

As a result, between April 1962 and March 1963, two civilian cabinets tried to find a middle way between the populism of the UAR days and the demands of the business community. They did all that amid continuous rumors of an impending coup. Prime Minister Khaled al-Azm, a staunch opponent of military interference in politics, announced his intention to hold an election in the summer of 1963 in order to put an end to the situation that had reigned since the dissolution of the UAR which saw unelected cabinets serving at the pleasure of the military. To ensure that power remained in the hands of the army, a cabal of Baathist, independent, and Nasserite officers joined hands to topple the government.

2

THE BAATH IN POWER, 1963–66

O N THE NIGHT of March 7–8, 1963, tanks and infantry began to move on Damascus. Residents of the capital awoke on the 8th to what were by now familiar sights: armed units taking up positions around key government offices and radio and television stations; roadblocks manned by soldiers; military vehicles moving slowly through the streets, their loudspeakers calling on the citizens to stay at home and remain indoors. Politicians and officers affiliated with the previous regime were arrested; others fled abroad. Thus began the Baath rule in Syria.

The results of the 1963 coup were long-lasting. From that point on, the commercial and landowning elite, once the undisputed master of Syria, could no longer hold the reins of power. Much had happened in the previous decades to shake its central position in Syrian society: the defeat in 1948, the succession of military coups, the rise of the Baath, and the dislocation brought by the union with Egypt. But the *coup-de-grâce* had been the economic reforms of 1962 that emphasized the plutocratic nature of the post-union coalition. The 1963 coup was a soft one; so unpopular was the regime that there was no resistance.[1] What followed next was far more bloody and violent. Soldiers shot their fellow soldiers and Muslims butchered Muslims as the struggle over the shape of the Syrian economy intensified.

Shortly after the March 1963 coup took place, Syrian businessmen expressed their fear that the Baath regime would nationalize large parts of the economy. Assuming the worst, they started to withdraw their money from the country. To stop the capital flight, the government first put a limit on the amount of funds that could be transferred abroad and, in May, nationalized all the banks to increase control over capital movements. In June a new agrarian reform law was announced which put stricter limits on land-ownership. In September and October the Baath convened two party congresses, which adopted resolutions calling for an end to the leading role of "the bourgeoisie" in the economy. The resolutions described Syria's businessmen as "allies to the new colonialism." Having in mind a radically different economic model, the resolutions spoke about workplace democracy through self-management by workers and the collectivization of farms. Full nationalization of all sectors of the economy was envisaged as the best way to promote industrialization and economic independence. Both congresses exhibited the mass attendance of party members from rural backgrounds. They were eager to use the power recently won by the Baath to unleash a thoroughgoing social and economic transformation.[2]

Life in Syria's main cities was changing fast, with farmers and workers taking senior positions in the state bureaucracy and asserting their authority over their past masters. As if in a mirror image, a mass exodus of educated urban Sunnis from Damascus took place. Professionals and white-collar workers crossed the border to Lebanon, especially Beirut. Business owners bypassed the measures imposed by the regime and smuggled their money abroad. In January 1964 Syria's government had to admit that the economy was in a state of crisis. Lacking capital, it had to adopt austerity measures and sharply limit the import of goods. Having issued through chambers of commerce several warnings to the government to change course, the conservative coalition between the *ulema* and business groups now waited for the right opportunity to channel popular resentment out into the streets. This opportunity arrived in February 1964.[3]

The riots of February and April that year were the general rehearsal for the even larger riots of May 1967. Students, shop owners, religious figures, and business associations used these events to vent their anger. In February clashes between Baathist and Islamic students in the coastal town of Banyas were followed by a commercial strike in nearby Homs. Businessmen who were identified by the authorities as strike leaders were arrested within twenty-four hours, tried, and jailed. In mid-April the riots spread to Hama, which was known to be a stronghold of large landowners and religious conservatism. Following a confrontation between high-school students and security forces in Hama, a local religious leader, Sheikh Muhammad al-Hamid, called from his pulpit for a jihad against the regime. Massive street demonstrations ensued with protesters calling for the downfall of the Baath regime, the "enemy of Islam." The Muslim opposition erected roadblocks, stockpiled weapons, and beat up any party official they found in the streets.

During clashes with security forces, a Baathist militiaman, an Ismaili named Munzir al-Shimali, was caught by the crowd. He was killed and his body was mutilated. In response, the army sealed the city, imposed a curfew, and sent troops into the old quarter. The National Guard commander ordered tank fire into the densely populated parts of the city. After two days of street fighting, the insurgents, armed with light weapons, blockaded themselves in the Sultan Mosque. Prime Minister Amin Hafiz and his chief of staff, Salah Jadid, took the unprecedented step of ordering tanks to shell the mosque. As a result, the minaret from which the rebels fired upon government forces collapsed, killing dozens of people.[4]

Visiting Hama on April 18, Hafiz ordered troops to execute any person who took part in the riot. Yet the commercial strike kept spreading to other cities, most crucially to Damascus, where large lines formed in front of the few bakeries and food shops that remained open. In an ominous move, military units were spread across key locations in the city. The Lawyers Association decided to join the opposition and went on strike. It presented the government with a petition calling for an end to one-party rule and for free and fair elections. Similar petitions were submitted by doctors' and engineers' associations. After several days of standoff, the regime launched a typically heavy-handed response. Government troops moved through Damascus smashing padlocks from shuttered stores and posting guards to keep them open. Business leaders rumored to be involved in unleashing the strike were arrested and a decree threatened shop owners with the confiscation of their property and a court martial. By the end of April the strike in Damascus and the riots in Hama had ended. Throughout it all, the regime remained intransigent. The pace of the nationalization of companies only increased during the riots. By mid-1965, the government owned three-quarters of the Syrian economy (up from about one-quarter in early 1963). Responding to another wave of riots in January 1965 during which the mosques emerged yet again as a focal point of opposition activity, the regime assumed full authority to dismiss and appoint preachers and religious teachers.[5] But while the regime demonstrated its coercive abilities, unrest continued to simmer below the surface.

The Reign of the Military Baath, 1966–67

On the night of February 22, 1966, Colonel Salim Hatum, a Druze from Jabal al-Druze, aged 38, and Colonel Izzat Jadid, an Alawite and cousin of Salah Jadid, who was the chief conspirator, used an official holiday to make their move. They marched their units – a commando battalion (under

Hatum's command) and a crack cavalry unit (Jadid) – from the Kaboun and the Harasata camps, both on the northern outskirts of Damascus, into the capital. At 5.30 a.m. the following day the denizens of Damascus awoke to the ominous rattle of small-arms fire. With the help of Jadid's T-54 tanks, the thousand men under the command of Hatum stormed the residence of President Amin Hafiz and the government guesthouse. Most fighting took place around the residence of Hafiz, where the president himself commanded the elite units of the Desert Guard. Ironically, both Desert Guard units and Hatum's battalion were manned largely by Druze soldiers.

In a three-hour-long battle around the presidential residency the two sides exchanged intensive fire. As Druze killed Druze, the tanks shot volleys into the building. To better their positions, the attackers mounted the roofs of adjoining buildings to pour bullets into the residence. During the fighting, air force MiGs patrolled the skies over Damascus in twos and fours. Across the street from the Hafiz residence, American defense attaché Colonel Frederick S. Wright and his wife were pinned down in their apartment while bullets and shrapnel peppered their rooms. The fighting lasted until noon. Only after his villa was shattered and his children injured (his daughter lost her eye as a result) did Hafiz leave the building and surrender himself. All in all, around a hundred men were killed in the heavy fighting there and in other incidents throughout the city. At the end of that day the military wing of the Baath was able to take up the reins of government.[6]

The causes of this coup were the same as those of almost any other Syrian coup: the rural–urban divide, sectarian strife, inequality, and the stubborn refusal of officers to obey civilians. All of these tensions were evident within the Baath itself. The rural supporters of the Baath were greatly dismayed when Aflaq and Bitar acquiesced to Nasser's dictate and dissolved the Baath in 1958. That these two middle-class Damascenes, Aflaq and Bitar, would give up on the party so easily was seen as a sign of their untrustworthiness. Coming from a hardscrabble background, officers, teachers, workers, and students saw the party as their vehicle for social mobility. And the influence of that segment of the party was growing rapidly. In the following years, more and more activists from minority and rural backgrounds came to dominate the apparatus and this tendency grew even stronger after the March 1963 coup when the number of party members quintupled.[7]

They became known as the "regionalists" because they wanted to focus on "the Syrian region of the Arab nation," while the followers of Aflaq and Bitar were known as the "nationalists" as their first priority was to unite the

Arab nation. The regionalists cared far less about Arab unity and far more about implementing a radical transformation of the Syrian economy. As a would-be middle class, the regionalists were strong adherents of state inter-vention, the redistribution of land, and nationalizations because the growth of state agencies and industries could supply them with secure employ-ment. They were also much more likely to stress the secular nature of Baath ideology as they were seeking to root out the decades-old cultural hierar-chies that blocked their way to the status they coveted. The nationalists, on the other hand, tended to come, like Bitar and Aflaq, from a Sunni urban background. The two men also sought to accommodate the Muslim Brotherhood, the landlords, and the business community. These social and ideological differences created two competing factions unequal in their power. The regionalists were aligned with the military while the national-ists only had the intellectual authority of Michel Aflaq to lean on.[8]

The March 1963 coup itself was partly organized by the military committee – a shadowy body created in 1960 while several Baathist officers were languishing in the boredom of the Egyptian capital during the UAR days. The leading members of the committee hailed from minority backgrounds: Salah Jadid, Hafez al-Assad, and Muhammed Umran were Alawites, while Abd al-Karim al-Jundi and Ahmad al-Mir were Ismaili. Once the UAR fell apart, in 1961, these officers came back to Syria. Between 1961 and 1963 the military committee surreptitiously recruited dozens of minority officers. This clandestine network became active during the March 1963 coup, and in the months that followed its members succeeded in purging their Sunni urban rivals from the ranks, appointing hundreds of Alawite, Druze, and Ismaili officers, many of them their direct relatives, in their stead. The architect of this strategy was Salah Jadid, who served as chief of staff between August 1963 and September 1965. There was no rapport between the Bitar and Aflaq duo and the officers who, like the rest of the regionalists, were peasants' sons with a burning desire to rectify age-old inequalities. Continuing the pattern of military opposition to civilian supervision, from 1963 to 1966 the military committee made appointments within the army its exclusive domain, elbowing out the civilian leadership of Aflaq and Bitar.[9] Once Jadid's control over the army was complete and his alliance with the regionalists solidified, he was ready to deal with his party rivals.

Aflaq and Bitar used a tactical mistake made by Jadid to appoint Bitar as prime minister in December 1965. Bitar made it clear that he would put an end to the wave of nationalizations and demanded that the army stop interfering in politics. Both initiatives were inimical to the radical line of the military committee. A coup against the civilian wing of the Baath Party was thus on the cards from early 1966. After President Amin Hafiz had been arrested, Jadid and his supporters controlled Syria. This was a milestone in Syrian history. For the first time, the Sunni urban majority was ruled by minority officers. Jadid, barely 40 years old, the mastermind of the coup, was probably proud of his achievement. Yet, demographically, the new regime had a narrow base of support now that it had removed the senior Sunni Baath members, such as Bitar and Hafiz, who used to be the party's public face. It had only a limited appeal among students and farmers and was still to develop as a mass party. Moreover, the preference of the military Baath to speed up the pace of social reform and put Arab unity on the back burner was inimical to the interests and worldview of the Sunni urban middle class. As a result, the regime's hold over the main cities was tenuous.[10]

The economic situation was dire even before the military Baath came to power and it kept deteriorating after the February 1966 coup. The regime denounced Iraq, Jordan, and Saudi Arabia as "reactionary servants of world imperialism" and vowed publicly to undermine them. All three reacted by implementing an economic blockade against Syria. That had a negative effect on an economy that was dependent on trade with the Arab world.[11] In addition, the regime accelerated the pace of agrarian reform, with 70,358 hectares distributed to new owners in 1966, up from 20,476 hectares in 1965. Yet the dislocation in the agricultural sector also decreased productivity. Between January and May 1967, food prices jumped by more than 33 percent and black markets proliferated. Businessmen continued to withhold their investment, slowing down economic activity. They kept doing so even when in the summer of 1966 government legislation prohibited "economic sabotage" and authorized up to fifteen years' imprisonment for transgressors. The growing external debt forced the government to devalue the Syrian pound, severely curtail imports, and levy new taxes.[12]

Syria's government tried to counteract the economic slowdown by increasing its investment in large state-owned enterprises. Annual governmental investment in Syrian industry rose from 113 million Syrian pounds in 1965 to 181 million in 1966. The government fast-tracked construction works in the high dam on the Euphrates. A cluster of irrigation works was to be built around the dam and an ambitious land reclamation scheme was also to be launched. Major investments were made in pipeline construction, railway extension, and port expansion. But the government's ability to implement all these programs was highly limited. Trained personnel had already started leaving after 1963 and the trickle became a flood post-1966. Moreover, worried that the bureaucracy was filled with "class-enemies," the new regime purged urban Sunnis from government service. If that was not enough, the proletarian brigades headed by the hot-tempered Khaled al-Jundi were terrorizing those qualified officials who remained in their jobs. The end result of all this was that the shortage of qualified personnel stymied the regime's ability to implement any of its ambitious programs.[13] It comes as little surprise, then, that most of the foreign reports from Syria presented a picture of a highly unpopular regime: the public was described as restless and inattentive to official Baath speakers during mass rallies.[14]

In such circumstances the alliance between the Muslim Brotherhood and conservative business groups grew ever stronger. A year before the military Baath came to power, a leading religious figure, Sheikh Karim Rajih, explained to a surprised Baathist officer why he was opposed to nationalizations: "Socialism scares away capital holders and those with an entrepreneurial spirit. It deprives the individual of any motivation to work." Rajih was a close associate of Sheikh Hasan Habanaka, the religious leader of the al-Maydan neighborhood in Damascus, which emerged in the spring of 1966 as a stronghold of Islamic opposition. In late April 1966 demonstrators in al-Maydan welcomed Habanaka, who had just come back from pilgrimage to the holy sites in Mecca, by shouting slogans such as "No communism, no Baathism; we want Islam." In November, Salah Jadid took care to visit Habanaka to promise him that Syria was not turning Communist despite its burgeoning ties with the Soviet bloc. Habanaka reportedly answered that Syria *was* going Communist, and he would not keep silent about it.[15]

But far worse was the fact that Jadid could not rely on the support of the army. He and his minister of defense and commander of the air force, Hafez al-Assad, had grown apart ever since April 1966 when Assad discovered that Jadid had tried to remove his supporters from air force command, the locus of Assad's political power, while he was away in Moscow on official business. The animosity had escalated in early May. Gunfights between Assad's and Jadid's supporters broke out, during which Assad's brother, Rifat, was seriously wounded. On the same day that these incidents took place, a time bomb was discovered in an office next to Jadid's.[16]

The conflict between Jadid and Assad may have started due to these incidents but it quickly developed into an ideological confrontation along lines that by then should have looked familiar. Following the 1966 coup, Assad aligned himself with the right wing of the Baath. He resented the attempts made by Jadid and his ally, Ibrahim Makhus, to create a revolutionary alliance with the radical regimes in Algeria and Egypt. Assad was well aware that the price of cooperation with Egypt would be the return of

Egyptian forces to Syria; as someone who championed the military's interests, he opposed that. Assad also thought that Jadid and his allies should
accommodate the needs of the private sector. Jadid firmly attached himself
to the "regionalists," took a radical line in social and economic affairs, and
devoted himself to the painstaking task of building loyal and ideologically
motivated party cadres.[17] The conflict also involved the officers vs. civilians
dimension: while Assad insisted on remaining an officer with a command
position, Jadid was a civilian (he left the army in 1965 after serving as a
chief of staff) and championed the right of the party to supervise the army.
Throughout this period, Jadid, despite his attempt to hide behind the title of
"assistant to the general secretary of the Baath Party," remained Syria's
strongman and placed his allies in key positions: Yusuf Zuayn was made
prime minister, Ahmed Sawidani became chief of staff, and Abd al-Karim
al-Jundi, known to be cruel and brutal, head of the secret services.

Nevertheless, Assad persisted, and proved resilient and cunning. It was
well known that while Assad enjoyed the support of the air force, Jadid was
predominant among land forces. In early June 1966, land forces laid siege to
airfields after information reached Jadid regarding a coup being hatched by
Assad and his supporters. At the end of July, Jadid loyalists arrested Assad
and brought him to the Ministry of Defense, where he was confronted by
an irate Jadid. When Assad supporters learned of this, they threatened to act
unless Assad was released within twelve hours. Assad was let go after six
hours, but only because he promised Jadid not to act against him.[18]

Shortly afterward, rumors started spreading about a coup conspiracy that
would be led by Assad and Colonel Salim Hatum, who commanded the
troops during the battle against Amin Hafiz's guard on the morning of the
1966 coup. Hatum was disgruntled because his determination on that day
had not been rewarded by the regime. The reason behind that slight was that
Jadid considered Hatum to be a hothead who could have ended the clash with
Hafiz's troops without so much bloodshed. Hatum struck an alliance with the
remnants of the supporters of Aflaq and Bitar among the troops. He also
contacted Assad, and believed that he had received his blessing for the coup.

Hatum's plot was as dramatic as it was reckless. He was able to secure the
support of the Druze community, which historically resided in Jabal al-Druze
(the Druze mountain), by convincing them that he and other officers were
discriminated against just because they were Druze. Baath Party members at
Jabal al-Druze sent Jadid a memo elaborating on these claims and threatened
to disobey party orders until the matter was settled. Jadid decided to deal
with the matter personally and arrived at Suwayda, regional capital of Jabal
al-Druze, on September 7. Once there, Hatum's forces arrested Jadid.[19]

At the same time, forces loyal to Hatum mobilized in Harsata and in the north, where the commander, Talal Abu Asali, a fellow Druze, was an ally of Hatum. It was at this point that Hatum overplayed his hand. He called Assad, demanding that several of Jadid's supporters be purged from the ranks and a number of his own supporters be appointed to senior positions. Once Hatum turned the coup into a sectarian affair in which Druze officers formed a coalition against the Alawites, Assad, an Alawite himself, had no choice but to throw his support behind Jadid. He refused to give in to any of Hatum's demands and sent military units, including a rocket battalion, to Suwayda, threatening to rain utter destruction on the city. Planes hovered menacingly over Jabal al-Druze. Hatum and Asali quickly realized that they could not win. It was there and then that they decided to flee to Jordan. Nevertheless, there were reports of scattered fighting in Homs, Aleppo, Harsata, and Qabun on the following day.[20]

The Jadid dictatorship narrowly survived, but its confidence in its ability to control the armed forces was rudely shaken. In the following days a wide campaign of arrests took place among Druze officers. Their interrogations revealed that a large number were aware of the plot yet did not alert the authorities. Assad's complicity with the conspiracy was also uncovered.[21] As a countermeasure, the government announced in early October its intention to enlarge the National Guard, a Chinese-style popular militia. According to official pronouncements, the National Guard would join forces with the proletarian brigades, which, following the Hatum coup, reappeared in the streets of Homs, Hama, and Damascus after a brief lull in their activity. Both were to function as a political army. To make things crystal clear, the government announced that the role of the military would be limited from then on to defending Syria against an invasion. In addition, security measures around party headquarters were strengthened. It was now guarded only by the forces Jadid could trust: the proletarian brigades, the National Guard, and the secret services. Yet, in November, *al-Hayat* reported that no more than 3 percent of the population were willing to serve in the National Guard and even that diminished number was achieved only after recruits were threatened with loss of income. However, the regime, apprehensive of additional upheavals, did not distribute any light weapons among the volunteers and they were asked to carry out their mission unarmed. Nevertheless, many officers within the ranks saw the National Guard as a direct threat to military control over the state.[22]

All this explains why, on the eve of the May 1967 riots, Jadid and his men felt exposed and defenseless. The regime had to face the Islamic opposition when it was deeply unpopular and the support of the army was qualified. It was no coincidence, for instance, that Mustafa Tlass, military governor of the Homs area, refused to obey orders and repress the Muslim Brotherhood during the wave of unrest in May 1967. He was, after all, a confidant of Assad. Jadid had good reason to fear that Assad might use the instability to launch a coup. He was really on his own this time and the Islamic opposition, mobilized and armed, could smell the blood in the water. There was only one desperate card that Jadid could play. He had no other choice.

3

PLAYING THE ISRAEL CARD

ISRAEL AND SYRIA squared off over a rather mundane border dispute. At the end of the 1948 war Syrian forces were able to hold on to a strip of 65 square kilometers beyond the territory allotted by the UN to the Jewish state. The ceasefire that, after bitter and protracted negotiations, both sides agreed to sign in 1949 stipulated that, following the withdrawal of Syrian forces, the disputed territory would remain demilitarized and the affairs of the disputed area would be managed by an armistice committee composed of Israeli, Syrian, and UN representatives. The Syrian interpretation of the truce was that Israel could not use that territory until there was a final agreement about its status. The Israeli interpretation was that it had full sovereignty over the area.

What made things even more complicated was the fact that both Israeli and Syrian farmers owned land within the militarized zone. Theoretically there were ways to settle the matter peacefully, yet both sides approached the problem with a good measure of ill will. Israeli units expelled some of the Arab population that remained in the demilitarized zone. Israeli farmers endeavored to till all the fields in the disputed area, including those under Arab ownership, while Syrian units used their fortified positions atop the Golan Heights to rain fire on them. The Israeli army responded several times by launching punitive raids against Syrian positions. Nevertheless, up to 1963, a tense status quo was maintained, which was far more stable than that which transpired after the 1963 Baath coup.[1]

The notion that the dispute with Israel might be turned into an asset in inter-Arab conflicts emerged in 1959. In that year it was revealed that Israel was about to embark on an ambitious National Water Carrier (NWC) project, involving the construction of a 130-kilometer-long pipeline from the Sea of Galilee in the north of Israel to the Negev Desert in the south. Stormy discussions in the Arab press described the project as a strategic threat to the Arab nation: as the NWC would increase the amount of arable land, it would allow Israel to absorb more Jewish immigrants. Akram Hourani, representing the Baath in the joint cabinet of the UAR, tabled the matter in December 1959. He proposed launching a guerrilla campaign against the NWC site. Nasser, who chaired the meeting, rejected the idea out of hand, explaining that the Arabs were not strong enough to confront Israel.[2] It was probably there and then that the Syrians realized the Israeli issue might be used to embarrass Nasser.

During the following years Nasser did his best to be seen as doing something about the issue while actually not doing anything at all. He convened several forums of the loose association of Arab countries known as the Arab League to discuss the matter, only to postpone actual decisions for further discussion. But when the UAR disintegrated in 1961, the Israeli project became a shield with which the Syrians defended themselves against Nasser's attempts to meddle in their affairs. Indeed, Nasser never forgave the Syrians for seceding from the union and unleashed a campaign of propaganda and covert operations against them during 1961–63. For instance, an Egyptian intelligence officer, Abd al-Magid Farid, was sent to Beirut to set up his headquarters and focus on training Syrian and Palestinian mercenaries to plant explosives in Syria as well as establishing Nasserite cells within the Syrian army. As bombs blew up in public facilities in Damascus, Homs, and Hama, Nasserite officers planned a coup in July 1962. During that month there were also large pro-Nasser demonstrations in the main cities. At the height of these tensions, the Syrian government became so concerned that it closed its border with Lebanon to make it harder for Egyptian operatives to contact their agents.[3]

Nasser, then, even in the post-UAR era, posed a threat to any government in Syria. He may have mistreated Syrian officers and politicians but he remained popular with workers, peasantry, and even the urban middle class. After all, he was the first ruler of Syria to impose a land reform and defy the Sunni commercial elite of Aleppo and Damascus. And he was still seen as the best hope of creating a united Arab nation.

The Syrian government had to find a rebuttal to Nasser's allegation that by seceding, Syria had betrayed the Arab cause. Akram Hourani, one of the staunchest supporters of the breakup, threatened Nasser in a May 1962 article that if he did not desist from public attacks on Syria, he, Hourani, would divulge defamatory information about him. When Egypt continued its public attacks, Hourani proceeded and published the protocol of the UAR cabinet meeting from December 1959 in which Nasser had refused to take action to subvert the building of the NWC. Hourani called Nasser a coward and a traitor. This was a lesson that the Baath would seek to teach Nasser again and again: if he accused them of betraying the cause of Arab unity, they would accuse him of betraying the Palestinian cause.[4]

On March 10, 1963, two days after the Baath coup took place, popular demand for a reunion with Egypt flared up. Stormy demonstrations in Damascus, covered extensively by Egyptian media, demanded a return to unity talks. In early April there was another round of riots, followed by resignations of six Nasserite ministers from the cabinet. The government had to declare a state of emergency and impose an eighteen-hour curfew in Damascus. Yet Nasser had support not just among the public, but also inside the Syrian army. The Nasserites were part of the cabal of officers that sanctioned the March 1963 coup and at this stage the Baath needed their support. Bitar, who led the post-coup government, always wanted to renegotiate with Nasser a revival of the UAR, albeit one in which power would be shared more equally. Now, thanks to the support of the Nasserite officers, Bitar could pursue a rapprochement with Egypt. Nasser, though, was harsh and unforgiving. He made it clear that he would not cooperate with the Baath unless and until his representatives gained an equal share of the seats in the Syrian cabinet. Eventually, a unity agreement between Nasser and the Baathists was signed on April 17, 1963.[5]

Two weeks later, however, the military wing of the Baath, which opposed the unity agreement, struck. For its members, the negotiations with Nasser were just a charade – a way to pass the time until the Baath ensconced itself. Now more secure in its position, the military wing ordered the purge of dozens of Nasserite officers from the ranks. The agreement with Egypt became a dead letter. In response, on July 18 a pro-Nasser Syrian officer, Colonel Jasim Alwan, aided by Egyptian intelligence services, led other likeminded officers to a bold attack on Damascus's radio station and military headquarters, which, unusually for a Syrian coup, took place in broad daylight. Amin Hafiz, minister of the interior, submachine gun in hand, ordered troops to open fire on Alwan's forces and unleashed the air force against them. Hundreds died in the fighting and twenty-seven Nasserite officers were executed the following day.[6]

Egyptian media reacted harshly, calling Hafiz *al-Saffah* (the butcher). At the end of July, during a speech in Alexandria, Nasser, in a blatant attempt to egg on the Muslim opposition in Syria, dubbed the Baath a party of irreligion and heresy. It was not long before the Baath regime delivered its

response. In August 1963 Colonel Salim Hatum told the Israeli spy Elie
Cohen (Hatum was unaware of Cohen's true identity: Cohen presented
himself as a businessman) that Syria was about to initiate border incidents
with Israel "to teach Nasser a lesson in courage." Hatum made it clear that
Syria had no intention of entering a full-scale war with Israel, because it was
clear that the Israeli army would have the upper hand. Rather, according to
Hatum, Syria sought a few border skirmishes that would embarrass Nasser.[7]
Of course, this admission by a Syrian senior officer did not represent the
views of the Baath as a whole. The civilian wing of the Baath, led by Bitar
and Aflaq, was more cautious and believed provoking Israel would end in
Syrian military defeat. Indeed, in January 1964 Colonel Hatum told Elie
Cohen that the Syrian General Staff had planned to hit the northern Israeli
city, Tiberius, in retaliation for recent border clashes with Israel. Had it not
been for the "cowardice" of Aflaq and Bitar, added Hatum, Tiberius would
have already been bombed.[8]

The military Baath, then, was determined to initiate border clashes with
Israel to wrong-foot Nasser: if he failed to come to Syria's aid (an option he
tended to favor), he would be accused of running away from the battlefield.
To avoid public humiliation, Nasser would have to stop interfering in the
country's internal affairs and acknowledge Syria as an independent and
separate entity. (Indeed, two years on from the dissolution of the UAR
Nasser still had not agreed to the establishment of an Egyptian embassy in
Damascus.) So, beginning in 1963, Syrian forces reacted harshly when
Israeli tractors attempted to enter the demilitarized zone and put Israeli
settlements under heavy fire. Such incidents were, however, more frequent
under the military Baath: during the three years of joint civilian and military Baath rule (1963–66) there were 169 border incidents, whereas the
Syrian army under the military Baath was involved in 177 skirmishes in a
little less than half that time (March 1966–May 1967).[9]

Syria also started its own project to divert the Banias, a tributary of the
Jordan River which originated in its own territory (other tributaries flowed
through Lebanon and Jordan). This was the Syrian response to the building
of the NWC. Ostensibly, by diverting the Banias the Syrians could block the
supply of water to the Sea of Galilee and transform the NWC into a white
elephant. In reality, the diversion works smacked strongly of being a propaganda ploy. They would involve the digging of a massive 73-kilometer-long
canal, 3 meters deep, in a mountainous terrain. Twenty-five kilometers of
the planned canal ran parallel to the Israeli border and within a short
distance of it. There was no realistic chance of building that part of the
canal without Israeli agreement, which, obviously, was not going to be

forthcoming. Furthermore, the success of the Syrian diversion project was dependent upon the building of complementary projects in Lebanon and Jordan. Both countries, militarily weak as they were, feared Israeli retaliation. They made only token efforts to participate in the diversion scheme and, in fact, shirked from doing their "Arab duty."[10]

Moreover, there were grave doubts about whether the project was technically feasible. The chosen path necessitated digging tunnels totaling 4.5 kilometers, yet Syria's inefficient bureaucracy failed to manage more modest projects. It was also clear that even if the Syrians succeeded in completing this enormous undertaking, the planned canal would not actually have significantly blocked the water supply to the Israeli lake. As Dr. Munif al-Razzaz, general secretary of the Baath Party and a member of its civilian wing, admitted to *Le Monde* in 1965:

> We started too late and we will not be able to disrupt in any way Israeli plans to use the Jordan's water ... Our plan, even after its implementation, would decrease the water available for Israel only by an insignificant amount ... I can say candidly that in our opinion [by "our" he was apparently referring to the civilian Baath] we should not play this game.

Yet the Syrian diversion works continued. Every time the Israelis attacked Syrian diversion sites, the Syrians denounced Nasser for doing nothing to help them as they led the fight against Israel. Expressing this view, in May 1964 the Syrian president, General Amin Hafiz, ratcheted up official rhetoric by calling upon the Arab masses to join the struggle against Israel "either to drag Nasser into war [with Israel] or denounce him for his cowardice."[11]

In 1963 the military wing of the Baath embarked on yet another scheme that would embarrass Nasser. Again, against the wishes of the civilian wing of the Baath, Jadid and his allies in the army allowed the Palestinian Fatah organization to train and establish camps on Syria's territory. By that point Fatah had been in existence for several years, having been established in 1959 by Palestinians in their thirties and forties who held degrees from Egyptian universities, and who had reached the conclusion that Arab countries would not liberate Palestine for the Palestinians – only they could do it. The new movement vowed to launch a long-term guerrilla campaign against Israel that would eventually weaken the Jewish state.

For both Aflaq and Bitar, the existence of a separate Palestinian movement was inimical to the Pan-Arab ideology of the Baath. A secret pamphlet written in September 1965 by the civilian Baath further argued that Syria was not ready for "a [popular] liberation war" and urged the Baath Party not to repeat "the mistakes of 1948" when Syria had been defeated. Another pamphlet written a week later by supporters of Jadid sharply criticized the position of the civilian Baath. It argued that Syria must not postpone the battle with Israel as the power of the latter was on the rise, adding, "We should not fear losing in a battle in which we have not yet begun." Another Baath official was more candid and explained that the aim of Syrian support for Fatah operations was to "rub Nasser's nose in the mud of Palestine."[12]

Fatah was headed by 35-year-old Yasser Arafat, a Palestinian who, up to that point, had spent most of his life in Cairo and gained basic military training during the 1950s while serving in the Egyptian army. An energetic organizer, albeit an uninspiring public speaker (especially in English, which remained mediocre throughout his life), and with frantically rolling beady eyes, Arafat excelled in raising money from wealthy Palestinian business-people living in Kuwait. Much of the money was channeled into hiring Palestinians with a criminal record, especially in smuggling, to launch Fatah's first operations. While others in this fledgling movement thought that actual guerrilla operations should wait until Fatah gained more volun-teers (they were known in the movement's lingo as "the rational camp"), Arafat was for an immediate launch of operations, arguing that the reverse was correct: a successful campaign would beget more volunteers (his camp was dubbed "the radicals"). At a crucial meeting in the summer of 1964, Fatah's radicals carried the day. And, as it turned out, Arafat was right: Fatah operations captured the imagination of Palestinian youth and they rallied to become part of the armed movement.[13]

In Fatah ideology, the fight against Israel was to be the spark that ignited Palestinian national awareness. The cycle of Fatah operations and Israeli responses, so the Fatah founders believed, would instigate an escalation of violence that would force Arab countries attempting to avoid confrontation with Israel, such as Jordan and Egypt, into entering the battlefield and liberating Palestine. Fatah activists and writers held up Cuba, Algeria, and Vietnam as examples of what a successful guerrilla campaign could achieve. But all this was largely the creative borrowing of ideas that would justify the violent road that Fatah had already been following. The main motivation for Fatah activity was existential – not intellectual.[14]

Fatah was established to address the plight of the 750,000 Palestinians who had become refugees after the defeat of Arab armed forces in the 1948 war in Palestine. As Jewish units kept advancing and conquering more territory, urban and rural Palestinians fled in fear to neighboring Arab countries – an exodus aided and abetted by the Jewish forces with a number of massacres and expulsions.[15] Deprived of their homes (as the newly established Israeli state opposed their return), for decades Palestinians had found themselves living in miserable refugee camps in Jordan, Lebanon, Egypt, and Iraq. They were marginalized and disenfranchised in every Arab country except Jordan; the top jobs in politics, the military sphere, and business eluded them.[16] They became a people without a home. And Arafat and his comrades-in-arms stood no chance of achieving anything of significance for themselves unless they took matters into their own hands and forced the issue on Arab governments.

Moreover, at the time, various other Palestinian movements, such as the Egyptian-sponsored Palestinian Liberation Organization (PLO), were competing with Fatah over the right to represent the Palestinian nation. Established in 1964, the PLO was better funded and relied on a very different cadre than that of Fatah. Its leadership emerged from the remnants of the influential landowning families in pre-1948 Palestinian society; Palestinian politicians who were co-opted by the Jordanian monarchy and became parliament members and mayors; and the professional class of lawyers, doctors, university professors, and engineers that emerged in Gaza and the West Bank. One of the founders of Fatah, Mahmoud Abbas, who later became the chairman of the Palestinian authority, described PLO founders as "the sons of [upper-class] families and traditional figures." The armed struggle offered Fatah's young activists the best chance of outshining the more moderate and establishmentarian PLO. Indeed, up to 1966, the PLO opposed guerrilla operations against Israel. In that sense the decision of the military Baath to support Fatah was a decisive intervention in an inter-Palestinian dispute. The military Baath helped Palestinian supporters of the armed struggle vanquish their civilian foes.[17]

In December 1965 Fatah began a series of guerrilla attacks against Israel, planting explosives near water pipelines, water pumps, warehouses, and power plants as well as mining roads, highways, and railroad tracks. Fatah's first operation – planting a few fingers of dynamite next to a pumping station, which were easily spotted and dismantled after failing to explode – was emblematic of those to follow. Out of 113 Palestinian sabotage acts, only 71 were moderately successful, but they were brilliantly marketed as resounding victories by Arafat's Number 2, Khalil al-Wazir. After the 1966 coup, the Syria–Fatah alliance grew stronger and the number of Fatah operations doubled: between 1963 and 1966, when the civilian Baath was still influential, Fatah units were involved in thirty-eight sabotage operations; during the fifteen months of military Baath rule, that number rose to seventy-five.[18]

The increase in the number of operations had everything to do with the decision of Assad and Jadid to arrange for soldiers of the 68th Battalion – an all-Palestinian commando unit – to become part of Fatah forces. Long an arm of Syrian intelligence services, 68th Battalion soldiers had been trained to conduct reconnaissance missions inside Israel. (After Yasser Arafat had been arrested by Lebanese police, Syrian intelligence services intervened to request his release as he worked for them.) Syrian military intelligence was also Fatah's main supplier of weapons and explosives. By the autumn of 1966 it was evident that, thanks to its guidance, Fatah operations were improving: units carried more mines, bombs were timed to allow the fighters a stealthy retreat, and Fatah units had better intelligence concerning how to reach their targets. In early 1966, Syrian intelligence even attempted to take full control of Fatah by installing Yousef Urabi, a Palestinian captain working in its ranks, as its head. To establish facts on the ground, Urabi announced to all Fatah cells that he was replacing Arafat. In return, the ever-ruthless Arafat ambushed Urabi together with Wazir and killed him in a shoot-out on May 9.[19]

Ahmed Sawidani aided Fatah first as the head of military intelligence and, from 1966, as Syria's chief of staff. He had been posted to Moscow as a military attaché between 1958–61 and had made several trips to Beijing where he encountered the military writings of Mao and North Vietnamese Minister of Defense Võ Nguyên Giáp's work on guerrilla tactics. In an April 1966 interview with the Egyptian press, Sawidani averred that there was no use trying to confront Israel with conventional forces as in that sphere Israel was clearly superior. Only a sustained campaign of small operations would force Israel to submit to Arab demands.

Indeed, on the face of it, there was much to connect Fatah and Baath leaders. The central figures in both groups were young and ambitious. The Palestinians were marginalized in Arab society as much as the religious minorities (from which Baath officers hailed) were in Syria. Many of the Baath officers who supported Jadid served on the Israeli front and were scarred by the numerous border incidents, which the Syrians usually lost.[20]

Yet, despite its many declarations of support for the Palestinian struggle, the Syrian military kept Fatah on a short leash. The incarceration of Fatah leaders in May 1966 was a case in point. A Fatah unit had launched a guerrilla operation against Israel from the Golan Heights, and in doing so had contravened an unwritten agreement between Fatah and the Syrian authorities according to which Fatah fighters could cross into Israel only from Lebanon or Jordan, not over the Israeli–Syrian border. The reason for this tacit understanding was that the military Baath did not want to give Israel a pretext to hit Syria – an embarrassing admission in the context of Syria's uncompromising rhetoric on the Israeli issue. Moreover, by channeling Fatah operations to the West Bank, the Syrians hoped to embroil King Hussein of Jordan, with whom the Baath were in open conflict, in a war against Israel. In May 1966, Fatah fighters not only violated this understanding by entering Israel from Syria, they also did so without informing army headquarters. Syria's Minister of Defense Assad had Fatah's leaders thrown into Mezze prison. They were released more than a month later and only after they had promised Assad not to breach Syrian instructions again.[21]

Ensnaring Nasser

The first war scare manufactured by the Jadid regime came in May 1966, immediately after the Jadid–Assad conflict broke into the open. Syrian media reported claims that Israel was about to attack Syria, allegations that were repeated by the government in September after the Hatum rebellion. Syrian President Nur al-Din Atasi even wrote to Nasser notifying him of reliable information that Israel was about to attack.[22] This letter was also the result of Jadid having concluded that his regime's base of support was too narrow, and that an alliance with Syrian Nasserites might stabilize it. From that point onward, contact with Nasser intensified. Nasser's main demand was for more Nasserite ministers to be included in Syria's cabinet; by October 22, 1966, a new government, which included four pro-Nasser ministers, was appointed in Damascus. In addition, and to ease Nasser's fears, Syrian Foreign Minister Ibrahim Makhus invited foreign diplomats to his office to present them with copies of an order to the army to cease Palestinian infiltration into Israel. A few days earlier, Syrian Minister of Information Jamal Shia had declared that the Syrian Baath Party saw Nasser as the natural leader of the Arab world. Finally Nasser assented, and a military treaty between Syria and Egypt was signed on November 1.[23]

It might have been assumed that the Baath regime would quit while it was ahead, but the opposite happened. Success had gone to the Baath leaders' heads. Once the Syrians had returned to Damascus, the Nasserite ministers were expelled from the government. The official rhetoric celebrated the treaty with Egypt and claimed that Syria was a revolutionary locomotive that would drag other Arab radical regimes – Iraq, Algeria, and Yemen – into a union that would replace the Arab League. Secret leaflets sent to Baath activists maintained that from this point Syria would spearhead the Arab struggle against Israel and shift from the defensive to the offensive. In early

May 1967, Ahmed Sawidani told the leader of the PLO, Ahmad Shukeiri, that he had received an ultimatum from his Egyptian counterpart demanding that Syria put an end to Fatah operations. Sawidani, however, bragged that he was ignoring it. The Baath Party supported Fatah, explained Sawidani, and would not stop doing so even if it brought about the occupation of Damascus. Ibrahim Makhus assured Shukeiri that Syria knew exactly what it was doing: Israel would not dare attack Syria now that it had Egyptian backing.[24]

Indeed, Fatah operations and Syria's border incidents with Israel only intensified after the signing of the treaty, pushing the region further toward war. On November 11, 1966, an Israeli patrol drove over a land mine that had been planted by Fatah fighters. The Palestinians, according to their pact with the Syrians, had taken care to enter Israel through the West Bank. The Israeli decision was to mount an asymmetric response that would avenge the planting of this land mine and others in previous months. On November 13, a column of tanks and half-trucks carrying 600 Israeli soldiers entered the West Bank village of Samu in broad daylight and blew up a hundred buildings. Deeply humiliated, Jordan embarked on a campaign aimed at shaming Egypt for doing nothing while the Israelis were invading the kingdom.

On April 7, 1967, the Syrians contributed once again to the escalation. On that day, a border clash between Syrian and Israeli forces quickly turned into a mutual exchange of fire. Wishing to up the ante, the Israeli Air Force sent its planes to bomb Syrian artillery. Without blinking an eye, Assad ordered his MiGs to confront them. Due to the conflict between Jadid and Assad, the Syrian government, fearing a coup, had ordered the air force to keep the planes unarmed, so the MiGs confronting the Israeli Mirages were armed only with dummy missiles. Seven of them were unceremoniously downed.[25]

After that incident, the military Baath regime became edgy. A secret pamphlet to Baath Party members dated April 20, 1967 claimed that Israeli troop concentrations had been spotted on the Syrian border and that this was "an initial stage before embarking upon a wide attack to smash the Syrian armed forces." It further claimed that the dogfight on April 7 was part of a "vast conspiracy." The current quiet along the ceasefire lines was therefore illusory, averred the pamphlet – merely the calm before the storm. The government had called up reserves for a compulsory six months' service and conducted daily alarm drills in Damascus, "a thing that creates a war psychosis among the denizens of the city," reported a Czechoslovak diplomat.[26]

All this lent credence to the efforts of the Jadid regime to solve the crisis with the Muslim Brotherhood, which started on April 25, 1967, again employing the Israeli bogeyman. On May 8, 1967, two Syrian secret service agents were sent to Cairo to meet with Nasser. They alleged that Syrian scouts, who had penetrated deep into Israeli territory, had spotted a significant military build-up. They had received similar information, they added, from the Lebanese intelligence services. In reality, there was no Israeli build-up. The Syrian agents were most likely sent to trigger an Egyptian response that would change the conversation in Syria, which at that point was focused on the clash between the regime and the Muslim Brotherhood. On May 11, Syrian media had begun a propaganda campaign to alert the people to "the imperialist conspiracies threatening the Syrian revolution." An official statement published that day had claimed that the Anglo-Americans, the Israelis, the Saudis, and the Jordanians were all involved in preparations to attack Syria and other radical Arab regimes. The statement was sent to all "Arab, progressive and friendly governments."[27]

Thus, between May 8 and 11, the military Baath kicked off a major public campaign aimed at shifting the Syrian public's attention from the confrontation with the Muslim Brotherhood to the danger posed by Israel. The practice of inventing and inflating the Israeli threat for internal and external purposes was by then well established, only this time the trick backfired. A unique set of circumstances caused the Syrian cries of "wolf" to ignite the Middle East.

4

THE SPY WHO CAME BACK FROM
THE COLD

O N APRIL 14, 1967, Murad Ghaleb, Egypt's ambassador to Moscow, met with Vladimir Semyonov, the Soviet deputy foreign minister. Semyonov, who was heavily involved in directing Soviet policy in the Middle East, was troubled by recent events on the Syrian–Israeli border. The aerial battle between Syrian MiGs and Israeli Mirages above Damascus on the 7th was still fresh in his mind, and in his evaluation of the Baathists' behavior he did not mince his words, calling them "over-eager adolescents" who were bandying the word "revolution" about far too much. The main thing Semyonov requested from Ghaleb was that the Egyptians calm the Syrians down by reassuring them that Cairo had their backs.[1]

Semyonov was preaching to the converted. The Egyptians themselves were well aware that they had to do something. The confrontation between Syrian and Israeli aircraft ended with six MiGs downed; the Israelis lost none. The meager capabilities of the Syrians made them a running joke in the Arab world. In their defense, the Baath regime lost no time in accusing Cairo of not helping out. After all, just five months earlier, in November 1966, Syria and Egypt had signed a military treaty in which each vowed to defend the other should it be attacked. On the face of it, Egypt was in breach of the agreement.

The argument that Cairo used to justify itself was technical. Allegedly, Egyptian planes could not store enough fuel for the flight to Syria and back. If Syria was so eager to receive military support, Egyptian propaganda pointed out, it should allow Egyptian pilots and planes to use Syrian airfields. (This had been a familiar Egyptian refrain since 1965.) Implicitly, what the Egyptians wanted was to regain their ability to shape Syrian policies, which they had lost after the breakup of the union in 1961. Had Egyptian planes been sent to Syria in the spring of 1967, it would have been to prevent future border clashes between Israel and Syria rather than to defend Syria.[2]

General Muhammad Sidqi Mahmud, commander of the Egyptian Air Force, was the first Egyptian official to visit Damascus following the April debacle. Having met with Assad, Mahmud was taken aback by the desperate mood that had taken over the Syrian leadership. He submitted a report to the Egyptian vice president, Marshal Abd al-Hakim Amer, in which he recommended, in strong language, that some arrangement be made that would ease Syrian minds.[3] The next senior Egyptian to try his hand at stabilizing an unstable situation was the Egyptian premier, Suliman Sidqi, who arrived in Damascus on April 20, at about the same time as Semyonov was discussing his concerns with Ghaleb.

Suliman Sidqi came accompanied by Egyptian officers. Their task was to create a mechanism that would end Syrian brinkmanship. Among other things, the Egyptians demanded that the Syrians put an end to Fatah operations, allow the permanent presence of Egyptian squadrons in Syrian airfields, and put the Syrian Air Force under de facto Egyptian command. Ever divided, the Syrian leadership could not agree on a response to the Egyptian gambit. While Minister of Defense Hafez al-Assad was opposed to it, undoubtedly concerned about losing control over the air force – his support base – Salah Jadid, the nominal leader of the Syrian junta, was willing to accept the Egyptian plan. Assad seems to have won the debate and Damascus rejected the proposal. In short, Sidqi's visit settled nothing. Furthermore, seventy Syrian Nasserites had been arrested for reacting too enthusiastically to Sidqi's arrival – yet another sign of the mutual, persistent suspicion that both Cairo and Damascus had for the other.[4]

Three days after Sidqi left Damascus, Anwar al-Sadat arrived in Moscow. Later, in the 1970s, Sadat would reveal himself to be a bold strategist who led Egypt in both war and peace, only to be assassinated by members of the Muslim Brotherhood in 1981. But that audacity was still far in the future of this 49-year-old man, who had begun his life in a poor village deep in the Nile Delta. In 1967, Sadat was occupying the largely ceremonial role of speaker of the National Assembly. He arrived in the Soviet capital on April 28 en route to North Korea for a goodwill visit. While in Moscow he met with Semyonov for an innocent chat. Semyonov told him about a meeting that had taken place a few days earlier, between Soviet Premier Alexei Kosygin and the Israeli ambassador, Katriel Katz. Katz had come to deliver a letter from Levi Eshkol, the Israeli prime minister, which accused Syria of provoking the recent incidents on the Syrian–Israeli border. Kosygin was not impressed and reprimanded Israel for concentrating troops on the Syrian border. Katz denied the existence of such concentrations and reminded Kosygin that Eshkol had invited the Soviet ambassador to visit the northern front with him, to see for himself that the whole affair had been a figment of Syria's imagination. Semyonov, recounting the Katz–Kosygin conversation to Sadat, dismissed Israel's denials and added that the Soviet Union had "the means to know what the situation was without a visit to the front line. [Israeli] units on the front line could be mobilized anytime, but the Soviet Union has the capability to know what is the real situation on the ground"[5] – a cryptic response, suggestive of sources inside Israel that were delivering top-secret information to the Soviets. Years later, Vadim Kirpichenko, one of the KGB's old Middle Eastern hands, was even blunter, claiming that the Soviets had a mole inside the Israeli government.[6]

Enter Victor Grayevsky, the servant of two masters. His first act on the Cold War stage was performed ten years earlier, in 1956. He had come to call on his lover, Lucia Baranowski, the wife of Poland's deputy prime minister. She worked as a secretary for Edward Ochab, who was the first secretary of the Polish United Workers' Party. Visiting Lucia in her office at party headquarters, Grayevsky spied a chubby red booklet bearing the title "The 20th Party Congress, the speech of Comrade Khrushchev." It was the 26,000-word speech in which Nikita Khrushchev, the Soviet party chairman, gave for the first time a full account of the mass murders committed under his predecessor, Joseph Stalin. The speech was delivered in front of hundreds of delegates from all corners of the Communist world. Many of them were taken aback by the severity of Khrushchev's attack on Stalin. It was for this reason that scattered pieces of information about the speech had found their way to Western intelligence services, and they were eager to lay their hands on a copy of the full text. Grayevsky, who at the time was a senior editor at the Polish News Agency, was aware of this and asked Lucia's permission to borrow the booklet for a few hours. Concealing it under his overcoat, he left the building, uninspected by the security guards. His curiosity as a journalist got the better of him, and he started reading the speech. But as the realization dawned that the document in his hands was a damning accusation of Soviet Communism, he decided he ought to return it before he got into trouble. On his way back to party headquarters, however, he had had a change of heart.[7]

A year earlier, in 1955, Grayevsky had gone to Israel to visit his ailing father, who had immigrated in 1949. Grayevsky was greatly impressed with what he saw, and he was planning to follow in his parents' footsteps. As he walked back to headquarters, all this came flooding back to him, and a new decision was formed, one that would shock the world. "I acted out of impulse," Grayevsky later recalled. "With hindsight, I know I was young and foolish. If they were on to me . . . I don't know if they would have killed me, but I would have spent considerable time in jail." Rather than party head-quarters, Grayevsky headed toward the Israeli embassy in Warsaw. Polish police officers and soldiers were circling the building, but Grayevsky none-theless knocked on the door. He asked to see an Israeli diplomat he had met previously, and then simply handed him the document, saying, "See what I've got." The Israeli diplomat "went white in the face, then red, and then he changed colors again. He asked to take the booklet for a minute, then came back after an hour and a half. I knew he was taking pictures," claimed Grayevsky. After receiving the speech, the Mossad, Israel's service of external intelligence, hastened to deliver the goods to the CIA. Two weeks later, quotes from the Khrushchev speech appeared in newspaper articles around the world.[8] No Kremlin leak had embarrassed the Soviet Union and demor-alized the Communist movement worldwide as much as Khrushchev's secret speech.

A year later, thanks to the strenuous efforts of Israeli officials who had feared for his safety, Grayevsky was in Israel. His services to his adopted country were not about to end. After he arrived, in 1957, the Shin Bet, Israel's internal security service, took pains to get Grayevsky employment at the Israeli broadcasting service and the Foreign Ministry – both were merely a cover, part of a well-planned ruse to deal with the problem of Communist espionage. During the 1950s and 1960s, Soviet intelligence officers posted to Israel were successful in netting several high-level spies, among them a senior adviser to the Israeli prime minister. Almost every East European diplomat seemed to be an operative, and the relatively inex-perienced Shin Bet, which was also suffering from a shortage of manpower, had a hard time tracking them all. The arrival of Grayevsky in Israel helped launch a counter-intelligence offensive.[9]

Upon arrival, Grayevsky was first enrolled in a six-month Hebrew-language course. As if by chance, several Soviet diplomats were studying in the same class. Grayevsky, fluent in Russian, quickly befriended them. One of the Soviets, a junior intelligence officer called Veleri Osachi, showed great interest in him, having learned that Grayevsky was working in the Israeli Foreign Ministry. Grayevsky reported back to the Shin Bet, and his handlers encouraged him to proceed. Grayevsky started meeting with Osachi regularly, and within a short time the Soviets regarded him as such an asset that he was invited to meet his contact at the inner sanctum of Soviet intelligence operations in Israel – the Russian compound in Jerusalem.[10]

The Shin Bet closely monitored Grayevsky's meetings with the Soviets, and was thereby able to map the activity of Soviet intelligence and uncover several spies. Grayevsky, on his part, dutifully reported his meetings with the KGB and even handed over the cash he had received from them. At one time, his reward amounted to $1,000, a huge sum in frugal and socialist Israel. Reuven Hazak, Grayevsky's handler, almost fainted when the sweaty pack of dollars landed in his lap. As the Shin Bet was closing in on the Soviet spy network in Israel, Grayevsky's handlers worried that the KGB would suspect that their prime agent had been compromised. To allay the Soviets' probes, Grayevsky, code-named "Apollonia" by the Shin Bet, was instructed in the mid-1960s to pass on a protocol of a meeting between Nasser and Soviet officials, to demonstrate his loyalty and access to classified materials. The protocol was genuine – Israeli intelligence laid its hands on it using its electronic capabilities.[11] The KGB must have been greatly impressed. If ever the Israeli intelligence wanted to run a disinformation operation targeted at Moscow, Grayevsky would be its perfect instrument. An opportunity presented itself in May 1967.

Inventing Aggressors

Spooking the Syrians so that they would behave was something the Israelis had been considering doing from early 1967. In January, Aharon Yariv, head of military intelligence, wrote a memo to Yitzhak Rabin, the chief of staff, which focused on how to convince Syria to stop supporting Palestinian guerrillas. Yariv's main recommendations were: "A. To declare that we would act against any terror-supporting government ... B. *Alternatively: leak this information to the Syrian intelligence.*" A month later Israel had passed on a message to Syria "through third parties" according to which Syria would be punished severely if Fatah operations continued. Obviously, this threat failed to convince the Syrians. By late April, the feeling among Israeli decision-makers was that enough was enough. Fatah operations increased by the day and became more and more daring. On May 7, the cabinet convened to discuss the situation on Israel's northern border and decided to warn the Syrians, through the Americans, that if they dared "to continue their provocations ... Israel would respond with a military operation."[12]

On May 9, Eshkol participated in a meeting of the Knesset security and foreign affairs committee. Though theoretically the committee was supposed to keep its discussions secret, in reality it was somewhat porous. Eshkol shared with committee members his opinion that Syria should receive a "serious blow" and added that "the time for revenge has come." Most attendees were in agreement with him on this. There is little doubt that the contents of this debate were leaked and they became known to Soviet intelligence (which passed the information to the Egyptians). Nevertheless, the campaign of threats had just begun.[13]

On May 11, speaking to members of his party, Eshkol said that Israel was taking the recent incidents seriously – there had been fourteen Fatah operations in the previous months – and would respond in a manner "as severe as on 7 April." Two days later, when speaking on state radio, he warned that "there will be peace and quiet on both sides of the border or none." Chief of Staff Yitzhak Rabin gave interviews to several media outlets between May 13 and 15 in which he reiterated the same position. The military pundit of *Yediot Ahronot*, an Israeli daily, who was known as having good sources, wrote on May 12 that "after the latest warnings by Israeli leaders, the most senior of whom was Mr. Eshkol, there is no doubt that Israel would react soon to Syrian terror acts against it." He added that this would be a big operation but would not include occupying territories "that are far and away from the Syrian border." He wrote, no doubt reflecting the opinion of the officials he had spoken to, that Russia and Egypt would intervene only if Israel occupied Damascus. The *New York Times* carried a similar story the next day. The message coming out of Jerusalem was unmistakably clear: Israel would use the next border incident to conquer the Syrian area closest to the border, namely the Golan Heights.[14]

On May 12, the Soviet Politburo received information from an agent "close to Israeli headquarters" indicating that the Israeli army had completed preparations for an operation against Syria. The unnamed informant further elaborated that any serious incident near the Syrian–Israeli border would be used by Israel to unleash an attack. That source also claimed that air and ground forces would participate in the operation and that a large contingent of paratroopers was preparing to be dropped on Syrian territory. Further suggesting that the source was a human agent, General Aleksandr Sakharovsky, head of the KGB's foreign intelligence department, stressed that the accuracy of the information could not be ascertained.[15]

Several contemporaries expressed the suspicion that Israeli intelligence was behind the information that Moscow received. Both Georgy Kornienko, a senior Soviet diplomat, and Murad Ghaleb, the Egyptian ambassador to Moscow, related in their memoirs their belief that the source of the May 12 intelligence report had been an Israeli double agent. Interestingly, they articulated these suspicions five years *before* Grayevsky who, in the last year of his life, decided to break his silence and reveal his part in the clandestine struggle between the Soviet and the Israeli intelligence services.[16]

Moreover, on May 12, Aharon Yariv, interviewed by the foreign press as "a senior military official," expressed his opinion that the only solution to Damascus's defiance would be "a military operation of a great size and strength." Yariv added that Israel needed a type of action that would alert the Syrians to the dangers of "a probable or possible or imminent all-out military confrontation" with Israel. Yariv also devoted considerable time during the interview to explaining that the Soviet Union was unwilling or unable "to temper Syrian actions."[17]

Clearly Yariv was referring to the prime minister himself. Eshkol was a firm believer in a dialogue with Moscow and argued that building a bridge to the Soviet Union would help improve relations with the Arab world. Furthermore, while Yariv believed that the Soviets would not lift a finger to forestall an Israeli–Syrian confrontation, he was not controlling Grayevsky. The Shin Bet was, though, and it was answerable to the prime minister alone. In other words, Eshkol could ignore the opinion of his head of military intelligence if he wanted to, and order the Shin Bet to use Grayevsky to persuade the Soviets that this time Israel's threats were real. As a matter of fact, Eshkol's adjutant, Yisrael Lior, noticed that "Eshkol evinced, for some reason, a special interest in Shin Bet surveillance of the Soviet embassy in Israel . . ."[18]

Grayevsky, for his part, never admitted that he was the source of the May 12 warning. Obviously, doing so would have been embarrassing in the extreme. If Israel was behind the rumor of an impending attack on Syria, it had only itself to blame for the regional crisis that unfolded in the next few days. If this was a disinformation operation, it had clearly backfired. Then again, it is hard to imagine that the Soviets had any other source of information. They had only seventeen diplomats posted to Israel, all of whom had been closely monitored. Indeed, in the summer of 1966, the Soviet ambassador to Israel complained that the Israeli secret services were constantly shadowing the embassy's personnel. Moreover, John Hadden, head of the CIA station at Tel Aviv during the 1960s, had maintained that the very few Soviet spies active in Israel at the time were "bottled up by Israeli counter-intelligence." Even if Soviet diplomats were not under surveillance, getting access to sensitive information in Israel during the 1960s was heavy lifting even for military attachés from friendly countries. Lieutenant Lynn P. Blasch, who was the American assistant naval attaché in 1967, described Israel as "Iron Curtain country as far as military information was concerned."[19]

Grayevsky did admit that he was sent, at a later stage of the crisis, to tell his KGB contact that Israel would attack Egypt if it did not comply with Israeli demands, thus confirming that he had indeed been used to deliver threats to Arab countries through the KGB.[20] Moreover, the intelligence report received by the Soviet Politburo on May 12 was a stern warning that Israel would attack unless Syria behaved. This message was in line with the latest pronouncements by Israeli Prime Minister Levi Eshkol.

The Soviets' most plausible and reliable source was an Israeli double agent operating out of the prime minister's office. Eshkol believed that the Soviets could help manage Arab–Israeli tensions. What the Soviets received from their Israeli source was a conditional threat. The original report mentioned no date for the purported Israeli attack and did not refer to the size of the invading force. In the following forty-eight hours, the report had changed its nature as it passed through Syrian and Soviet hands. Various parties were ready and willing to lie in order to turn the threat into a war scenario. Why? The answer to this question is similar to the one given in Agatha Christie's *Murder on the Orient Express*: everybody had a motive, and everyone was involved.

With this hot potato on its hands, the Politburo decided on May 12 to alert the Syrians. The ambassador to Damascus, Anatoli Barkovski, was instructed to meet with Syrian Foreign Minister Ibrahim Makhus and warn him. In his conversation with Makhus, Barkovski talked about the possibility of an Israeli attack that would be more severe than that of April 7 – an almost verbatim reiteration of Eshkol's threat from May 11.[21] The Soviet intervention fell like manna from heaven on the Syrian Baath. Ever since May 8 the regime had been claiming that it was about to be attacked by a number of hostile regional players, including Israel, Jordan, and Iran. This had been a rather obvious attempt to draw the attention of the Syrian public away from the regime's confrontation with the Muslim Brotherhood, and to focus the minds of the citizenry on the unifying theme of national security. The Syrians, who from atop the Golan Heights had a good view of Israeli positions and were regularly eavesdropping on IDF radio communications, knew that there were no Israeli troop concentrations on their borders.[22] Nevertheless, they corroborated the Soviet report.

About twenty-four hours elapsed between Barkovski's conversation with Makhus in Damascus and the arrival of Sadat in Moscow on May 13. Sadat was on his way back from North Korea, and was making another courtesy call in the Russian capital. The visit proved much more consequential than Sadat had expected. His first meeting was with the foreign minister, Andrei Gromyko, and their conversation revealed just how hazy

Soviet and Egyptian knowledge was regarding what had transpired in Syria. Gromyko started by claiming that "reactionary forces" were active in the Middle East, especially along the Syrian–Israeli border. Sadat recalled that, when in Korea, he had heard rumors about a coup attempt in Damascus. Gromyko responded by saying that he had no information about a coup attempt in Syria, although there was evidence that a conspiracy had been afoot, but had been uncovered. Semyonov, who was also present, said that there was an attempt in Syria to organize a merchants' strike and that an anti-Islamic article had been published in the local press. Most probably, mused Semyonov, the Americans had a hand in this. All this led Sadat to observe that the Syrians liked to play with dangerous declarations about Israel. He did not say that the Syrians were doing so at that point, but he implied it. Sadat reiterated the Egyptian position: Egypt was willing to help Syria, but Syria was unwilling to let Egyptian planes and pilots use its airfields. Egypt's hands were tied.[23]

The events in Syria were discussed further in Sadat's next meeting, with the chairman of the Presidium, Nikolai Podgorny. According to the minutes, Podgorny told Sadat that "Syria is in a difficult situation, and we are helping it deal with it. And we had informed President Nasser in Cairo regarding the intelligence we have." Podgorny did not elaborate on the nature of that intelligence and quickly moved on to discuss the prospects of the Egyptian oil industry.[24]

If Sadat was not worried at that point, his concerns crescendoed during the farewell party thrown in his honor. The ubiquitous Semyonov arrived after speaking informally with the "white neighbors" (the KGB, in Soviet Foreign Ministry parlance). Semyonov's contact at the KGB told him that, based on information received from the Syrians, Soviet intelligence now believed that Israel was preparing a ground and air offensive against Syria, to be carried out between May 17 and 21. Semyonov must have understood the implications of that information. In the previous months, he and other Soviet diplomats had worked hard to avoid a Middle Eastern conflagration. Now it seemed the powder keg was about to blow. When he arrived at the party, Semyonov grabbed Murad Ghaleb, the Egyptian ambassador to Moscow, by the elbow. He told him what he knew and then added that while Egypt should prepare itself for some tense times, it must stay calm and be careful not to be drawn into a conflict with Israel. Semyonov explained that the Syrians had received a similar message, urging them to show restraint and not to provoke Israel into attacking. He ended by saying that the Soviet Union's next step would be to bring the whole matter before the UN's Security Council (indeed, that was what the Soviet diplomats would do in the following days).[25] Ghaleb hurried across the room to talk with Sadat. He suggested that Sadat, who was scheduled to take an early flight back to Cairo the following morning, inform Nasser about it then. Sadat, however, instructed Ghaleb to send the news to Cairo immediately.

Ghaleb's telegram, which was intercepted by the CIA, arrived that evening and struck the Egyptian capital like a bolt of lightning. General Abd al-Muhsen Murtagi, who in the following days would be appointed commander of the Egyptian land forces in Sinai, recalled a tense atmosphere. On the evening of May 13, the air was thick with rumors of an impending Israeli attack. First, there were the threats from Jerusalem. Added to that was Syria's insistence that it was facing immediate danger. On the 12th, twenty-four hours before Ghaleb's telegram reached Cairo, the Syrian minister of information, Muhammad Zubi, passed on his government's request to Egypt to implement the joint defense agreement, signed in November 1966, and start military consultations to stop the Israeli invasion. The request was also transmitted through the more official channel of the Joint Arab Command (JAC), which had been established by the Arab League to coordinate Arab military activities.

When he saw Syria's appeal to Egypt for military assistance, the head of the intelligence branch at the JAC, a Syrian, commented that it appeared that the Syrian government was engaged in a political maneuver designed to strengthen its position, and that it was unlikely that any armed conflict between Syria and Israel would occur. At the time, his opinion was ignored. The Syrians continued to sound the tocsin during May 13 as well. Foreign Minister Ibrahim Makhus wrote to his Egyptian counterpart that an imperialist conspiracy was being hatched against Syria and he hoped that Egypt would not stand aside. In the afternoon, the Syrians sent another missive alleging that an Israeli attack was imminent.[26]

Murtagi wrote in his memoirs that, on the night of May 13, the Egyptian military intelligence was unsure of what the Israelis would do. There were reports about Israeli troop concentrations, but it was unclear which country was the target. Was it Jordan? Egypt? Perhaps Syria? The telegram that, unbeknownst to the Egyptian intelligence, was partly based on what the Syrians had told the Soviets seemed to erase all doubt. Rather than seeing the information coming from Moscow as an echo of recent Syrian claims, the head of the Egyptian military intelligence thought this was a corroboration based on the KGB's excellent sources. Moreover, at about the same time that Ghaleb's telegram reached Cairo, Mohamed Fawzi, chief of staff of the Egyptian armed forces, was contacted by Ahmed Sawidani, his Syrian counterpart. Sawidani claimed that Israel had called up the greater part of its reserve forces and was mobilizing fifteen or so brigades on the Syrian front. For the Egyptians, the last piece of the puzzle seemed to have fallen into place.[27]

And so, two disinformation operations that were run in parallel converged to create a plausible story. The Israelis wanted the Syrians to believe that this time they meant business and used a double agent to deliver a threat to Syria, through the KGB. The Syrians, for their part, wanted the Soviets to think that they were about to be attacked, and claimed that they knew when the Israeli attack would take place. To ensure that some regional crisis would arise, the Syrians had fabricated the existence of Israeli troop concentrations and delivered this false information to the Egyptians. Within twenty-four hours, Egyptian intelligence realized it had been duped. But during the night of May 13–14, the threat of an imminent Israeli attack on Cairo's ally seemed real enough.

The Egyptian president decided it was time to take action. Nasser phoned his vice president and commander of the armed forces, Abd al-Hakim Amer, and summoned him to his private residence for an urgent discussion. The fateful meeting lasted well beyond midnight. At this particular point in their long political partnership, Nasser and Amer mistrusted each other but were also dependent on each other. The mood in the room must have been thick with suspicion and despair. The long years of economic hardship and political turmoil had taken their toll on both of them. This was not how their revolution had begun. Fifteen years earlier, Egypt's chances had looked much brighter.

5

THE CORRUPTION OF THE
REVOLUTION

NASSER CAME TO power in July 1952, after leading a successful blood-less coup against a corrupt monarchy. Political instability had reigned during the previous seven years, and Egypt was in a constant state of crisis. The source of political turmoil had been the younger generation. Egypt's system of higher education – the best and the most advanced in the Arab world – produced hundreds of new graduates every year, but the country's crony capitalism, which was dominated by several family-owned monopolies, could not create enough jobs for all of them. Their parents had sent them into the campuses to ensure that they would escape a life of hard labor, under a scorching sun, in Egypt's vast cotton fields. Disgruntled and unemployed, these youths now roamed the streets of Cairo and Alexandria in their thousands, demanding change.

In the minds of those educated youngsters, the source of Egypt's troubles was the alliance between the British army, which occupied a vast military compound along the Suez Canal, and the big landowners, also known as pashas. University graduates wanted the British gone, the pashas removed from power, and people who represented their own interests at the helm. In addition, they demanded that the state expand in size, tax the rich, and actively promote growth (the pashas preferred a *laissez-faire* policy and low taxation). They hoped that state intervention would create new jobs for them, mainly within the government sector. There were no more than a few thousand of them, concentrated in the large cities, but that was where politics happened, since the vast rural areas remained relatively dormant. Their education, in a society rife with illiteracy, conferred upon them leadership status. And so, they could punch above their weight.[1]

At first, unemployed university graduates thought that Nasser and his military junta would adopt policies that would be beneficial to them. Fairly quickly, these hopes were dashed. Nasser believed at the time that the best way to lead Egypt forward was to align with the US. He and his deputies had contact with the CIA prior to the coup, and after they had taken power, American advisers could be observed in every ministry. Nasser believed for a while that the US would bankroll Egypt's future development and did his best to create a business-friendly environment: he put a freeze on the salaries of government officials, cut the budget, and took a harsh line toward the trade unions. This policy, implemented between 1952 and 1954, had made Nasser extremely unpopular. The university graduates were out in the streets to protest the hire and salary freezes. Workers and students joined the fray. All ridiculed Nasser as an American stooge, and he earned the nickname "Colonel Jimmie."

Nasser remained steadfast, as he believed that a capital infusion from Washington would help him buy the support of all those who were agitating against him. But the Eisenhower administration was in no hurry to supply Nasser with the $100 million he requested. Nasser was asked to sign a formal alliance treaty with the US, and when he refused, fearing this would further solidify his image as American lackey, negotiations with the Americans became deadlocked. On the other hand, Iraq, which showed a willingness to sign a military treaty with the US and even to convince other Arab countries to do the same, was offered the aid package that Cairo had been denied.[2]

A political crisis that lasted from February to April 1954 nearly toppled Nasser. It was then that Nasser understood he needed to reconsider his domestic and foreign policies. From 1955 on he took a different path. Salaries of government officials rose, the state bureaucracy expanded, governmental intervention became prevalent, and some businesses were nationalized. In his foreign policy, Nasser began to stray away from Washington's shadow. In 1955 he went to the Afro-Asian conference in Indonesia to declare that Egypt would take an even-handed approach to the East–West conflict. At the end of that year he also signed a large arms deal with the Soviet bloc. Further, Nasser was now actively fighting against the creation of an Iraq-led and US-backed regional defense alliance, and applying pressure on Syria and Jordan to refrain from joining the so-called Baghdad Pact. In a step that magnified his status as the hero of the Arab world, in 1956 Nasser nationalized the Suez Canal Company, in protest of the refusal of the British and the Americans to grant him the loan he sought to fund the construction of a high dam at Aswan.[3]

These decisions traced a new strategy that Nasser would continue to pursue until his dying day: rather than ingratiate himself with the Americans, who, in his view, had been ungrateful, he would strive to become the region's chief. Anyone who wanted to get things done in the Middle East would have to go through him. Nasser would use this position to "milk" both superpowers. The achievements of this policy were remarkable. Between 1952 and 1965 Egypt received $1.7 billion in aid from the US and its European allies, as well as $1.4 billion from the Soviet bloc. These sums funded about one-third of the costs of Egypt's five-year plan, which brought about an impressive 5.5 percent annual rate of growth.[4]

The drawbacks had been significant as well. For most of Nasser's time in power, Egypt was embroiled in an Arab cold war against the conservative monarchist regimes in Jordan and Saudi Arabia. The Jordanian and the Saudi kings, whose authority emanated from their claim to be servants of Islam, and who were reigning over societies with wide income gaps, feared that Nasser's secular and socialist ideology would undermine their standing at home. Accordingly, they were unwilling to submit to Nasser's hegemonic ambitions and fought him tooth and nail. Between 1956 and 1958 Jordan and Saudi Arabia were well rewarded for their efforts by Britain and the US. But afterward, the US lost its appetite for confrontation with the Egyptian dictator and acquiesced in his regional leadership.[5]

Nasser's plan to use foreign policy to advance Egypt's development goals went further than that, though. Through various Arab, African, and international conferences, Nasser tried to promote inter-Arab, inter-African, and Asian–African trade. The reasons were not hard to fathom. Soviet and American aid provided only partial funding to the new factories. Egypt also had to take loans from institutions such as the World Bank. Export revenue was therefore crucial for paying back the loans. As will be shown later, the quality of Egyptian-made products was abysmal, but the Egyptian planners nevertheless thought they could push Egyptian-made textiles, shoes, tires, furniture, refrigerators, air-conditioners, radios, carpets, cement, canned fruit, and even Ramses cars into Third World markets. There was also the desire to diversify Egypt's trade partners, born of the travails of the 1956 Suez Crisis. Britain, France, and the US opposed Nasser's decision to nationalize the Suez Canal Company, which was jointly owned by British and French shareholders, and they responded with the imposition of a painful embargo. The US, whose corporations had investments throughout the Third World, also disapproved of the precedence. Nasser set a goal for the Egyptian planners: to wean Egypt's economy from its dependence on Western markets by directing one-third of its exports to Arab, Asian, and African economies.[6]

The first opportunity to implement this blueprint came knocking in early 1958 when Syrian officers came to Cairo to promote a full union between the two countries. It has long been debated why Nasser accepted the Syrian invitation. After all, he had passed on such Syrian proposals in the past. It is clear that economics, no less than politics, was on his mind. Even before an agreement had been signed, Nasser told an interviewer that Syria should become a market for Egypt's finished goods while supplying Egypt with wheat. Likewise, development plans for the union, prepared by Egyptian planners, envisaged a division of labor between the two parts of the newly named United Arab Republic (UAR): the Egyptian district would increase its industrial production whereas Syria would concentrate on the further development of its agriculture.[7]

Nasser's first decree as president of the UAR unified Syrian and Egyptian tariffs. In the following three years, cheap Egyptian textiles flooded the Syrian market, pushing out Syrian products and forcing Syrian textile factories to operate below their capacity. Special regulations forbade importing into the UAR products that might compete with Egyptian ones. At the same time, revenue from the export of Syrian farm products had funded Egypt's industrialization drive. No wonder that Syrians of various stripes wanted to break from the union. One Baathist summed up the experience of the Syrians under the UAR: "We [Syrians] wanted unity, and they wanted a colony." The Syrian chambers of commerce and trade published a statement shortly after the dissolution of the UAR asserting that Egypt had sought "to weaken [Syria's] economic potential, block its way to industrialization, and convert it into a backward country supplying agricultural products and raw materials to Egypt and, at the same time, open Syria's markets to Egypt's manufactured goods."[8]

Nasser's foreign policy also sought to create regional trading blocs in the Arab world and Africa, which Egypt, being the most industrialized country in those two regions, was sure to dominate. In 1953, and also in 1961, Egypt used the forum of the Arab League to table a proposal to create an Arab common market. A year later, Egypt, together with Morocco, Guinea, Ghana, and Mali, signed an agreement to create an African common market. Seeking to advance its commercial ties with Africa, Egypt, itself an aid recipient, had loaned $65 million to several African countries (African recipients could use the money only to purchase Egyptian products). In the 1950s and 1960s, Cairo was the main venue where African representatives discussed schemes to integrate African economies by creating unified African mail and railway systems. Cairo also became a revolutionary mecca, hosting representatives of African underground movements who swore to do battle with pro-Western regimes.[9]

Any trade bloc, such as an Arab or an African common market, was to be surrounded by high tariff walls, designed to encourage trade between its Arab or African members and make imports from non-members prohibitively expensive. Western countries were the most vulnerable to such an arrangement and, when threatened, they fought back by bribing African and Arab countries not to join such schemes. Egypt, with its meager resources, could not compete alone with economic giants such as the US, the UK, and France. It had to seek partnerships with other Global South countries that had an interest in eliminating Western commercial competition. And so, in the 1950s and 1960s, Nasser cultivated friendships with Third World statesmen such as Jawaharlal Nehru, Zhou Enlai, Kwame Nkrumah, and Josip Broz Tito. Afro-Asian and Non-Aligned conferences convened with great fanfare, often in Cairo, to call on "small states" or "non-aligned countries" to unite against "imperialism." Each of these forums begot an economic committee in which plans to increase trade between Third World countries were discussed.[10]

Finally, there was the Egyptian intervention in the civil war in Yemen, which commenced in September 1962. The Yemeni Free Officers, who modeled themselves on Nasser's movement in Egypt, found themselves besieged by forces loyal to the imam, whom they had deposed in the name of Arab republicanism. When the Yemeni officers called upon Nasser to intervene, he decided to support them. "Operation 9000," as it was code-named by the Egyptian army, started as a limited and cautious police action involving only 2,000 men. But the Saudis, who resented the fact that Nasser was meddling in their backyard, were quick to supply weapons and funds to the imam and the tribes loyal to him. The ensuing civil war in Yemen became a proxy war among the heavyweights of the Arab world. Soon, Nasser found himself in the precarious position that the US had encountered in Vietnam: the escalation logic of guerrilla warfare had led him to invest more and more resources and to augment his troops. By 1965, Egyptian forces stationed in Yemen numbered 70,000, about 50 percent of the whole army.

On the face of it, the intervention only hurt Egypt's development needs. The running cost was about $100 million per year, at a time when Egypt desperately needed hard currency.[11] But when the commander of the expeditionary forces pleaded with Nasser to reconsider his Yemen policy, he responded: "Withdrawal is impossible ... This is more a political operation than a military one ... I consider it to be a counter-response to the separation from Syria."[12]

Indeed, following the dissolution of the UAR, Nasser was determined to preserve his image as the regional boss. In his mind, this was the key to persuading the Soviet Union and the US to maintain the high level of aid given to Egypt. Yemen was a good way to remind the superpowers of Nasser's nuisance value. With its proximity to Saudi Arabia's vast oilfields, Yemen was a lucrative asset. And whoever controlled Yemen also controlled the strategic Bab el-Mandeb Strait, through which any tanker from the Gulf was obliged to pass.

Egypt's Balance of Payments Crisis

In 1962, basic products started to disappear from the markets. The long list included flour, wheat, rice, corn, oil, meat, lentils, sugar, dairy products, salt, olives, fish, cigarettes, and fruit. Sometimes these products would be available at the beginning of each month, only to become scarce again in the following weeks. When they did become available, long lines, familiar to anyone who lived under a command economy, would form in front of the shops. The black market flourished. Most Egyptians' standard of living steadily deteriorated. Once in a while, the press would announce that the president had decided to deal actively with the supply problem and would sit down with his cabinet to solve the matter. A temporary boost to the availability of foodstuffs was granted from time to time, especially ahead of the month-long Ramadan holiday with its nightly feasts. But the supply crisis persisted, and worsened considerably, from 1965 onward.[13]

Another problem was the quality of the products that came on the market. Egypt under Nasser sought to manufacture internally what the country had to import from abroad. The government protected home-grown corporations from foreign competition and forbade the import of competing brands. But the made-in-Egypt goods, which now monopolized the shelves, gave the citizens no reason to be proud. According to a story in an Egyptian daily, flies were found in jars of jam, cockroaches in boxes of white cheese, mice in sugar tins, and dirt at the bottom of eye-drop bottles. Shoes became worn after two weeks' wear and sweaters fell apart after the first wash. The journalist concluded with a thought: "Would it not be better for the good reputation of our country and of our products if we confined ourselves to four or five good quality industries, instead of having twenty or fifty bad ones? An English proverb says: 'Jack of all trades and master of none.'"[14]

People did not just grumble; they were looking for someone, or something, to blame. The most immediate culprit was the Yemen war. The stationing of tens of thousands of troops, 2,600 kilometers from Egypt's borders, obviously seemed to the average Egyptian a costly and unnecessary undertaking. The war clearly affected public morale. With 10,000 dead by the time it ended, the conflict touched every community in Egypt. Although official media described the Yemen campaign as an unqualified success, the public had ample proof that something went afoul. The imam-supporting tribesmen showed no mercy toward Egyptian captives. Often they would decapitate their victims, or release them after chopping off their ears and noses. Corpses were buried in coffins to hide the fact that they were headless. Earless and noseless invalids were a familiar sight. The popular rage pointed at the president. A man who attended a funeral for a deceased soldier heard the father muttering: "May God burn your heart, oh Gamal [Abd al-Nasser], as he had burned mine."[15]

The public's resentment was also directed at the amount of time and resources expended by the regime in order to maintain a high profile on the world stage, in particular the loans to African countries and the money spent on convening Arab, African, and Afro-Asian conferences in Cairo. One popular form of public protest was the clandestine printing of not-so-subtle political cartoons that passed from hand to hand. One of them, seen by a foreign visitor in 1964, depicted a cow with large udders, dripping milk into Yemen, North Africa, and the African continent. The same cow also relieved itself, and the caption read, "For the Egyptian people." Another cartoon from 1965 portrayed the Suez Canal as a pipeline through which dollars were passing. Nasser was depicted standing at the end point, grabbing all the dollars and tossing them toward Yemen, Aden, Syria, and Algeria.[16]

Nasser tried to defend his foreign policy in a speech he gave in October 1964. He argued that the loans to African countries had helped open African markets to Egyptian goods, and had mitigated Israel's growing influence in Africa. At the end of 1965, Nasser's confidant, Mohamed Hassanein Heikal, editor of the leading daily *al-Ahram*, argued in an editorial that Egypt's foreign policy was not costing the country all that much. The overall financial burden of the Yemen war – $500 million – had been fully covered by a recent Soviet commitment. Heikal argued that Egypt was gaining much by pursuing an active foreign policy; the superpowers provided Egypt with wheat and weapons because they recognized its nuisance value. But the people were not listening. As one contemporary observer noted, no one read Heikal's articles, since they were viewed as "philosophy with no beginning and no end."[17]

Heikal, however, had a point. The problem was not Egypt's foreign policy, adventurous though it had been. The real issue was the gross mismanagement of Egypt's economic affairs, a sphere in which Nasser had been far less audacious. To begin with, Egypt's five-year plans proved to be too ambitious. Working to deal with the high fertility rate (800,000 babies were being born every year) and raise the national standard of living, planners had assumed that Egypt would be able to build both light and heavy industry, and expand social services such as health and education at the same time. Such a daunting task required talented bureaucrats, the co-operation of the private sector, and strict discipline. The regime possessed none of these. Rather than select the most qualified academics to serve in government, Nasser promised every university graduate a position. The government's payroll had doubled between 1960 and 1967 to comprise one-third of the workforce. A million officials were in the service of the state in 1967, and they constituted 60 percent of university graduates. As one scholar noted: "Clearly Nasser perceived state institutions . . . as incubators for a new class of citizens whose interests were tied to his ruling party."[18]

In 1961, frustrated by the lack of cooperation, and seeking total control of the society, Nasser nationalized the two-thirds of the economy still held by the private sector, including banks and newspapers. This decision led to a further deterioration of the Egyptian economy. Many of the managers of the state-owned companies were former military officers, who had neither knowledge of nor experience in running an enterprise. Rather than a juggernaut, which would push forward an efficient industrialization drive, state bureaucracy had become a hurdle in the path of future growth. Factory managers claimed that "the center" kept issuing contradictory and illogical instructions. These inefficient bureaucrats cost the state budget a fortune, as their salaries had increased by 102 percent during the 1960s.[19]

Manufacturers who were awarded a captive market by the state had no incentive to improve the quality of their goods or to make production more efficient. The attempt to push these second-rate finished goods into Arab markets had largely failed. Arab countries refused to cooperate with Egypt's attempts to create an Arab market, especially after the Egyptians had tried to exploit Syria economically. African countries were willing to use Egyptian credits to import Egyptian goods, but had never been able to send back to Egypt anything it needed. A World Bank report from July 1966 noted that the most glaring failure of the Egyptian government was that exports increased only 20 percent, rather than 30 percent as planned, while imports rose at a higher pace. As a result, the attempt to turn Egyptian factories into a source of revenue had floundered.[20]

From 1962 onward, external debt hovered over the Egyptian economy like a menacing cloud. Resultantly, there were reports about factories closing because the government could not afford the cost of importing a few spare parts. In September 1964, the president of the World Bank, George Woods, announced that Egypt would not be receiving new loans. The regime became defensive. In several of his speeches Nasser reminded his listeners that Egypt had traveled a long road under his stewardship. New roads and factories were constructed. Egypt expelled the British forces from its territory in 1954 and became truly independent. Nasser was willing to admit he had made mistakes and that problems remained. He singled out the high birth rate and excessive consumption. Hypocritically, Nasser denigrated the steep rise of state employees' salaries, for which he was directly responsible. He even advised the Egyptians to have fewer children and to consume less food. Otherwise, Nasser warned, Egypt would sink deeper into debt and would not be truly independent. Sacrifices were still required, Nasser insisted, as the revolution still faced threats from the imperialist West.[21]

In October 1965, when the supply crisis reached new heights, Nasser decided to change course. He installed Prime Minister Ali Sabri as the head of the ruling party, and appointed Zakaria Muhi al-Din in his stead. Al-Din, known for his pro-Western proclivities, was to head a no-nonsense government of experts that would scale back Egypt's industrialization drive. Al-Din tried to convince Nasser to cut the budget, raise taxes, and end the Yemen war to address Egypt's ballooning $1.4 billion external debt. Nasser feared that such steps would make his regime even more unpopular. Nevertheless, he permitted al-Din to raise taxes moderately. However, at the first sign of opposition, Nasser decided to sabotage al-Din's efforts and allowed Ali Sabri to organize demonstrations against the government. Differences of opinion between al-Din and Nasser came to a head in September 1966 when an IMF delegation came to Cairo to negotiate a new loan. It made demands similar to the ones al-Din had articulated in the past year: devaluation of the Egyptian pound; fighting inefficiencies in the state-owned industries; scaling back development goals; taking deflationary measures; and cutting defense spending. When the delegation left empty-handed, al-Din resigned in despair.[22]

That year, the Egyptian economy received another blow when the Lyndon B. Johnson administration made the decision to stop selling subsidized wheat to Egypt. Egypt had always relied on American imports to feed its population since cotton, a profitable cash crop, dominated the fields. Wheat was a crucial ingredient of the local diet, with the traditional pita bread accompanying every meal. The Americans' withdrawal meant that Egypt's import bill would greatly increase. Its nominal patron, the Soviet Union, had become stingier after Khrushchev's ouster in October 1964. The

new leadership in the Kremlin insisted on timely debt payments and refused
to extend new loans. Egypt had no choice but to pursue loans from private
banks; the interest rates they demanded were exorbitant, but Egypt took the
loans nonetheless. From late 1966, Egypt was left without a viable economic
strategy. In January 1967 it had defaulted on its payments to the IMF and
was in arrears on payments to France, Britain, and Italy. In March, the
managing director of the IMF threatened Egypt that if it would not settle its
$8 million debt it would be expelled from the IMF and lose access to
Western financial markets.[23]

Egypt's regime felt so vulnerable it was willing to sacrifice long-term
growth for political breathing space, and dealt with the growing debt by
cutting new investment in industry and agriculture by 20 percent, rather
than raising taxes. At the same time, public housing, transportation, education, health services, and defense spending increased. Reports by foreign
visitors to Egypt depicted widespread discontent but no organized opposition. Rank-and-file Egyptians still saw Nasser as the undisputed leader of
their country. And those who opposed Nasser still faced a considerable
obstacle: an army of 200,000 secret agents spying on every utterance by
citizens against the regime, bugging phones, homes, and offices, and going
through mail.[24]

Despite it all, there was evidence of growing unrest. In the summer of
1965, Mustafa Nahhas Pasha, the former leader of the Wafd party (disbanded
in 1952, immediately after Nasser rose to power), had passed away, twelve
years after he had disappeared from the public eye. Hundreds of thousands
of mourners followed his coffin, chanting pro-Wafd slogans in an act of
defiance against the regime. In September, a Muslim Brotherhood underground was uncovered by the security services. The audacity of its members,
who were planning to assassinate Nasser and Amer, as well as blow up
factories, power stations, railway stations, and TV and radio buildings,
surprised the government. These Brothers were armed and had apparently
received instructions and money from abroad (the Egyptian secret services
claimed the CIA had a hand in this). Most of the Muslim Brotherhood
arrested were townspeople from Cairo, Alexandria, Suez, and Heliopolis.
Surprisingly, nearly two-thirds of the detainees were students, teachers,
professionals, and low-level bureaucrats. Nasser had stuffed the civil service
with educated people to gain their loyalty. But by 1965, many were fed up
with and alienated from a regime that was increasingly failing to live up to
expectations.[25]

Even the villages, the preserve of the typically apolitical *falaheen* (Arabic
for farmers), were showing signs of unrest. Since the late 1950s, the falaheen,

more than any other group, had to bear the burden of Egypt's audacious development goals. The state had given them no tools with which to increase their productivity and let their annual incomes decline from $330 in 1954–55 to $200 in 1961–62. While the salaries of state employees were continually pushed up, the farmers' standard of living, and particularly their diet, was deteriorating. All this was part of a deliberate policy that sought to tax agriculture to fund Egypt's industrialization. However, the falaheen were not going to remain quiescent for long. The first sign came in the shape of rural support for the Muslim Brotherhood underground. When the police tried to arrest a Brotherhood member in Kerdasa, near Cairo, two police officers were killed, and the police had to place the whole village under curfew.[26]

Two activists from the ruling party, the Arab Socialist Union, were murdered in the villages of Kamshish and Bani Muhammad Sultan, for pleading the case of landless farmers. The murderers came from the ranks of two large landowning families. Incredibly, after more than a decade of extensive land reform, the power of landowners had not been broken, and they still held whole villages under their thumb, using extortion and violence. The murder cases shocked the public and exposed the weakness of the Egyptian state.[27] Nasser, always fearful of losing popular support, saw these incidents as ominous and sought refuge in outright repression. Ultimately, there was only one organization strong enough to quash the Muslim Brotherhood and break the power of landowners in the rural area. It was the army. But relations between Nasser and Field Marshal Abd al-Hakim, supreme commander of the armed forces, had long been strained.

Going from Bad to Worse: Civil–Military Relations in Egypt

They started off as the best of friends. Relations were so intimate that Nasser named one of his sons Abd al-Hakim, while Abd al-Hakim Amer named one of his sons Gamal.[28] Both conspired, back in 1952, to launch a military coup that would change Egypt for the better. Once in power, Nasser appointed Amer, the man he trusted the most, to be Egypt's chief of staff. Amer, barely 33, tall, tan, and handsome, was only a colonel when he had been appointed, vaulting over four ranks to become Egypt's most senior officer. But no sooner was he in place than Nasser started suspecting that Amer was not following his orders.

The first cause of friction was the policy toward Israel. Amer wanted a harder line and advocated forceful reactions to border incidents. Nasser, who wanted to avoid confrontation with Israel, felt he had lost control over his army. Palestinian reconnaissance units, trained by the Egyptians, were sent into Israel without his knowledge. To get to the bottom of this, Nasser instructed two of his confidants to create secret cells within the ranks, which would report to him directly. Nasser took the time to meet with the officers who were part of this network to ensure their allegiance. They were encouraged to gather incriminating information on their fellow officers and to ascertain loyalty.[29]

The tensions between the two men widened during the 1956 Suez Crisis. At the end of October, Egypt faced a tripartite military assault by British, French, and Israeli forces. The operation was in retribution for Egypt's nationalization of the French- and British-owned Suez Canal Company in July. Israel had come along for the ride to punish Egypt for its sponsorship of Palestinian infiltration into its territory. Upon learning of the mortal danger to Egypt's security, Amer collapsed. Nasser, known for having nerves of steel, took the command from Amer and orchestrated an Egyptian Dunkirk: a forty-eight-hour pullout operation from Sinai that saved his army from annihilation by the Israelis.[30]

His failure as military commander made Amer feel increasingly insecure. Nasser had never showed much loyalty to those close to him, and in the years since 1952 had ousted all those who might have outshone him. Amer must have realized that he might meet the same fate. Moreover, Amer did not feel comfortable in his own skin. None of the men who were involved in the 1952 coup was highly educated, but Nasser, who was a voracious reader, soon acquired the aura of a multifaceted man and could easily converse with (and impress) world leaders. Amer, the son of a landowning family from the countryside, had never possessed this skill. One anecdote might illustrate this. In 1965, Amer was preparing for a state visit to Paris. The prospect of conducting small talk with his French hosts, among them President Charles de Gaulle, made him anxious. Amer asked his second wife, the actress Berlenti Abd al-Hamid, to cobble together short summaries of important French novels for him to bring up when conversing with his hosts. Nevertheless, the French found him dull and unimpressive.

The insecurity that such experiences generated in him may explain why Amer never dared to remove Nasser from power. At one time Amer told a fellow general that if he were to launch a coup against Nasser he would quickly gain domestic support. However, he had no idea how to explain this step to the Arab world and the Communist countries, which was another way of expressing his sense of inadequacy when it came to diplomacy. Indeed, even when Amer's power was on the rise, foreign policy remained mainly Nasser's purview.[31]

One thing that Amer had learned from his rapid promotion from colonel to general was that politics trumped everything in Nasser's Egypt. After all, Amer's appointment was based on his loyalty to Nasser, rather than on his skills. Amer now sought to implement what Nasser had taught him. More a politician than a military man, he strived to turn the army into his base of support and thus maintain an effective Number 2 status within the regime. When Nasser demanded that Amer replace the officers responsible for the Egyptian army's dismal performance during the Suez Crisis, the latter refused, arguing that he could not act against "his own men." Amer had also showered officers with travel grants and fast promotions. Officers were invited to all-night parties in Amer's several villas to ensure their loyalty and satisfaction. If military men committed a crime, Amer made sure that they would not be prosecuted. Thus, Amer had placed himself at the center of a patronage network that was to secure his survival – more the leader of a gang than a commander-in-chief.[32]

Nasser viewed Amer's maneuvers with great alarm. One of his tactics was to put Amer in charge of various civilian tasks, to lure him away from building his power base within the army. One such assignment was governing the Syrian province after the establishment of the UAR in 1958. When the UAR fell apart in September 1961, Nasser wanted Amer to accept responsibility and resign: he was trying to use that debacle to bury Amer's career. Amer, though, was not going anywhere. In the struggle that ensued, between September 1961 and December 1962, Nasser discovered that he was no longer Egypt's strongman. In January 1962, his intelligence agency uncovered a plot by pro-Amer officers to launch a coup against Nasser if he tried to remove Amer. The president decided to bide his time and wait for a better opportunity. Meanwhile, he complained to his associates that the military had become a state within a state.[33]

In November 1962, Nasser went out on a limb and launched his most ambitious attempt yet to get rid of the recalcitrant Amer. He created a new institution, the Presidential Council, with the sole purpose of putting a veneer of legitimacy on Amer's ouster. On the 21st, on Nasser's instructions, the Council convened to pass a bill that would put all military promotions, transfers, and pensions under its purview. Amer stormed out of the meeting, enraged. He wrote a letter of resignation, which was leaked to army units on December 1. In it, Amer called for free and democratic elections, as if this were the cause of conflict between him and Nasser. Meanwhile, reports started coming in to Nasser about groups of officers who were mobilizing their units in advance of a possible coup, and paratroopers were observed demonstrating in front of Nasser's residence, pointing their machine guns at the house. Only the air force remained loyal to the president. As a precautionary step, a senior officer, Ali Shafiq, instructed an artillery battery to point its cannon toward Nasser's house and warned that if even one aircraft tried to interfere, the president's home would be demolished.[34]

On December 11, Nasser and Amer met for a *mano a mano* confrontation that lasted nine hours; the outcome, however, was a foregone conclusion. Nasser had only theatrics on his side; Amer had the army. Indeed, as Amer pointed out, the political stability of the armed forces depended on him personally, and his dismissal might lead to chaos. Eventually, Nasser had to capitulate. Amer got what he wanted: the Presidential Council's decision was annulled, and Amer was declared vice president and deputy supreme commander. As Nasser himself admitted to his associates, Amer had successfully concluded a silent coup. The attempt to remove Amer had ended up consolidating the field marshal's power.[35]

Meanwhile, the Yemeni Free Officers gained control over Sanaa in October 1962 and called on Egypt for help. By sending troops to Yemen, Nasser provided Amer with the means to enlarge his fiefdom. The military was using the war in Yemen to isolate itself from the pernicious effects of the economic crisis, already evident in 1962. At a time when the state budget was facing severe pressure, the defense budget rose from 7.1 percent of the GNP in 1961 to 12.2 percent in 1964. In 1965, as funds for economic development were being scaled back, Minister of Economics Abd al-Munim Kaisounni declared that the defense budget would not be cut.[36]

Furthermore, officers and soldiers serving in Yemen received a 50 percent increase over their base salary. Wives of serving officers enjoyed a generous stipend, an apartment of their choice, priority in the installation of telephone lines, and a car for personal use. Their children could enter schools and universities regardless of their academic achievements. Yemen veterans also had precedence in land grants and in purchasing Egyptian-made cars. At a time when there were harsh restrictions on imports of luxury goods, Egyptian soldiers and officers could import, duty-free, any item they could lay their hands on in Yemen's markets and send it back home, free of transportation costs. These items included Japanese radio transistors, Swiss watches, televisions, cameras, refrigerators, washing machines, and gas stoves. Troops at the front exploited that perk so enthusiastically that special port facilities had to be constructed to handle the traffic. Amer and his men also used their enhanced position to appoint officers to various posts within the state bureaucracy: chairmen of the boards of large state corporations, mayors, governors, and diplomats. Amer's network of patronage was thus further extended.[37]

Naturally, Amer applied pressure on Nasser to prolong Egyptian involvement in Yemen, always demanding additional resources. He had to, because Nasser's support sometimes wavered. For instance, in January 1963, Nasser ordered plans for a withdrawal from Yemen within sixty days. By March Nasser was even blunter: "The Yemeni war is over," he said in a closed meeting. In September 1964, during the Arab League summit in Alexandria, Nasser tried to come to terms with Saudi Arabia over Yemen (though, eventually, this initiative failed). Amer had different views. Whenever the marshal spoke about the war he sounded upbeat, as if victory was just around the corner. Talking with the Soviet ambassador in February 1965, Amer waved off the proposal of the Tunisian president, Habib Bourguiba, to mediate between Egypt and Saudi Arabia. Bourguiba would never get anything out of King Faisal, Amer argued contemptuously. The Egyptian army, he boasted, was about to perform operations in Yemen that would convince the royal opposition that it could not continue the war indefinitely. However, if Saudi Arabia persisted, Amer threatened, Egypt would respond by expanding the war into Saudi territory. Egypt could supply the Saudi opposition tribes with weapons and money, Amer mused, and they in turn would bring down the Saudi monarchy.[38]

Yemen was just one of Amer's trump cards. The more the economy deteriorated, the more Nasser needed the army. Historically, the mere sight of military units stepping out of their barracks was one of the most efficient ways of quelling disturbances and demonstrations. The military took the lead in confronting the uprising of the Muslim Brotherhood by arresting 27,000 suspects in just twenty-four hours in August 1965. Those in custody ended up in army camps, and many were subjected to severe torture. Likewise, military police were deployed to enforce ruthlessly a new land reform. Their role was to enter villages, locate the big landowners, and then beat them in front of the villagers so as to destroy their authority. No fewer than 4,000 families were affected by "anti-feudalism" measures. Land and assets seized during this campaign amounted to $300 million. Contemporaries saw both campaigns as excessively brutal and inhumane. One Egyptian journalist claimed that the Egyptian military had become an occupying force, much worse than the British military.[39]

This, alongside the enormous privileges enjoyed by the military in a time of collective belt-tightening, engendered resentment. Rumors spread about Amer's wild lifestyle and his lust for women, alcohol, and hashish. A popular joke making the rounds in 1966 told of Amer being found by the police late at night, in a dark alley, completely inebriated. The police officer tries to arrest him, but Amer resists, stating who he is and asking to be left alone. The officer does not believe the drunk in front of him is Amer, so Amer suggests he call Nasser to prove it. The officer phones the presidential office, and Nasser tells him to question the man about the precise number of soldiers and planes in the Egyptian armed forces. The man replies that he had no clue. "Release him," Nasser says. "He is indeed Amer."[40]

Persistent diplomatic reports indicated that tensions between Amer and Nasser were rising during 1966 and 1967. In February 1967, Shams Badran, minister of war and Amer's henchman, met with Nasser to tell him that Amer wanted to lead the republic "because the country is complaining." Nasser told Badran he would be willing to step down only if Amer resigned from the command of the armed forces. In the next three months, however, such demands ceased as Amer became immersed in the campaign against the big landowners. By giving Amer increased powers in the civilian sphere, Nasser distracted him and kept the danger of a military coup at bay.[41]

Meanwhile, Nasser was arming himself politically. In 1962, he realized that he had painted himself into a corner. Amer had a base within the army. Nasser had popular support, but no apparatus to mobilize it. That December, he established the Arab Socialist Union (ASU), which was to be Egypt's only party. The more the tensions between Nasser and Amer increased, though, the more the ASU seemed too large and incoherent. Nasser and his men wanted something more secretive and with more organizational muscle. From 1965 on, both Ali Sabri, who had been forced to leave the premiership, and Shaarawi Gumaa, the interior minister, took it upon themselves to create two clandestine platforms: the Youth Organization (YO) and the Vanguard Organization (VO). The younger members, who joined the YO, and the older ones, who joined the VO, were all sworn to secrecy. Regional governors and government officials were relieved of their duties so they could devote themselves full-time to leading Nasser's shadow army. The members of these movements were aware of their goals: the central activity of the YO summer camps was preparing for the possibility of a military coup.[42]

The main attraction of the YO and VO was also what drew officers into Amer's patronage network: the members were promised appointments and promotions in the government sector. Their benefactors, Nasser, Sabri, and Gumaa, encouraged them to act as a security apparatus rather than an ideological movement. YO and VO members were instructed to infiltrate civilian associations, as well as the military, and gather incriminating evidence on civilians and officers. In April 1967, a Soviet delegation, headed by Communist Party Secretary Nikolai Yegorychev, met with Shaarawi Gumaa and received a thorough briefing from him. What they heard astounded them. Gumaa explained that Egypt now had two parties: a clandestine party and a public one. The task of the clandestine party, according to Gumaa, was to "reach maximal readiness for an eventual political crisis." The Soviet report further elaborated that "The special section [of the VO] . . . which is devoted to mobilization is, according to the view of members of the [Soviet] delegation, akin to a military staff."[43]

By 1967, the number of YO and VO members had reached 250,000, too large a number to remain hidden from the watchful eyes of military intelligence. Amer was aware of YO and VO activity and had tried several times to shut the organization down, arrest the members, and remove Ali Sabri. Ultimately, despite his immense power, Amer came up short. Ali Sabri, whom Amer considered an inveterate enemy, was a wily organization man, as was Gumaa. Nasser stood behind them four-square and, really, Amer had bigger fish to fry.[44] And so it happened that relations between Amer and Nasser were as acrimonious as ever on the eve of the Six-Day War. This would have a direct impact on Egypt's incoherent policy during the crisis of May and June 1967.

6

SLIDING INTO WAR

Following the dissolution of the UAR in 1961, the Arab–Israeli conflict became a cog in the wheel of the Arab cold war. The Syrians were willing to get their noses bloodied by Israel, as long as it embarrassed Nasser and weakened him. To prevent this, and to lock the Syrians into a set of hard and fast rules, Nasser instituted the Arab League summits. The idea was to summon Syria and other Arab countries together and apply peer pressure to force Damascus to comply with Egyptian demands. One of the events that spurred Nasser into action was the conference of Arab chiefs of staff on December 7, 1963. Syrian and Iraqi representatives had devised a plan for a military operation against Israel's waterworks, and demanded that Egypt take part. The Egyptians refused. A few days later, the semi-official Egyptian weekly *Ruz al-Yusuf* reported that Syria and its allies in the Arab world were "aiming to drag Egypt into a war with Israel to knife it in the back."[1]

The January 1964 Arab League summit in Cairo played out according to the script. The summit converged on a solution that demanded long-term planning under a Joint Arab Command (JAC). It also adopted a less belligerent method to use against Israel, that of building diversion sites, which would deny the country access to water. Seemingly, Nasser did not see the exercise as having any value other than throwing the Syrians a bone. The Syrian leader Amin Hafiz, who participated in the conference, appeared a comic figure, walking around with a pistol in his jacket pocket and taking care to show it to everybody.[2]

That September, the second Arab summit in Alexandria began with a report by an Egyptian officer, Lieutenant General Ali Ali Amer, on the impossibility of a confrontation with Israel. If the Arabs tried to attack Israel, the report argued, they would have France, the UK, the US, and perhaps even the UN arrayed against them. It would be unrealistic to expect the USSR to support the Arabs on this issue. Arab countries would not be able to defend themselves: the Syrian army was ill-equipped, the Jordanian army too small. There was no quick fix to either of these problems. Amin Hafiz had been isolated again. When he claimed that he could liberate Palestine in no more than four hours, Ahmed Ben Bella, the Algerian leader, said to him sarcastically, "If you can liberate Palestine in four years, rather than four hours, we will be by your side." Ben Bella had been one of the firm opponents of the Syrian call for immediate war with Israel. A year later, at the Casablanca summit of 1965, Nasser tried to convince the Syrians to stop their diversion works and hinted that if Israel attacked Syria, Egypt would not come to Damascus's rescue.[3]

In those years, Nasser also made speeches explaining that he had no intention of doing battle with Israel in the near future. While attending the second National Palestinian Conference in January 1965, Nasser argued that "we must postpone the diversion of the Jordan River's tributaries and give up on the water, which is precious to us all, until we can defend ourselves." He further maintained that "We should not fight according to the timing that Israel sets." Speaking in Moscow in August, Nasser stated that the Arabs needed to wait for the right convergence of international circumstances, adding: "Those who seek to exploit the issue and yell 'the Israelis attacked us' as the [Syrian] Baathists are doing, do it for show and nothing else. This is not the way to achieve cooperation." In November, he warned: "Israel is not an easy problem and those who demand unwise attacks against Israel, serve the Jewish country a victory on a plate . . . war is not a game. And if you can't be confident of your victory, why take the risk?" Behind closed doors, Nasser was even blunter. In 1964, during a private talk with his confidant, journalist Mohamed Hassanein Heikal, Nasser said that the Israel issue would not be resolved in his lifetime. The most important thing for Egypt was to defend its borders and deter an Israeli attack on other Arab countries. In September 1965, Nasser allegedly told King Faisal: "We do not now possess a joint plan for the liberation of Palestine, and we do not possess the means to achieve that aim, supposing that we had a plan. So my estimation is that the struggle between us and Israel is a hundred-year problem . . ."[4]

Egyptian officials were all on the same page. In July 1964, Kamal al-Din Rifat, Egypt's deputy prime minister, met with French journalists for an off-the-record conversation. He admitted that Nasser was repeating the mantra of an inevitable war with Israel only to maintain Egypt's leadership in the

Arab world. Several Arab governments, he complained, were waiting for Egypt to misstep and then to accuse it of treason. Rifat conceded that there was no military solution to the conflict with Israel. Time must run its course, he concluded. Likewise, in the talks that Amer conducted in Paris in October 1965, he said that Syrian efforts to divert the waters of the Jordan were acts of passion, and there was no chance that anything the Syrians did would prevent Israel from completing its national water-carrier project. Arab unity is a myth, Amer had admitted ruefully, but it must be respected.[5]

While Nasser had been trying to establish a framework for long-term planning, which would postpone the war indefinitely, Fatah and its Syrian backers proffered a battle plan focusing on the immediate future. As opposed to Nasser's call to wait for the right moment and reach the necessary level of military preparedness, in 1963 the Fatah mouthpiece *Falestinuna* (Our Palestine) thundered enthusiastically:

> We announce to the whole wide world that we shall implement our revolution with sticks and knives, old pistols, and rusty shotguns to teach a lesson to all those who suffer from nightmares about Israel's tanks and planes. Everybody says that Israel would blow Gaza up, slaughter the Palestinians, and invade the Arab countries. Israel, Israel, Israel. But nobody thinks about what *we* can do – how we shall burn orchards, demolish factories, blow up bridges, and cut off main roads.[6]

In November 1966, Nasser found himself arguing the whole matter anew. The reason was an Egyptian–Syrian summit convened to sign a joint military treaty. Nasser arrived reluctantly at this reconciliation with the Syrian Baathists. In the previous year, the institution of Arab summits fell apart after Nasser found out that Faisal, the Saudi king, was scheming to create something called "the Islamic Congress" to rival the Arab League. Faisal had already made trips, at the end of 1965, to the Shah of Iran and to King Hussein of Jordan, to plan a conference in Mecca. As he was visiting Tehran, King Faisal declared that Iran and Saudi Arabia "should unite in fighting the elements and ideas which are alien to Islam." Nasser felt his leadership in the Arab world was again being challenged by the Saudis.

He was equally frustrated that he could not use the summit meetings to persuade the Saudis to agree to a peace treaty, which would have enabled him to extricate himself honorably from Yemen. In addition, the Soviets were leaning on Nasser to bury the hatchet with the Syrians and establish an alliance of progressive Arab countries, together with Iraq and Algeria. Indeed, the shift in Nasser's foreign policy occurred after the visit of the

Soviet premier, Alexei Kosygin, in May 1966. It is likely that the Soviets had promised to reward Egypt's compliance with an easing of credit terms and more weapons supplies.[7] A month after Kosygin left Cairo, Nasser declared that Egypt would cease its Arab summit policy as he despaired that anything positive could be achieved by cooperating with the reactionary Arab regimes.[8] After three months of additional haggling between Nasser and the Baathists, the road to the treaty lay open.

On November 1, a senior Syrian delegation arrived in Cairo. While Nasser wanted to use the talks to preach moderation to the Syrians, Syrian Prime Minister Yusuf Zuayn wanted to discuss the concept of the popular war of liberation. Zuayn, Foreign Minister Ibrahim Makhus, and Chief of Staff Ahmed Sawidani argued that the Arabs had no chance of winning unless they embraced the concept of the popular war as it was practiced in Vietnam and Algeria and promoted by China. In essence, they claimed that due to overwhelming US support for Israel, the Arabs could never win the arms race against the Jewish state. The Arabs had superiority in numbers – 100 million Arabs as opposed to 2 million Jews – and thus the Arab countries should unleash guerrilla warfare against Israel along the armistice lines. If Israel decided to conquer Damascus and Cairo, it would find itself wallowing in the mire of a low-intensity conflict, the very same situation that was sapping US power in Vietnam. Makhus went even further and demanded the overthrow of the reactionary regimes in Jordan and Saudi Arabia before the liberation of Palestine. But Nasser categorically opposed them. The Egyptian president asserted that Israel would not accept a guerrilla war on its borders. Rather, it would quickly push the conflict toward a conventional confrontation with the Arab armies. Unleashing a popular war, Nasser claimed, was akin to inviting Israel to take a stroll all the way to Damascus and Cairo. Nasser also rejected the idea of a war against Jordan and Saudi Arabia.[9]

In an attempt to educate the Syrians, Nasser told them that there were only two issues that were absolutely crucial for American policymakers with regard to the Middle East: oil and Israel. Any attempt to jeopardize either would put Syria and Egypt on a collision course with Washington. Seconding Nasser, Abd al-Hakim Amer added that the United States was now militarily stronger than ever and it no longer feared the Soviet Union. Amer warned that by waging war at that time, Syria and Egypt would fail the progressive forces in the Arab world and give imperialism a perfect opportunity to obtain a quick victory. Countering the Syrian example of Vietnam, Nasser pointed to Taiwan, where Maoist China had accepted the status quo rather than unleashing a popular war. Zuayn responded sarcastically, "If so, we will have to wait for a hundred years." But Nasser parried: "Your talk about a popular war does not suit this time and place."[10]

Regardless of the intensity of the discussions, Nasser decided to sign a military treaty with Syria. However, aware of the danger of escalation, he insisted on a get-out clause. After the Syrian delegation had left Cairo, an editorial in the Egyptian daily *al-Ahram* claimed that "this treaty does not obligate Cairo to respond automatically to any retaliatory raid [by Israel] against Syria." Also, the agreement stipulated that any response to a security threat was to be the result of joint consultations.[11] Nevertheless, the following weeks would show that this caveat was ineffectual. The Baath regime ignored Nasser's lectures and encouraged Fatah to increase its attacks on Israel. Those actions goaded Israel into launching a raid on the West Bank village of Samu on November 13. It took place in broad daylight and went on for hours. The Egyptians stood by and did nothing.

Following the raid, Jordanian and Saudi radio stations began a propaganda campaign, accusing Nasser of adopting a defeatist attitude toward the Palestinian problem. A week after the Samu operation, Jordanian Prime Minister Wasfi al-Tal held a news conference in which he attacked Syria and particularly Egypt because "the responsibility of supplying air coverage to southern Jordan belongs to the Egyptian Air Force." In a speech in the Egyptian parliament, Nasser responded by suggesting that the inhabitants of Jordanian villages on the frontier be supplied with weapons so that they could defend themselves.[12] Regardless of the elaborate explanations, Egypt was evidently embarrassed by its inactivity during the Samu raid. The next development in this sordid tale, the dogfight between Israeli and Syrian planes on April 7, 1967, which ended in a decisive Israeli victory, supplied fresh fodder to Nasser's enemies in the Arab world. Egypt was humiliated again.

Bit by bit, Syrian policies and Fatah operations pushed Nasser to change his position on irregular warfare. An Egyptian intelligence memo written in February 1965 noted that too many members of the new political entity had been former members of the Muslim Brotherhood (which was true). In the next two years, Egyptian propaganda tried to portray Fatah as a stooge for Israel and the West, and Egypt's media avoided all discussion of Fatah operations against Israel. Egyptian authorities in the Gaza Strip placed Fatah activists under surveillance to make sure they would not be able to launch operations from Gaza (and at the end of 1966, some of them were jailed). In July 1966, a meeting took place between Fatah and Egyptian leaders. The Egyptians maintained that although Fatah activities against Israel were courageous, they must become "part of overall Arab planning

for the liberation of Palestine." Kamal Rifat, a senior officer in Egypt's intelligence services, argued in a public speech that Fatah operations "do not
threaten Israel's existence." At the end of 1966, another meeting took place.
The Fatah leader Khalil al-Wazir suggested to Shams Badran, Egypt's
minister of war, that a terror network be created in southern Israel. Fatah
would supply manpower while the Egyptians provided logistical support.
Badran refused to discuss the proposal seriously.[13]

Nasser helped found the Palestinian Liberation Organization (PLO) in
1964 precisely to avoid this kind of entanglement. The PLO was supposed
to represent the Palestinian people but also to be wholly dependent on
Egypt's goodwill. Nasser appointed Ahmad Shukeiri, a voluble lawyer, to
head the PLO because he thought he would serve as a pliable tool, which
he did prove to be. Up to 1966, Nasser instructed Shukeiri to keep himself
busy by creating a Palestinian army whose military activation was to await
the war with Israel that Nasser never planned to start. However, in
October 1966, concerned that the PLO was losing the battle for Palestinian
hearts and minds to Fatah, Nasser allowed Shukeiri to initiate guerrilla
activities against Israel. PLO units were to emerge from the West Bank
to embarrass King Hussein, who at the time was attacking Nasser viciously
through Jordanian media outlets. The PLO did launch two operations
that month, but Nasser's leash was tight. He did not allow it to lead the
way in guerrilla activity, and PLO sabotage acts remained few and far
between.

From February 1967 onward, the Egyptian media changed their tune
and supported Palestinian operations against Israel. This endorsement was
a very qualified one, however. Nasser was willing to countenance Fatah
activity as long as it was launched from the territory of other Arab countries. In terms of the struggle for leadership in the Arab world, it was far
preferable to be viewed as supportive of the Fatah operations that in fact
Nasser had been powerless to stop. Still, the ban on Fatah activity in Gaza
remained in force and, in early May 1967, Lieutenant General Ali Ali Amer,
the Egyptian who headed the Joint Arab Command, issued an ultimatum
demanding that the Syrians put an end to Fatah operations from their soil.[14]

In retrospect, Nasser's precarious position and slowly shifting policies
concerning the Palestinian issue demonstrated that the Syrians were
winning. Nasser, while truly wishing to avoid any confrontation with Israel,
had found himself toeing the Syrian line. It was just one more example of
Nasser's slipping grip on affairs in the region. In mid-May, though, he made
a last desperate attempt to assert his leadership and gain the upper hand in
the Arab struggle for regional supremacy.

A Fateful Decision

The fact that Nasser's meeting with Amer on the night of May 13 was lengthy clearly suggests that they disagreed. Although there was no protocol, both protagonists' versions tell largely the same story. Amer and Nasser were discussing a plan they both knew well. It involved sending Egyptian troops into Sinai. The desert peninsula, which had been separated from Egypt by the Suez Canal, remained demilitarized following an informal agreement reached between Egypt and Israel after the second war between them in 1956. As a result of the agreement, UN Emergency Forces (UNEF) were placed along the Israeli–Egyptian border and were credited for the decade of tranquility that had ensued.

Nevertheless, that agreement had already been breached once before, in February 1960. Then, just as would become the case in 1967, the Syrians had issued a warning that Israel was about to launch a massive attack. Since Syria and Egypt were a single political entity at the time, Nasser responded by sending troops into Sinai, to make Israel think twice. However, both the Egyptian mobilization and the entry of its troops into Sinai remained a secret. Israel responded by alerting its forces to be at a high state of readiness but did not publicize the fact. Both Nasser and Israeli Prime Minister David Ben-Gurion were eager to avoid escalation. Once Nasser started to withdraw his forces, Israel did the same. Bit by bit, each army withdrew from the border until the crisis was finally defused.[15]

Nasser and Amer seemed to be revisiting this affair in 1965 when they were overheard toying with the idea of sending into Sinai an Egyptian brigade that had just come back from Yemen. At that point it proved to be no more than humorous chit-chat. The subject was further discussed before the Arab League summit in Casablanca which took place that year. Arab countries were already accusing Egypt of using the UNEF to avoid war with Israel. A high command meeting, with Nasser in attendance, discussed the question and decided that if Egypt were to deploy its troops in Sinai, it needed to create two additional divisions to compensate for the troops stationed in Yemen. The matter was left hanging until December 1966. Amer was at the time on an official visit to Pakistan and had sent a telegram suggesting that the best reaction to Jordanian propaganda against Egypt was to ask for the withdrawal of UNEF troops, and to send Egyptian units into Sinai. Nasser decided not to respond to the telegram and to wait for Amer's return to find out whether the additional divisions, discussed back in 1965, were indeed formed. He also commissioned staff reports on how to request the UNEF's withdrawal and on what the international repercussions might be. After Nasser had received that report, he shelved it.[16] In short, in the previous two years, the issue had come up, mostly on Amer's initiative, and Nasser had procrastinated and dithered as much as he could.

On the evening of May 13, Amer and Nasser again revisited the issue. Amer laid out his plans to send the Egyptian army into Sinai and to demand the immediate and full withdrawal of UNEF.[17] The circumstances in which Nasser found himself made it impossible to wave off these demands. Firstly, Amer's grip on the armed forces meant that his demands could not be ignored. The relations between the two men were strained, and Amer had ways to enforce his will. The second issue was the nature of the intelligence alert. Nasser had accused the Syrians more than once of crying wolf. However, this time the cries for help from Damascus seemed to be validated by the Soviet intelligence services and a sustained campaign of threats originating from Jerusalem. The third issue was the propaganda war in the Arab world. An Israeli attack on Syria, accompanied by Egyptian inaction, would cause Nasser endless embarrassment. The fourth issue was time, which was of the essence. The Egyptian army needed at least seventy-two hours to deploy its troops in Sinai.[18] If Nasser had wanted to force Israel to cancel the operation against Syria, which, according to the information from Moscow, was set for May 17, he had to send Israel a signal *before* it launched its attack. Therefore, an order needed to be given that evening to have troops in Sinai by May 16.

The final thing to consider was whether Egypt's army was prepared for a confrontation. During the meeting, Amer insisted that it was battle-ready. Nasser probably did not know any better: although he did spy on the armed forces, it seems that most of that effort went into discovering good material for blackmail rather than systematically inquiring into military capability.[19] In 1963 Nasser had told an American visitor that Egypt's radar system was inefficient and, as a result, Israeli planes could easily fly sorties over Cairo and the Suez Canal.[20] It is unclear whether he knew that in the four years that had elapsed, the air force had tried to fix the problem and failed; Egyptian radar was still unable to detect planes flying at an altitude lower than 500 meters. And it is more difficult to determine whether Nasser was aware that there had been a wide-ranging purge of qualified officers in the summer of 1966, so that Amer could fill these positions with his less-than-qualified confidants. Another piece of information that might have caused Nasser to think twice was the fact that land-force exercises had been canceled altogether in the previous years due to the high cost of the Yemen operation. Moreover, six months earlier, the operations branch of the armed forces had passed a memo to Amer which argued that as long as Egypt was involved in Yemen it should avoid war with Israel. The memo underlined that while a third of the Egyptian army was stationed in Yemen, the military did not have the requisite number of troops to execute its plans.[21]

If Nasser did not know, Amer certainly did not volunteer the information. In any case, commanders like Amer tended to hold a rosy view of the army's abilities – a consequence of their seclusion at headquarters, with no real contact with the troops. General Abd al-Muhsen al-Murtagi, an Amer intimate, declared in October 1966 that Egypt's armed forces could teach Israel a lesson it would never forget. That same month, General Sidqi Mahmud, commander of the air force, boasted that Egyptian planes could defend the skies of any Arab country. In January 1967, Murtagi, during an interview for the daily *al-Gumhuriya*, made the assertion that "we have acquired wonderful knowledge in battles [in Yemen]. We [will] increase our knowledge by expelling Israel from our Arab land."[22]

The path of least resistance for Nasser was to accept some of Amer's demands while rejecting others. Nasser agreed to deploy the army in Sinai. He was also willing to go along with the idea of requesting the evacuation of UNEF troops, though what he was really after was their redeployment: he wanted them gone from most of the Israeli–Egyptian border, except for the two major flashpoints, Sharm al-Sheikh and the Gaza Strip.[23] As long as UNEF forces continued to guard these spots, war could be avoided. And that was also the essence of the maneuver that Nasser had signed up for. It was to be a calculated show of force: brinkmanship – without resorting to war.

The tension between what Amer wanted and what Nasser planned was to adversely affect the efficiency of the Egyptian operation. When Amer convened the General Staff at 11 a.m. on May 14, he ordered the generals to put all units on high alert and to start moving troops into Sinai. The plan by which the army was to proceed was code-named "Qaher": a defensive plan aimed at deploying Egyptian troops along three well-fortified defense lines, each backing the other. Nevertheless, Amer, in a move that confused the attendees, ordered the officers to be ready for an offensive maneuver, for which the troops had never been trained. Chief of Staff Mohamed Fawzi, one of the few Nasser loyalists within the ranks, was dispatched to Damascus. Before leaving, Fawzi instructed the logistics branch to take measures to prevent the mobilization from hurting the economy and to prepare for a long standoff with Israel, the scenario preferred by Nasser.[24]

On May 15, Fawzi made his way to Damascus to meet with Ahmed Sawidani, the Syrian chief of staff, and Hafez al-Assad, minister of defense. He was instructed to update the Syrians on the impending movement of the Egyptian forces and to tell them that Egypt would only intervene after a deep invasion and occupation of Syria by Israel, or if Israel bombarded the

Syrian Air Force. Border skirmishes would not constitute a reason for Egypt to get involved. The Syrians seemed alarmed by what Fawzi told them. Apparently, the Baath regime did not expect such a substantial response on the part of the Egyptians. Indeed, Damascus did not seem a city on a war footing; in fact, the Syrians had been demobilizing, sending home some of the reservists they had recruited in the preceding weeks. All this aroused Fawzi's suspicion, and he asked to see aerial photos of the front taken in the previous two days. To his surprise, Fawzi discovered that they showed no Israeli troop concentrations, and when he returned to Cairo he shared his dramatic findings with Amer, who seemed neither surprised nor interested. By that time Egyptian military intelligence had already flipped its assessment, realizing that the alert about Israeli troop concentrations was fabricated. They had sent an analysis to headquarters, and recommended waiting for more accurate information.[25]

However, by May 15, the die was cast. It had everything to do with the orders Amer gave the army. If Amer still retained thoughts of taking Israel by surprise, he should have instructed the troops to move stealthily and quickly on the roads that circumvented the cities and which had been paved in the previous years especially for that purpose. What had actually happened was that troops had been marching through the main streets of Cairo with great fanfare since the late morning hours of the 15th. So, by the time Fawzi returned from Damascus and Egyptian military intelligence changed its assessment, it was too late. Egypt was publicly committed to the redeployment of its troops. Reversing course could have been humiliating for the regime. Nevertheless, there is no evidence that Amer shared with Nasser the information he had received from Fawzi.

What appeared to be so orderly and impressive in urban settings turned quickly into one of the messiest redeployments in military history. Soon after the troops left Cairo it started to rain and did not stop for the next forty-eight hours. Only two main roads led to the Canal, and they became jammed with vehicles that were slipping in the mud and colliding with each other. Even Amer admitted to a fellow officer that the logistics were rather amateurish. The army had to call up reserve forces to compensate for the troops stationed in Yemen. This had not been practiced for several years and the system was creaking. Reserve soldiers were sent to their positions without uniforms or weapons. New units were created using reserve soldiers who had never been trained. Yet reserve forces accounted for half the manpower deployed in Sinai. Later on, when units from Yemen began to arrive, their officers insisted on bringing to the desert the refrigerators that they had imported. By May 16, one infantry division and three armored brigades entered Sinai and they were ordered to maintain pre-jump positions. An attack on Israel was to begin immediately if Israel were to invade Syria.[26]

Around 2 p.m. on May 16, Major General Indar Jit Rikhye, Indian commander of UNEF, was planning to escape his hot and humid office and head to the golf course. Just as he was preparing to leave, he received a surprising phone call from an Egyptian officer informing him that an important message from Egypt's military headquarters was coming via a special courier, who was already en route. The letter, written according to Amer's instructions, reached Rikhye only at 10 p.m. Contrary to Nasser's intentions, the letter carried an explicit request for a full UNEF withdrawal. When he found out about this, Nasser asked that the letter be corrected to reflect his request for a redeployment, but when he called Amer about it Amer told him it had been too late to make the amendment. Over the next few days, this discussion became moot. A complex story unfolded, at the end of which it became evident that UN Secretary General U Thant was unwilling to accept a request for a partial withdrawal of UNEF. It was all or nothing, he insisted; either Nasser sought a complete withdrawal of UNEF, or he canceled his letter. By May 18, Nasser, reluctant to lose face in the Arab world, was forced to ask for a complete withdrawal of UNEF.[27]

At 9 p.m. on May 21, Nasser called a high-level meeting of officials from the party, the cabinet, and the chiefs of staff. Nasser devoted the discussion to the problem of the Straits of Tiran, through which ships sailing from the Red Sea to Israel had to pass. Following the 1956 war, an informal agreement had been reached between Israel and Egypt according to which Israeli ships would be free to sail through. In the years since, Israel's naval link to the Persian Gulf via the Straits of Tiran had become economically significant, as Israel started importing more and more of its oil from Iran – on the eve of the war, as much as 90 percent. Already in March 1957, Israeli Foreign Minister Golda Meir declared in the UN that the closing of the Straits would be construed as a *casus belli*. As long as UNEF was present in Sinai there was no danger of that happening – a UNEF unit was based in Sharm al-Sheikh, where the Straits could be locked by the positioning of a single cannon. However, as UNEF was withdrawing from Sharm al-Sheikh in mid-May 1967, it became imperative that the Egyptian army take over Sharm's military installations. But could Egyptian troops reach the spot and countenance with equanimity the free movement of Israeli ships? Again, the danger of losing face in the Arab world presented itself.[28]

Initially, Nasser made no plans for his troops to reach Sharm al-Sheikh; indeed, the original redeployment plan said nothing about sending troops there. But now the topic presented itself in all urgency. Nasser opened the meeting by saying that, in his view, there was no other choice but to implement the same set of rules that applied during the years 1948–56, when the Straits of Tiran had been closed to Israeli navigation as Egypt did not acknowledge Israel as a legitimate entity. All the same, Nasser explained, he was aware that this decision would considerably raise the likelihood of war. He was therefore posing the question to the armed forces. If the army was not battle-ready, then he, Nasser, would think of creative ways to deal with the political embarrassment. Amer answered decisively: "I stake my neck on it. Everything is perfectly ready." Amer even claimed that if the army got no clear orders, the soldiers might shoot ships carrying the Israeli flag out of patriotic zeal. He said nothing of the fact that four days earlier, on May 17, during a military conference over which he had presided, Egyptian generals had been against the closing of the Straits of Tiran since the troops were not ready for war and too many units were still in Yemen. At that point, Amer had intervened and told the generals that no one was thinking seriously about sending troops to Sharm al-Sheikh. Not for the last time in the course of this crisis, Amer withheld vital information from Nasser.[29]

On the morning of May 22, Amer issued a command to close the Straits of Tiran to ships flying the Israeli flag as well as to oil-carrying tankers. Generals such as Fawzi and Salah al-Din Hadidi, commander of military intelligence, were surprised by Amer's order. The "Qaher" plan made no mention of sending units to Sharm al-Sheikh, and the feeling among high-ranking officers was that the leadership was playing politics with military strategy. Units that were needed to man defense lines in northern Sinai had to be sent to Sharm al-Sheikh, the southernmost corner of Sinai, 500 kilometers away.[30] However, the decision to close the Straits served Amer's purpose of pushing forward his favorite design – the "Fajer" (Dawn) plan.

The assessment of Amer and his cronies in the General Staff was that Israel would respond to the closing of the Straits with a limited incursion (indeed, at that point, this was exactly the kind of plan the Israeli General Staff was debating). Amer argued that Egypt should not wait passively for Israel to strike; it should respond to Israel's attack with one of its own. "Fajer" called for a three-pronged invasion into southern Israel, the final goal being the conquest of the port city of Eilat.

In the coming days, Amer would insist on pushing more and more troops into the peninsula. Rather than an orderly deployment along three defense lines, Amer wanted more units on the front lines to prepare the ground for an offensive against Eilat, the Eilat–Beersheba road, and a diversionary attack on Israeli settlements near the Gaza Strip. The air force was to supply additional support by commencing Operation "Assad" (Lion):

a bombardment of airfields in southern Israel. Amer ordered that detailed instructions for the execution of these plans be written and distributed to front-line units. Yet Amer's orders were divorced from reality. Egyptian troops had been trained for over a decade to execute defensive plans, not an offensive one – something that Amer, who rarely took an interest in training activity, was unaware of.[31]

On May 19, Amer was interviewed by a leading daily and declared: "I want to say it clearly so that no one can have any doubt . . . that Egypt would strike with all its might against any aggression. It is time to put an end to the provocative policy of Israel . . ." Amer's protégé, General Murtagi, made a similar statement that day: "Our troops are at the highest state of alert and are ready to initiate a battle outside of our borders." These utterances were even brasher given Nasser's silence. He had not given any speeches since the crisis started. On May 21, the day he recommended the Straits of Tiran be closed, Amer made a tour of the front and judged the troops sufficiently ready for the execution of "Fajer."[32]

Nasser, however, still thought that a confrontation with Israel might be avoided. When he met with Syrian Foreign Minister Ibrahim Makhus on May 16, Nasser warned him that Syria should tread carefully and not provoke Israel into war because "he [Nasser] wanted Israel to have a chance to walk back from the crisis." Nasser also believed that if he could persuade Washington that war in the Middle East would be inimical to its interests, confrontation with Israel could be prevented because Israel would not dare start a war without American approval. Egyptian officials were thus instructed to deliver the following message to any American diplomat: Egypt was strong and ready for battle, but if the US were to restrain Israel, peace would prevail.[33]

Since Nasser attached so much importance to what the US would say to Israel, he tried as best he could to dictate the Soviet position. Apparently his thinking was that a Soviet commitment would deter the US from intervening, as it would not want to risk a superpower conflict over Israeli shipping in the Straits of Tiran. On May 22, Nasser took a step to embroil the Soviet Union further. Although the Soviet ambassador Pozhedaev wanted to meet with Nasser in the morning, Nasser intentionally delayed and saw Pozhedaev late in the evening, after he had made his sensational declaration about the closing of the Straits. Pozhedaev was eager to inform Nasser that the Central Committee of the Soviet Communist Party had issued a statement of full support for Egypt's request for the removal of UNEF. But the Russian was surprised when Nasser told him about the step he had just taken. Nasser demanded that the Soviet Union stand behind his decision to close the Straits. He emphasized that he wanted the statement to be made by the USSR government rather than the Soviet news agency Tass. The Americans, Nasser argued, must know that the Soviet Union would defend Egypt, and observed that this was the key to ending the crisis peacefully. Israel, Nasser explained, was nothing but the US's puppet, and if the US decided to sit this one out, so would Israel. The Soviet warning, Nasser insisted, must therefore be addressed to Washington, not to Israel.[34]

Nasser's plot was clearly a case of the tail trying to wag the dog. Egyptian positioning between May 15 and 22 yielded contradictory results. While Nasser was trying to conduct a diplomatic campaign that would allow Egypt to get away with its unilateral abrogation of the 1956 understanding with Israel, Amer was preparing the ground for an offensive. While Nasser was trying to restrain the Syrians, spook the Americans, and squeeze a commitment out of the Soviets, Amer was beefing up the front lines in Sinai with more troops, and sending more planes into airfields in Sinai. Egypt's military maneuvers were undermining its diplomacy, and the Israeli generals could see that. They used Egypt's actions in Sinai to advance their long-planned offensive. And, as in Egypt, civilian decision-makers were unable to stop them.

THE PHONE CALL

Every national security crisis begins with a phone call. This one was no different. The recipient was Yitzhak Rabin, Israel's chief of staff, who was at a party in the home of a wealthy businessman in Jerusalem. The villa was surrounded by an enormous garden where the revelers congregated. The mood was celebratory. It was the night of May 14, the eve of Israel's nineteenth Independence Day. "Long live Israel!" toasted the guests as they raised their champagne flutes. Rabin was engaged in conversation with current and former officers about the war they had fought together in 1948 when the phone rang. "Yitzhak, it's for you," someone yelled. On the line was Rafi Efrat, Rabin's assistant. "Ahrale Yariv wants to talk to you about the latest news from Egypt," Efrat informed him in his German-accented Hebrew. "I'll connect you in a second."[1]

Aharon Yariv, known to all as "Ahrale," was Israel's head of military intelligence. He had started receiving worrying reports as early as the night of May 13. As Nasser was inviting Amer to a private meeting at his residence, Yariv deliberated whether to go out to see a movie with friends. Eventually, he decided to stay at home near a secure line. In central Tel Aviv, a few dozen kilometers from Yariv's house, Captain Ehud Ramot was standing in the intelligence ops center – Yariv's brainchild, inaugurated only a week before. Above his head a large sign read: "Those you have spared at night will show you no mercy during the day." The somewhat cryptic message was meant to relieve junior officers of their hesitations regarding waking senior officers. Ramot, though, required little prodding. His desk was overflowing with hot news. The eavesdroppers from Unit 848 intercepted calls from Damascus to Cairo in which Syrian officials alleged that Israel had concentrated troops on their border. There were scattered pieces of information about the Egyptians' preparations for mobilizing their army and crossing the Suez Canal. Around midnight Ramot called Yariv, who listened attentively. "What does the head of the Egyptian desk think?" Yariv inquired. "He thinks it's an Egyptian drill," Ramot answered. Yariv gave the order to call a staff meeting in his office at 6 a.m. After he had hung up, Yariv went to bed. He tossed and turned for a few hours but could not sleep, and rose early. A short man with sandy hair, Yariv was a health fanatic and kept a strict routine, obsessively diarizing his fluctuations in weight (even if they amounted to no more than a few hundreds of grams). After practicing some yoga, he took a cold shower, dressed, and ordered his driver to head for Tel Aviv.[2]

Throughout the day of May 14, news about Egyptian troop movements kept dogging Yariv. He made sure that the intelligence ops center kept Rabin informed, but at the end of that day Yariv decided to talk with his commander directly and found him at the Independence Day party. Yariv told Rabin that the Egyptians were responding to Soviet information and Syrian fears. His assessment was that the Egyptians were flexing their muscles, nothing more. After that phone call, Rabin proceeded to the prime minister's office. Yariv and the prime minister had arranged to meet there ahead of the traditional Independence Day spectacle taking place at the Hebrew University stadium. When Rabin arrived, Eshkol and his wife Miriam, thirty years his junior, were already standing on the veranda. From that vantage point, Eshkol, a bespectacled 72-year-old who had the appearance of a kind uncle, could see the stadium; the roar of the crowd rose from below. The atmosphere was festive and expectant. Rabin approached and said something about Egyptian troop movements toward Sinai. Eshkol looked at him in surprise, but said nothing. The two did not discuss the matter further that evening.[3]

Long after Rabin and Eshkol retired to their homes, a phone call from the ops center woke Yariv again. One battalion had already crossed the Canal and entered Sinai; another Egyptian division was making preparations to do the same. "Keep up the good work," said Yariv, and put down the phone. He travelled to Jerusalem early on May 15 and met Rabin at 9 a.m. in the lobby of the luxurious King David Hotel. Eshkol was present, as well as many other dignitaries, gathering there before heading out together to watch a military parade. After talking with Yariv, Rabin drew Eshkol into a corner of the lobby. By this point, Rabin had a more detailed picture to paint. The Egyptian army was at the highest state of alert. It had been ordered to deploy in Sinai according to the "Qaher" plan, which Israeli intelligence knew well. Rabin added that the Egyptian chief of staff,

Mohamed Fawzi, had been sent to Damascus to update the Syrians. As far as we know, said Rabin, Fawzi had demanded that the Syrians not provoke Israel into war. Nevertheless, if more Egyptian troops entered Sinai, Israel might need to call up reserves. "We cannot leave the South[ern front] without additional troops," Rabin maintained. Eshkol listened but did not seem overly concerned. A pattern had been set: Rabin would apply pressure to respond militarily to the Egyptian threat, while Eshkol played for time. After that short conversation, Eshkol, Rabin, and Yariv set off for the stadium in central Jerusalem, where 18,000 spectators were waiting eagerly.[4]

While Rabin and Yariv sat on the bleachers to watch their army march, they were receiving updates about the march of a different army at a different location. The ops center in Tel Aviv had installed a phone system in the stadium in advance to feed reports to Rabin and Yariv, and the news kept coming in waves: Egyptian forces were marching through the streets of Cairo, on their way to Suez; the first line of defense in Sinai had already been manned; Egyptian missile ships had taken positions along the Canal; the Syrians had moved tank battalions into the Golan Heights.[5]

Once the military parade was over, Eshkol and Rabin went on to the Bible Quiz, another traditional Independence Day event, featuring contestants from all over the world. Before entering the auditorium, Rabin approached Eshkol. For the first time, Rabin requested permission to call up reserve soldiers. Eshkol resisted. He valued his headstrong chief of staff but was suspicious of his rush to judgment. Calling up reserves would be the first step on a slippery slope, and in the preceding years, Eshkol had invested a lot of time and effort in preserving the peace.[6]

Waging Peace

Even before taking office, Eshkol had been displeased with the state of Soviet–Israeli relations. According to his testimony, he asked Ben-Gurion, who seemed to revel in anti-Soviet rhetoric, why relations with the Soviet Union had to be so bad. After all, for a brief moment the Soviet Union had been generous with the Zionist movement: voting in the UN, in November 1947, for the establishment of a Jewish state; green-lighting Czechoslovak arms sales to Israel when it was fighting the Arabs in 1948; and allowing East European Jews to immigrate to Palestine, just when the Israelis needed to man their front lines. Three years later, though, the romance had gone sour. In 1950 Israel chose, under American pressure, to take sides in the Cold War and expressed its support for America's intervention in the Korean civil war. From that point onward, relations cooled considerably.

Stalin's persecution of Jewish Communist officials in 1952 further increased Israeli animosity.[7] Following Stalin's death in March 1953, Soviet foreign policy assumed an increasingly pro-Arab tilt.

Nevertheless, Eshkol wanted to resuscitate the moribund relationship. He took over as prime minister shortly before Kennedy's assassination and saw great promise in JFK's détente policies. Indeed, in January 1966 Eshkol declared in the Knesset: "Israel is opposed to the so-called Cold War and wants to see it end."[8] Eshkol believed that a détente between the superpowers could mitigate Arab–Israeli tensions. His hope was that the superpowers, as part of their reconciliation, would reach an agreement that would put an end to the regional arms race, which both the Soviet Union and the US fueled by supplying weapons to their proxies.[9]

Eshkol also thought that Israel should play an active role in this process by courting Moscow and serving as an intermediary between the superpowers. A case in point was Eshkol's decision to intervene in a dispute between the US and the Soviet Union over the latter's $50 million debt to the United Nations. The Soviets were unwilling to pay their dues to the UN, complaining that UN money was invested in peacekeeping missions that they did not support, such as those in Korea and the Congo. This was alarming news for Israeli diplomacy. UN peacekeeping forces had an important role to play in Israel's disputes with its Arab neighbors. They served as a buffer between Israeli and Egyptian forces in Sinai and helped mediate border disputes with Syria. Eshkol feared that if the Soviet Union left the UN, the organization would break down. In one meeting with Secretary of State Dean Rusk, Israeli Foreign Minister Abba Eban tried to convince Rusk to create a special fund into which the Soviet Union would pay its debt – knowing exactly where the funds would go.[10]

Between 1963 and 1966, Eshkol did all he could to set the rapprochement in motion. In 1964 he declared his recognition of the Oder–Neisse Line, the post-World War II border between Germany and Poland, which granted the latter additional territory. Although West Germany disputed the Oder–Neisse Line, Eshkol said that it should be accepted as a permanent settlement and should not be changed by force.[11] On several occasions, Eshkol met with the Soviet ambassador and expressed his desire to improve relations, particularly in the economic sphere.[12] Eshkol was probably alluding to the delicate matter of oil. Israel, devoid at the time of energy resources of its own, was wholly dependent on imports from Iran, which, in Eshkol's view, was charging exorbitant prices. To break Iran's stranglehold on the Israeli market, Eshkol wanted to buy oil from the Soviet Union as well.[13]

Meeting with senior members of his party in 1963, Eshkol asked them to moderate their references to the Soviet Union in their Knesset speeches. He even talked about searching for opportunities to vote with the Soviet Union at the UN. Likewise, during a conference with senior officials to discuss the Soviet Union's refusal to allow free Jewish immigration, Eshkol asked attendees to avoid portraying the USSR as anti-Semitic in official pronouncements, but rather to emphasize the humanitarian aspects of letting people travel freely.[14] His foreign minister, Abba Eban, made a public speech in 1965 in which he called upon the Soviet Union to become a partner in securing the stability of the region. If that were not enough, Eban had met with the Soviet ambassador and pointed out to him how far-reaching his statement was: while no Western country had been willing to acknowledge Soviet interests in the Middle East, emphasized Eban, Israel was.[15]

Eshkol was aware of Moscow's strong opposition to nuclear prolifera-tion and entertained the thought of calling for the creation of a nuclear-free Middle East. As Eshkol explained to Golda Meir in 1964, he was certain that no Arab country would cooperate with this initiative, but he was hoping to make a good impression on Khrushchev. A year earlier, Eshkol's confidant, Eliezer Livneh, discussed the proposal with a Soviet diplomat. To whet Moscow's appetite still further, Livneh added that Israel would be willing to use the Jewish lobby to help the Soviet Union receive loans from the US. In January 1966, Eshkol wrote a letter to Soviet Premier Alexei Kosygin congratulating him on his success in mediating a peace agreement between Pakistan and India. Toward the end of the letter, Eshkol reiterated his government's desire to reach a regional agreement on the denuclearization of the Middle East. The same month, Abba Eban met with Soviet Foreign Minister Andrei Gromyko and put to him the same position. Since his previous probes had met with no response, Eshkol decided to up the ante by leaking to the Soviets, through his intelligence adviser, Isser Harel, informa-tion to the effect that Israel intended to build an atomic bomb. Harel's contact was a Communist member of the Knesset, Moshe Sneh, who had direct channels to the leadership of the Soviet Communist Party. According to Sneh's assistant, at one point Sneh even received an official letter from Eshkol authorizing him to facilitate a dialogue between Israel and the Soviet Union on the nuclear issue.[16]

The pattern of pursuing discreet diplomacy to avoid war was evident also in Eshkol's policy toward Jordan and Egypt. As with the Soviet Union, Israeli diplomats used the reputation of the Jewish lobby on Capitol Hill to persuade the Jordanians and the Egyptians to do business with them, the implication being that good relations with Israel were the gateway to better relations with Washington. The contact in Amman was none other than King Hussein. That the monarch would be willing to meet with Israelis while his country had not officially recognized Israel's right to exist sounded almost too fanciful. But King Hussein was merely following in the footsteps of his father, King Abdullah, who held a series of clandestine meetings with Zionist leaders, Golda Meir being the most senior of them, between the 1920s and 1940s.

Jordan – a conservative monarchy, poorly endowed with natural resources, and with a largely agricultural economy – was a weak state surrounded by strong and hostile neighbors. During the 1950s and 1960s, both Nasser and the Baath regime in Syria sought to undermine Hussein and bring his regime down. With so few friends in the region, Jordan could not ignore Israel. Israeli policymakers reached the same conclusion. Although somewhat partial to the idea of taking the West Bank from Hussein, in the late 1950s Ben-Gurion came to believe that a friendly kingdom on Israel's eastern border was his safest bet. This was the lesson he learned in 1956. In that year, Ben-Gurion had tried to expand Israel's borders by joining the Anglo-French operation against Egypt. Within a week, the IDF controlled the whole of Sinai. But then President Eisenhower applied strong pressure on Israel to withdraw, which it did in early 1957. Ben-Gurion's conclusion was that any attempt to expand Israel's borders would meet a wall of American resistance. In 1960, when, inconceivably, Hussein contemplated an invasion of Syria, an Israeli emissary promised him that Israel had his back. In 1961, Ben-Gurion met with President Kennedy and urged him to support King Hussein financially.[17]

Kennedy refused to accept Ben-Gurion's advice. Hussein's kingdom seemed to Kennedy to be an ancient relic, and his administration had turned a cold shoulder to the king. In 1962, the US cut its yearly subsidy to Jordan to $39.5 million, down from $40.5 million in the previous year, and reduced that sum even further in 1963 to $37.1 million. In April 1963, when pro-Nasser riots had rocked the kingdom, Kennedy had released no official statement, and State Department documents from the period reveal that American policymakers considered with equanimity an annexation of Jordan by Nasser's Egypt.[18]

At the time, Washington was Jordan's main financial backer, a burden it assumed in 1957 having inherited it from a bankrupt British Empire. The subsidy amounted to one-third of Jordan's annual budget. Indeed, forty years after gaining independence, Jordan was still economically non-viable. The US's receding support was, therefore, a serious issue for the ruler of a small kingdom. Fear had sent Hussein scurrying into the arms of the Israelis, who had been seeking talks with a senior Jordanian official ever since 1960.[19] The first meeting between King Hussein and Yaacov Herzog, general director of the prime minister's office, took place in September 1963 in the private residence of Hussein's personal (Jewish) physician. The first item on the agenda was Hussein's troubled relations with Washington. His friends, rather than his enemies, were the source of his predicament, Hussein complained. The Americans were supporting Nasser without reservation, and were taking Jordan "for granted," he maintained. Herzog quickly steered the conversation toward a practical conclusion. Realistically speaking, Herzog said, Hussein could not allow himself to sign a peace agreement with Israel. It was better to create a backchannel through which the two sides would exchange intelligence regularly, to form a regional anti-Nasser bloc that would include Israel, Jordan, Iran, and Turkey, and to coordinate the use of the Jordan River's water. Israel, Herzog promised, would act as Jordan's lobbyist in Washington. Israeli diplomats would appeal to members of Congress, senators, and journalists to support an increase in American aid to Jordan. Further, Israel would seek out private US companies and convince them to invest in the kingdom. Hussein could not ask for more. He readily agreed to Herzog's proposal.[20]

The meeting had immediate consequences. Golda Meir, the Israeli foreign minister, who was in New York at the time, was informed of the tacit understanding. She called Avraham Harman, the Israeli ambassador to Washington, and instructed him to start lobbying on Jordan's behalf. Later, Meir met with American Secretary of State Dean Rusk and recommended that the US expand its aid program in Jordan. In a meeting that took place a month after his talks with Hussein, Herzog appealed to Deputy Assistant Secretary of State for the Near East John Jarnegan to ensure that Hussein's upcoming visit to Washington would be a success. Talking with State Department officials in June 1964, Herzog argued that the administration needed to put more thought into "accelerating the growth rate in Jordan. It is a critical matter. It is regrettable that every year you cut back your aid to Jordan."[21]

Herzog and Hussein met twice in 1964. In May, Herzog updated Hussein regarding Israel's efforts on Jordan's behalf in Washington. The two also coordinated their countries' water development projects, and made sure that they did not get in each other's way. In doing so, Hussein was undermining the Arab League's resolution to disrupt the building of Israel's National Water Carrier. Whilst in Arab League meetings Hussein claimed that the dam he was building would be part of the scheme to divert the water of the Jordan River away from Israel, in reality he had made an agreement with Herzog to share it. When Herzog and Hussein met again in December, Hussein was able to calm Herzog's mind with regard to the recent resolutions of the Arab summit in Alexandria. Contrary to what he had stated at the summit, Hussein assured Herzog that he had no intention of letting Iraqi forces enter his country and take up positions near the border with Israel. Hussein also averred that, regardless of the conclusions in Alexandria, he would prevent the PLO from establishing a military presence in his kingdom.[22]

Herzog and Hussein did not meet during the following year. Yet communication with Amman was vital, as Fatah units launched more and more operations from Jordan's territory in 1965. Eshkol therefore decided to use American diplomats as mailmen, and they delivered letters to Hussein in which Eshkol urged cooperation so that Israel and Jordan might start "to guard the border together." Eshkol reined in his army to give Hussein and his security services the time they needed to hunt down Fatah forces. By early 1966, Eshkol declared his policy a success and proclaimed Fatah to be "comatose, dying."[23]

According to Meir Amit, head of the Mossad in the 1960s, a third opportunity to use tacit diplomacy to improve Israel's relations with its neighbors came knocking on Israel's door in 1964. A European businessman who had been heavily involved with Egypt's development projects offered his services to the Mossad. The Mossad knew that the man, whose name Amit had chosen not to disclose, was a business partner of Muhammad Khalil, a brigadier-general in the Egyptian Air Force (EAF). Khalil, a colorful figure with an appetite for women and whisky, was heading Egypt's weapons-development program and, as such, had access to both Nasser and Amer. The Egyptian government often used him as unofficial conduit to Western governments.[24]

From the very start, the businessman suggested a package deal that would enable Israel to "Jordanize" its relations with its southern neighbor – that is, to earn Egypt's goodwill by helping it navigate the dire economic straits in which it found itself. In February 1965, in a meeting with a Mossad representative, the businessman claimed that Nasser was aware of his mission and had given it his blessing. By the end of 1965, the businessman introduced his Mossad contact to Khalil.[25] On February 1, 1966, there was a breakthrough in the talks, when Khalil met with none other than the Mossad's chief in an undisclosed European location. Amit said that Israel would be willing to arrange a $30 million low-interest loan for Egypt and, echoing Herzog's talks with Hussein, he suggested that Israel would use its influence on Capitol Hill to help Egypt receive American aid. In exchange, he wanted Egypt to moderate its anti-Israeli propaganda and allow non-Israeli ships to move merchandise to Israel through the Suez Canal. Khalil then flew back to Cairo to discuss the matter at length with Abd al-Hakim Amer. Amer was apparently excited by Amit's offer, but then threw a spanner in the works: he insisted that the next meeting with Amit take place in Cairo. Adding a splash of Arab hospitality, Amer suggested that Amit come to Egypt as his personal guest.[26]

Amit – like Eshkol – was willing to contemplate such a daring trip, but Eshkol's cabinet thought that Amer's proposal could be a trap. The Mossad contacted the European businessman who had initiated the backchannel to announce that Amit would not come to Cairo but Israel would still move forward with the loan. The businessman was disappointed, as were Khalil and Nasser. The businessman told the Mossad in March 1966 that he had reported their offer and that Nasser had decided to scuttle the whole affair. The backchannel to him was now a dead end.[27] By then, however, Nasser had more pressing problems. The businessman told the Mossad that shortly before Nasser had decided to kill the talks he had tendered his resignation. It was his assessment that the Egyptian president would not survive for long at the top.[28] If Nasser was indeed fighting for his political life, he certainly could not allow himself to continue the talks with the Mossad or reproach Amer for setting an improbable venue for the next meeting with the Israelis.

The Mossad, the military intelligence, and the Foreign Ministry kept on thinking about establishing some sort of "red-line" arrangement with Egypt. In two sizable meetings that took place in November 1966 and January 1967, officials from those agencies agreed that whilst Nasser was not ready to make peace with Israel, he was obviously reluctant to fight it. They therefore recommended that Israel find a way to maintain contact with the Egyptian president. Such a mechanism, they argued, could prove critical during regional crises. At such perilous turning points, Israel would need to coordinate with Nasser to find steps that would enable both countries to avoid war.[29]

By 1966 the mood surrounding Eshkol was one of sanguinity. The dialog with Moscow and Amman, and the almost successful attempt to start one with Nasser, suggested that the Middle East was becoming a friendlier place. It was not just about what had been said behind closed doors; the speeches that Arab leaders were making sounded different. In April 1965, Habib Bourguiba, Tunisia's president, called on Arab states to start negotiating directly with Israel. Gamal Abd al-Nasser gave several speeches between 1965 and 1967 in which he argued that war with Israel was not a realistic policy. Eshkol's advisers dubbed this emerging trend "Arab realism," by which they meant a de facto recognition of Israel. At the end of 1965, the annual assessment of military intelligence also acknowledged "Arab realism" as a recent phenomenon.[30]

Eshkol's peace offensive was rooted in a dovish worldview. His daughters attested that he had taught them from a young age to see the Arabs as equal to Jews, and to oppose any racist attitudes. Indeed, one of Eshkol's first actions as prime minister was to cancel the travel restrictions for Arab citizens. In 1966 he abolished the military rule imposed on Israel's Arab citizens since 1948. As Eshkol explained back in 1963, he believed that peace with the Arab world was possible and that Israel should take concrete steps to promote it. He once confessed in a closed meeting, "I feel good among Arabs ... I have no [emotional] complex, certainly no hatred." In 1965 Eshkol outlined his peace plan, which called for direct negotiations with Arab countries, economic cooperation with Jordan, and Arab–Israeli research in the fields of agriculture and water desalination. Such a plan, Eshkol told Knesset members, "is not pie in the sky. Current political and economic integration in Western Europe would have seemed impossible twenty years ago. We are approaching the twentieth anniversary of the 1948 war. [Regional cooperation] is possible [in the Middle East] as well."[31]

Nevertheless, between 1963 and 1967, the Israeli army had initiated several armed raids and countless border incidents. By the spring of 1967, these operations shattered the illusion of a pragmatic truce between Israel and the Arab world. Eshkol certainly wanted to pursue a softer line. However, he was not the master of his own house. His old nemesis was breathing down his neck, berating him at every turn, accusing him of selling Israel down the river. This was not the regular collision of egos so rife in politics. It was a blood feud.

8

DEFYING ISRAEL'S FOUNDING FATHER

ESHKOL WAS BORN in Russia in 1895 and immigrated to Palestine on the eve of World War I. His generation dreamed of creating a socialist society in Palestine that would in time become the homeland of a Jewish nation. During the 1920s, Eshkol and his comrades worked tirelessly to create a hierarchical and disciplined socialist party, and saw their dream realized when the Workers' Party of the Land of Israel (Mapai, according to its Hebrew acronym) was established in 1930. Gradually, through the 1930s and 1940s, David Ben-Gurion emerged as its leader. Born in Poland in 1886, Ben-Gurion soon tired of working as an agricultural day laborer and exhibited more interest in writing articles, making speeches, and engaging in politics. His passion, tactical agility, and ruthlessness in particular ensured his steady rise to the top. Along the way, he had to make peace with the small group of party activists who controlled Mapai's apparatus – essentially, Mapai's party bosses. Eshkol was one of them. Later, Golda Meir became another leading member of the group.[1]

During the 1930s and 1940s, conflicts between them and Ben-Gurion over spheres of influence ended with an unofficial pact. Ben-Gurion agreed to focus on security affairs and foreign policy, while the party bosses assumed the seemingly mundane task of running the party and dealing with social and economic issues – an arrangement that concentrated a lot of power in their hands.[2] This power emanated principally from their control over the Histadrut (Hebrew for self-organization). It was a Jewish trade union, the largest in Palestine before World War II. One shrewd observer wrote that the secret of the Histadrut's immense power was that its leaders were able to convince the public that it was a boring affair. In fact, it was a formidable enterprise. Histadrut officials, most of them from Mapai, channeled Jewish contributions from abroad to establish a vast array of social services: schools, health clinics, hospitals, labor exchanges, and sports clubs. The Histadrut not only unionized workers from all spheres of the economy, provided for their health, and educated their children; it also employed them. With funds received from the World Zionist Organization, the Histadrut opened factories, which it owned and operated. The most important of them was Solel Boneh, the largest construction company in Palestine.

Through their control of the Histadrut, Mapai's party bosses could secure jobs and social benefits for hundreds of thousands of breadwinners. People owed them favors and the party bosses knew how to translate their gratitude into votes. Once, in a burst of outrage, Golda Meir referred to Mapai's leadership as Tammany Hall. But this should not be thought of as a pejorative. Just like the Democratic Party machine that had been dominant in New York politics for over a century, Mapai emerged in an immigrant society. Pre-independence Palestine absorbed wave after wave of penniless Jews. In many cases they had no connections and needed help. Mapai and the Histadrut could be there for them, if they were willing to show political fealty.[3]

This pattern continued after the Israeli state was established in 1948. If, during the British mandate years (1917–47), the Histadrut was a state-in-the-making, then after 1948 it existed as a shadow state, filling all the holes in the young country's safety net. As in pre-independence times, Mapai's party bosses considered their control of the Histadrut crucial for the party's success and, just as important, for their own dominance within Mapai. Indeed, thanks to this arrangement, Mapai received the largest share of the vote in every election cycle. However, in the post-independence era, the informal pact between Ben-Gurion and the party bosses began to unravel.[4]

During the war of 1948, Ben-Gurion, as both prime minister and minister of defense, oversaw the successful offensives that led the Jewish armed forces to victory over their Arab foes. As a result, he gained a popular mandate no other leader enjoyed before (or since). Consequently, Ben-Gurion was no longer willing to co-rule with the party bosses – also known at the time as "the middle generation" – but rather plotted to replace them with young Defense Ministry protégés such as Shimon Peres and Moshe Dayan. He also spoke openly about his desire to nationalize various functions of the Histadrut, such as health and education. A realization of these plans could have emasculated the last group of leaders within Mapai who could challenge Ben-Gurion. But the party bosses had no intention of going silently into the night.[5]

The tension between the party bosses and the Ben-Gurion camp became particularly evident before the 1959 election. Ben-Gurion's young disciples, who became known in the media as "the youngsters," although most of them were well into their thirties and forties, wanted to be positioned at the top of the party's list for the Knesset, a sign of seniority. The middle generation suspected that this would be the first step in Ben-Gurion's master plan to elbow them out of the party. As had often happened in Mapai, participants in the power play camouflaged their intentions by donning ideological garb. The party bosses claimed it was wrong to parachute the newcomers into senior roles; they must wait their turn and start on the lower rungs.

Ben-Gurion's protégés, supported by a growing group of young party activists who were disgruntled by the middle generation's total control over the party apparatus, claimed that Mapai was ossified, old, and gray. They pointed out that internal elections within the party were rigged. Secret ballots rarely took place. The party bosses usually based decisions about appointments and promotions on deals among themselves, and the party's elective bodies functioned as an elaborate puppet show. The youngsters, particularly Dayan, criticized the Histadrut and claimed that the inefficiency of its factories was a drag on the national economy. His generation, Dayan proclaimed, had fought valiantly for the country in 1948, while the party elders sat in their Histadrut offices. Golda Meir retorted that Dayan sounded as if he wished to establish a military dictatorship.[6]

Ben-Gurion watched the struggle between the party veterans and the youngsters from the sidelines, ostensibly taking an impartial position. Eventually he was able to place Dayan, Peres, and Abba Eban in the party's line-up for the Knesset. After all, this was 1959: Ben-Gurion was at the height of his power. Three years earlier he led Israel to another resounding military victory in the war of 1956 against Egypt. For that reason, Ben-Gurion was front and center in Mapai's 1959 election campaign. The party's slogan was "Say yes to the Old Man!" (Ben-Gurion's popular nickname). Dayan and Eban were touted as the Young Turks and were sent by the campaign managers to tour the country and increase voter turnout. It worked. Mapai gained forty-seven seats in the Knesset – its best result ever. After the elections, Ben-Gurion made Dayan the minister of agriculture, Peres was appointed deputy minister of defense, and Eban a minister without portfolio. For the time being, the party bosses had to accept this reality. Still, their representatives in the government – Eshkol as finance minister, Meir as foreign minister, Pinhas Sapir as minister of trade and industry, Zalman Aran as minister of education – had more prominent positions than the youngsters.[7]

Moreover, one year after the elections, Ben-Gurion played into their hands when, drunk on his own success and power, he embarked on an elaborate scheme. The long and painful strife that Mapai was about to go through, because of Ben-Gurion's political gamble, revolved around a Pandora's box that had first been opened back in 1954. That summer, Egyptian security services had uncovered an Israeli spy net. Its members were Egyptian Jews who had been trained by Israeli military intelligence. Their mission was to engage in a campaign of sabotage by planting explosives in cinemas and post offices. Whoever authorized the operation – his identity remains a mystery to this very day – hoped that it would derail Egyptian–British negotiations over the final evacuation of British troops from the Suez Canal base. The operation was concocted because the military establishment in Israel thought, mistakenly, that the British presence along the Suez Canal provided a buffer between Israeli and Egyptian troops.[8]

Officially, Israel denied responsibility for the acts of sabotage and described the trials of its Egyptian-Jewish spies as a blood libel. However, Moshe Sharett, Israel's then prime minister and foreign minister, made inquiries and discovered to his surprise that someone had authorized this operation without running it by him. His defense minister, Pinhas Lavon, claimed that he had no prior knowledge of this affair either, and laid all the blame on the shoulders of Benjamin Gibli, the handsome chief of military intelligence. Gibli, for his part, alleged that Lavon had given him a direct order to set the operation in motion. A judicial committee composed of only two members investigated the scandal in utmost secrecy. Eventually, it submitted an anodyne report in which it stated that the nature of the evidence did not allow the culprit to be named.[9]

Neither Lavon nor Gibli was willing to take responsibility and resign. Each was scheming to implicate the other and demanded his opposite number's removal. The General Staff supported Gibli, and Lavon's authority was seriously impaired. For more than six months, "the mishap," as the affair became known, had been a topic of intense debate within Mapai. Sharett and the party bosses invented various schemes to shuffle the deck in ways that would satisfy both Lavon's vanity and the military leadership's demands. None of them succeeded.[10]

Up until February 1955, the whole matter was kept under wraps; the public had no inkling of the crisis that was paralyzing Sharett's government. But in February 1955, Shimon Peres, then director general of the Ministry of Defense, and Nachman Karni, the military's spokesman, leaked information related to "the mishap" to the press to force Sharett to act. The party bosses were desperate to prevent publicity. Any media discussion of what had happened in Egypt was bound to open a can of worms. In the two years that Sharett served as prime minister, from 1953 to 1955, he lost control over the military. Israeli generals resented Sharett, a dovish politician who sought to rein them in and who believed that tacit diplomacy could quench the fire of the Arab–Israeli conflict. Rather than obey its new master, the military derailed his policies. Thus, forces were dispatched beyond the border for a host of reasons: training, revenge, and retribution. The army's actions on the border constantly undermined the feelers Sharett was putting out. When Sharett gave the army a clear instruction to stop, they ignored it. "The mishap," then, was not an accidental slip, but rather emblematic of the pathological nature of civil–military relations in Israel. If this became known, Mapai's reputation as a governing party would have been ruined.[11]

To put an end to the rumor mill, the party bosses demanded Lavon's resignation in February 1955 and called Ben-Gurion back from his temporary retirement in a remote kibbutz in the desert. The public and the press accepted this reshuffle without much probing. Ben-Gurion had been so popular that his return to the helm, after two unsteady years under Sharett, was accepted with relief. It was one of the largest cover-ups in Israel's history.

For five years, the 1954 "Spygate" lay dormant. The protagonists were compensated so that they would keep their silence. Gibli left his position as head of the military intelligence, but still served in various other command positions before finally retiring from the ranks in 1961. In 1956 the party bosses handed Lavon the powerful position of chairman of the Histadrut as compensation for his defenestration two years earlier. Lavon was a strong and effective chairman, which did not win him any points in Ben-Gurion's book. Moreover, Lavon clearly stood with the middle generation in their fight against the youngsters. In 1959, two weeks before the internal elections in the Histadrut, Lavon criticized Ben-Gurion and Dayan for their anti-Histadrut broadsides. He said they were hurting Mapai's campaign. "If Mapai loses its majority in the Histadrut," argued Lavon, "Mapai is done for." After the general elections later that year, Lavon spearheaded the opposition within the party to the appointment of the youngsters as ministers. He also fought against Ben-Gurion's attempts to invite into the coalition right-wing parties that wanted to see the power of the Histadrut curbed. He was assisted by Eshkol, who announced that if Ben-Gurion tried to create a governmental coalition hostile to the Histadrut, "[Ben-Gurion] would have to form a coalition without Mapai." The confrontation between Ben-Gurion and the party bosses intensified during the following year, causing one participant to observe that "Mapai was on the verge of a split from which two parties would emerge: the Histadrut party vs. a military party."[12]

In early 1960, Lavon discovered that new evidence had surfaced that could help him clear his name. In May, Lavon met with Ben-Gurion and told him he wanted a public exoneration. Ben-Gurion, though, had no intention of giving Lavon what he wanted, instead demanding that "the mishap" be investigated by a judicial committee. Ben-Gurion had a perfect alibi: at the time the whole affair occurred, in early 1955, he was out of power. Apparently he hoped that a judicial committee would unearth the cover-up in which Eshkol and Golda Meir were deeply implicated, and thus destroy their careers.[13]

Eshkol put himself at the forefront of the efforts to block Ben-Gurion's ploy. He knew he was on fairly safe ground in opposing Ben-Gurion. Gibli's former secretary, Dalia Karmel, became Eshkol's lover and disclosed to him that, back in 1954, Gibli had ordered her to forge a letter "proving" that Lavon had instructed him to activate the spy network in Egypt. Eshkol's first success in his struggle with Ben-Gurion was to maneuver the Old Man to agree to the establishment of a ministerial, rather than a judicial, committee. The prosecutor general, on behalf of the committee, was able to get hold of Karmel's testimony, which was reason enough for the ministerial committee to acquit Lavon. Ben-Gurion, however, was not going to let the story end there.[14]

The committee submitted its report in December 1960. Ben-Gurion was irate. He claimed that it had no legal standing. Lavon could be exonerated only by a judge, he said, and he demanded Lavon's immediate ouster. As was his custom, he resigned as prime minister to cow the party into submission. Eshkol decided to accept Ben-Gurion's demand. Sacrificing Lavon to prevent a judicial process was a small price to pay for the party bosses, who were now engaged in a struggle for survival. In addition, Lavon had made himself a pariah within Mapai by pleading his case to the Foreign Affairs and Security Committee of the Knesset in the preceding months. During four emotional sessions, Lavon gave his version of the affair. He described in detail the perjuries that officers had allegedly committed in order to frame him and criticized Mapai's leadership for covering up the injustice. Worst of all, he divulged his assessment that the renewed discussion of "the mishap" was part of the leadership struggle within Mapai over the future of the Histadrut. The party bosses could not forgive Lavon for washing Mapai's dirty linen in public.[15]

On February 4, 1961, members of Mapai's central committee convened to remove Lavon from his position as Histadrut chairman and from the party's line-up for the Knesset. They were greeted by young students carrying banners claiming that Israeli democracy was under threat. Ironically, this was a mark of Eshkol's success. The public followed the political imbroglio closely, but newspaper coverage was hampered by severe censorship. Since the allegations against Lavon could not be spelled out, people viewed Ben-Gurion's demand to oust Lavon as the whim of a vengeful old man. Academics and intellectuals published newspaper columns describing Ben-Gurion's long rule as a danger to democracy. Suddenly, his unquestioned hold over the Defense Ministry was challenged. Israel under Ben-Gurion, pundits claimed, had succumbed to a new religion: "Security-ism." In Lavon's testimony before the Knesset he drew attention to the "economic imperialism" of the Ministry of Defense.[16]

Lavon was referring to the fact that as minister of defense, Ben-Gurion had concentrated in his hands immense economic power. The defense budget, which in 1957 was $100 million, grew each year by 14 percent and reached $200 million in 1963. Employees in Israel's arms industry constituted 10 percent of the workforce. Ben-Gurion also supervised one of the largest infrastructure projects in Israel's history: the construction of a military nuclear reactor at Dimona, the cost of which was estimated to be $180 million. Israel had spent an additional $200 million on long-range missiles capable of delivering a nuclear warhead. The Ministry of Defense also controlled Arab workers' access to the labor market, since all Arab citizens were under military rule.[17] Formerly, all that had passed without scrutiny. Now it was a matter of public debate.

After Lavon's dismissal, Ben-Gurion withdrew his resignation and tried to form a new coalition, but to no avail. So discredited was his leadership that his former coalition partners refused to negotiate with him. Ben-Gurion had no choice but to call fresh elections. The 1961 elections were the last in which Ben-Gurion headed Mapai. This time, his star was waning, his reputation in tatters. In an attempt to shift the narrative, Ben-Gurion released a photo of himself and Peres waiting for the experimental launch of the first Israel-made long-range missile, Comet 2. The newspapers greeted that spin with disdain.

Mapai lost five seats at the polls, but it was still the largest party in the new Knesset. Once again, Mapai's potential partners refused to negotiate with Ben-Gurion. Reluctantly, he took the unprecedented step of asking Eshkol to form the coalition for him. Ben-Gurion presided over the new government, but his position was much weakened. His coalition partners monitored his actions more closely than ever. The party bosses continued to wrong-foot him at every turn. For instance, when it was revealed that

German scientists with a Nazi past had been working on the Egyptian missile project, Golda Meir was quick to use this story to skewer Ben-Gurion, the architect of the historic reconciliation with West Germany.[18]

In June 1963, Ben-Gurion, frustrated and beleaguered, resigned his position as prime minister. He was 77 years old. Eshkol, who had been running the party from behind the scenes during the previous two years, was anointed by Mapai as Ben-Gurion's successor. But the Old Man did not quite disappear from the scene. On the contrary, he appeared to be itching for a comeback, casting a giant shadow over Eshkol. In late 1964, Ben-Gurion unearthed some new material on "the mishap" and used it to provoke a renewed interest in another judicial investigation into the matter, demanding that Mapai's central committee consider it afresh. Again, the ostensibly mild-mannered Eshkol proved more capable than his former mentor and employed a trick that had worked so well for Ben-Gurion: on the eve of the central committee's meeting, Eshkol resigned. The message was clear: should the party back him, he would withdraw his resignation; if not, the party would face a succession struggle. It worked. The central committee decided to back Eshkol's decision to refrain from re-investigating "the mishap."[19]

Following the confrontation with Ben-Gurion, Eshkol initiated talks with the left-wing Ahdut Ha-Avoda (Unity of Labor) party in December 1963 to discuss a possible merger. Previously, the presence of the irascible Ben-Gurion at the top precluded such an endeavor. In the late 1940s and early 1950s, Ben-Gurion purged left-wing officers associated with Ahdut Ha-Avoda from the ranks, and his attacks on the Histadrut further alienated workers' parties. Now that Ben-Gurion was out of the picture, Eshkol could invite Ahdut Ha-Avoda to form a new political bloc with Mapai. But that was not the only reason Eshkol had wanted Ahdut Ha-Avoda by his side. The average age of the Mapai leadership was over 60. These leaders may have been great organization men, but they were also dull and uncharismatic. If the party bosses wanted to compete with Ben-Gurion's protégés, such as Dayan and Peres, who were both considered handsome and articulate, they had to come up with their own youngsters. Ahdut Ha-Avoda had a cadre of young leaders with military backgrounds, such as Yigal Allon, Yisrael Galili, and Moshe Karmel. All of them were more hawkish than Eshkol, but he saw them as boosting his arsenal. Ben-Gurion, who understood better than anyone what Eshkol was doing, vehemently opposed the merger with Ahdut Ha-Avoda. But, despite his resistance, by November 1964 the new "Alignment" between Mapai and Ahdut Ha-Avoda was a done deal.[20]

Ben-Gurion did not give up. As the party convention of February 1965 approached, he challenged Eshkol's authority again and tabled a motion to annul the merger. Eshkol, Golda Meir, and Aran, who led the efforts to defeat Ben-Gurion on the convention floor, prepared a special surprise for the Old Man. Moshe Sharett, who Ben-Gurion brutally forced to resign from his position as foreign minister in 1956 and marginalized within the party in the following years, was called upon to deliver a speech. At the time, Sharett was dying of lung cancer in the Hadassah hospital in Jerusalem. Traveling to Tel Aviv, according to Sharett, was "a mad adventure involving all sorts of risks . . . it was not clear, up to the last minute, if I would be able to do it." However, Sharett could not resist the temptation to draw the dagger and sink it in the heart of his old nemesis. Wheeled into the convention hall by his son, Sharett made a trenchant hour-long speech in a quivering voice accusing Israel's founding father of hubris and telling "half-truths." At first the audience was mesmerized, but then Ben-Gurion supporters began to heckle the speaker. Sharett nevertheless persisted in making a mockery of Ben-Gurion's demands. When he was done, Golda Meir kissed the exhausted Sharett on the forehead. The convention defeated Ben-Gurion's motion, yet 40 percent of the delegates voted with him. It was a sign that a large minority was still loyal to the Old Man.[21]

The next stage in the struggle involved Ben-Gurion's camp ceding from the party and a "comrade trial" of Ben-Gurion taking place. Ultimately, Ben-Gurion was excommunicated from the party. The split between the Histadrut and the military party was now final. They would face each other in the general elections in November 1965. The Ben-Gurion list for the Knesset, known as Rafi (a Hebrew acronym for the Israel Workers' List), could be read as a "who's who" of security bigwigs. Among Rafi's supporters and Knesset candidates were three ex-chiefs of staff (Jacob Dori, Moshe Dayan, and Tzvi Tzur), one former head of military intelligence (Chaim Herzog), and a former director general of the Ministry of Defense (Shimon Peres). Ben-Gurion planned to leverage his charisma and reputation to slaughter at the polls the party he had fathered. Likewise, Eshkol and his supporters had no intention of pulling their punches.[22]

The warring camps stopped at nothing. Ben-Gurion claimed the Mapai platform was tainted with "Marxist ideas" and that Eshkol was weakening the nation's morale by conjuring "illusions of peace." A Mapai leader responded by calling Rafi "a Neo-Fascist group." Ben-Gurion tried to convince the sitting chief of staff, Yitzhak Rabin, to join Rafi. Mapai retaliated by flexing its financial muscles: it drew upon secret funds and handed out cash to precinct officers to secure votes. A Mapai mayor who had dared to join Rafi lost his job after more than a decade of service. Workers in the military industries, suspected as natural Rafi voters, were invited to a rally with Histadrut officials, who called on them to "overcome their inhibitions [to support Eshkol]." Finance Minister Pinhas Sapir, who headed Mapai's campaign, applied pressure on business owners to open their wallets for Mapai, and they did. Mapai's election budget reached $50 million, the largest ever. It funded the best get-out-the-vote effort in the country. "On election day," a popular weekly reported later, "a [Mapai] juggernaut was at work, destroying on its way from North to South all the other parties."[23]

On election night, Sapir, a bald-headed giant of a man with a thundering voice, was at party headquarters in Tel Aviv, following the results with bated breath. When it became clear that things were going well, tears of joy started rolling down his cheeks. Party workers poured cheap wine into paper cups and hoisted Sapir on their shoulders. Singing reverberated down the corridors as it became apparent that the Mapai party machine was more formidable than any man, even if he happened to be Israel's founding father. Mapai gained five seats and remained the largest faction in parliament. Rafi won just ten seats, as opposed to the thirty that Ben-Gurion had dreamed of. Eshkol could easily form a coalition without Rafi, and he did. Ben-Gurion, the man who had it all, had been relegated to the backbenches.[24]

As an opposition party, Rafi kept touting its security expertise, suggesting that Eshkol had no understanding of national security affairs and that he was "soft" with the Arabs. In early 1966, Ben-Gurion accused Eshkol of a mysterious error that put Israel in great peril. At no point did Ben-Gurion disclose what he had in mind. He declared that he was willing to talk about the issue only in the Knesset committee for foreign and security affairs. However, its chairman, an Eshkol supporter, never invited him to testify. Ben-Gurion was not much peeved by this. He seemed to relish the opportunity to accuse Eshkol without specifying the reason.[25]

In the years leading up to the Six-Day War, the Syrian Baath and the Palestinian Fatah resurrected the Rafi threat to Mapai. When the borders were burning, the security expertise of the Rafi leaders was again an electoral asset. If Eshkol had authorized military strikes, Dayan and Ben-Gurion cried that he was using excessive force. If he did not resort to military measures, Rafi described Eshkol as weak. Eshkol was damned if he did, and damned if he did not.[26]

9

EXPANDING ISRAEL'S BORDERS

IN JULY 1963, a month after he entered office, Eshkol conducted a series of discussions with the General Staff. He found out, to his surprise, that the generals were eager to use the next war to expand Israel's borders. Chief of Staff Tzvi Tzur argued that Arab leaders were hell-bent on destroying Israel, and therefore Israel had the right to use the next war to achieve strategic depth. The army, Tzur maintained, must be reinforced so that in the next war its various units would be able to conquer Sinai, the West Bank, and northern Lebanon. Deputy Chief of Staff Yitzhak Rabin concurred. Ezer Weizman, the commander of the air force, maintained that "security-wise the IDF has to expand [Israel's] borders, whether it fits the government's approach or not." Rabin, Weizman, and Yeshayahu Gavish, head of the training branch, worried that Israel would not be able to keep up with the regional arms race. Weizman prophesied that within five years, Israel "would have to think seriously about launching a preventive war." Gavish made it clear that, in his opinion, if King Hussein lost his throne, or if Arab armies entered his kingdom, Israel would have to conquer the West Bank. Other officers who participated in the debates shared the same thoughts. Eshkol, clearly taken aback, warned the generals to stop thinking about changing Israel's borders. The government, he promised, would "turn the world upside down" in its quest for peace, although "it sounds quixotic nowadays."[1]

Eshkol may have been surprised, but the generals were merely reiterating concepts that had already been formed in the 1950s. These gave expression to the unease percolating through the ranks following the end of the 1948 war. During that war, Israeli armed forces were able to defeat a coalition of Arab armies soundly and were on the verge of conquering areas beyond the borders of Mandatory Palestine. For instance, at the end of the conflict in 1948, Israeli forces easily invaded the northern part of Sinai and withdrew only after Britain issued an ultimatum. At that time, Israel was also on the cusp of conquering the West Bank, stopping only because the cabinet voted against Ben-Gurion's recommendation. Ben-Gurion and the generals were left with the bitter taste of missed opportunities.[2]

Consequently, Ben-Gurion was in the habit of describing the post-1948 borders as "unbearable." In his eyes, Israel's meandering border with the Kingdom of Jordan was especially repugnant. Jordan's hold over the West Bank created a large enclave that bulged into Israel's populated coastal areas. Although Ben-Gurion's public speeches described Israel as a small state under siege by powerful neighbors, behind closed doors he depicted Israel as a developed country surrounded by a backward and hopelessly disunited Arab world. Rather than a threat, Ben-Gurion saw the Middle East as an open vista, beckoning Israel to use its military superiority to expand its borders.[3]

Responding to Ben-Gurion's prodding, officers at the IDF's Planning Department drew contingency plans that called for the creation of more "natural" and defensible borders. These were to run along geographical barriers such as the Litani River and the Golan Heights in the north, the Jordan River in the east, and the Suez Canal in the south. A memo authored by the Planning Department in August 1950 referred to these areas as "Israel's Strategic Living Space [*Merhav Mihya*]." Another contingency plan from June 1953 mentioned the availability of oil as well as valuable minerals in Sinai. Yet another spoke about conquering not only the whole Kingdom of Jordan but also "extending fingers" into the Saudi oilfields. These plans formed the bedrock of strategic thinking within the IDF and became the launch pad for Israel's participation in the 1956 Suez Crisis.[4]

About a year before the crisis began, in October 1955, Dayan called for a special meeting of the General Staff to discuss a possible confrontation with Egypt. The moderate Moshe Sharett was still serving as prime minister, but it had already been made clear that Ben-Gurion, the hardliner, was about to form a new government and replace him. At the outset of the meeting, Dayan said that he had decided "to call this meeting so we can discuss what we want to demand of the [new] government." He explained that Israel would have little difficulty in finding a pretext for a strike against Egypt and, therefore, "we should be ready to conquer the Gaza Strip, the demilitarized zones [on the border with Egypt and Syria] and the Tiran Straits ... And we should think of a triple-stage plan ... in the second stage we will reach the Suez Canal; in the third stage we will reach Cairo ... whether we will implement all three stages or just one of them depends on how the war objectives would be defined." Dayan added: "As to Jordan, there [is a] two stage [plan]: the first is [to reach] the Hebron line. The second [is to take] the rest [of the territory] up to the Jordan River. Lebanon is last on our priority list, but we can reach up to the Litani. In Syria, one [line may reach] up to the Golan Heights, and the other [goes] up to Damascus."[5]

At first, Ben-Gurion opposed Dayan's expansionist plans because he thought Israel should not start a war without an alliance with one of the superpowers. When it became clear that Britain and France not only acquiesced to an Israeli campaign against Egypt but would actually support Israel militarily, Ben-Gurion became quite enthusiastic. At the end of September 1956, Ben-Gurion told Dayan that he hoped the outcome of the anticipated military operation would be Israeli control over the west coast of the Gulf of Aqaba. By the end of October 1956, Ben-Gurion's appetite had grown; he opened talks with the French to sound out their opinion on a future Israeli annexation of the West Bank, the southern part of Lebanon, and the Straits of Tiran.[6]

In early November 1956 Israel easily conquered Sinai, but by February 1957 it had to withdraw all its forces from the peninsula following pressure applied by the American president, Dwight Eisenhower. Ben-Gurion's view had shifted once again. He now believed that in the current international situation, any Israeli attempt to conquer and annex territories was doomed to failure, and he told his generals as much when the topic came up for discussion at a January 1959 General Staff meeting.[7]

However, the General Staff had never let go of the plan to expand Israel's territory. The contingency plans from 1953, which envisaged the annexation of Sinai, the West Bank, and the Golan Heights, were updated and rewritten in 1957. Yitzhak Hofi, who was head of the operations branch in the early 1960s, boasted that in other countries, the government dictated the army's objectives, but in Israel, since the government had supplied no directive, the military created its own strategic plan. Actually, as had been shown, Ben-Gurion did instruct the military and ordered it to avoid war. Nevertheless, the Planning Department in the General Staff kept its war plans very much intact, merely producing a new version in 1963.[8]

Riots erupted in Jordan during April that year, and they seemed to portend the kingdom's collapse. In early May, Ben-Gurion met with Deputy Minister of Defense Shimon Peres and Minister of Agriculture Moshe Dayan. Both men believed that an overthrow of Hussein would supply Israel with a pretext to conquer the West Bank. Within the military, preparations to take over the West Bank went into overdrive. The military's attorney general, Meir Shamgar, began the meticulous process of crafting a codex of laws that Israel would enforce in the West Bank once it had been conquered. His men got hold of thick copies of Jordan's legal code and had them translated so they would know which laws to abolish and which to uphold once the military ruled over the those lands. They also decided to divide the West Bank into eight administrative districts, to be served by four courts.

In addition, the industrious Shamgar had turned his mind to the training of reserve soldiers in the intricacies of military law in occupied territories. In the summer of 1963, Shamgar and his men started teaching a special course on the topic to reserve officers. Among the subjects discussed were the lessons the army had learned from its short occupation of Sinai and the Gaza Strip in 1956. To complete these preparations, in December 1963, Chief of Staff Tzvi Tzur appointed Chaim Herzog, the former head of military intelligence, to command a new unit that would administer the occupied territories. Herzog, already in the reserve service, recruited economic advisers and administration experts to draw up detailed plans for military rule of the West Bank. To ensure that Herzog would hit the ground running, military intelligence sent him reports on Jordanian politics and translated articles from the Jordanian press.[9]

Eventually, the riots in Jordan died down and Hussein remained on his throne. Yet preparations for the occupation of the West Bank did not stop. Herzog continued to serve as the future military governor of the West Bank until the summer of 1967. Shamgar and his men taught more courses to reserve soldiers and officers. The topic of military rule was now part of the curriculum at the army's higher college for military studies. Someone in the IDF also produced booklets with detailed instructions to future governors about how to deal with civilian populations; they were to follow the Geneva Convention, which had been translated into Hebrew. The governors were also instructed to start the occupation with a few days of curfew, during which weapons would be confiscated and those under suspicion would be arrested. Many copies of these booklets were printed and they became part of a kit that all judges and prosecutors were to receive when the occupation commenced. The kits also included translated copies of The Hague and Geneva treaties, as well as legal literature in English, such as the *Manual of Military Law* and Gerhard von Glahn's treatise *The Occupation of Enemy Territory*. These kits were packed in boxes and stored in the basement of the general prosecutor's office in Tel Aviv. They could be distributed at a moment's notice.[10]

The Origins of Military Expansionism

Most of the generals serving in the General Staff during the 1960s were *sabra* – that is, the Palestine-born generation, thus named after a cactus common to Israel's flora. Military expertise was the only quality that granted them a seat at the table, and that heightened their motivation to advocate for territorial expansionism. Their problem was the longevity and stamina of Israel's founding fathers and mothers, such as Ben-Gurion, Eshkol, and Golda Meir, who continued to hold higher offices into their old age. The sabra realized that their route to the top in the Histadrut or Mapai was blocked. Their parents' generation controlled the heights of public life and had no intention of letting go.

The role that the founding fathers allotted to the sabra was to fight for the Jewish state's existence from a young age. By the 1930s and 1940s, the sabra had been able to leverage their military expertise to challenge the older generation. By adopting ultra-patriotic positions, they were able to wrong-foot the elders and thus gain a voice of their own. Indeed, the pressure they applied had forced Ben-Gurion to change his position and declare independence in 1948, making a confrontation with the Arab world inevitable. And the sabra were the ones who carried out many of the forced evictions of Arabs from Palestine during the 1948 war.[11]

The same state of affairs existed in the 1960s. The average age of cabinet members in Eshkol's government was 64, as opposed to 43 in the General Staff. Out of eighteen ministers, only one was born in Palestine, while out of eighteen generals serving in the General Staff only five were born in the diaspora. In the minds of the generals, the age difference meant that they were superior to the older politicians. Just like Dayan, senior officers believed they were the brave new Jews who fought to make Israel a reality, while all the politicians had done was sit and talk. Eshkol's cabinet was dovish and moderate. More than once, the ministers had applied the brakes when the generals wanted to escalate. The generals saw this as evidence that the ministers were neurotic diasporic Jews, afraid of their own shadow. In fact, in General Staff meetings, the generals referred to cabinet ministers as "the Jews." Oddly enough, they used the word pejoratively. Eshkol, for his part, referred to the generals as "the Prussians." In short, the chasm between the civilians and the military men in Israel was wide indeed.[12]

What made the chasm even wider was the political background of most of the officers. Out of the eighteen serving generals, twelve served in the Palmach (a Hebrew acronym for strike forces). The Palmach was the elite force of the Jewish army in the pre-independence era. Its officers developed a strong camaraderie in their youth, forged by many nights by the campfire, mischievous thefts, plowing the fields and, of course, armed clashes with the Arabs. They saw themselves as belonging not just to an armed militia, but to a tribe, with unique costumes, language, and culture. In essence, the Palmach was a settlement militia. Numbering no more than 5,000 at its peak, Palmach members were based in agricultural communes, known as kibbutzim, and earned their upkeep by working on the land. At other times, they trained to become professional soldiers. The Palmachnik epitomized the warrior-farmer, a role prevalent in settler societies.[13]

In the pre-statehood era, the Palmach was affiliated with Ahdut Ha-Avoda, which meant that the generals serving on the General Staff in the 1960s were infused with its particular ideology. As the story goes, Ahdut Ha-Avoda was once part of Mapai until it ceded in 1944. Ahdut Ha-Avoda liked to think of itself as a more socialist and patriotic version of Mapai. For instance, its ideological leader, Yitzhak Tabenkin, had opposed any plan to divide Palestine between Arabs and Jews ever since the 1920s. The truth of the matter, though, was that Ahdut Ha-Avoda was merely an interest group representing the kibbutzim. It ceded from Mapai because Ahdut leaders believed they were not getting a fair share of the pie. In the following years, Ahdut Ha-Avoda presented itself as an alternative to Mapai and competed with it in elections to the Knesset and the Histadrut, though it never really came close to threatening Mapai's hegemonic position. In fact, as soon as the state was established, Ahdut Ha-Avoda started to decline.

At first, the kibbutzim could rely on the immigration of East European Jewry to expand their geographic breadth and reach. The kibbutzim drew young Jews through the youth movements, which were active throughout Europe. But that great reservoir of manpower was wiped out during the Holocaust, and Ahdut Ha-Avoda arrived at a demographic cul-de-sac. No wonder that one of its leaders, Yitzhak Ben-Aharon, argued in 1966 that "since the establishment of the state, kibbutzim members are depressed. It is as if the kibbutz was pushed to the wayside."[14]

Previously, Ahdut Ha-Avoda had forcefully argued for giving the kibbutzim vast resources. The kibbutzim were intentionally established in frontier areas, and they bore the brunt of the clashes with the Arab population before and during the 1948 war. These settlements functioned as resourceful outposts of the Zionist enterprise, making the land of Palestine Jewish by the sheer tenacity of their hold on the ground, despite inclement weather and hostile neighbors. But after the state had been established, the kibbutzim lost their vanguard role. Between 1955 and 1967, Ahdut Ha-Avoda was able to found only one new settlement. Most of the new frontier settlements in the 1950s were established by the state and were populated by Jews who had emigrated from Arab countries. The kibbutzim used their new neighbors only as a source of cheap labor. They never considered accepting them into their communes and transforming them into a source of demographic growth.[15]

Palmach Generals and the March toward War

In the minds of kibbutz members, their movement was undergoing a deep crisis. Without the establishment of new kibbutzim and with no new members, the movement faced a slow death. How could they persuade the state to give them more resources? Then again, some things had been working out for Ahdut Ha-Avoda. Kibbutz members were disproportionately represented within the ranks of the military: in 1956, half of all fighter pilots were from a kibbutz. In 1966, 22 percent of Israel's officers were kibbutz members, four times their demographic weight in the general population (about 5 percent).[16] And the kibbutzim were still located in frontier areas.

The most ardent advocate for employing security language to obtain more for the kibbutzim was Yigal Allon. Allon was the quintessential sabra. He was born in 1918 in a small, impoverished village in the Galilee, surrounded by an Arab population. His father was a Russian Jew who had immigrated to Palestine at about the same time as Eshkol had. He celebrated Allon's bar mitzvah with a gesture that was typical of the relationship between fathers and sons in Palestine – he gave young Allon a gun and sent him to guard a faraway field. Under the cover of darkness, Arab horsemen crept into the plot and started carrying away stacks of hay. That night was the first time, but not the last, that Allon shot at Arabs. Five years later, he joined the Jewish armed forces and fought with distinction. He spoke Arabic and knew the Arab workers who had worked on his father's land well. As a military commander in the late 1930s, he used to punish Arab villagers harshly, including demolishing suspected Arab attackers' homes, to deter them from killing Jewish settlers. Later on, as commander of the Palmach brigades during the 1948 war, he showed cunning and acumen in confronting numerically superior Arab units, invading both Lebanon and Egypt with his troops. He had also ordered the forced expulsion of tens of thousands of Arabs from villages in the Galilee and the coastal plains.[17]

In 1949, Ben-Gurion, worried about Allon's affiliation with Ahdut Ha-Avoda, removed him from his position as commander of the southern front, and forced him to resign. Only 30 years old, Allon was quickly recruited by Ahdut Ha-Avoda. His valor in battle had made him a revered and popular figure. With his shock of curly black hair neatly combed back, and a handsome face dominated by drooping eyelids that gave him the air of a sleepy gazelle, Allon was a charismatic figure and an able speaker. He was one of the few in the Israeli labor movement to make an effort to earn an academic degree. He spent the years between 1950 and 1952 at the University of Oxford reading politics, philosophy, and economics, and in 1957 he participated in Henry Kissinger's famous international seminar at Harvard. As part of his attempt to establish himself as a national figure, in 1959 he authored a book in which he presented his views on Israel's national security.

One of the book's main arguments was that the kibbutzim performed an invaluable service during the war of 1948. They functioned as small fortresses and stood in the way of the advance of Arab armies. The kibbutzim, Allon insisted, could perform that service again. The personal qualities of kibbutz members and the strong solidarity inculcated by communal life made them uniquely effective warriors. The settlements created by the state and populated with Jews from Arab countries, Allon maintained, were not up to the task. The establishment of new kibbutzim therefore had to be supported by the state, especially in the Negev and the Galilee. To make this a reality, the state should encourage graduating high-school students to spend their military service in the kibbutzim, thereby helping to expand existing settlements and create new ones. Although Allon did not say it, the adoption of that policy would have helped his party gain new vitality. Allon's security agenda fitted neatly with the interests of kibbutz members. Many of them were complaining about a shortage of working hands. Sending army recruits to work and live in the kibbutzim, as if reviving the Palmach days, would provide the perfect solution.[18]

One of the things Allon had emphasized in his book was that the kibbutzim should enforce Israel's sovereignty by cultivating their plots right up to the border. This was a recipe for trouble on Israel's northern border, especially in the three demilitarized areas, where the Syrians disputed Israel's claim to the territory. As Avraham Yoffe, commander of the northern command, admitted in 1963, the insistence on working these plots was "more political than agricultural. The land isn't worth the trouble." As attested to by several contemporaries, the plots in question had no economic value. Nevertheless, both Allon and kibbutz members in the north insisted on sending their tractors into the disputed plots. Often, Syrian units responded with heavy fire. Every barrage of artillery that landed on Ahdut Ha-Avoda settlements seemed to prove that the kibbutzim were still Israel's shield and armor. Allon, who joined the cabinet in 1961, quickly became the most hawkish voice in government meetings. A settler himself (he lived in a kibbutz in the north that was outside the range of Syrian artillery), he supported the demand to cultivate the plots next to the border's wire fence, and he never encountered an operation against Syria that he did not like.[19]

Allon had a strong supporter for the advancement of this agenda in the form of Yitzhak Rabin. Rabin had been born in Jerusalem in 1922, the son of immigrants from Russia and the Ukraine. His mother was active in the labor movement in Tel Aviv, and was known as "Red Rosa." His father, Nehemiah, was an active member of Ahdut Ha-Avoda. Rabin joined the Palmach at the age of 19, and for a few years lived in a kibbutz. He was a serious, hard-working officer, and he knew how to write neat staff papers, something that most Palmach officers simply could not do. He quickly became Allon's protégé and was his deputy in many of the battles that Allon led during the 1948 war. However, immediately after the war Rabin's devotion to the Palmach almost cost him his military career. In mid-1949, Ben-Gurion decided to dismantle the Palmach, being concerned about its close association with Ahdut Ha-Avoda. Palmach commanders decided to respond with a protest march in Tel Aviv. Jacob Dori, the chief of staff, gave an order that forbade IDF officers and soldiers from participating in the march. Rabin found himself caught in a dilemma, but his conscience urged him to go. Ben-Gurion, though, decided to intervene. He called Rabin to his house on the day the march was to take place and talked to him at length. The time to leave for the march was nearing, but Ben-Gurion seemed content to talk some more. Rabin became impatient. Was this Ben-Gurion's way of stopping him from participating? He decided to tell Ben-Gurion that he was going to the march and explained why. Ben-Gurion used one last trick: would Rabin join him for supper? Rabin declined and scurried away so he would not be late. He was later court-martialed for defying orders but got off with a light sentence.[20]

Between 1956 and 1959 Rabin served as commander of the northern front, a role that put him in direct contact with the settlers in the north and their disputed plots. During the 1956 Suez Crisis, Rabin used the mayhem in the south, and the fact that the world's attention was directed elsewhere, to drive 3,000 Arab farmers off the lands of the demilitarized zones and into Syria. Set against the expulsions he effected under Allon during the 1948 war, this was small fry. Nevertheless Rabin was proud of his achievement, and admitted he had used "not-so-delicate methods" to convince the Arab inhabitants of the area to leave. He made the Arab farmers sign a document in which they stated that they were moving to Syria of their own volition and then razed their villages. Afterward, the vacated plots were given to nearby kibbutzim.[21]

By the time Rabin arrived at the northern front, a tense status quo had settled over the demilitarized zones. The zones comprised a maze of Israeli- and Arab-owned plots. A tacit agreement between the Syrians and the Israelis recognized a de facto division of the territory: 15 percent to the Syrians, 85 percent to the Israelis. Syrian farmers and Israeli settlers often plowed their plots, side by side, with no conflict. As Rabin well knew, the livelihood of some of the villages on the Syrian side of the border depended on cultivating their plots in the demilitarized zones. Nevertheless, under his command, Israeli units took an uncompromising position and shot at every Syrian farmer who tried to cross the border. During a General Staff meeting in 1958, Rabin was candid about the aim of his policy; it was, he said, "to expand our control over the land." He was willing to submit a proposal to the UN's armistice committee to reach a settlement with the Syrians. If the Syrians refused to accept his proposal, which Rabin thought was highly likely, "we will grab [the Syrians] by the windpipe." In that year, the number of border incidents between Syrian and Israeli units increased, due to Rabin's policy of plowing and tilling as much land as possible.[22]

In 1960, as a brigadier-general, Rabin wrote a detailed memo on how to build up the Israeli army and increase its capability to conquer new territories in the next war. Rabin's memo argued for the creation of a lethal and agile war machine, typified by mobility and maneuverability. Once the war started, Rabin reasoned, the IDF would have no more than four to six days to fight before the superpowers, through the UN, imposed a ceasefire. To complete the mission in time, the Israeli Air Force had to achieve air superiority within forty-eight hours of zero hour. Then the cavalry would charge, taking over as much land as possible. He therefore recommended giving precedence to the purchasing of tanks and aircraft. If budgets had to be slashed to make funds available, then defensive measures such as mines and fortifications would have to bear the brunt.[23]

Rabin's appointment as chief of staff was confirmed in the cabinet in December 1963. Allon thought it a much-deserved promotion since Rabin "had a lot of knowledge and experience both in staff and field work. [Rabin] is judicious and able." Indeed, Ahdut Ha-Avoda received the news of Rabin's appointment with much enthusiasm. Between 1949 and 1950, 176 officers affiliated with Ahdut Ha-Avoda resigned from the army, 41 of whom held the rank of major. Ben-Gurion's dismissal of Allon persuaded these officers that under Ben-Gurion (as minister of defense) their way to the top would be blocked. And yet, about eighty ex-Palmach officers continued to serve in junior positions, and during the 1950s they rose steadily through the ranks. Rabin turned out to be the most successful among them, and as chief of staff he promoted many of his brothers-in-arms. The most consequential of these appointments was that of David Elazar, known to all as "Dado" since his Palmach days. Rabin sent Dado to command the northern front in November 1964.[24] Together, Rabin and Dado pushed Israel toward a confrontation with Syria. Allon cheered them on from his cabinet seat.

Dado was no sabra, yet he spent a lifetime becoming one. He was born in 1925 in Sarajevo, the capital city of mountainous Bosnia, to a harsh and violent father. His mother died when he was 6 and he moved with his father to Zagreb, where he later joined a Zionist youth movement. In 1940, when he was 15, he left Zagreb for Palestine and joined a kibbutz. At age 21 he joined the Palmach, despite the disapproval of his kibbutz colleagues who wanted him to stay on and help lead the commune. However, Dado knew in his bones that a confrontation with the Arabs was near and he wanted to play a leading part in it. He got more than he bargained for. As a young officer he participated in some of the bloodiest battles of the 1948 war. He saw many of his friends die, their funerals taking place almost every day, usually in the morning. No matter how tired the soldiers were, they were ordered to accompany the dead to their last resting place. After the ceremonies, Dado and a decreasing number of young men would be back at it, defending the only route to Jerusalem, where a large Jewish population was under siege. Others broke down, collapsed from exhaustion, or shirked their duty. But not Dado. He was tough, energetic, and daring. Rather than recoil from battle, he relished the fight.[25]

During the war, Dado rose quickly through the ranks. His coolness under fire won him many adherents, and he ended up as a battalion commander. Like Rabin, Dado participated in the march protesting the breakup of the Palmach. So too did he end up with an official reprimand, but his promotion was not affected. After the war, Dado occupied staff positions, which he did not like. Life as a pen-pusher did not suit his taste or his talents. When, after much debate over how the cavalry should be deployed, the IDF made massive use of tanks to break through the Egyptian fortifications in Sinai during the 1956 campaign, Dado saw his chance. He had no doubt that from now on tank divisions would become the army's ramming device and so, up to this point an infantry officer, he requested to be moved to the armored forces. He spent eight months learning how to drive a tank, operate its guns, and command a platoon. Between 1958 and 1964, Dado became one of the architects of Israeli cavalry doctrine.[26]

Much thought was devoted to the Soviet doctrine that the Syrian and Egyptian armies had adopted. Based on copious intelligence reports, IDF planners now realized that in both Sinai and the Golan Heights, Israeli forces would face three fortified lines of defense. Trenches, barbed wire, mines, machine guns, and heavy artillery would defend the lines. Sandwiched in between, infantry troops, armed with anti-tank weapons, would ambush Israeli tanks. If the military wanted to expand Israel's borders, it had to find a way to break through these defenses. While Arab defense lines were formidable, these fortifications were also a sitting target. Israeli officers, Dado among them, planned to attack these lines by outflanking and flying above Arab fortifications. To maintain the element of surprise, tank units were trained to fight at night and drive through seemingly impassable terrain. Aircraft were to bomb Arab defense lines and land paratroopers behind them.[27] Israeli plans were afoot.

10

CONFRONTING SYRIA

ON AUGUST 12, 1964, following several incidents in the demilitarized zone, Rabin and Haim Bar-Lev, the head of operations branch, met with Levi Eshkol. Rabin wanted to set a date on which a tractor would drive into a disputed plot. If the Syrians shot at the tractor, the IDF would escalate and bomb Syrian positions from the air. Rabin's argument was that the Syrians were interfering with the cultivation of land that was clearly within Israeli territory. Moreover, Rabin elaborated a domino theory, according to which the Syrians, if they were not stopped at that point, would try to take control of more territory. Eshkol wanted to know whether there was any legal justification to what Rabin was proposing. Rabin harrumphed: "It's Jewish land ... Our actions in the demilitarized zone are not based on any legal principle."

Eshkol told the two generals emphatically that he was unwilling to use the air force for such purposes. Eshkol was ready to send armored tractors into the demilitarized zones and authorize Israeli units to hit Syrian tanks with artillery fire, but nothing beyond that. "You are putting us needlessly in harm's way," he told the generals sternly. Nevertheless, Rabin and Bar-Lev insisted. "If the Syrians see that we resist," Bar-Lev argued, "they will not shoot at the tractors." Puzzled, Eshkol asked, "And shall we continue to do this endlessly?" Rabin then showed his cards: "If they shoot [at us] again we will have to conquer the [Golan] Heights." Finally, Eshkol voiced what the three men knew: "I understand it's a piece of land [but right now] it's more a matter of prestige and honor. [This plot] has no economic value."[1]

A few months later, Rabin appointed Dado to head the northern command. On November 2, 1964, his first day on the job, Dado was told by his staff that the Syrians were preventing the completion of a patrol road on a hill leading northward to Kibbutz Dan. Dado's response surprised the officers: "We will drive through this road tomorrow!" They knew that acting on this decision meant a confrontation with Syrian forces, as indeed happened the next day. Israeli tanks used the incident as an excuse to shoot at Syrian tanks, but they missed. Dissatisfied, Dado kept sending more patrols down the same road. The ground forces' presence in the area was enhanced and the air force was put on high alert. Finally, on November 13, the Syrians took the bait and opened fire. This time the Israeli tanks' aim was true. The Syrians responded by shelling nearby kibbutzim. Rabin picked up the phone and called Eshkol. He wanted authorization to send in the air force.[2]

Things had changed quite a bit for the prime minister since the summer. Now he was in the midst of a struggle with Ben-Gurion. Two weeks earlier, Moshe Dayan, Ben-Gurion's ally, resigned from the cabinet. Two days before Rabin's phone call there was a stormy meeting of Mapai's central committee, in which Ben-Gurion's trenchant opposition to the merger with Ahdut Ha-Avoda had been discussed. When Eshkol took Rabin's call he might have been thinking about the up-or-down vote on the merger, which was to take place two days later. It was far from certain that Eshkol would win. If he wanted to prevail, he had to show he was tough, maybe even tougher than Ben-Gurion, who had rarely allowed the use of aircraft in previous border skirmishes. Eshkol agreed immediately to Rabin's request. He asked no questions. He did not try to limit the extent of air force intervention. He gave Rabin a blank check.[3]

The air force threw fifty planes into the sky, nineteen of which participated in the battle and bombed Syrian positions. It was a turning point in the Israeli–Syrian conflict. Two days later, on November 15, the Central Committee vote concluded with a convincing victory for Eshkol; Ben-Gurion, his pride wounded, announced his resignation from the Central Committee. However, Ben-Gurion made it clear that he would continue to demand a new inquiry into "the mishap." Rabin met with Eshkol, also on November 15. He told him that Dado was pleased with the results of the November 13 confrontation and sought to exploit it. Northern command wanted to send more troops down that road, including tanks. Rabin said his inclination was to refuse Dado's request and leave the Syrians to lick their wounds. Eshkol's response surprised Rabin. He told him that Dado had been right and that he, Eshkol, wanted to see an operation that would remove Syrian positions from that area.[4]

Dado's Plan

Colonel Pinhas Lahav, Dado's logistics officer, could not fathom his commander's insistence on sending tractors to plow land that had little economic value. He once asked Dado: "Why are we doing it again and again? Gosh, it would have been cheaper to fly wheat kernels from California, wrapped in cotton and packaged in cellophane, and it would not cost us human lives!" Dado's response was to reiterate Rabin's domino theory: if the Syrians got their way in the demilitarized zone, they would push forward into the Galilee. By fighting them on the border, he was keeping the Syrians at bay.[5] Other people heard differently. "[Dado's] idea was that Israel should have the Golan Heights," recalled Colonel Immanuel Shaked, Dado's operations officer. "Dado liked to say: 'We should live large, not small! We should not ask the Syrians for permission to plow.'" Rehavam Zeevi, assistant to the commander of operations branch, had the same impression: "Dado had a very clear plan, to liberate the Golan Heights ... He talked about it night and day, repeated it endlessly during General Staff discussions." Beyond that was Dado's consuming ambition to become the next chief of staff. If he could take the Heights for Israel, he would have bettered his chances.[6]

The settlers in the north were naturally inclined to support Dado's policy, but he took no chances. He invested a lot of time in showing kibbutz members that their interests were near to his heart. One time, the general had been invited to Kibbutz Neve-Oz, where the comrades told him at length about their difficulty protecting the dairy farmers on their way to the cowsheds, especially in the early hours of the morning. Dado patiently discussed the practical details of dairy farming with the civilians while some of his staff officers napped. Others were incredulous. After leaving, Dado's underlings accused him of wasting their time on "nonsense." Dado retorted: "It may be a trifling matter for you, but this is a big issue for them." And Dado's colleague Zeevi got the impression that his friend was not acting out of kindness: "He cultivated his relationship with the kibbutzim not just because they were wonderful people, but because Dado realized they were the largest interest group in the country. Since he aspired to enter politics once he retired from the ranks, he saw them as his natural 'electoral base.'"[7]

Water Wars

During the years 1964 and 1965, two things played into the hands of Dado and Rabin, and helped them sell the confrontation with Syria to the government: the Syrian effort to divert the tributaries of the Jordan River, and the tensions between Mapai and Rafi.

Ostensibly, the Syrian diversion project was a mortal threat. The Jordan River is Israel's lifeline, as important as the Nile is to Egypt. If it were to be blocked, Israel would face a severe challenge. The devil was in the detail, though. If things went without a hitch (and they did not), Syria was to gain 112 million cubic meters of water upon completion of its diversion scheme. This may sound a considerable amount, but in fact in 1953, under the hawkish Ben-Gurion, Israel had accepted a formula for the division of the Jordan's waters, allotting 132 million cubic meters of water to Syria – that is, 20 million more than Syria had been counting on gaining from its diversion project.[8]

The provenance of this plan was in early 1953, when Israel and Syria exchanged blows over Israel's attempt to build a diversion canal near the Syrian border. President Eisenhower responded by appointing Eric Johnston as his personal envoy to the Middle East. His mission was to find a compromise that would divide the Jordan River's waters between all riparian countries. After two years of intensive shuttle diplomacy, Johnston presented a plan, which Israel accepted. Though the technical committee of the Arab League found Johnston's proposal acceptable in principle, it did not endorse the plan formally. Israel's name appeared in the document, and approving it meant acknowledging its existence, which the Arab countries refused to do. After some delay, Ben-Gurion announced in 1959 that, having received no response, Israel would go forward with its NWC project, and would take no more than the amount of water allotted to it by the Johnston formula.[9]

From this perspective, Syria's diversion project should have been a non-issue. Like Israel's, it conformed to the Johnston formula, although the Baath propaganda misleadingly represented it as a deathly blow to Israel's existence. Moreover, there were good reasons to suspect that the Arab diversion project would fail to meet the ambitious goals set in Arab League meetings. For the Syrian blueprint to succeed, Jordanian and Lebanese cooperation was essential. Two tributaries of the Jordan River, the Wazzani and the Hasbani, passed through Lebanon, while a third, the Banias, flowed through Syria. A fourth tributary, the Dan, runs only through Israel and no Arab country could do much about it. The Arab plan envisaged the diversion of the Wazzani and the Hasbani into the Banias. Since Syria had no natural basin to use for storing the joined streams of the Hasbani, Wazzani, and Banias, the combined flow of all three tributaries was to be diverted to Jordan, where a large dam would block the water from reaching Israel. If all the plans had come together, the combined projects would have diverted

about 200 million cubic meters of water. However, even that did not constitute a threat to Israeli interests. The combined flow of the Jordan's tributaries
produced an annual average of 672 million cubic meters, of which Israel,
according to the Johnston formula, was to receive 450 million. Had the Arab
diversion projects been completed, Israel would have still received about 472
million cubic meters, a little more than it had agreed to back in 1955.[10]

Moreover, the completion of the Arab diversion plan was very much in
doubt. For Jordan, the most convenient place to build the dam was at
Mukhayaba, just 3 kilometers from the Jordanian–Israeli border. It would
have been easy for Israel to derail this plan. Moreover, Jordan knew that
American funding for the project would come through only if it abided by
the Johnston formula; this was the reason that Jordan had cooperated with
Israel. As we saw earlier, King Hussein promised Jerusalem that his planned
dam would draw from the Jordan no more than the Johnston formula had
prescribed. The rest would flow to Israel. It was far better for the Jordanians
to complete the dam, which they regarded as crucial to the development of
their economy, than to get into a fistfight with Israel over water that Jordan
did not really need. Likewise, the Lebanese had no interest in serving Syrian
vanity. There was little love lost between Lebanon, led by a Christian, pro-
Western elite, and radical Syria. Lebanon had no need of the Wazzani
waters; the Litani River amply supplied its farms. Also, Lebanon was a small
country with a weak army and it could not seriously contemplate a confrontation with Israel. For that reason, farmers in southern Lebanon were
applying pressure on their government not to honor the obligation it had
given in Arab summit meetings to join in the diversion scheme.[11]

From March to June 1965, Rabin tried to persuade Eshkol to authorize
the IDF to launch either a land or an air attack that would hit the Lebanese
diversion sites. Rabin lobbied for these operations, although he knew it
made no sense for the Lebanese to complete their project until the Syrians
had done so. Without the diversion of the Banias to the Kingdom of Jordan,
the Hasbani and the Wazzani would flow directly to Israel through the
Banias. At that point, the Syrian project was not even close to completion.
Moreover, the Lebanese asked French diplomats, in late 1964 and early
1965, to deliver a secret message to Israel: Lebanon had no intention of
completing the diversion works it had started; these had been done only to
appease Arab public opinion. Nevertheless, Rabin was insistent. However,
Eshkol resisted his pressure and preferred to work through diplomatic
channels. Israeli ambassadors in Paris and Washington were instructed to
approach the respective foreign ministries to protest Lebanon's actions.
State Department officials were unimpressed. They said that the Lebanese

waterworks had posed no risk to Israel and that the Lebanese were proceeding slowly, doing the least that they could. The French were franker, calling the Lebanese diversion works "a joke." On July 14, during a public speech, Rabin made a veiled threat toward Lebanon. And that was that. By the end of July, Lebanon halted its diversion project completely.[12]

And so, from an early stage, the Syrian diversion project was hampered. Without Lebanese and Jordanian cooperation, it was akin to a bucket with two large holes. Baath Syria found itself saddled with a thankless job: performing a challenging and incredibly costly (it had been estimated at $500 million) engineering project, only to divert the water to a conservative Arab state whose regime it thoroughly despised, namely Jordan. The maintenance costs of the project, once completed, were reportedly high as well. Israel's own NWC, the major pipeline that drew water from the Galilee to the Negev, took fifteen years to complete. It was reasonable to expect that Syria's project would take as long, if not longer. Given all this, it made sense for Israel not to respond to Syria's provocations but rather let its northern foe start a project it would probably never complete, and bear the costs of this futile exercise. Moreover, from their positions the Israelis could see that the Syrians were not serious about the matter. They cherry-picked the easiest parts of the project and started with them, leaving the harder parts untouched. One segment of the diversion route was described by an Israeli observer as being so difficult that "trying to dig a diversion canal here is akin to attempting to light a match in the eye of the storm."[13]

Most of this story was public knowledge in Israel at the time. As early as 1965, the daily press carried such sensitive details as Lebanese non-cooperation with Syria and the Jordanian promise to build their dam in a way that would not breach the Johnston formula. In a public debate that took place in mid-April 1965, Yisrael Barzilay, the minister of health, said that in view of Lebanese and Jordanian reluctance to participate in the project, Israel should not rush to take action. Israel could easily afford to wait six or even eight years to see whether the Arab project would become a reality.[14]

It was no surprise, then, that when Moshe Dayan, the minister of agriculture, was asked in March 1964 about the Arab diversion project, he answered that it was impractical and would not benefit any Arab country. When Eshkol commented on the same topic in January 1965, he was equally skeptical that these plans would ever become a reality. That month, during a General Staff meeting, Aharon Yariv, the head of military intelligence, reported that a reconnaissance flight over possible diversion sites detected nothing out of the ordinary.[15] In the following months, though, the

Ben-Gurion/Eshkol conflict had escalated and the Arab diversion project became a political football.

In November 1964, two days after he resigned from the government to join Rafi, Dayan was still skeptical that Lebanon, Jordan, and Syria would overcome their political differences and pull the diversion project together. If it did happen, Dayan recommended that Israel accelerate its effort to desalinate seawater to compensate for the water the Arabs might divert. In January 1965, however, Dayan was already changing his tune. He described the Arab diversion efforts as a dire threat and demanded that the IDF take action. In April, his tone grew shriller; in an op-ed, he maintained that "we have to shoot at any [Syrian] tractor [working on diversion sites] . . . and stop any attempt to implement the plan." In response, Eshkol shifted his position. He met with Rabin in March 1965 and green-lighted operations against Syria's diversion sites. Eshkol was even worried that the Syrians would refuse to play along and avoid border skirmishes. Rabin replied that it would be very easy to provoke the Syrians.[16]

From March 1965 on, Rabin and Dado's policy of working in the disputed plots received the prime minister's blessing. The General Staff meticulously planned each incident. A date was chosen, preferably with fair weather so that the air force could be deployed. Two operations centers were set up. One at the rear, in Tel Aviv, supervised air force activity. Another, at northern command, directed Israeli artillery and tank fire. Civilians in frontier settlements were told to enter their shelters. Aircraft hovered in the sky, ready to respond at a moment's notice. An Israeli tractor was sent to one of the flashpoints. If the Syrians did not respond, Israeli tanks shot at them. When the Syrians shot back, Israeli artillery directed its fire to a diversion site and hit Syrian tractors and bulldozers. The first operation of this kind took place on March 17, 1965, ten days *after* Israeli military intelligence had reported that the Arab diversion project was progressing slowly and Arab countries were not making a serious effort to push it forward.[17]

The elections that would determine the fate of Rafi and Mapai were to take place in November. Aharon Yariv had no doubt that, as election day approached, Eshkol would become increasingly "trigger happy." Indeed, Eshkol authorized two additional operations against the Syrian diversion sites on May 13 and August 12. On May 10, during a government meeting, several ministers expressed their reservations. Zerach Verhaftig, the minister of religious affairs, argued that "the gain . . . isn't worth the trouble," and Zalman Aran, the education minister, claimed that Israel could wait until the project was done and then launch a large-scale operation. Golda

Meir and Sapir were also opposed. Eshkol put his foot down and declared, "the world would not stand on its head if we blew up some tractors." When a vote was taken, Eshkol prevailed, but only by one vote.[18]

During the election campaign, Eshkol gave speeches in which he touted his government's resolute policy against the Syrian diversion efforts. This was his response to Rafi's spin, which sought to represent him as too moderate and dovish. On October 23, during a radio broadcast, Eshkol claimed: "For a long period we have restrained ourselves, while the Syrians sought to steal our water and harass our settlements. But when they used their topographical advantage to attack our settlements we did not hesitate to use our Air Force to respond, and brought about an end to the attempt to rob our water." Six days after the elections, which resulted in Eshkol's victory, Rabin's assessment was that "at this rate [the Syrian diversion project] will take another ten to twenty years [to complete]." One month later Rabin went further, saying during a public lecture that the Syrian diversion works were proceeding at a "symbolic pace and so may take another thirty years." Nevertheless, in the following months Rabin tried to persuade the cabinet to allow him to bomb other diversion sites. Up to the summer of 1966, the cabinet did not acquiesce to Rabin's requests and, now that Rafi was on the ropes, Eshkol was under no pressure to prove his security credentials.[19]

11

THE SELF-INFLICTED RECESSION

MOSHE ZANDBERG, ADVISER to Finance Minister Pinhas Sapir, and
David Horowitz, the governor of the Bank of Israel, were watching
the numbers with alarm. In 1963 the deficit in Israel's balance of payments
was $448 million; by 1964 this figure grew larger still, reaching $572 million.
They agreed that it was time to make deep cuts in the state's budget, especially in infrastructure spending. Horowitz did not believe that Eshkol and
Sapir would take the plunge. "You go ahead and plead with these two 'devel-
opmentalists' to cut down on development," he growled. Horowitz, tongue
in cheek, promised Zandberg a gold coin, recently minted to celebrate the
Bank of Israel's first decade, if he succeeded in convincing the prime
minister to go along. Horowitz knew what he was talking about. During
Israel's first decade, Eshkol and Sapir, his protégé and ally, had adopted
growth-first policies. Using loans and grants from Germany and the US, the
two made the state the main engine of economic growth. They channeled
resources to Histadrut factories, subsidized and protected entrepreneurs in
the private sector, and manipulated the Israeli currency to help exporters.
The results were impressive indeed: Israel's economy grew on average by
10 percent each year.[1]

The deficit was clearly a symptom of problems created during the years
of fast growth. The companies and corporations that Sapir and Eshkol had
helped to thrive became addicted to trade protections and subsidies. They
refused to function without them and protested each time the government
tried to lower tariffs and expose them to foreign competition. As monopolies in the home market, they were often inefficient and tended to hire more
workers than they actually needed. This phenomenon had to be tackled.

Still, had he wanted to, Eshkol could have inflicted a far milder recession on Israel. Though the deficit in Israel's balance of payments had increased, so had its foreign currency reserves, although at a more modest pace than in previous years, and by the end of 1964 the reserves stood at $500 million. In other words, Israel could have settled at least some of its debts.[2]

IMF officials believed, and had been saying to Israeli officials since the early 1960s, that it was time for Israel to remove its trade protections, stop manipulating the currency, end subsidies, and let Israeli corporations face the music. But unlike Egypt, Israel was under no immediate threat of being cut off from the financial markets. On the contrary, the IMF considered Israel a success story on a par with Japan. Eshkol could have kicked the can down the road, leaving the unpopular task to another year. But what could brook no further delay was the matter of the Histadrut. Eshkol had spent four long and bitter years defending the Histadrut from Ben-Gurion's nationalization schemes. But now, the Histadrut was falling apart. Prosperity had brought unemployment down to around 3 percent. Workers, who no longer feared redundancy, constantly demanded wage increases. The job of the Histadrut was to enforce wage restraint. Workers, however, ignored its dictates. Wildcat strikes were becoming more common, increasing from thirty-four between 1960–61 to almost double that, sixty-three, during 1962–65, and 1966 alone saw fifty-five such strikes. Even more worrying was the tendency of workers to cede from the Histadrut by creating factory-level "action committees" to negotiate directly with their employers. If this pattern persisted, the Histadrut would no longer be able speak for all the workers.[3]

This was a long-standing problem. Since the late 1950s, the Mapai leadership would gather at the beginning of each year and vow to enforce wage restraint, only to see this resolve evaporate under the pressure of a restless workforce. The rising costs of labor pushed up the prices of Israeli products, making them increasingly uncompetitive in world markets. The year 1964 offered a convenient opportunity to put an end this pattern. Several large infrastructure projects, such the NWC and the reactor at Dimona, were winding down, and so all the government had to do was avoid initiating new ones. Long-term loans, which Israel received from Germany and the US, were about to expire. These facts alone could have been wielded to convince the ministers to accept budget cuts, and Eshkol would have been spared from talking about the awkward matter of the Histadrut's plight.[4]

For all those reasons, Eshkol listened attentively to what Zandberg had to say. He had one overriding concern. "Could you assure me," he asked Zandberg, "that the public would feel the effects of the cuts only *after* the election?" Zandberg promised that this would be the case. In October 1964, the ministerial Committee for Economic Affairs started discussing the growing deficit in the balance of payments. Both Sapir and Horowitz described the situation as urgent. Horowitz quoted at length from an IMF report on the state of Israel's economy. The report underlined Israel's external deficit and urged the government to cut its expenses. During the following months, the committee adopted a series of resolutions, the most important of which was not to start new infrastructure projects and to cap the growth of the next budget at 8 percent (it grew by 26 percent in 1963 and by 18 percent in 1964). Nothing of this had been leaked to the press. When the budget was officially published, it turned out that Zandberg had written it using such dense gobbledegook that no one could understand the significance of the numbers therein.[5]

During the 1965 election campaign, Eshkol could still argue that the economy was in a sterling condition. Indeed, due to contracts already signed in 1964, wages climbed during 1965 by 18 percent. After the elections, Eshkol's government enjoyed a comfortable majority in the Knesset and had four full years ahead of it. It had plenty of time to enact unpopular policies without worrying about the wrath of the electorate. The public was first informed about the new economic policy only in February 1966 when Sapir announced it. In that speech, Sapir also introduced new taxes: income tax was raised by 2 percent, tariffs on cigarettes and alcohol by 20 percent, gasoline prices went up by 33 percent. Food subsidies were canceled. A week later Eshkol endorsed Sapir's policy on the radio, calling on all sectors of Israeli society to acknowledge that the country had been living beyond its means for too long. This reality, Eshkol claimed, had been masked by the generous aid received from Germany and the US. Hard times were ahead, Eshkol warned, but in the end, Israel would become economically independent.[6]

Though Sapir and Eshkol talked stridently about the deficit in Israel's balance of payments, it was evident that increasing the number of unemployed was the goal they had in mind. Curiously, Sapir and Eshkol did not enact a devaluation of the Israeli pound. Devaluation is a fairly common measure of pro-export policies; it pushes the value of the currency down relative to other world currencies, making all products nominated in that currency cheaper and more competitive on world markets. By weakening the local currency, devaluation also makes imported products more expensive, and consumers in the devaluating country purchase less of them. In short, devaluation boosts exports and reduces imports: the very medicine that a country with a deficit in its balance of payments needs. Indeed, in 1962, when Eshkol was still minister of finance, he had tried to improve

Israel's balance of payments through a massive devaluation of almost 50 percent. However, when in September 1966 the government discussed anti-recessionary measures, Sapir opposed devaluation. He also rejected the call to pay unemployment benefits to those out of work (Israeli law did not guarantee them). When informed that there were 40,000 people out of work, Sapir reportedly replied that his economic program required 95,000 unemployed. By early 1967, that number reached 100,000, and the unemployment rate tripled to 12.5 percent.[7]

If the recession had been unleashed to halt labor militancy and strengthen the authority of the Histadrut, it was a success. The number of strike days per year decreased from 207,000 in 1965 to 156,000 in 1966 and 58,000 in 1967. The number of wildcat strikes went down by 50 percent. However, the recession also severely damaged Eshkol's image. The Israelis liked Eshkol as long as he was the smiling, avuncular face of the boom years. Industrialists liked his subsidies and tax incentives. Workers liked him when he honored indexation agreements. Academics liked him when he bloated the state bureaucracy to ensure their employment. Nobody liked Eshkol when he became the face of a harsh recession. His economic policy hit Jews who emigrated from Arab countries, many of whom were employed in the construction sector, particularly hard. Workers were also hurting as factories laid off their employees, now that they were exposed to competition from foreign goods.[8]

The first sign of trouble arrived from Ashdod, the southern town where the government had spent a fortune building a new harbor. Now that the harbor was ready, construction workers were being laid off. On May 1, 1966, blood was spilled during the festivities of International Workers' Day when hundreds of unemployed workers confronted the police. They raided the Workers' Committee headquarters, smashed windows, and ransacked the place, but not before removing the red Histadrut flag and tearing it to pieces. Then they moved on to the municipal offices. The police were outnumbered and called for help. Four hundred police officers, from all over the south and as far as Beersheba, rolled into town wearing helmets and wielding batons. To finally subdue the demonstrators, mounted police officers rode into the crowd. "Everyone who was there – had been beaten up," reported an excited journalist, adding: "During a battle of fists, stones, and batons, the protesters were trampled by the four horses that galloped marvelously along the street." Sixty people were arrested, twenty were wounded. Such sights were seen in the following months across the poorest cities: Dimona, Acre, Beit Shean, Petah Tikva, Lydda, Ramla, and Nazareth. In some of those towns, unemployment had reached 20 percent.[9]

Those who had been university-educated, most of them Jews of European extraction, fared far better than the workers. While wages in general decreased by 0.4 percent in 1966, those of salaried employees went up by 19 percent. At the height of the crisis, in December 1966, only 819 academics throughout Israel were unemployed; by May 1967, there were half as many. Still, by their standards, they were going through lean times. The urban middle class stopped purchasing home appliances, carpets, and furniture. People refrained from buying shoes and clothes and consumed less butter, fresh meat, cakes, and foreign-made chocolate. Tel Aviv, the cultural and business heart of the country, was less vivacious, its cafés and restaurants quiet. Real estate prices in the big cities dropped. The middle class did not like any of that. It turned angry, though non-violent as compared to the workers.[10]

Haaretz, a liberal daily, led the attack. Fifteen percent of the urban Jewish public read it and it was highly regarded among politicians, businessmen, and academics. By the early 1960s, the newspaper was gingerly aligning itself with Ben-Gurion, but not because it had concurred with his demand to investigate "the mishap" – it was rather a case of "the enemy of my enemy is my friend." *Haaretz* was privately owned, unlike the great majority of Israeli newspapers which were owned by political parties. Its owner and chief editor, Gershom Schocken, and his writers strongly believed in *laissez-faire* economics and vehemently objected to the outsized role played by the Histadrut in Israel's economy. Following the merger between Ahdut Ha-Avoda and Mapai, *Haaretz* was increasingly concerned that Eshkol might take the country down a more socialist path. So enamored was the newspaper with Ben-Gurion's challenge to the Mapai establishment that two members of its editorial board had joined Rafi. The inclusion of all the workers' parties in the new coalition, created by Eshkol after the 1965 elections, troubled the editors even more. *Haaretz* saw an opportunity in the recession and increased its attacks on Eshkol. In December 1966, the newspaper conducted a poll in Jerusalem, Haifa, and Tel Aviv, and later published the results on its front page as the lead story: 42 percent of the participants wanted to see Eshkol replaced; only 22 percent supported him.[11]

Eshkol criticized *Haaretz* in a Knesset speech, claiming that the newspaper had "some strange tendency" to put a negative spin on everything. Schocken, Eshkol stated, had never "accepted the existence of this country," and for that reason he "systematically poisons the souls of his readers." However, other polls conducted around that time produced similar results. A poll of August 1966 showed that 77 percent of responders had a negative opinion of the government's economic policy. A poll carried out by Rafi in October indicated that Eshkol's approval ratings were down by 50 percent; those of Ben-Gurion had doubled. In December, a self-published book came out. Titled *All the Eshkol Jokes*, it became an immediate sensation. Typical jokes went like this: "What's the argument between Eshkol and Nasser? Nasser claims that Israel could be destroyed only by using military means, while Eshkol argues that you can do the same thing using peaceful methods," and "They've hung up a sign at Israel's international airport saying, 'The last one to leave is requested to turn off the lights.'" The latter joke referred to the fact that 1966 was the first year since the state's establishment that had ended with a negative immigration ratio: more people left the country than came to settle in it.[12]

There were further humiliations to come. The unemployed continued to demonstrate against Eshkol throughout early 1967. In March, a talk Eshkol gave at the Hebrew University's student club turned into a spectacle of public disdain. The students heckled him, booed, and whistled as Eshkol tried to answer their questions. One student asked him why he was not resigning and another accused him of "knowingly lying" to the audience. Reactions in the press suggested that Eshkol was now perceived as a lame duck – a leader who had good intentions but who was unable to command authority or elicit compliance. In April, Eshkol managed to convince Sapir to adopt some anti-recessionary measures, but that proved too little, too late.[13]

The Star of David Line That Never Was

Fatah guerrilla attacks on Israel started in January 1965, with the unsuccessful attempt to plant explosives near a water facility in northern Israel. During that year Fatah operations were few – seven in total – and largely ineffective. Their number and lethality had increased since February 1966, when the military Baath faction gained power and took Fatah under its wing. There had been forty-two Fatah guerrilla attacks since early 1965, and sixty-four during 1966. They resulted in the killing of eleven Israelis and the wounding of sixty-two.[14]

Up to the summer of 1966, Israel responded to Fatah attacks by launching several retaliatory raids, mostly against Lebanon and Jordan. The raids targeted water facilities and led to the demolition of two Jordanian villages. Syria was punished only once, by another bombing of a diversion site.[15] In July 1966, Chaim Yaari, a senior diplomacy editor at the Mapai-owned daily *Davar*, wrote an article questioning the wisdom of Israel's responses. He started by pointing out that Fatah operations up to that point were few and far between. Overreaction, in Yaari's opinion, would be a mistake. While the government should certainly do something about it, the question remained whether cycles of Fatah attacks and Israeli retaliation raids were indeed in Israel's best interests. It was not clear at all, Yaari argued, that retaliation raids were effective. Syria's main towns were located far from the front, and their denizens were not much perturbed by Israel's bombing of Syria's forward positions. It was hard to fathom why Fatah's foot soldiers would care if Israel shot up Syrian tractors; *their* lives were not in danger. Is it really that hard for the IDF to seal the border? Yaari wondered. Of course, no one could seal off Israel's 1,000-kilometer-long border completely, but Fatah commando units were entering mostly through a narrow area, 70 kilometers wide, not all of it passable. This area included the Syrian border, especially its tangent points with Lebanon and Jordan. As ordered by its Baath masters, Fatah kept entering through these points, making sure that Israel's wrath was directed at Lebanon and Jordan rather than Syria. The army, Yaari concluded, could do more to guard the border by using the tried and tested method of constructing a barbed wire fence, paving patrol roads, and setting ambushes.[16]

Rabin, however, referred to defensive measures as "nags." He used that term in a General Staff meeting he had convened during August to discuss the conflict with Fatah. More people joined the debate, but the solutions they offered remained the same. Motti Hod, the commander of the air force, suggested that Israel occupy the Golan Heights. He believed this would make it harder for Fatah to cross the border. Yeshayahu Gavish, commander of the southern front, wanted a frontal clash with Syria but emphasized that Jordan and Lebanon needed to be punished as well. Ariel Sharon, head of the army training branch, opined that the only solution was a war that would end with territorial expansion in the east and the north. Dado and Rehavam Zeevi waxed nostalgic about the 1956 campaign against Egypt, which came about partly as a response to Egypt's decision to train and arm Palestinian groups in order to send them on sabotage and espionage missions inside Israel. After the 1956 war, the Egyptians stopped these operations. Dado and Zeevi insisted that Israel should do to Syria what it did to Egypt in 1956. Rabin took a somewhat more moderate tone, arguing for a series of operations against Syrian military targets.[17]

In August, Rabin was interviewed by the military's weekly *Ba-Mahane* (In the Barracks). He created an uproar by declaring, "the response to Syria's actions . . . should be against those who commit these acts of sabotage and the regime that supports them . . . here [our] aim should be to change the regime's policy . . . in essence, we need to confront the Syrian regime." With this sentence, the chief of staff had crossed the line. International and national responses were adverse. Eshkol scolded the brash general and released a statement to clarify that "the state of Israel does not interfere in the internal affairs of other countries and their regimes."[18]

September 1966 was as uneventful as early October was bloody. On the night of the 7th, explosives went off in the heart of Jerusalem, destroying two houses and injuring two civilians. On the 8th, a mine exploded in the north, killing four police officers and wounding two. Though the tracks led to the Jordanian border, military intelligence had no doubt that Fatah units had come from Syria. Writing the next week in *Davar*, Chaim Yaari was still wondering whether the military was doing all that it could to guard the border. Couldn't the military initiate something along the lines of "Tegart's Wall"?

Yaari was referring to the barbed wire fence that Sir Charles Tegart, a British police officer with expertise in subduing anti-colonial rebellions, had recommended constructing in 1938. Its purpose was to halt the stream of ammunition and armed volunteers that had been arriving from Syria and Lebanon to help the Palestinians in their rebellion against British rule in Palestine. Along the fence, the Histadrut-owned company, Solel Boneh, had built several forts and small fortified positions. As of the summer of 1938, the British army vigorously patrolled the wall and this reduced the movement of Arab volunteers across the border significantly. It led to the suppression of the Arab Revolt in northern Palestine and pushed the rebellion further to the south. Stretching along 75 kilometers, its total cost in 1938 was $450,000. In 1966 money, the price tag would have been $1 million, about half the cost of one French-made Mirage plane, and Israel had ordered thirty of those in early 1966. Though the British army dismantled Tegart's Wall once the rebellion had been subdued, the forts built thanks to Tegart's insistence survived and were used by the Israeli police. They served as a solemn reminder that there were defensive methods to fight against irregular warfare.[19]

The discussion over defensive vs. offensive measures was about to heat up. On the night of November 12, a jeep carrying soldiers on their way to ambush Fatah units drove over a mine. Three paratroopers were killed and six were wounded. The following morning, the General Staff convened to discuss what to do. Yeshayahu Gavish, the commander of the southern front, suggested an attack on the village of Samu, which might have been a haven for the Fatah unit responsible for the attack. Gavish proposed attacking Samu in broad daylight using tanks and armored troop carriers. The scale of the proposed operation surprised Eshkol's military adjutant, Yisrael Lior, who was present.[20]

The military had been planning an operation along these lines for a year. The assumption behind the plans was that a noisy operation would humiliate King Hussein to the degree that he would have to fight Fatah more vigorously. In June 1965, Rabin argued that Hussein could prevent at least 95 percent of the attacks launched from his territory but was not doing so. On October 3, Rabin and Yariv tried to sell Eshkol exactly that kind of operation. Eshkol had authorized smaller raids on Jordan in the previous month, but in his view what the generals suggested might bring about the fall of Hussein "and maybe even war." Eshkol therefore blocked the operation.

Undaunted, the General Staff continued to discuss the very operation that Eshkol had opposed. In a meeting of the General Staff on October 4, Yariv candidly admitted that it was hard to obtain intelligence on Fatah operations before they occurred. He argued that Israel could solve this problem by forcing Jordan "to finish the Fatah off." The method he proposed was to "take over a piece of [Jordanian] territory ... using significant numbers of tanks and aircraft, all in broad daylight, to hurt the regime and its prestige." About two weeks later, Rabin gave a speech at the IDF's higher military college in which he argued that Israel should no longer fear Hussein's downfall because Jordan would not become a Nasserite satellite (he gave no explanation as to how he had reached that conclusion). Rabin admitted that "the desired solution is that Hussein would remain, and Fatah activity would stop," but he hastened to add that "we have to make Hussein choose: either he puts an end to Fatah activity or he loses his throne."[21]

So Gavish's proposal in November 1966 came out of the blue for Lior but not for Rabin, who fully endorsed it. Rabin told Lior they should waste no time: he wanted to see the prime minister immediately and ordered a helicopter. The two men arrived in Jerusalem at 1 p.m. "Rabin presented his case," recalled Lior. "His words were harsh. It was clear from his tone, words, and manner of speaking that we had to act. Rabin left no other option." At first, Eshkol was not persuaded. A month earlier, on October 12, Eshkol had told the Knesset's foreign affairs committee that "Jordan has continued to act forcefully to thwart Fatah activity." He argued that Syria was interested in "entangling Israel in a clash with Jordan" and added that he did not want "to end up making life easy for Syria." Israel, Eshkol argued, should let Hussein deal with Fatah as best as he could. Furthermore, just two days prior to the November 12 incident, Eshkol had sent a letter to Hussein in which he applauded Jordan's counter-terror activities and promised that Israel would not attack Jordan.[22]

Eshkol knew very well that the operation that Rabin proposed would damage his tacit cooperation with Hussein. At the same time, since the summer his economic and security policies had suffered a withering attack. Rafi described him as being too weak, economic pundits as being too harsh. In the previous month, the criticism came from his own party: the secretary of Mapai's young vanguard wrote an op-ed article in a popular daily in which he argued that the coalition must be broadened. Rafi and the right-wing Herut, the writer asserted, should be invited to join the government as it was no longer able to gain the trust of the people. Only a week earlier, headlines in the press highlighted polls showing a marked decline in Eshkol's popularity. As on other such occasions, Eshkol responded by taking a more hawkish position. He decided to bring the operation before the cabinet.[23]

This time, most of the ministers supported taking action. A month earlier, after two mines had exploded, cabinet members had opposed a large-scale land and air attack on Syria and agreed to take the diplomatic route. Israel submitted a complaint to the Security Council; nothing came of that. Now, most ministers thought it was time to get tough. Rabin's report that the Jordanians, fearing an Israeli raid, had moved a battalion to the environs of Samu did not deter them. Still, three ministers considered the operation as proposed by the IDF to be too large and risky. Allon, on the other hand, demanded that the chief of staff's recommendation be approved without amendments. To appease the doves, Eshkol suggested that the resolution include a time limit, a directive to avoid shooting at civilians, and that only necessary force should be used to complete the mission. Rabin said he would "see what he could do" and left the room. Ultimately, the military ignored the instructions of the ministers. The invading force included six infantry platoons, combat engineers, and commandos in addition to thirteen tanks and fifty armored troop carriers. They stayed in the Samu region for four hours, during which time they demolished a hundred buildings, attacked two adjoining villages, got into a fight with a Jordanian battalion, and killed fourteen Jordanian soldiers and four civilians. A request for air cover led to the downing of one Jordanian Hunter. The cabinet approved an operation; the military took it as permission to start a mini war.[24]

Eshkol was irate. He summoned Rabin back to Jerusalem. Rabin seemed exhausted and nervous, red-eyed from not sleeping the previous night, and he chain-smoked. He explained that the presence of Jordanian troops in the area had caused him to increase the number of units participating in the operation. It was clear that he himself had been surprised by the level of destruction. Behind all this lay a sad reality: Rabin was losing control over his generals. Back in July, he was annoyed that a sortie to bomb a Syrian

diversion site ended in the downing of a Syrian MiG. Talking with the
pilots a few days later, Rabin stressed that "we need to act according to rules
and laws . . . because this is an order and we are an army . . . there were
several moments here that I would not like to define as insubordination but
I would also not want them to be repeated in the future." After Samu, Rabin
used the same aggrieved tone when he talked to his officers: "A retaliatory
raid needs to serve a certain aim; it's the continuation of politics by military
means. It should be limited and measured and this should affect the way we
use our troops. I regret that after 12 years of retaliatory raids this point is
not clear."[25]

In stark contrast, Gavish, commander of the southern front, was pleased
with how the operation had turned out. He later recalled:

> we learned that we know how to move large forces in the area and use
> effective firepower . . . we established that we could conquer the West
> Bank in a very short time using just a few armored columns. If the
> enemy had been presented as strong during training, then after Samu we
> comprehended that this was not the case . . . Samu was the first time that
> paratroopers were deployed together with tanks and armored troop
> carriers. The experiment was a success and an important lesson for our
> doctrine.[26]

The public at home and abroad was confused. Was not Syria the one that
stood behind Fatah activity? Israeli spokesmen had been very clear about it
and promised retribution. Then why did the IDF attack Jordan? American
diplomats were just as puzzled by what seemed like an erratic response.
Hussein was an American ally and Israel knew that. How come Washington
had not been consulted on this? Secretary of State Dean Rusk threatened
the Israeli ambassador that the US might reconsider its decision to sell
tanks and planes to Israel. That was a daunting prospect. The American
threat was leaked to the American and Israeli press and a *New York Times*
story speculated that the main reason Eshkol had authorized the operation
was that he was politically weak.[27]

Although Eshkol defended Rabin from his critics at the cabinet meeting,
he knew as much as anyone that the Samu operation had got out of control.
Eshkol told his wife after the Samu raid, "write down in your diary that,
unlike my predecessor, I am not the representative of the army in the
government!" Allegedly, after learning about the destruction left in the
IDF's wake, Eshkol also quipped: "We intended to pinch the mother-in-law
[Syria] but we ended up beating the bride [Jordan] to a pulp." Nevertheless,

in the following month he continued to strike a strident tone. December 1966 was a low point in his term, with another slew of polls showing how unpopular he was, and rumors in the press that he was about to capitulate and invite Rafi into the government. However, Eshkol found a way to change the conversation. A month after Samu he declared that Israel might attack Jordan again if Fatah operations were launched from its territory. He told a group of professors who had come to criticize his policies, "the Americans thought they would have it easy with me. I don't mind them thinking that way, but enough is enough ... Of course we acted against Jordan, but hadn't we warned them? ... Shall we sit silently while our civilians are being killed and our homes destroyed?" In late December, Eshkol repeated on two occasions that his policy was to use planes against the Syrians every time they fired at a Jewish settlement.[28]

But Samu's most enduring effect was to reignite the public debate about the best means to deal with Fatah operations. Eshkol had already urged the General Staff to use defensive means to deal with the problem and promised to fund the construction of barbed wire fences and patrol roads. The army was dragging its feet. Now other public figures made an intervention. Uri Avnery was the editor of the provocative weekly *Ha-Olam Ha-Ze* (This World) that improbably mixed gutter press with new-left politics. In 1965, Avnery, running as an independent candidate, was elected to the Knesset. A military history buff, he avidly followed the news about a technology both the French and the Americans were deploying to confront the infiltration of guerrilla fighters.

The French had completed their Morice Line in 1957. It was intended to stop the flow of volunteers and ammunition from Tunisia to the anti-French rebellion in Algeria. The formidable line, stretching along 250 kilometers of the Tunisian border, consisted of "an eight-foot electric fence charged with five thousand volts; on either side of this was a fifty-yard belt, liberally sprinkled with anti-personnel mines and backed with continuous barbed wire entanglements." Seismic and acoustic sensors on the fence helped alert the French to any breach, and guided either artillery fire or helicopter-borne infantry. According to some estimates, the Morice Line reduced infiltration by as much as 90 percent. It was built during the peak years of the Israeli–French alliance, and Israeli generals were acquainted with it (they specifically discussed the Morice Line in a General Staff meeting at the end of January 1967). In 1966, the Pentagon sought to create a more sophisticated version of the Morice Line on the border between North and South Vietnam, to stop the southward ingress of Vietcong and North Vietnamese units. Since Secretary of Defense Robert

McNamara was an enthusiastic supporter of the project, it became known as the McNamara Line.[29]

Avnery had a chance to share his thoughts when the Knesset debated the Samu raid. Taking to the podium, he explained why he thought retaliation raids were harmful and counterproductive. Some Knesset members taunted him. "Do you have a better idea?" Yes, Avnery said: building a fence. "People laughed at me," he recalled. Not one who despaired easily, Avnery published a detailed plan for the creation of a fence along the Syrian and Jordanian borders in his weekly. Being a good copywriter, he invented a name for the yet-to-be-constructed barrier: the Star of David Line. It caught on. One month later Rabin referred to the possibility of building a fence as "creating a Star of David line."[30]

Avnery was not the only journalist paying attention to this matter. A week or so after Samu, the *New York Times* reviewed the issue at length. A story written by the paper's Jerusalem correspondent started with Eshkol's statement in the cabinet, on November 20, that "a major effort will be launched to seal Israel's border against Arab infiltration." The correspondent's source claimed that "patrols will be increased, ambushes set, and fences and lights used where suitable." Indeed, at the time, Eshkol and his foreign minister, Abba Eban, were making such statements in the hope of mollifying Washington's anger. The article, looking into the current state of these efforts, observed that while some fences existed along the border, "for the most part, Israeli hills in border regions melt into adjacent Arab hills." The *Times* also drew a map based on sixty-nine Israeli reports of sabotage by Fatah units. The correspondent observed that there were four areas where infiltration usually took place: in Israel's most northerly point, at the tip of the Galilee "finger," where the Syrian and Lebanese borders met; south of Jerusalem; between the Arabah and the Dead Sea; and west of Nablus and Tel Aviv. Israel had built a 5-kilometer fence in the Jerusalem area, but not in the others.[31]

A week later, a State Department source had a chat with the Washington correspondent of *Maariv*, Israel's most-read daily. The source claimed that from then on Washington would apply pressure on Israel to make a more serious effort to close the border. This was in response to the angry telegrams the State Department received from its embassies in Damascus, Amman, and Riyadh after the Samu raid. The source described Israel's claim that sealing its borders was impossible as "ridiculous and defeatist." The source also argued that since most of the area in question was arid and flat, Israel would have a much easier job than the Americans had had in the jungles of Vietnam. The State Department continued the offensive three

days later with another leak to the *New York Times*. This time, the anonymous official was more specific. Washington was considering selling Israel
"the latest acoustical and radar equipment," originally developed for the
McNamara Line in Vietnam. A team of scientists at Harvard and the best
minds in the Pentagon were working at the time on cutting-edge technology that could detect infiltrators and pinpoint their exact location. The
source admitted that the technology was expensive – it might cost "up to
$1 million per mile to be any good." Still, Washington promised to sell the
equipment on the most generous terms possible, and if the Israelis carefully
selected the areas in which they deployed these sensors, it might not cost
them that much.[32]

Four days later Rabin exploded with anger. Speaking at a General Staff
meeting, Rabin referred to the *New York Times* story as "an American spin
... it's a classic PR stunt to pacify public opinion in the US." The reality,
Rabin claimed, was just the opposite: "Not only are they not offering us
equipment, but they are also preventing it from [reaching] us ... We sent
Yoske [Yosef Geva, the Israeli military attaché] to the Pentagon and they
didn't know anything about it. Our request for information about these
devices has been declined." As the discussion progressed, it transpired that
the real problem was not American non-cooperation but rather Israeli
resistance. Rabin was worried that, following the Samu debacle, the cabinet
would not authorize additional raids. "We can't make the defensive method
the main axis [of our policy]," Rabin complained. If the government invested
in electrical fences, Rabin warned, "[the ministers] would turn Israel into
another ghetto."[33]

A week later, on December 12, 1966, Eshkol decided to participate
in a General Staff meeting. Contrary to what he told Israeli journalists,
Eshkol did not want to approve more retaliatory raids and he certainly
did not want further friction with the Americans. He started by pointing
out that many Americans had asked him, "why Samu?" Yariv responded
by presenting the thesis that he and Rabin had developed in the last few
months. While Egypt, Lebanon, and Jordan argued that Fatah operations
would lead to war, Syria insisted that Palestinian guerrilla activity would
not lead to a confrontation, Yariv explained. If Israel did not act, Yariv
asserted, "we would undermine Nasser's thesis." Rabin concurred. Some
defensive measures could be adopted, Rabin said, but the question was
whether "we would build a Maginot line." Eshkol was not impressed by
any of these arguments. He complained that the army was not guarding
Jerusalem properly. He insisted that infrared sensors be purchased in large
quantities. Most importantly, he wanted a staff paper elaborating on where

fences should be erected along the border, and what it might cost. Eshkol promised to cover any expenses necessary to make the border more secure.[34]

A General Staff meeting that took place the next day in Eshkol's absence made it clear that he would not receive that staff paper. The generals were willing to contemplate setting more ambushes, enhancing patrols, and using acoustic and infrared sensors. They even considered erecting more fences around frontier settlements. What they were unwilling to do was to put up a barbed wire fence on the border itself. In another General Staff meeting with Eshkol, after the prime minister had effectively bullied them, the generals explained their reasons. Dado admitted, "I don't know where to put [the fence], whether to include the demilitarized zones or not." Zeevi agreed. Why not build a fence along border areas that were not in dispute? Eshkol wondered. That provoked another of Rabin's outbursts. Technical measures, he claimed, would not end Fatah's operations, "even if we get another 500 pairs of binoculars, buy 200 infra-red sensors, and build a 100-kilometer-long fence."[35]

Indeed, why would the Israeli generals put time and effort into entrenching a border the legitimacy of which they had never accepted? A border that they aimed to change at the next available opportunity? This was the reason the military resisted Eshkol's attempts to nudge it toward adopting a defensive solution to Fatah incursions. Rabin, Dado, and the others had no intention of letting Eshkol turn the offensive machine they had painstakingly built over more than a decade into a mere border militia. For that reason, the General Staff was also working to kill the American proposal to help with the creation of the Star of David Line.

At the end of December, an anonymous source, probably none other than the Israeli military attaché, Yosef Geva, spoke with the *Maariv* correspondent in Washington. The source said that the conversations that had taken place up until then between Israel and the US on border defense were merely a "probing exercise" that would probably end in nothing. Although American officials referred to these talks as "promising," what they offered was impractical. Currently, the source claimed, American-made sensors could barely distinguish between a roaming hyena and a Fatah infiltrator. The source was referring to the sensors that a Senate Armed Forces Committee report described as having "made a dramatic contribution toward saving a significant number of American lives in Southeast Asia." The source also asserted that the cost of these sensors was prohibitive; deploying them along the Jordanian and Syrian border might cost as much as $400 million. Electronic devices, the anonymous official argued, could not solve political problems, and using them was akin "to giving an aspirin to a cancer patient."[36]

In the following months, Geva continued to stonewall the negotiations with the State Department over anti-infiltration technology, arguing that "to give [these sensors] undue weight as part of a 'static' defense policy would limit Israel's sovereign right to defend itself by whatever means it deems necessary." Like Rabin, Geva complained that "undue emphasis on anti-infiltration technology would create a defensive ghetto psychology, which would encourage increased Arab harassment and foster a defeatist attitude in Israel." Thanks to Geva's efforts, these talks remained fruitless.[37]

Resuming the Confrontation in the Demilitarized Zones

In the summer of 1966, the Syrians did something that perplexed Rabin and his colleagues: they proposed a ceasefire in the demilitarized zones. In exchange, the Syrians wanted the IDF to stop shooting at Syrian farmers, who entered the demilitarized zones to cultivate their plots or graze their herds. The cabinet decided to accept the offer, which made Rabin extremely frustrated. If the Syrians were still providing a haven to Fatah operators, Rabin asked, why shouldn't Israel punish Damascus by ending the ceasefire? At the same time, the kibbutzim were applying pressure on Eshkol to end this arrangement. They claimed that the ceasefire brought about the loss of 198 acres which were taken over by Syrian farmers. On visiting one of the kibbutzim, Eshkol gained the impression "that the comrades there are on tenterhooks." Members of the northern kibbutzim demanded that Eshkol order the IDF to open fire on Syrian farmers entering the demilitarized zones so that they could cultivate "all of the plots."[38]

In December 1966, the coalition of Palmach generals and settlers won a victory when Eshkol gave Rabin permission to breach the ceasefire. When the new policy was discussed in cabinet in January, Allon demanded its approval. Other ministers again raised questions about the danger of escalation. Specifically, they opposed the use of aircraft. Minister of Health Yisrael Barzilay reminded everyone that Egypt had a military treaty with Syria and might rush to its rescue. Eventually the cabinet allowed only cultivation of undisputed plots in the demilitarized zones and forbade the use of airplanes. But in the following weeks, the military would ignore these limitations. The Syrians responded by renewing their fire toward each and every Israeli tractor entering the demilitarized zones, and lifted the ban on the passage of Fatah units to Israel through their border. The rate of Fatah attacks went up in 1967, reaching a crescendo of seventeen sabotage acts during May and June 1967.[39]

Rabin was pleased. In a General Staff discussion on January 23, 1967, Rabin argued that "border incidents are a goldmine we should exploit." Eshkol, who was present, wondered if Rabin was considering the ramifications of his proposal: "Shall we conquer Syria? And what do we do after that? ... We will kill seven million Syrians?" Rabin brushed Eshkol's doubts aside. The main thing, he said, was to launch a Samu-type operation against Syria, to teach it a lesson. Eshkol retorted that in such a case "all the Arabs, including Jordan," would unite to fight Israel. Rabin reminded him that nothing of that sort had happened after Samu; Israel attacked Jordan while Egypt and Syria stood on the sidelines.[40]

At the end of February, Rabin and Eshkol had another opportunity to air their differences, this time at a gathering of senior military officers. Eshkol spoke first. He said that while Arab countries were seeking to annihilate Israel, Israel was aiming to deter them from going to war. The IDF's planning, Eshkol argued, emphasized the importance of starting the next war with a pre-emptive strike, but "we don't have a plan to destroy Syria." He warned the officers, "God forbid that anything should happen with Syria!" and added, "I know there are plans and planning [for war with Syria] ... and looking at them makes my heart heavy." Rabin on the other hand sounded no notes of caution. He argued that "the problem isn't what the Arabs can do to us, but rather to what extent we can use our strength to exploit the disunity in the Arab world."[41]

Rabin also boasted that the IDF's budget for construction had doubled in the last two years. His economic adviser, Rabin recalled, told him recently that "we are going to have a year of prosperity." The recession, Rabin explained, did not affect military planning. That was true in an even wider sense. As in Egypt, the officers were unaffected by the recession; their salaries had not been cut. Indeed, when Eshkol suggested just a week earlier that generals take a 2 percent pay cut, to set an example, all bar two of the members of the General Staff refused even to discuss the issue. Senior officers had access to subsidized housing and tended to cluster in the same neighborhoods, the most famous of these being the beautiful Zahala, in Tel Aviv's north, where Rabin lived. At a time of growing economic difficulties, balls, banquets, feasts, and celebrations were common in various units of the IDF. Senior officers regularly visited fancy restaurants in Tel Aviv. While Israelis of all walks of life had to tighten their belts, the defense budget grew from 9.5 percent of the GDP in 1965 to 10.4 percent in 1966 and 17.7 percent in 1967.[42]

During January and February 1967, Israeli and Syrian officers conducted talks about the renewal of the ceasefire in the demilitarized zones. The negotiations went nowhere, which rather pleased Rabin. In his assessment, the failure of the talks would confer legitimacy on a large operation against Syria. Opportunity knocked at the end of March, when a Fatah unit blew up the water pumps of a kibbutz in the Galilee. This act of sabotage coincided with another awful month for Eshkol: students at the Hebrew University booed and jeered when he tried to make a speech, and members of his party were calling for his resignation. As usual with Eshkol, in times of trouble he grasped for the image of a tough leader. Eshkol told Rabin that he wanted to make the Syrians pay, but he felt like doing something new, something creative. However, he said, he did not want to start a war. He authorized the chief of staff to pick a date and send a tractor to a disputed plot. A few days later, on April 5, Rabin informed Eshkol that the upcoming incident might involve the activation of the air force. Eshkol was fine with that.[43]

The IDF waited for a fair day, and it came on April 7. Israelis and Syrians had been exchanging both light and heavy fire during the morning hours when the UN proposed a ceasefire. The Israelis accepted, and so did the Syrians, but with one caveat: that Israel withdraw the tractor. Rabin refused to accept this condition, arguing that the plot in question was under full Israeli sovereignty. At noon, Eshkol and Rabin talked on the phone. Eshkol backed up Rabin's decision and authorized the use of the air force. Between noon and late afternoon, the confrontation escalated considerably. On that day, the IAF sent half of its planes into the air, and they encountered Syrian MiGs eager to engage them. Seven of them were downed. Two Syrian MiGs were shot down over Damascus after Israeli Mirages went after them in hot pursuit. Having won an air battle, the Mirages made a victory loop over Syria's capital. As the Israeli Air Force was pounding Syrian fortifications, kibbutz members left their bomb shelters to watch the Syrian planes dropping from the sky like confetti. One of them exclaimed excitedly, "this is [the work of] our neighbor from Deganya Bet [a nearby kibbutz on the Sea of Galilee], Air Force Commander Motti Hod, who came to attack those who try to harm his neighbors." As Hod admitted afterward, "I didn't like the fact that the Syrians were bombing the Jordan Valley," where he resided.[44]

The use of firepower during the April 7 incident dwarfed Samu. On that day Israeli Air Force planes flew 171 sorties and lobbed 65 tons of bombs at the Syrians. It had been the largest air battle since the 1948 war. Eshkol was no less responsible for the scale of the confrontation than was Rabin. By 3 p.m., Rabin wanted to call it a day and order the tractor to retreat, but Eshkol blocked him: he wanted the tractor to work until dusk. Three more Syrian MiGs were downed in the next hour. By this time, Eshkol was already at the air force's ops room – his third visit since becoming prime minister:

Eshkol liked being there while his pilots were engaged in daring exploits. Hod took advantage of the fact that Rabin was in the north and away from headquarters to get authorization directly from Eshkol. The prime minister nodded enthusiastically whenever he was asked to approve another sortie. Three weeks after the incident, Eshkol stated in an interview with *Maariv*: "I gave the order."

Rabin was also pleased by the outcome of the engagement. He wanted to use the momentum and cultivate more disputed land, but the government rejected his proposal.[45] However, he remained undaunted. He told his generals on April 24 that Israel should continue confronting Syria until the Baath's fall from power. Rabin said that he would soon tell the commander of the UN observers in the north that Israel would not accept any Syrian presence in the demilitarized zones, including that of farmers. "If [the Syrians] try to interfere," warned Rabin, "there will be blood."

Following more Fatah operations, the cabinet convened on May 7 to discuss the situation in the north. The decisions taken there were a compromise between hawks and doves. On the one hand, the cabinet decided that if Syria continued to support Fatah, the IDF would launch "a limited operation" against Syria. On the other hand, the cabinet decided to deliver a warning to Damascus through a third party. After that meeting, Eshkol, Rabin, and Yariv started a very public campaign of threats against Syria. They should have known they were playing with fire. Headlines in the Israeli and international press reported anti-Baath riots in Syria; one of them read, "Syria is on the verge of exploding."[46]

Nonetheless, they persisted. Rabin wanted to prepare the public for the war he had been planning against Syria. On May 8, he met with Yariv and told him that one of Israel's next moves should be to destroy the Syrian navy. Yariv was alarmed: "But this is not a retaliatory raid. This means war." Rabin just shrugged.[47] Eshkol added fuel to the fire with his own statements. He was probably trying to kill two birds with one stone: show the public how tough he was and spook the Syrians enough so they would keep the border quiet. But the movement of Egyptian troops into Sinai shattered Eshkol's and Rabin's elaborate plans.

12

RABIN'S SCHLIEFFEN PLAN

"GROUPTHINK" IS A term developed by political scientists to describe a situation where policymakers prevent themselves from seeing reality clearly. They convince each other that a certain falsehood is true, and facts that do not align with that belief get tossed aside.[1] Israelis talk about the "concept," meaning much the same thing. The "concept" became infamous in Israel six years after the Six-Day War, when the country was still trying to understand how its intelligence services, considered to be the best in the world, could have missed the fact that Syria and Egypt (aided by Libya, Iraq, Kuwait, Saudi Arabia, Morocco, and Jordan) were preparing a surprise attack on Israel. The official conversation revolved around the "concept," which was more like a soothing mantra that Israeli intelligence had kept repeating to itself: Egypt would not attack Israel unless and until it had acquired heavy bombers, and Syria would never start a war with Israel without Egypt's participation. However, on October 6, 1973, Egypt's president, Anwar Sadat, ordered his troops to attack – without the much-vaunted bombers. Syria followed suit.[2]

The fact that such "concepts" had prevailed before was conveniently ignored. In Israel, assessments of the intentions of Arab states have always been politically skewed. The head of military intelligence was deemed to be Israel's chief assessor. Just like any other general, his promotion depended on the goodwill of the chief of staff or the prime minister. It was far easier for him to adopt the views of those higher-ups than to sound a dissenting voice. Thus, during 1955 and 1956 for instance, Yehoshafat Harkabi, then head of military intelligence, stubbornly argued that Nasser's Egypt was preparing for war and was absorbing quickly and efficiently the weapons it had purchased from the Soviet Union in September 1955. This assessment mirrored that of Chief of Staff Moshe Dayan, who was eager to confront the Egyptians. Harkabi's analysis also corresponded with the nightmarish portrayal of Nasser as an Arab Hitler, heard in many speeches by Ben-Gurion. When Israel invaded Sinai in October 1956, ostensibly to prevent the rise of a formidable Egyptian war machine, the Egyptian army quickly folded and retreated. Egyptian ground troops were neither highly motivated nor well trained. The assessment of the Egyptian threat turned out to be exaggerated. In fact, Ben-Gurion and Dayan knew about the poor quality of the Egyptian army. They let Harkabi "cook" the intelligence to legitimize the war.[3]

Four years later, in February 1960, military intelligence gave no warning regarding the entry of three Egyptian divisions into Sinai. It did not know that the Syrians had asked the Egyptians to help them or how many troops entered Sinai or, for that matter, where they were. At that time, Ben-Gurion was eager to avoid a conflict with Egypt. It was the eve of a crucial trip to the US to meet with the president, who had forced Israel to retreat from Sinai after conquering the peninsula. Ben-Gurion had no desire to anger Eisenhower again or to embark on another war without his blessing. The military intelligence, under Chaim Herzog, was under no pressure to inflate the threat and, if anything, it took it too lightly. The response of the military intelligence during the "Rotem Crisis," as it had become known, was slow and lethargic, which made the General Staff rather exasperated.[4] When Yariv became a senior officer in the military intelligence, he commissioned an investigation into the sources of these two instances of intelligence failure.[5] However, as soon as he assumed office, Yariv succumbed to the pattern of politically tailored assessments.

The fact that his boss, Rabin, had made him his right-hand man certainly influenced Yariv's assessments. Although Yariv had served in the British army in the pre-statehood era, ex-Palmach officers considered him a member of their tribe; one of them fondly depicted him as "a light British cannon refurbished in a Palmach workshop." Yariv knew Rabin when both had participated in battalion commanders' training in 1949, and they continued to work together as they rose through the ranks, mainly by taking on staff (rather than combat) positions. They established mutual trust and liked each other. Both Rabin and Allon worked hard to convince Eshkol to appoint Yariv as chief of military intelligence at the end of 1963. One of the first to give Yariv the happy news was Allon, who hugged him and said, "We made it!" It was clear that Yariv owed his promotion to the Palmach lobby. Later, a congratulatory call came from Rabin himself.[6]

In the following years, Yariv produced the assessments that legitimized Rabin's bare-knuckle tactics against the Syrians. The concept fathered by Yariv and Rabin argued that the IDF could localize its confrontation with Syria because Egypt, preoccupied in Yemen and governed by a level-headed leader, would never intervene. Yariv stuck to his guns, even after the secret correspondence between Amer and Nasser – in which Amer recommended sending the Egyptian army into Sinai – had been intercepted by Israeli intelligence in November 1966. Since Nasser did not act upon Amer's recommendation, Yariv saw the whole affair as a validation of his basic assessment. Likewise, Rabin was so certain that Egypt was solidly in the moderate Arab camp that in April 1967, as he was urging the General Staff to prepare for an "all-out confrontation" with Syria, he suggested that Israel would contact Nasser to brief him about Israel's intentions. Egypt "must know what our plans are," he said, and should not learn about them from the Syrians. Another tenet of Yariv's concept was that Syria was a rational entity that could be taught a lesson, although he apparently knew this was fiction. During one General Staff discussion, in late 1966, Yariv admitted that the Syrian Baath was "a coalition of ethnic groups plus armored units, an air force, and troops at the front."[7]

After Nasser had moved his forces into Sinai, the whole matter blew up in Rabin's and Yariv's faces. Rather than deterring Syria, their policy forced Nasser to take a stand and support his northern ally. Rather than localizing the conflict with Syria, the military's belligerent line had created a regional conflagration. Both Yariv and Rabin argued forcefully for their concept in General Staff meetings and cabinet discussions. Not everyone agreed with them. Dovish ministers tried to stop them. Generals who headed the central and southern fronts resented the fact that priority was given to the northern front. Eshkol had always suspected that the offensive measures the two generals were advocating would not stop Fatah but rather ensnare Israel in a war against the Arab world.

Yet, Yariv and Rabin persevered. Nasser's decision pulled the rug from underneath their theories and humiliated them, but Yariv proved the more flexible of the two. On May 19, he started to shift his position, effectively admitting his mistake. That morning, Yariv acknowledged, in a typically vague manner, that "there is willingness [in Egypt] to go very far toward a confrontation, and even initiate it." The reason for the change in Yariv's assessment was intensive eavesdropping by the Israelis. The Egyptian Air Force's communication networks were being watched very closely. As a result, Israel started to learn about Amer's brainchild, Operation "Assad," which targeted Israel's airfields. Israeli intelligence still believed that the odds of that attack materializing were low, since Egypt's expeditionary force in Sinai was not yet large enough to mount a follow-up attack. Nevertheless, from that point onward, Yariv supported launching a strike against Egypt.[8]

Rabin, conversely, tried to salvage the original plan. He did all he could to minimize the extent of the confrontation with Egypt. He then came up with a military blueprint that had never been tried or practiced before, something which perplexed everyone who came into contact with it. His idea was to launch a surprise air attack on Egypt, and then take advantage of air superiority to occupy Gaza. Rabin argued that Gaza could then be used as leverage to force Egypt to undo its unilateral decision to close the Straits of Tiran. The idea of using that small and troubled piece of land as a bargaining chip was so improbable that only Rabin supported this plan. "Why would we want all those refugees?" Eshkol inquired on May 20, when he first heard Rabin's proposal.[9]

From May 15 on, Rabin argued repeatedly that Israel should assume that a war with Egypt would also mean a war with Syria. Syria would not sit on the sidelines, Rabin maintained. The Syrians, he believed, would respond to the Israeli attack on Egypt with a massive barrage of artillery fire on Israeli settlements in the Galilee. As it transpired later, the Syrians were far from being enthusiastic participants in the war that eventually came. But Rabin latched on to that assessment as it provided him with the policy he had always advocated: war with Syria. Rabin's Gaza operation was akin to the Schlieffen Plan, which the German General Staff implemented at the outbreak of World War I. Its aims were to hit France decisively at the beginning of the war and free the German army to clash with the Russians. This was Germany's way of avoiding a two-front war. Rabin's plan aimed to knock out Egypt as economically as possible, and by doing so provoke Syria to join the war. Then Rabin would unleash the might of the IDF on Damascus.[10]

Rabin's single-minded commitment to the Syrian campaign was evident from the early stages of the crisis. On May 17, when it was still believed that the entry of Egyptian forces to Sinai was nothing but a show of force, Rabin said that his order to deploy more tanks in the south was only to deter Egypt from responding to an Israeli attack on Syria. On that day, Rabin met with Eshkol and asked for authorization to use tanks, artillery, and even the air force against the Syrians if any brush with them occurred. Eshkol refused, instructing Rabin to use only preventive measures and avoid escalation at all costs. Eshkol's perspective on the crisis was in stark contrast to that of his chief of staff. Speaking in the Knesset's foreign affairs committee on May 17, Eshkol said:

I want to keep the status quo for [another] 50 years ... I announce here: we are not planning a war; we did not want a war, before or even after the Egyptians had entered Sinai ... we do not want anything from our neighbors but the status quo ... and we need to avoid war now and maneuver accordingly.[11]

Eshkol continued to uphold that line in the coming days. He wanted to leave nothing to chance, and on May 18 asked Rabin to assign 2,000 troops solely for the purpose of patrolling the border with Syria and setting ambushes along it. In this way Eshkol wanted to ensure that no Fatah unit would be able to infiltrate Israel and spark a conflagration. Moreover, talking to the political committee of Mapai, Eshkol said, "I would now refrain from responding to any incident on the [Syrian] border that did not involve a significant loss of lives."

On May 22, Eshkol went public with this position, trying to scale back his belligerent declarations of the previous week. Speaking in the Knesset, Eshkol declared: "I want say to Arab countries that we do not want to attack [them]. We have no interest in impinging upon their safety, territory, or legal rights. We will not intervene in their internal affairs, their regimes, and the relations between them ..."[12]

The cabinet supported Eshkol and on May 23 decided to respond to Nasser's challenge by sending Foreign Minister Abba Eban to Washington. Eban's task was to ascertain Washington's next step. Did it have the wherewithal to assemble a multinational armada that would break the Egyptian blockade? At least, that was what American diplomats promised their Israeli counterparts. However, the cabinet's decision was contrary to what Rabin had wanted. He recommended going to war at once. The ministers were inquisitive and incredulous. They thought Rabin's war plan too risky and preferred to exhaust diplomatic channels first. Rabin probably hoped that Eshkol would pull his chestnuts out of the fire for him; Eshkol had defended Rabin in the past when dovish ministers attacked him. But not this time. Eshkol calculated that it would take a week for the next tanker headed for Israel to reach the Straits of Tiran. Until that time he was content to experiment with other ways of solving the crisis.[13] By gambling on diplomacy, the cabinet was prolonging Rabin's agony. Four ambitious generals were putting incessant pressure on him. Each wanted his own command to share the glory of the coming victory.

As could be expected, Dado was gung-ho. He believed that he was now within reach of conquering the Golan Heights. One piece of land had always been on his mind: the northern tip of the Heights, where the Syrians had failed to build fortifications, judging the slope leading to the plateau too steep for any sane general to climb. Dado thought this was the chink in Syria's armor. He planned a short, decisive battle in which his tanks and infantry would storm the area and then widen the breach in the Syrian line. After initial success, troops would advance on the Heights' regional capital, Quneitra. That was only one aspect of an overall plan code-named "Makevet" (Sledgehammer). The plan also envisaged using helicopters to land infantry and commando units behind enemy lines in the southern part of the Heights.

Dado had been working on various versions of this plan ever since he took the post at northern command in 1964, and he was eager to implement it. He introduced "Makevet" during a crucial General Staff meeting that took place on May 22. At that time, Rabin was unwilling to let Dado make further preparations, fearing he would reveal his hand too much. How could Rabin explain that while Egypt was concentrating troops in Sinai, he was still planning a campaign against Syria? Perhaps as a way to get back at Rabin, Dado called Rabin's Gaza-first plan, code-named "Atzmon," "an act of folly" and "a grave error." Apparently, Dado did not realize that Rabin had been trying to ensure an eventual confrontation with Syria.[14]

Another general who opposed "Atzmon" was Yeshayahu Gavish. An ex-Palmach officer, Gavish was born in 1925 to a low-income family that lived in Tel Aviv. They resided in a ramshackle hut, so close to the sea that one winter the waves swept away all their belongings. One of his most vivid childhood memories was of his mother carrying buckets of cold seawater to fill an iron tub, into which little Gavish was dunked daily. He carried this sense of deprivation into his military career. Although Gavish shared a similar trajectory to Dado, it was clear who Rabin's favorite was. Dado got the "hot command," where all the action had been. Gavish got the southern command in late 1965. When Rabin appointed him, he told Gavish cheerfully, "there is nothing there. No enemies, no infiltration. The Egyptian army is focused on the war in Yemen." Gavish's heart sank. He knew he was being relegated to the sidelines.[15]

Nevertheless, he closely followed intelligence reports on what was happening on the other side of the border, and used this information to argue that his command should receive more resources. Gavish tried to prove that the Egyptian army would emerge out of Yemen hardened and battle-ready. He found proof of his thesis in the fact that Egypt was still reaping the fruits of a large arms deal it signed with Moscow in 1958. As a result, it had received modern weapons, such as the T-54 and T-55 tanks. Gavish told whoever cared to listen that the quiet on Israel's southern border was deceptive and that Rabin and Yariv were wrong: there was no way Egypt would sit out a fight between Israel and Syria. The confrontation with Syria, Gavish had insisted, would end in a war with Egypt. Gavish argued for this position most forcefully during a General Staff meeting in November 1966, after Syria and Egypt had signed a military pact. Nobody listened to him.[16]

When Egyptian troops started rolling into Sinai on May 15, Gavish felt his assessment had been vindicated. However, Rabin seemed unresponsive. Gavish wanted an immediate mobilization of all reserve forces to prepare an assault on the Egyptian army. Indeed, like Dado, Gavish had a plan, which would make him known as a bold military leader. He was not the first to come up with it: the bragging rights belonged to Allon, who argued in a book he authored that if Israel tried to occupy Sinai, the US would force a withdrawal, as it did in 1956. The IDF's next invasion of Sinai should therefore focus on annihilating the Egyptian forces rather than taking over territory. Plans drawn up within the IDF since 1958, the year in which Allon published his book, described the same maneuver, with slight differences.

It started in northern Sinai, the most logical region for the Egyptians to place the majority of their troops – the rest of the desert being too mountainous for tanks and other vehicles to maneuver in. The most important goal of the IDF planners was to turn that area into a killing zone from which Egyptian troops would not be able to escape. Israeli divisions were instructed to perform a pincer movement that would envelop the Egyptian troops from both the north (moving through Rafah along the Sinai shore) and the south. Once this was done, Israeli units were to rush to block the Mitle and Gidi passes – two openings in Sinai's central mountain ridge, which were the Egyptian army's exit points. After ensconcing themselves on the slopes of the mountains, Israeli troops were to shoot anyone who tried to cross the passes. Air and land attacks were to ensure the complete destruction of all military materiel. IDF planners had assumed that conquering Sinai would take six days, but also that the offensive might be stopped by the superpowers sooner than that. This grand maneuver in the desert, which involved the complex coordination of the air force, hundreds of tanks, artillery, and the movements of three divisions, all aimed at routing the Egyptians, became something of a holy grail for Israeli generals. Six months before the war, Dado, giving a talk in a northern kibbutz, confided that each night before he went to sleep he had only one prayer: that Nasser would order his army to enter Sinai. There and then, Dado promised his audience, the IDF would kill anything that moved.[17]

After two years in which all the glory went to Dado's exploits in the north, Gavish was eager to take his chance to shine, but the chief of staff and the prime minister seemed willing to let that opportunity pass. When Eshkol and Rabin made a tour of the south on Saturday, May 20, Gavish did his best to explain that the time to pounce was now. UN emergency forces were already leaving their posts along the border and intelligence reports indicated that the chances of conducting a successful campaign were fading with each passing day. Egyptian units were digging in, blocking major roads in Sinai. There was also a lot of mine-laying activity. Although all this information suggested the Egyptian army was adopting a defensive formation rather than preparing to attack, Gavish claimed that Israel's security was under dire threat. Eshkol was unimpressed. When Gavish told him that 6,000 soldiers held Abu-Ageila, a major Egyptian compound that blocked the road to the passes, Eshkol "said in his language, 'das ist Gantzen?' [This is all?]" Eshkol's Yiddish did not sit well with Gavish.

"Eshkol showed little understanding in military affairs," Gavish complained in his memoirs, "and failed to comprehend the situation. The terminology – division, brigade, artillery, armored units – meant nothing to him." The more he talked with Eshkol and Rabin, the more Gavish became frustrated:

> If the Prime Minister did not understand the severity of the situation, who in Jerusalem and at Headquarters in Tel-Aviv did? Who would make decisions? I started to realize we would not get help from this person [i.e. Eshkol] ... The Chief of Staff, who sat by the Prime Minister, did not intervene. Only listened ... All my attempts to explain that we could attack safely and gain swift victory with our five armored brigades were to no avail.[18]

While Rabin and Eshkol toured the south, a discussion was underway at headquarters in Tel Aviv. The topic was "Axe 1" – an ambitious plan to take over the whole of Sinai. When Rabin was presented with the blueprint, he asked that the planners focus on the more modest plan, "Atzmon," to conquer only the Gaza Strip. Gavish, who was there, exploded:

> I was strongly against it. I felt that what Rabin wanted was a limited retaliatory raid as if the IDF was not strong enough to make a bigger move. If the Egyptian army responded that would be very good; we would smash it. But what if they didn't respond? I demanded that we take Al-Arish [in northern Sinai] ... Rabin hesitated ... His concept of war was highly limited ... In my view, it was Rabin who recommended that the government make an effort to resolve the crisis through diplomatic means, rather than war.[19]

Another general who was there to oppose "Atzmon" was Uzi Narkiss, head of central command. Short, energetic, red-haired Narkiss carried in his heart the memory of how he and his Palmach brothers-in-arms failed to conquer East Jerusalem in 1948. Not a day had passed in which he did not think about launching an attack to take Jerusalem. On the eve of the 1967 Independence Day, the following dialogue took place between Narkiss and his friend, the poet Haim Guri:

> *Guri:* Tell me, Uzi, how long can we continue to teach the Bible to our children, while most of the biblical land is out of our reach?
> *Narkiss:* I can't answer this question officially, but let me tell you this: we have not given up. We can aspire, we can hope, we can dream.

As the crisis crystallized, Narkiss's mood improved. Like Dado and Gavish, Narkiss believed this could end well for him. He told his colleagues, "It's a great opportunity to do something with the Jordanians. We should not miss it!" To his staff officers he prophesied, "Within 72 hours we can drive off all the Arabs from the West Bank."[20]

For a number of reasons, Narkiss believed that *his* command should get priority, and not the south. The superpowers would allow only a few days of fighting. While Israel might not be able to defeat the Egyptian army in such a short time, it could take over the West Bank. However, even if the IDF did conquer Sinai, Israel would be forced to withdraw. Still, according to Narkiss, the Jews had a historical claim on Judea and Samaria. No power would drive them away from there. Taking the West Bank would remove the Jordanian threat to Jerusalem and Tel Aviv, and establish a line of defense on the Jordan River. Despite all that, he still could not bring himself to agree with Rabin's "Atzmon" plan, which seemed bizarre to him. He later wrote, "I was certain the army could not settle for half-measures and must strive to annihilate the Egyptian army."[21]

The fourth general to apply pressure on Rabin was Ezer Weizman, his deputy and chief of operations. Tall, mustachioed, noodle-shaped, and impulsive, Weizman spent most of his years in the air force. On a good day, he could be charismatic, charming, and bright. But when crossed or opposed he was prone to volcanic eruptions of rage. As befits a pilot, he was a scion of Zionist aristocracy. His uncle, Chaim Weizman, had led the Zionist movement for many years and then became Israel's first president. His mother's family founded one of the first Zionist settlements in Palestine at the end of the nineteenth century. He commanded the air force for eight years, between 1958 and 1966 – the longest term of any air force commander – and was considered one of its founders. Unlike other generals in Rabin's staff, Weizman did not serve in the Palmach and was close to the right-wing Herut party.

In his lectures to officers and soldiers he likened Israel to a beautiful girl and Arabs to potential rapists. During a speech in the high military college he asked his listeners, "Are you, as officers in the IDF, willing to accept that the Wailing Wall, the very heart of this nation, is under foreign occupation?" As a pilot, he felt that Israel's small dimensions were like a "cage ... where you must land such a short time after you take off." Intervening in a General Staff discussion four months before the war, Weizman stated, "if an Arab gets killed – it's a good thing."[22]

Weizman testified in his autobiography that he never tired of telling his pilots that "the current borders are not sacred ... we *must* change them in the next war." He well understood that achieving total air superiority would be key to promoting territorial changes. Free from the harassment of enemy planes, the Israeli Air Force (IAF) could bomb and shoot at Arab land forces, making it easier for army divisions to rush forward and take as much territory as they could. Air force officers had already concluded in the early 1950s that the best way to achieve this would be to launch a surprise attack against Arab air forces. It was not a novel idea: this trick had worked well for the German Luftwaffe during World War II. Twice it had destroyed East European air forces while they were on the ground. The Germans had done it to the Poles in September 1939, and even more spectacularly to the Russians in June 1941. (German planes had destroyed 800 Soviet aircraft in one day.)[23]

By 1955, the IAF already had a blueprint for a raid on enemy airfields that would catch the other side unawares. In the following years it continued to perfect the plan. IAF planners knew their daring ploy would work, because Arab air forces, and the Egyptians' in particular, were weak. In the decade between 1957 and 1967 Egypt had accumulated more aircraft, more radar systems, and constructed more airfields (from eight in 1957, there were twenty-three by 1967) than any other Arab nation. But the technical competence of maintenance and air crews had remained low. The Egyptian radar system proved faulty, as Israeli planes easily penetrated Egypt's air space numerous times in the pre-war decade. Tapping into the wavelength of the Egyptian radar systems, Israeli engineers had also invented a way of spying on the very images that Egyptian radar operators were seeing on their screens. Israeli planes would then be sent into Egypt's airspace to test the abilities of its radar, with Israeli intelligence being able to tell in real time whether or not they had been detected. The process produced an elaborate map showing where Egyptian radar coverage was patchy. Flight routes into Sinai were planned accordingly.[24]

Weizman was single-mindedly devoted to the idea of a stealth attack. He vigorously lobbied both Ben-Gurion and Eshkol to provide enough aircraft for the IAF to destroy all Arab air forces on the first day of the next war. Some people, like Eshkol's adjutant, Lior, thought that Weizman was setting an overly ambitious goal. Nevertheless, under Weizman the IAF's budget had increased by 66 percent, from $28 million in 1958 to $42 million in 1966. Seventy-five Mirage planes were ordered from France just for that purpose. Weizman's efforts to promote that plan did not end here.[25]

In 1961, a tense discussion took place between Weizman and his superiors. For the first time, President Kennedy had offered Israel the chance to acquire a sophisticated weapons system: a new surface-to-air missile dubbed "the Hawk." Israeli leaders were eager to purchase the Hawk for political reasons. They interpreted Kennedy's generosity as an important sign of American commitment to Israel's security. The question was not whether to purchase the Hawk, but how many batteries to buy. Weizman recommended purchasing only a few; the Hawk was quite expensive and Weizman realized that it would compete for the scarce resources the IAF needed to build its armada. Weizman's greatest concern was that the politicians, faced with a choice between gambling on risky air raids or relying on the sophisticated Hawk to defend Israel's skies, would choose the latter. That would mean no glory to Weizman and an end to his dream of an expansionist war. Eventually, Weizman won the argument. Israel purchased five Hawk batteries and the budget allocated to Weizman's beloved Mirages was saved.[26]

In 1963, Weizman's air raid plan came under another threat. He was about to be promoted to chief of operations, a job that would make him a candidate for the position of chief of staff. Becoming such would have created a historic precedent, as he would have been the first IAF commander to reach the pinnacle. Weizman, ever ambitious, was more than willing to take on the challenge. However, he was consumed with worries about the fate of the IAF after his departure. Would the next IAF commander be as committed as he was to an offensive doctrine? Would he abandon Weizman's great stealth attack? Weizman felt that only Motti Hod, his protégé, would continue to develop the IAF according to his vision. But Hod, 37 years old at the time, was considered too young and Rabin wanted to appoint an older officer. Weizman tried to bypass Rabin and spoke directly with Eshkol. Pleading on behalf of Hod, Weizman told the prime minister that Hod might be young, "but he would screw the Arabs good and proper." Eshkol, perhaps taken aback by Weizman's crude language, was not persuaded.

Weizman then did something that surprised everybody. He declined the offer to become chief of operations and asked to remain as commander of the IAF. His wish was granted and his rival, Haim Bar-Lev, was appointed. Two years later, in 1966, Weizman got what he wanted. Hod was promoted to IAF commander, Weizman to chief of operations, and Bar-Lev was dispatched to study at France's École Militaire. Weizman was now in a position to promote his hawkish designs and help the IAF launch its surprise attack, code-named "Moked" (Focus).[27]

The first clash between Rabin and his generals over his "Atzmon" plan took place on May 22, during a General Staff discussion. Dado, Narkiss, and Gavish together battled Rabin and his "think small" approach. Rabin, nevertheless, asked the operations branch to prepare a detailed outline of "Atzmon" and distribute it to front-line units. After Rabin left headquarters, Weizman ordered plans to be prepared for an attack to conquer Sinai, code-named "Kardom" (Axe). The clash between Rabin and his staff intensified during the next day. For Rabin, May 23 was a long day; it started at four in the morning with the news of Nasser's decision to close the Straits of Tiran, delivered to him by phone. Then followed in quick succession agonizing discussions with the prime minister, the cabinet, the government, the prime minister again, and finally the General Staff. Weizman doggedly shadowed Rabin throughout the day, insisting on participating in all the meetings. In each, he pressed for an immediate decision to go to war and for a general call-up of the reserve forces. Twice Weizman suggested launching Operation "Moked," even if the land forces were not ready to mount a follow-up attack on Egypt. At 10 a.m. the cabinet decided to give Eban time to sound out Lyndon Johnson, but Weizman insisted on convening another meeting with Eshkol at a secluded facility near Tel Aviv. Weizman pressed Rabin and Eshkol to authorize "Moked" on the spot, and went into technical detail to prove that his plan could work. Both Rabin and Eshkol explained that the cabinet's decision could not be ignored.[28]

At 5 p.m. that day, Rabin and Gavish clashed at a General Staff meeting. Gavish said it was time to decide which plan was to be executed, "Atzmon" or "Kardom." Gavish recommended taking Gaza even before achieving air superiority – because it was easy – and then "taking a serious chunk [of Sinai] without going too much to the south." Rabin resisted. He insisted on taking Gaza, and only Gaza. The demolition of the Egyptian army, Rabin claimed, could be done from the air. "Kardom," Rabin fumed, was not on the table. Lior, who was present, noticed something peculiar. All the generals were tired from endless staff meetings, but Rabin most of all. "This is not the same Yitzhak," he noted to himself. Lior was worried enough to seek out the prime minister and tell him about it. A few hours later Rabin had a nervous breakdown.[29]

In his memoirs, Rabin claimed that what truly lowered his spirits that day was not the arguments with Weizman and Gavish; it was his conversation with Minister of the Interior Moshe Shapira, which took place immediately after the morning cabinet meeting and probably lasted no more than five minutes. Shapira was the leader of Mafdal, the national religious party, and one of the chief doves in the cabinet. With his overbearing personality, he dominated debates and was a strong opponent of any use of military force. Rabin badly needed the cabinet to change its position. He did not feel he could prevail over his generals much longer. Had Shapira shifted his position, the rest of the cabinet might have followed. Although Rabin was known as a straight-as-an-arrow officer, he proved rather cunning in this instance. Before he met with Shapira, he had sent Chief Military Rabbi Shlomo Goren to convince Shapira that the IDF could win the war.[30]

It did not help. Shapira was harsh and unforgiving. He berated Rabin for dragging Israeli into the crisis. Ben-Gurion secured an alliance with France and Britain before going to war in 1956, Shapira reminded Rabin. No such thing existed now, and war was out of the question, he shouted. Rabin was at his wits' end. Shapira was the fourth politician he had met with during the last forty-eight hours. The day before he had talked to the heads of Rafi – Ben-Gurion and Dayan – and tried to sell them his "Atzmon" plan. He found no takers. Just like Shapira, Ben-Gurion argued that Israel could not go to war without a military alliance with a major superpower. "You've put the country in a tough spot. You bear responsibility," said the Old Man. Immediately following this talk, his spirits down, Rabin appealed to Yisrael Galilee, a minister without portfolio and Ahdut Ha-Avoda's Number 2. "Yisrael, the army needs to get clear instructions from the government. We cannot navigate in this fog," pleaded Rabin. (Rabin said "we" but was actually talking about himself.) Galilee promised to assist. In the evening, Rabin met with Dayan, who was at least willing to listen to the details of "Atzmon," but then he poured cold water on it. Dayan thought the plan too small and believed the IDF was strong enough to wage an all-out war on Egypt. Rabin muttered that he was sorry he had not hit Syria harder. Dayan asserted that this line of action would have made things even worse. Dayan looked at Rabin closely. He saw a man on the brink of despair.[31] And how could Rabin be otherwise? His attempts to dabble in politics had reached a dead end. He could not bring Rafi into the cabinet to support him and he failed to convince the leader of Mafdal. His staff was conspiring against him. Eshkol, again in a dovish mood, was of no help.

Increasingly anxious and beleaguered, Rabin found comfort in cigarettes and coffee. Nicotine calmed his nerves, caffeine kept him going. Since
the onset of the crisis he had not eaten or slept properly. Anyone who saw
him in the preceding days realized that something was wrong; on May 21
Abba Eban had noticed that the general was chain-smoking and very tense,
describing him as being "in a daze." By the end of May 23, Rabin was
exhausted mentally and physically. The sensation was familiar. He had
suffered from two bouts of nicotine poisoning in the past. After another
tense talk with Weizman, Rabin announced that he was feeling unwell
and left headquarters. Weizman then subverted Rabin's instructions. The
operations branch, which Weizman headed, sent out instructions to the
troops to prepare for a campaign in which the IDF would "destroy
the Egyptian air force, conquer the Gaza Strip . . . and be ready for an all-out
offensive to take Sinai."[32]

The official version, the one later told by Rabin and his wife, Leah, goes
like this: when Rabin got home, Leah noticed he was extremely pale.
Thinking that he was moments away from collapsing, Leah summoned the
chief medical officer, Dr. Eliyahu Gilon, to examine her husband. He told
the couple that in his view Rabin was suffering from nicotine poisoning.
However, all other reports from the time suggest that this version greatly
understates what had really happened to the chief of staff: namely, that Rabin
suffered a severe anxiety attack, from which he did not recover until the end
of the war. Rabin, it seems, was a unique creature: a general with weak nerves.
He himself left a clue as to what ailed him in his autobiography:

> My mother had a heart condition and I worried that a [heart] attack
> would end her life. Every time she had a heart attack, I would run as fast
> as I could to call a doctor, fearing that when I came back, I would find
> her dead. My sister and I spent our childhood in the shadow of this fear
> and took care never to make her angry.

A traumatic childhood begets an anxious individual, and Rabin did not
perform well in stressful situations. He led forces into battle only once,
during the 1948 war. He was no good at it, and Allon quickly brought him
back, to serve by his side as a staff officer. From that point onward, Rabin
served mainly in staff positions.[33]

Gilon, the physician Leah Rabin summoned, was not a psychiatrist. He
was a gastroenterologist. The main reason he was called was that he was
Rabin's personal doctor and the couple relied on his discretion. Gilon was
well aware of Rabin's condition and after the fact told Pinhas Sapir that he

had known for a long time that Rabin would be unable to withstand a national security crisis.

According to Rabin's account, Gilon recommended a sedative injection and plenty of rest. Worried about the effect of the drug, Rabin first summoned Weizman to his home. After struggling with him for the past week, Rabin was now willing to capitulate. In a weak and broken voice, he told Weizman that he believed he had made errors that brought grave danger upon Israel. Rabin suggested that he resign, and that Weizman take his place. Weizman cheerfully encouraged him and advised Rabin to take his time. Following that, Rabin received the injection. Weizman left as Rabin's body lay motionless on the mattress, submerged in a deep sleep. He wasted no time in betraying Rabin's trust. By 7 a.m. the next day, Lior knew the full details of the story. Weizman made it clear that Rabin would take a long time to get better and until then he, Weizman, was in command.[34]

Weizman came up with a new plan dubbed "Axe 2." It combined elements of all of the previous plans, beginning with an air attack, and then shifting to a multi-pronged assault on Gaza and the Egyptian army in Sinai. Barring the superpowers' intervention, the maneuver was due to end on the eastern bank of the Suez. In essence, Weizman had thrown Rabin's beloved "Atzmon" into the wastebasket. He ordered the generals to prepare a set of presentations for a meeting at 5 p.m., to be attended by the prime minister. With Rabin out of the way, the atmosphere during this discussion was different from all those that had preceded it. In the past week, Rabin had cast a melancholic shadow. He would recommend launching an attack against Egypt, but at the same time describe the dangers: he believed that northern settlements would be exposed to Syrian artillery in the first hours of the war, with the IDF unable to do much about it. The war, Rabin warned the ministers on May 23, would be no "walkover." Eshkol later said that Rabin had told him privately that the war might result in tens of thousands of casualties. The generals had always suspected that Rabin was sending the government the wrong signal. They wanted to meet with the prime minister to present their case more forcefully. Now, thanks to Weizman, they had their chance.[35]

They were brimming with confidence. Gavish said that with the forces under his command he could take on the Egyptian army and win. Most importantly, Dado argued that even though he would lack air support during the first hours of the war, he had enough firepower at his disposal to shut down Syria's artillery. He even suggested he could launch a limited attack on the Golan Heights. Narkiss, commander of the central front, asserted that he would be able to conquer the Mount Scopus enclave in

Jerusalem. Hod was the most optimistic and said he had no doubt Operation "Moked" would succeed. All of the speakers emphasized that war should start as soon as possible, otherwise the enemy would find out about Israel's plans for a surprise attack. "The IDF will be ready to launch a war, starting tomorrow," Weizman said. "The time to act is now." Lior's impression was that the generals expected Eshkol to authorize the campaign on the spot. Eshkol refused to budge. He said he was pleased that the military was certain of victory, but this was the time for diplomacy. With that, he left. Lior asked Eshkol later whether he would like to summon a joint meeting of the government and the General Staff to make a quick decision. The prime minister said no.[36]

Weizman, though, still believed that Eshkol would convene the cabinet and give him the authorization. He instructed the IAF to brief the pilots about their battle missions and ordered the southern command to complete preparations for an immediate attack. Gavish was concerned that Weizman was getting ahead of himself. He pointed out that he did not have enough time to complete the deployment of his troops. Weizman barked: "I'm the commander. I gave you an order. Do it!" It was going to be an arduous task. For "Axe 2" to succeed, two divisions had to swap places. Throughout the night of May 24–25, thousands of men and hundreds of tanks, trucks, and armored personnel carriers moved across the sands of the Negev, leaving great clouds of dust in their wake. Ariel Sharon, who commanded one of these divisions, later described the experience as "a mad race of intersecting paths." At 5 a.m. Gavish called Weizman. "Do we have a green light?" he inquired. "Well, not yet," Weizman harrumphed. Gavish and the other generals at southern command were irate. They had been hassled for nothing. Weizman's General Staff colleagues had always suspected him of being foolhardy and irresponsible. During that night, Weizman proved them right. Gavish and the other generals would start a campaign to remove him from command.[37]

What tripped Weizman up was his disdain for diplomacy. He did not grasp the importance of Abba Eban's visit to Washington. Eshkol did not intend to make any significant move until he had heard from his foreign minister. Eban left Israel in the early morning of the 24th. When the generals tried to convince Eshkol to start the war, Eban was still en route. Everything was riding on the results of his upcoming talks with President Lyndon Johnson. Would the White House consent to an Israeli attack on Egypt, or would it act to undo Nasser's unilateral move?

13

FROM YEMEN TO TEXAS

The Graveyard of Nasserism

A T THE END of March 1967, about two months before Abba Eban's plane descended on Washington, Yaacov Herzog came for a visit. Herzog's job title was General Director of the Prime Minister's Office. But this was not what he really did. He had no interest in social and economic affairs and left all such matters to his underlings. Instead, Herzog was Israel's expert on clandestine diplomacy. His portfolio included managing Israel's relations with Jordan, the Maronite Christians in Lebanon, and the tribal warriors in Yemen who conducted a guerrilla campaign against Nasser's expeditionary forces. Herzog, together with the head of the Mossad, Meir Amit, had been involved since December 1963 in a series of secret meetings in London, Paris, and Tel Aviv with representatives of the Yemeni imam, the most senior among them being Prince Abd al-Rahman Yihya, the imam's uncle.[1]

Yemeni representatives informed Herzog and Amit at the end of 1963 that they were running out of weapons and ammunition. The Saudis, they claimed, had stopped giving them military aid. They wanted Israel to supply them with money (specifically gold coins), lobby on their behalf in Washington, and attack Egypt so it would have to withdraw from Yemen. In exchange the Yemenis promised that once they got to power they would recognize Israel and sign a peace agreement with it. Amit detected an opportunity. Aid to the Yemeni rebels could tie Egypt's forces to Yemen and prevent Nasser from launching a war against Israel. After some hesitation the Mossad and the Israeli government decided to take the Yemenis up on their offer.[2]

The Israelis were not the only ones to take a gamble on the Yemeni royalists. The Conservative government in Britain knew that Egyptian intelligence services were fomenting trouble in its colony of Aden in the southern tip of Yemen. It therefore gave tacit support to a group of ex-commandos who acted as mercenaries in Yemen.[3] And so, in late 1963, Mossad agents, Saudi officials, and British mercenaries came together to help Yemeni royalists fight the Egyptians. Neal McLean, a former British intelligence officer and member of parliament, served as a go-between for the Israelis and the mercenaries. This alliance was to be shrouded in secrecy. Only a small group of people in Israel – the likes of Herzog, Amit, Weizman, Rabin, Golda Meir, and Eshkol – were in the know. Israel agreed to fund a consulate of the Yemeni opposition in Paris and to lobby on the Yemenis' behalf in Washington and West European capitals. Most importantly, Israel committed itself to airlift a steady supply of weapons and medicine to the tribal warriors in northern Yemen. The British mercenaries helped the Israelis send Mossad agents – Yemenite Jews who had immigrated to Israel in 1949 – to enter Yemen to find safe locations for a drop.[4]

The first flight took off on March 31, 1964. The plane was loaded with UK-made weapons that the Israelis had captured from the Arab armies in the wars of 1948 and 1956. The point was to make sure that the equipment could not be traced back to Israel. Only the imam and a few of his top brass were aware that Israel was behind this. One Mossad agent recalled that when one of the sheikhs saw the containers being dropped from the sky he exclaimed: "Look, even God is helping the Imam." Even the Saudis, who were told by one of the mercenaries that a supply to the royalists would pass through their airspace, did not know where the planes came from.

Nevertheless, eventually Israel's ploy became public knowledge. The imam spilled the beans in November 1965 while being interviewed by an Italian newspaper. "To thank Israel for all the help it had given me and my people in our war of liberation," he told the interviewer, "I have decided to award it all the mining concessions it would desire." His translator hastened to add, "How would we get along had Israel not given us credit? Who do you think paid for all the weapons, ammunition and cars that we have?" Now the Egyptians, who suspected all along that the Israelis were involved in Yemen and working against them, had proof. In early 1966, during the brief time in which Israel and Egypt were in dialogue through a Mossad agent, Amer said that a precondition to the continuation of the talks was that Israel would stop its airdrops in Yemen.[5]

In May 1966, after the fourteenth airdrop, British mercenaries asked Israel to temporarily halt the airlift. Saudi money had dried up following an oral agreement between Egypt and Saudi Arabia to dampen the flames of conflict, and the mercenaries had to leave Yemen. At that time it became known that Britain had finally decided to withdraw from Aden, annex several protectorates to the colony, and create a new entity: the Federation of South Arabia. The Israelis were quite worried. They thought that Nasser would be able to take over the Federation, thus gaining control of the strategic Bab al-Mandab Straits. Like the Tiran Straits, they were Israel's gateway to Africa and Asia. Someone in the prime minister's office, probably Herzog, prepared a staff paper on all the ways in which Israel could help strengthen the Federation. It recommended that Israel solicit the support of moderate Arab and African countries as well as France and the US. Israel, the memo argued, could help the Federation establish an intelligence service, an internal security force, and an air force, as well as to furnish the Federation with economic aid. A special task force within the Mossad was to be established to study these questions.[6]

And this was the reason that Herzog arrived in Washington at the end of March 1967. He wanted to sell this plan to the White House and get American backing for the creation of a consortium of moderate countries – Herzog apparently mentioned Iran, Saudi Arabia, Jordan, Ethiopia, and Kenya – devoted to strengthening the Federation of South Arabia. Israel was to lead this regional coalition from behind. It had already been working as a subcontractor of American foreign policy in the Third World, particularly in the Congo, training the soldiers and officers of the pro-American forces there (some officers and soldiers also trained in Israel). Israel's on-the-ground operation in the Congo was partially funded by direct White House transfers of $80,000 to Mossad accounts. (Later the State Department passed on an additional $7 million to Israel for that purpose.) Israel's planned operation in South Arabia relied on this shared experience.[7]

As with anything related to Israel's Yemen operation, it was all hush-hush. Herzog's meeting in Washington with Walt Rostow was organized by the Mossad and the Americans emphasized that the meeting was "outside official contacts." Nevertheless, it was agreed that after Rostow and Herzog had talked in private, the Israeli ambassador, Avraham Harman, and his aide would be invited into the room. What Harman heard when he entered startled him so much that his report bore the highest classification possible: "Eyes Only – Top Secret – Send by a special courier." According to Harman, Rostow said that what he had heard from Herzog "is very exciting" and added that he wanted to share some thoughts with the Israelis that he defined as "irresponsible." "A common coordinated action," argued Rostow, "carried out by the different factors in the region, ones with ability to help stop Nasser in Southern-Arabia, has a chance of being successful. In [Rostow's] opinion, it is possible that by then Nasser, who has become somewhat old, will decide that he might be taking too big a risk with an offensive initiative." Rostow, though, hastened to add that American support for the Israeli scheme would be "implicit."[8]

Rostow underlined that it would be important to have King Faisal of Saudi Arabia in on this. Herzog did not share the information with Rostow, but Israel had already contacted Faisal through Neil McLean, the liaison officer with the British mercenaries. In fact, Israeli officials had met with McLean a month earlier in Europe. What brought the two parties together was their shared assessment that the war in Yemen was about to get hot again. Faisal told McLean that he wanted to start supplying the monarchist rebels again but was concerned that the Egyptians would attack him in response. One month earlier, Egyptian planes had punished Saudi Arabia for giving aid and haven to the imam's troops and bombed the Saudi border city of Najaran. Worried about further attacks, Faisal was trying to talk King Hussein into sending a squadron of Jordanian aircraft that would protect Saudi airspace. Hussein claimed that such a step would leave him exposed to an Israeli raid (Samu had occurred only three months earlier), Egyptian air attack, or a Syrian incursion. Faisal wanted to know whether Israel would be willing to promise not to attack Jordan at that time and to commit to protect Jordan if either Syria or Egypt sought to harm it.[9]

The same day that Herzog met with Walt Rostow, Harman went to talk with Eugene Rostow, Walt's brother and under secretary for political affairs in the State Department. Rostow sat silently while Harman delivered his spiel, then said that he would try to sound out the French in his coming trip to Paris. Harman could only interpret this utterance as assent. All in all, Harman was under the impression that Washington was ready to jump onto the consortium bandwagon. Writing to Abba Eban the same day, Harman elaborated:

> As far as the [US] military is concerned we were given an indication that there would be a readiness to consider a number of unorthodox steps . . . In regard to the economic aspect . . . My impressions, from talking with officials in the Administration and some Senators, is that if this is the only problem, the US would find money if there were a way of channeling it [secretly].

Harman's analysis was that US officials in the era of Vietnam were loath to take on new responsibilities in the Gulf. But if Israel was willing to act as a loyal foot soldier, it was most welcome. Harman's punchline arrived toward the end of his letter to Eban: "I would say that one should approach the whole Aden–South Arabian problem in the spirit that it could become a graveyard for Nasser or Nasserism and therefore the stakes are high."[10] With the green light from Washington, the Israelis pursued the matter further. On April 12 Israeli representatives met with a group of Yemeni rebels who called themselves "the Third Force." The Israelis tried to find out whether they would be willing to sign a peace agreement with the Jewish state.

And then, two days later, Rabin landed in Tehran. While in public Iran was keeping Israel at arm's length, in truth the two countries had had a tacit alliance ever since 1961 when Ben-Gurion conducted a secret but fateful visit. Ever since, Iran had been supplying Israel with oil, receiving in return Israeli military technology and fertilizers. Israeli agronomists consulted the Iranian government on how to develop agriculture on arid land. Israeli construction companies such as Solel Boneh were involved large-scale public-housing projects, and when in 1962 the Qazvin province experienced a massive earthquake that killed 12,000 people, it was Israeli companies that were chosen to rehabilitate the area.[11]

Beyond immediate economic interests were the Israelis' regional isolation and the Iranian conservative monarchy's fear of the insidious influence of radical Arab regimes such as those in Syria, Egypt, and Iraq. Iran had also waged a border dispute with Iraq over the Shatt al-Arab River, intensified by the countries' mutual claim to become the hegemon of the Persian Gulf. Israel was a helpful ally to have in that regard. It trained Iranian soldiers, officers, and secret services personnel, and it shared its intelligence on Nasser's regional activities. Most importantly, Israel and Iran cooperated to inflame the Kurdish rebellion in north Iraq. Each wanted to tie down Iraqi forces so they would not be able to attack Iran or augment Jordan's military strength. Iran supplied access, and Israel the manpower and the weapons. As a result the Mossad had its very own station on Iraqi soil. Meir Amit was even able to travel there and meet with Kurdish rebels.[12]

Rabin's goal in coming to Tehran in April 1967 was to find out whether the Iranians would be willing to share the burden of confronting Nasser. In particular, Rabin wanted to know whether the Iranians would be willing to send troops to Yemen. As always, Rabin's sights were on Syria. Were the Iranians to commit their soldiers to Yemen, Nasser would have to send more of his divisions there. The Egyptian dictator's ability to respond to an Israeli operation against Syria would be truly limited under such a scenario. Rabin told the Iranians bluntly that "it is in our mutual interest to deal with [Iraq, Syria and Egypt]. We should contain Nasser in the southern Arab peninsula, neutralize the Iraqis and screw the Syrians." But the Iranians had it the other way around. The Shah and Prime Minister Amir-Abbas Hoveyda wanted to hear from Rabin when Israel would attack Syria. They were deeply worried by Nasser's actions in Yemen and were already scheming with Saudi Arabia and Pakistan to stop him. Israel, maintained the Iranians, was not doing its share. The Iranians were well aware of the Egyptian–Syrian military treaty that obligated Egypt to defend Syria and thought, therefore, that Israel should escalate its conflict with Syria. That way, Nasser would be forced to take his forces out of Yemen and shift them to Sinai. Rabin had to leave Tehran empty-handed.[13]

Surely the most interesting aspect of the story was the American willingness to let Jerusalem play the role of regional policeman. This episode was but one thread in the complex tapestry of American Third World policy. One of the main protagonists was Walt Rostow, the man who gave Herzog and Harman the go-ahead to turn Yemen into the graveyard of Nasserism.

Kennedy, Rostow, and the Politics of Foreign Aid

In 1950, Walt Rostow landed a job as a professor of economic history at the Massachusetts Institute of Technology (MIT). During the 1950s, together with Max Millikan, a professor of economics at the same institution, Rostow became one of the strongest voices in the American policy community calling upon the United States to take an active role in helping developing countries modernize and industrialize. Rostow assumed that all developing countries would pass through a process of modernization in the coming decades. This was bound to exacerbate social tensions and create dislocations. The process of modernization might end up with underdeveloped countries catching the disease of Communism. The United States must be involved in order to guide these societies toward the path of healthy capitalist prosperity. If the US abdicated that role, argued Rostow, it would find itself increasingly isolated with more and more Third World countries succumbing to the temptations of Communism. To do it the right way, the US must invest billions of dollars each year in the developing world.[14]

Thus Rostow preached social equality, urging his country to share its wealth with the world's poor and needy. Little wonder he crossed paths with a young senator from Massachusetts by the name of John F. Kennedy, who felt equally comfortable selling his liberal values using tough Cold War rhetoric. Like Rostow, Kennedy believed that the US should roll up its sleeves and work harder at developing the Third World. He supported the liberation of countries in Asia and Africa from colonial rule and was one of the first senators to call on the French to leave Algeria. He also sharply criticized Eisenhower's policy in the developing world as unimaginative and lacking in purpose.[15]

It was no accident that both the politician and the intellectual came from America's northeast. This was the heartland of US industry, and concentrated there were large corporations that produced the finest industrial machinery – exactly the kind of equipment that newly established factories in the Third World were likely to buy. Of course, US foreign aid always came with strings attached. Recipients of American loans and grants *had* to spend the money *only* on US-made equipment. In other words, foreign aid was a subsidy for industrial machinery producers in the US's northeast and the Midwest. Moreover, foreign aid created technological dependency among recipient states. Once they bought American equipment for a certain sector of their economy, they were hooked. They needed to buy spare parts (again, only from the US) to keep their production lines humming. Their workers, technicians, and factory owners got used to working with American technology. As Secretary of State Dean Rusk explained in 1965: "Aid is a two way street. It opens the recipient state to the products and investments of the donor. Its acceptance is a fractional surrender of sovereignty – an advantage which in the course of time can be built up into a position of commanding influence."[16]

The northeast and the Midwest badly needed that subsidy. During World War II the US federal government had purposefully invested in the creation of military industry in the south and west of the country, leading to a shift of industrial clusters in those directions. States such as Massachusetts (which Kennedy represented), New York, Illinois, Pennsylvania, Connecticut, Ohio, and Michigan were the biggest casualties, losing billions of dollars in yearly revenue.[17]

The idea of foreign aid as a stimulus plan for the American economy was captured in a memorable line that Rostow contributed to Kennedy's speech at the Democratic Convention: "This country is ready to start moving again and I am prepared to lead it." The emphasis was on "moving again," as the US was in a recession. By 1961, the year that Kennedy became president, the deficit in the US's balance of payments had reached $3.4 billion. As in Syria, Egypt, and Israel, the response of the Eisenhower administration was to take recessionary measures: the Federal Reserve increased interest rates and the government cut spending. The results were grim. With 5.5 million people unemployed, Kennedy had to address the issue in his inaugural address: "We take office, in the wake of seven months of recession, three and a half years of slack, seven years of diminished economic growth . . ."[18]

Kennedy's economic advisers were influenced by Keynesian ideas. They looked favorably on government intervention in the economy, especially to mitigate a recession. America's real problem, thought officials such as Walter Heller, chairman of the Council of Economic Advisers, was not the deficit in the balance of payments: that was just the symptom. The real problem was that the US was not growing fast enough. While in Western Europe economies were growing at an annual rate of 4.5 percent during the 1950s, the average rate of growth in the US from 1953 to 1960 was 2.6 percent. Luckily, the US had an immense privilege in the form of the dollar, a reserve currency that anchored the global monetary system. Governments were eager to hold it to back up their own currencies, and banks saw it as a safe asset since it was backed by gold. Kennedy's advisers argued that the US should issue more debt – i.e. print more dollars – to pay for the goods and services it was buying from other countries. In their view, the American financial position was so secure that the US could allow itself to engage in deficit spending to stimulate its economy. Kennedy's advisers claimed that as long as its economy grew briskly, the US would have no problem paying back its debts.[19]

Kennedy used deficit spending to stimulate the American economy in a number of ways, such as tax cuts, the promotion of a global reduction of tariffs and an increase in the foreign aid budget. Promising that the 1960s would be "a decade of development," in 1961 Kennedy pushed through Congress the biggest foreign aid appropriation since the Marshall Plan. The same year, the US committed itself to an Alliance of Progress with Latin America, promising to deliver $20 billion within a decade to develop the area. All this had practical implications for the Middle East. During his election campaign Kennedy had declared that "the Middle East needs water, not war; tractors, not tanks; bread, not bombs." He wasted no time in promoting modernization there. Kennedy kept American technical assistance to Saudi Arabia at a low level, delayed arms sales to Iran, and cut aid to Jordan, all to apply pressure on the Shah and the kings of Jordan and Saudi Arabia to appoint reform-minded prime ministers: Prince Faisal, who promoted female education and the abolition of slavery in Saudi Arabia; Ali Amini, who enacted land reform in Iran; and Wasfi al-Tal, who fought against crony capitalism in Jordan.[20]

Promoting Development and Peace

Kennedy's policies also affected the Arab–Israeli conflict. In 1962 the Kennedy administration signed an agreement with Egypt in which the US committed to deliver subsidized wheat to Egypt for three years. Kennedy's advisers were worried about the US losing its leverage over Nasser by pledging three years' supply in advance, but Kennedy turned such recommendations aside. One of the lessons that the Eisenhower administration drew from its experience in dispensing aid was that it was more beneficial to commit to long-term aid plans. The planning and implementation of economic projects in developing countries were long-view undertakings and Third World leaders needed to know that the US would back them all the way. That was the reason the Kennedy administration asked Congress in 1961 for a five-year authorization for a Development Loan Fund. The Alliance for Progress was another long-term commitment it made. Thus, by signing a three-year wheat-supply agreement, Kennedy was merely implementing the same policy he was enacting elsewhere in the developing world.

Nasser, for his part, returned the favor by promising to keep the Arab–Israeli conflict "in the ice box." This promise expressed the mutual understanding in Washington and Cairo that the conflict could not currently be solved by a peace agreement. The best that could be hoped for was to prevent it from erupting; in other words, to freeze it. By and large, Nasser stood by his word.[21]

In May 1963, Kennedy stated in a press conference: "We support the security of both Israel and its neighbors. We seek to limit the Near East arms race, which obviously takes resources from an area already poor ..." In his relations with Israel, Kennedy sought to bring about changes in Israeli security policies. He was the first president to offer Israel the opportunity to purchase the Hawk missile – a defensive weapon, and one that perhaps presented an alternative to Israel's avowed offensive doctrine. More famously, during the first half of 1963, Kennedy applied strong pressure on Ben-Gurion to allow American inspectors to visit the site of the nuclear reactor that Israel was building at Dimona. The reactor, which was constructed to manufacture the first Israeli nuclear bomb, was a classic example of a project that took resources away from development for the purposes of military build-up.[22] These visits were meant to ensure that, as Ben-Gurion promised Kennedy back in 1961, the reactor at Dimona was built for civilian use. Ben-Gurion, who was eager for Israel to have a bomb, dallied and parried as much as he could. Kennedy persisted and in mid-May 1963 sent Ben-Gurion his toughest letter yet, making clear that he would not budge and allow an Israeli nuclear bomb to jeopardize his administration's campaign against the proliferation of nuclear weapons. A month after receiving that letter, Ben-Gurion stepped down as prime minister. Several of his colleagues and advisers believed that Kennedy played a role in his decision to resign. The Old Man knew that he would have had to confront the US on this issue without any support from his cabinet. As a result of this crisis, the dovish Eshkol succeeded the hawkish Ben-Gurion.[23]

The Anti-Aid Rebellion

From the get-go, Kennedy's aid strategy came under sharp criticism in Congress. The president employed Cold War rhetoric to sell his expanded program to the American public, but the aid went to that conflict's so-called neutrals – those countries that intentionally sought aid both from the US and the Soviet Union, and refused to align themselves firmly with either of the Cold War camps. Such was the case of Jawaharlal Nehru of India, Kwame Nkrumah of Ghana, Sukarno of Indonesia, and Nasser himself. In addition, they sometimes acted against other regional allies of the US. For instance, Nkrumah's intelligence services tried to undermine the government of Togo, while Nasser's activity in Yemen angered Saudi Arabia.

That left the US administration open to accusations that it was squandering American money on unreliable allies. Liberal senators were appalled that Alliance for Progress money was being given to dictatorships in Haiti, Peru, and Argentina. These senators came from the kinds of agricultural or raw-material-producing states which had little to export to developing countries. Such foreign aid skeptics included William Fulbright (D-AR), Wayne Morse (D-OR), Ernest Gruening (D-AK), Albert Gore (D-TN), and Frank Church (D-ID). Republicans were generally opposed as well. They were disappointed that aid recipients had not reciprocated by giving US multinationals greater access to their markets and were queasy about using public investment to spur growth. When these two groups joined hands, Congress became gripped by what the American press termed a "foreign aid revolt." In 1963, Congress slashed Kennedy's original request for a $4.5 billion foreign aid appropriation to $3.6 billion.[24]

To be sure, the Kennedy administration was aware that aid recipients did not respond to aid with gratitude or use it wisely. Still, an argument was made that engaging with these countries was better than cutting them off. In a memo from February 1963, Robert Komer, Kennedy's intellectual alter ego in foreign policy affairs, argued that a proportion of US aid "is for such purposes as buying political leverage, *bakshish* [an Arabic term for bribery], buoying up feeble regimes, preclusion and the like ..." Komer, who served on Kennedy's National Security Council (NSC), also admitted that many of the countries receiving foreign aid did not have "development plans worthy of the name." However, Komer countered, "isn't it cheaper to try to keep Cambodia or Indonesia or Iran afloat and independent by hopefully judicious use of aid ... than let them slide and then mount some massive rescue operation as in Korea or Vietnam?"[25]

Kennedy himself was somewhat exasperated by the behavior of neutral leaders such as Nasser, Sukarno, and Nkrumah. But he was still willing to work with them. In one of his last press conferences he spoke about US–Egyptian relations. The context was another resolution by Congress that sought to limit his power to dispense foreign aid. Alaska Senator Ernest Gruening was able to pass an amendment to block aid to nations preparing aggressive actions against their neighbors. Without naming them directly, the amendment targeted Sukarno (who was embroiled in a confrontation with Malaysia) and Nasser. Kennedy argued, nonetheless, that the severance of aid would limit Washington's leverage when dealing with Nasser and might well produce the opposite effect than Congress wanted. He cited Eisenhower's decision to withdraw an American offer to finance the building of the dam at Aswan – a step that brought about the 1956 Suez Crisis.[26]

At any rate, by the time Congress confirmed a much-reduced foreign aid bill for 1964, Kennedy was dead. His vice president, Lyndon Johnson, a man with a different set of skills and instincts, took over. Gradually he would adopt a new and markedly different policy toward the developing world. For Third World leaders, there was no doubt that the three shots in Dallas that killed the youthful president truly changed history.

Lyndon Johnson and the American South

Looking at Johnson's biography, the assumption would surely be that he would have deeply empathized with the plight of poor countries. He grew up and built his political career in Texas hill country, one of the most underdeveloped parts of the US. He came from a humble background, his father eking out a precarious living from the family farm. Starting off as a high-school teacher who educated Mexican-American children, Johnson felt an affinity with society's underdogs. His wife recalled that when Johnson went to see *The Grapes of Wrath* movie in 1940, he "sat in his seat crying quietly for about two hours at the helpless misery of the Okies."[27]

As a politician, Johnson felt deeply that the economies of the southern and western states were dominated by the economic interests of the northeast. A Texas historian who used to advise Johnson vividly described the state of geographic inequality in 1937. Looking at a map of the US, he saw an L-shaped region stretching from Florida to California and from there to Canada where "millions of people would be playing a game with pennies, nickels, dimes and dollars, rolling them northward and eastward where they are being stacked almost to the moon." Another expert who was close to Johnson, economist Arthur Goldschmidt, claimed that in the 1930s the South had existed as "a kind of a colony of the US."[28]

Elected to Congress in 1937, Lyndon Johnson sounded like a leader of a developing country when he decried the looting of Texas's natural resources by northeastern business interests. During a radio address in 1939, Johnson complained that "Our public utilities in Texas are owned in New York. We have sold our Texas gas and oil to other corporations owned in New York ... We have sold our cotton to be processed with New York and London capital ... What resource haven't we sold to be processed somewhere else?"[29]

If there was one thing that gave Johnson hope, it was Roosevelt's New Deal. Roosevelt poured resources into building infrastructure and electrifying America's south and west. Roosevelt had a special liking for Lyndon Johnson. He observed that his administration's investment plan was changing the economic balance of power in the country and that Johnson "could well be the first Southern President." At the end of the 1930s Johnson's district was awarded $14 million in federal spending for various dams plus millions more for other purposes. Most of the cash ended up in the pockets of Brown & Root, a small road-building company, which was able to grow into a multimillion-dollar business thanks to Johnson's help. In return, George Rufus Brown and his brother Herman, who owned the company, funded Johnson's election campaigns. According to George, he and Lyndon Johnson formed an alliance and swore that "we will not let any of our friends or enemies come between us as long as we are alive."[30]

The federal cornucopia grew even more abundant once World War II came along, as billions of dollars were invested to develop the defense industry in such states as Georgia, Missouri, Texas, and California. The economies of southern and western states, hitherto dominated by a large agricultural sector, were transformed. Finally they had an industrial base of their own and were busy manufacturing the weapons that enabled Russia, Britain, and the US to win the world war. Their economies gained billions of dollars of income as a result. Johnson's patrons benefited directly from that process. Brown & Root built no fewer than 355 vessels during the war and emerged from it as a large engineering-construction concern. During the Cold War the Texas-based company became a major contractor for the Pentagon and built military bases from the Persian Gulf to South Vietnam.

By 1969 it was the largest construction company in the US. Brown & Root never forgot who set them on their way.[31]

In 1943, George Brown gave Lyndon Johnson $17,500 to buy a radio station in Austin. That asset became the basis of Johnson's Texas media empire that was estimated toward the end of his political career at $14 million. In 1948, Brown & Root funded Johnson's senatorial campaign. Because Johnson's victory was narrow (he won by a mere eighty votes), it was challenged in various Texas courts: Brown & Root also helped pay for the battery of lawyers who defended Johnson and convinced the court to ignore the claims of fraudulent returns. Once in the Senate, Johnson strived to create a regional alliance between western and southern senators that would further shift resources toward what was once America's periphery. Since these states' industrial growth was dependent on military industries, members of the western–southern coalition tended to support defense spending. In Johnson's view, Texas was the natural leader of that regional alliance and he himself its natural leader in Washington. Indeed, it was a coalition of southern and western senators who elected Johnson in 1953 to be the Senate minority leader and thus brought him to national attention.[32]

By 1960, Johnson felt his political base was wide enough for him to pursue a presidential campaign, but he lost, to his surprise, to John Kennedy, a candidate much less experienced in politics than he. Losing to a Boston patrician must have stung badly. Nevertheless, once offered the second place on the ticket, Johnson took it. Yet, the vice presidency did not suit him. Kennedy offered him the position only to make peace with the Dixicrats. He did not trust Johnson, and Kennedy's advisers, many of them Harvard graduates, made it known that they considered Johnson to be nothing more than a southern boor.

Picking Friends in the Global South

And so, when Johnson had a chance to leave Washington for trips abroad, he welcomed the opportunity. During his term as vice president, Johnson traveled to no fewer than thirty-three countries. Many such trips took him to the underdeveloped world, where he showed an unusual zeal to practice public diplomacy. In 1961, during a trip to Senegal, Johnson insisted on stopping his limousine in various villages. Treating the trip as if he was running a campaign, he forced the diplomats who accompanied him to walk in the oppressive heat, among mounds of feces, while he pressed the hands of stunned farmers. In one memorable scene, Johnson shook hands with a leper while a baby chewed on a ballpoint pen inscribed with "Lyndon

Johnson." In Dakar, stopping to tour another village, Johnson left the American ambassador sitting in the car while he walked among dead chickens and human excrement to greet the locals. In India, he enthusiastically jumped out of his vehicle when he spotted a local well and mesmerized onlookers by hoisting a bucket and describing how he had drawn water the same way many times before as young boy in Texas.[33] Once he reached power, though, his Third World policy belied his outward generosity.

Kennedy's engagement with the Third World did not sit well with Johnson and he seemed much less enamored with promoting the development of underdeveloped countries. He was an early critic of foreign aid and showed no real desire to fight for it in Congress. He thought that by engaging with the neutrals of the Cold War, the US was wasting its time and money. After traveling in the Middle East in late 1962, Johnson wrote a detailed report with policy recommendations. Unlike Kennedy, who pressured the Shah to introduce democratic and economic reforms, Johnson urged the administration to "accept the Shah, with his shortcomings, as a valuable asset." Moreover, according to Johnson, the US must tell regional allies such as Iran that "they are nearer and dearer to our hearts than are the neutralist states they fear we are wooing at the expense of our friends." Johnson was also explicit about the kind of aid these countries should receive: military aid that would enable them "to maintain their armed forces along the underbelly of the [Soviet] bloc."[34]

Johnson has been described by historians as arriving at the White House with little foreign policy experience. One of his biographers quipped that Johnson was "king of the river and a stranger to the open sea." Observers believed that this inexperience was the explanation for Johnson's less than adroit handling of the war in Vietnam. In truth, Johnson had firm views about foreign policy issues long before he became president. For instance, during his days as Senate majority leader in the late 1950s, Johnson supported Eisenhower's efforts to furnish aid to conservative Middle East monarchies such as Iran, Saudi Arabia, and Jordan. However, he was willing to endorse conservative regimes outside the Middle East as well. Already in May 1961, Johnson expressed his support for South Vietnam's strongman, Ngo Dinh Diem, who took up the cause of the big landlords rather than that of the small farmers. In August 1963 there was a high-level meeting that discussed Diem's fate. Kennedy's advisers were looking for ways to get rid of him, possibly by tacitly encouraging a local coup. Johnson, however, dissented. His argument was similar to the one he made regarding the Shah a year earlier: "[Johnson] recognized the evils of Diem but has seen no alternative to him. Certainly we can't pull out. We must reestablish ourselves and stop playing cops and robbers." Johnson's only other suggestion was to cut aid to Vietnam.[35]

Kennedy's death created a new opportunity for Johnson to change American foreign policy. But at first, he trod carefully. He retained all of Kennedy's foreign policy team although he knew some of them would oppose him. To JFK's men he said, immediately after the assassination, "You're the men I trust the most. You must stay with me." A few years later Johnson was more candid. He admitted that he believed at the time that without Kennedy's advisers to protect him, the eastern elite that dominated the media and the policy community would oppose him simply because he was a politician from the south.[36]

14

A SHORT TETHER

The Empire's Dying Embers

IT WAS A process. But, by the end of 1964, Kennedy's policy of engaging with the Third World had been jettisoned. Johnson chose to align the US's foreign policy with the declining British Empire in Asia and the Middle East. Up to 1963, the UK had been faced with the same situation in Aden and Singapore, both places where it had substantial military installations that anchored its ability to project power in the Persian Gulf and Southeast Asia respectively. These world regions accounted for about £800 million in annual profits for British firms, revenue that an economy afflicted with a growing external debt could not ignore. British policymakers believed that to make Southeast Asia and the Middle East safe for British business, British troops and destroyers had to stay. But political ferment in Aden and Singapore was threatening to inflate defense costs and embarrass the UK.[1]

After withdrawing from the Suez Canal in 1954, the British had turned Aden, their colony in the south of Yemen, into their strategic outpost in the Middle East. The headquarters of British Middle East Command were stationed there, as well as 22,000 troops. It was from Aden that the UK coordinated the efforts to deter Iraq when it threatened in 1961 to annex Kuwait. In 1952 the British built an oil refinery and by the 1960s Aden was the second busiest port in the world. Fast growth in the 1950s and 1960s drew in growing numbers of African, Indian, and Yemeni workers, who labored in the large refinery and military bases. This urban working class resented the British presence and demonstrated against it. The UK wanted to remain in Aden but the government in London knew that it would be accused of practicing imperialism if it clashed with the opposition. In Singapore, the problem was the educated urban Chinese who supported the socialist party, Barisan Sosialis, in growing numbers. The socialists propounded an anti-colonial ideology and were expected to call on the British to leave.[2]

UK decision-makers came up with a similar scheme for both cases. The recalcitrant movements in Aden and Singapore were to be submerged within larger political units – namely, federations. Aden was to become a part of the Federation of South Arabia, in which the conservative sheikhs from the surrounding protectorates, with whom Britain had long-standing relations, were to hold sway. Singapore was to become part of a greater Malaysia that was to be ruled from Kuala Lumpur by Prime Minister Tunku Abd al-Rahman, scion of the royal family and a reliably pro-British politician. This was a clever way for the British to deal with the anti-colonial zeitgeist. Rather than confront their opponents directly, they sought to empower local elites to do it for them.[3]

As long as Kennedy was in the White House, Washington turned a cold shoulder to British attempts to preserve their empire. Kennedy was a sharp critic of European colonialism. As president he applied pressure on France to grant independence to Algeria (which it did by 1961) and forced the Dutch to relinquish their claim on West Irian in Indonesia. He and his administration did not support British plans to create federations in south Arabia and Southeast Asia, much to the chagrin of the UK. Those federations were becoming an obstacle to better relations with Indonesia and Egypt, two countries that were at the heart of Kennedy's efforts to promote Third World development. Both Nasser and Sukarno asserted their roles as regional bosses and in harsh words decried Malaysia and the Federation of South Arabia as artificial creations and a guise for neocolonial policies. Egyptian secret services were giving aid and safe haven to opposition elements in Aden, and Sukarno ordered his army to start a guerrilla campaign against Malaysia, waged along the shared border on the island of Borneo. The Kennedy administration intervened to bring these conflicts to an end by mediating between Egypt and Britain and between Indonesia and Malaya. Three days before his death Kennedy discussed a "package deal" with Sukarno according to which the latter was to end the confrontation in Malaya in exchange for further funds for economic development. He was to be told that Malaya "was a temporary problem which should not be permitted to interfere with our long-range objectives."[4]

All this changed once Lyndon Johnson took over. He chose not only to support the British Empire but also to bankroll it. The reason for this would come to define his presidency as a whole: the Vietnam War. Johnson took a secret decision to escalate American involvement in Vietnam as early as

February 1964 by allowing US vessels to venture into North Vietnam's territorial waters and conduct raids on its shores. Johnson wanted British support for the American war, and for British forces to secure Anglo-American interests in the Persian Gulf and Southeast Asia while Washington was pouring its resources into Vietnam. As with the case of Israel, Johnson wanted the UK to assume the role of the loyal foot soldier. In that spirit, Secretary of State Dean Rusk told the British foreign secretary in March 1965 that due to "our relationship with you we will back you, if necessary, to the hilt [in Indonesia] and hope for your support in Vietnam." In June 1965, NSC staffer David Klein wrote to Johnson's national security adviser, McGeorge Bundy: "It is useful for us to have [the British] flag, not ours, 'out front' in the Indian Ocean and Persian Gulf – in areas where they have strong historical associations. For we might be very much better off to pay for part of their presence – if they really cannot afford it – than finance our own."[5]

This dovetailed with British policies. Britain's pipe-smoking prime minister Harold Wilson wanted to preserve the UK's world role. In the summer of 1965, Wilson declared in New Delhi that "Britain's frontiers lay on the Himalayas." There was one small snag in his plan: the economy. Since the 1950s British governments had had trouble funding a far-flung empire abroad and a generous welfare state at home. Britain, like other countries at the time, was suffering from recurrent balance of payments crises and its currency, the pound sterling, the anchor of its extensive financial industry, was constantly under attack by speculators. Lyndon Johnson came to the rescue. Between 1964 and 1967 the US organized no less than $4 billion in loans to save the British pound. The US feared that under pressure, the Labour government would yield to the speculators and devalue the pound. For the Johnson administration, financial and security concerns were linked. In the same way that British troops in Aden and Singapore were considered by American strategists as part of America's line of defense, sterling was considered the dollar's sandbag. With the Vietnam War's costs reaching $3.6 billion a year, the US's external deficit grew. It was clear to American officials that if speculators were able to defeat the Bank of England, they would move on to attack a weakening dollar. Thus, Johnson's decision to escalate the Vietnam War made the global leadership of the US dependent upon the stability of the British Empire and the pound.[6]

Swiftly, Johnson started turning against Sukarno and Nasser. At the end of 1963 the House of Representatives passed an amendment to the 1964 Foreign Assistance Act. It required the president to determine that aid to Indonesia was "essential to the national interest of the United States." Johnson signed the measure into law in mid-December, and by the start of 1964 he was confronted with what determination he would make. He had no intention of answering in the affirmative. On January 2, in a conversation with Secretary of Defense Robert McNamara, Johnson described Sukarno, who was challenging the British Empire in Southeast Asia, as a bully. Naturally, Johnson also refused Sukarno's request for a meeting and ignored entreaties by State Department officials that he would approve an aid program to Indonesia.[7]

The same dynamic played out when it came to Egypt. Nasser had developed a good working relationship with Kennedy based on lengthy correspondence. He feared Johnson from the beginning, since the Texan politician already had a reputation as a strong supporter of Israel. In February 1964, rumors reached Cairo regarding Johnson's alleged intention to slash economic aid to Egypt and increase military assistance to Tel Aviv. To show Washington that his bite was as bad as his bark, Nasser unleashed a barrage of propaganda on Egyptian radio that called on Libya to end the US military presence at the Wheelus airbase. The signal Nasser sent was clear: if Johnson pushed him, he would push back.

Johnson, though, was unimpressed. On April 2 the NSC convened to take stock of the Egyptian scene. The main speaker was Dean Rusk, exactly the kind of bureaucrat that Johnson liked: self-effacing, mild-mannered, and above all southern (Rusk hailed from Georgia).[8] He enumerated Nasser's bad record. The first item was not Nasser's attacks against the American base in Libya but the "sending of more troops into Yemen rather than withdrawing them, *exerting various kinds of pressure against the British.*" Likewise on April 9, Johnson told Rusk in a telephone conversation that Nasser "has not performed in Yemen, he is undermining us in the Wheelus base . . . I think it's important for Nasser to know that . . . he just mustn't take us for granted on these things." As with Indonesia, State Department officials tried to make the case that the Johnson administration was adopting a bad policy. The policy planning council warned that a sudden cut-off of US aid "could make Egypt into a sort of Middle Eastern China . . . [which] would turn to more radical policies . . ." John Badeau, the ambassador to Cairo and a Kennedy appointee, cited Nasser's moderate influence during the January 1964 Arab summit in Cairo to urge the Johnson administration to "continue to make those contributions to the [Egyptian] economy which will give us maximum political leverage." But such admonitions fell on deaf ears. On April 10, Johnson wrote the British prime minister: "I, of course, have no illusions about Nasser or the mischievous game he is playing." As for Nasser, he was escalating his involvement in Aden with Egyptian secret services supplying arms, finance, and training to the rebels.[9]

Meanwhile, the clash with Sukarno and cooperation with the British were both growing apace. After the American media called on Johnson to cut all economic aid to Indonesia, in late March Sukarno gave a speech in which he asserted that he would tell any country that tried to put conditions on economic assistance "You can go to hell with your aid" (Sukarno made sure to say it in English). In July, Johnson responded by receiving in Washington Sukarno's arch-enemy, Malaysian Prime Minister Tunku Abd al-Rahman. Sukarno, exasperated, made an Independence Day speech in which he counseled his people to prepare for a "year of living dangerously." The Indonesian ruler proceeded to recognize North Vietnam and strengthened his ties with Peking and Moscow.[10]

As US–Indonesian relations were moving toward a confrontation, Washington's relationship with Cairo was teetering on the brink of collapse. This time it was Nasser's intervention in the civil war in the Congo that raised Johnson's ire. The vast African country was torn by inner divisions and the legacy of Western intervention. After Belgium had granted the Congo's independence in 1960, it quickly moved to destabilize the country. The reason was Congo's newly instituted prime minister, Patrice Lumumba, who made preparations to sever economic and military ties with Brussels. Belgium enjoyed highly lucrative mining concessions, especially in the Katanga region, and had no intention of giving them up. The Western nation therefore supported anti-Lumumbist elements in the Congo and was implicated in Lumumba's assassination in 1961. Internecine fighting between the supporters of the deceased prime minister and his Brussels-backed opponents had shattered the Congo ever since.[11]

As in Indonesia and Aden, the Johnson administration took a firm stand in support of the European power. The CIA ran a secret operation to recruit and fund South African and Rhodesian mercenaries whose task was to bolster the corrupt and pro-Belgian Armée Nationale Congolaise (ANC), a local militia. The mercenaries came to the Congo armed with light weapons and resentment; in only the previous year, 1963, had the Organization for African Unity been established in Addis Ababa, heralding the awakening of the black continent. The broad-shouldered Boers and the lanky Englishmen from Rhodesia came to demonstrate that the white man was not going to be kicked out of Africa without a fight. They had little respect for their enemies and no inhibitions. When the mercenaries entered the Congolese town of Boende in late October 1964, they demolished houses, looted stores, and executed whomever they encountered in the streets. The carnage lasted for three days. Pictures of the mercenaries torturing their black victims, hanging them, and using the bodies as shooting targets reached the international press. The Egyptian connection to this story was the support that Nasser gave to the warriors in the pro-Lumumbist forces who were known as the Simbas. The Johnson administration disapproved of that.[12]

In the summer of 1964, units of the ANC, aided by the ruthless mercenaries, gained ground on the Simbas and started pushing them out of their strongholds. The Simbas were desperate. They wanted to buy some time so that African countries such as Ghana and Egypt would be able to send them military assistance. The Simbas thus threatened to execute all the Europeans in Stanleyville, a large city they controlled, if government forces did not halt their advance. As 1,600 men and women were held hostage, negotiations took place between a representative of the rebels and the American ambassador to Nairobi. While the Simbas sought to exchange their hostages for an American commitment to end assistance to the Belgians and their Congolese allies, the US demanded the immediate and unconditional release of all the Europeans in Stanleyville. Meanwhile, the Johnson administration and Belgium stepped up military preparations for a rescue operation codenamed "Dragon Rouge." On November 24, the dragon was unleashed when Belgian paratroopers and white mercenaries stormed Stanleyville. The paratroopers were able to save most of the hostages, and then opened the way to the ANC units and mercenaries who rampaged through town with ferocious rage, looting and killing thousands of people, some European hostages among them. Africa was agog. Stormy demonstrations erupted on the continent. "Hang Johnson" signs were sighted in a Nairobi rally.[13]

Two days later, a demonstration of African students studying in Cairo got out of hand. The students surprised the small contingent of Egyptian policemen that secured the area, marched on the American library in Cairo, and burned it to the ground as an act of retribution for the American involvement in the Congo. An indignant US embassy reacted strongly, demanding an apology and compensation. Nasser was embarrassed. He did not want to destroy his relations with his benefactor, but at the same time worried about appearing as if he was betraying the cause of national liberation movements in Africa. Finally, Nasser decided to offer the Americans both an apology and compensation but he preferred that this arrangement should not be publicized. For Lyndon Johnson, this was not enough. He made the Egyptian ambassador march to his office, then scolded him: "How can I ask Congress for wheat for you when you burn down our library?"[14]

Johnson, though, reacted differently when at the end of 1964 the American library in Kuala Lumpur was attacked not by citizens of another country but by Malaysians. The reason for their anger was that Malaysia had been offered a loan on terms that were inferior to those given to South Vietnam, South Korea, and India. The administration's response was to appease the Malayans by offering an $11 million loan at reduced interest rate (3 percent rather than 5) through the Export-Import Bank and another $5 million as a direct loan.[15] Of course, Malaysia was Britain's ally in Southeast Asia while Egypt was Britain's enemy in the Middle East.

In December 1964, the Egyptian minister of supply, worried about Egypt's dwindling reserves of wheat, met with the American ambassador to inquire whether negotiations for an additional $35-million wheat sale could begin. The ambassador, Lucius Battle, had, according to his report, a "very brief and very tense meeting" and said that he was "unwilling to discuss supplementary food aid shipment under the conditions that exist today." That encounter was relayed to Nasser by Prime Minister Ali Sabri on December 23 as Nasser was en route to Port Said to give a speech. Sabri embellished things somewhat, alleging that Battle had said that the US would cut food aid if Egypt did not moderate its behavior. In the twitchy atmosphere after the recent public clashes between Cairo and Washington, it was easy to believe that story. Like Sukarno three months earlier, Nasser snapped. Improvising on his prepared speech, Nasser proclaimed at Port Said: "The American Ambassador says that our behavior is unacceptable. Well, let us tell those who do not accept our behavior that they can go and drink from the sea ... We will cut the tongues of anybody who talks badly about us."[16]

The burning of the library became a turning point in Egyptian–US relations. The act was captured on film and photographs appeared in the newspapers. American voters were enraged. In the popular imagination the burning of the library played out as Nasser's personal act of ingratitude. And, a month later, Nasser had seemingly added insult to injury by making such a defiant speech. All this played into the hands of the anti-foreign-aid coalition in Congress that at the time was trying to bring about the immediate suspension of wheat shipments to Egypt. Johnson decided to foil their purpose, not out of any love for Nasser but because of the White House's traditional opposition to any attempt by Congress to tie its hands. Dean Rusk was sent to Congress to plead with legislators not to intervene because the administration would soon "shorten the string on Nasser."[17]

The Short Tether in Action

The Johnson administration made good on Rusk's promise. In February 1965, the Egyptian government was informed that, due to strong opposition in Congress, the last installment of the 1962 agreement, which Kennedy had

1 Michel Aflaq, the ideological leader of the civilian Baath, and Salah Jadid, chief of staff and the head of the clandestine military committee which removed Aflaq from power two years after this picture was taken.

2 Victor Grayevsky, the Israeli double agent, in the 1950s.

3 Gamal Abd al-Nasser (left, standing) and Abd al-Hakim Amer reviewing a military parade, July 1957.

4 David Ben-Gurion sits, dejected, as Levi Eshkol makes a speech during the 1963 ceremony at which Eshkol took over Ben-Gurion's position as minister of defense.

5 David Elazar, or "Dado" as he was known, as commander of the northern front. Tanks were his passion; no wonder one found its way onto his desk.

6 Amer, Soviet Premier Alexei Kosygin, and an interpreter during Amer's November 1966 visit to Moscow.

7 A meeting of the Israeli chiefs in Tel Aviv following the outbreak of war between Israel and the Arab states on June 6, 1967. From left to right, Motti Hod, Yitzhak Rabin, and Ezer Weizman.

8 Israeli Foreign Minister Abba Eban undergoing "the Johnson treatment," a cloud of cigarette smoke hovering over both, May 25, 1967.

9 On May 25, 1967, Eshkol (center, wearing the beret) toured the southern front. He already knew that several politicians were trying to remove him from his position of minister of defense. He told his adjutant, Yisrael Lior (far right) that he wanted a picture taken of him, Yigal Allon (second from right) and Rabin (third from right) together – and that it would be the only picture to appear in the press the next day. Eshkol wanted to be seen as leading a team of tough-minded generals. He got the picture he wanted.

10 Rabin (center) talks with Yeshayahu Gavish during the chief of staff's only visit to the front during the war. Gavish talked; Rabin smoked and asked no questions. Rabin then walked back to the helicopter seen in the background. His nerves could handle no more than that.

11 From left to right: Dado, Moshe Dayan, Eshkol, and Haim Bar-Lev try to plot the best way to take the Golan Heights on the final day of the war. Not in the picture, in every sense, was the chief of staff, Rabin.

12 From left to right, front row, are Uzi Narkiss, Dayan, Rabin, and Colonel Rehavam Zeevi, on their way on June 7 to the famous picture at the Lions' Gate. A few minutes later, at the gate, at the crucial moment when the photographer pressed the button, Zeevi turned backwards to inspect something and thus was erased from history.

signed with Nasser, would be postponed indefinitely, as would Egypt's request to negotiate a new multi-year deal. A State Department official informed the Egyptian ambassador, Ibrahim Kamel, that a renewal of wheat shipments to Egypt was dependent on Cairo's willingness to pull back from the Congo and Yemen as well as to moderate its stance toward Israel.[18] Though the rebuff must have stung Nasser, he could have drawn cold comfort from the fact that Egypt was not the only developing country to receive such notice from the US. Having won the 1964 elections, Johnson felt he had a renewed mandate to further mold America's policy in the Third World. Johnson decided that Kennedy's emphasis on long-term American commitments to sell subsidized wheat to developing countries had backfired. In his view, these countries had proved ungrateful. He was particularly irked by the refusal of developing countries to support America's war in Vietnam, which escalated considerably during 1965.

To be sure, it was not only the president who was growing more critical of foreign aid. Congress was as well. Two processes strengthened the already mighty anti-foreign-aid coalition. Since the Gulf of Tonkin resolution in August 1964, Congress had felt that it was losing its control over US foreign policy. The resolution was not a formal declaration of war on North Vietnam, but Johnson behaved as if it were. As time went by, it turned out that evidence for the alleged attack by the North Vietnamese on US ships at the Gulf of Tonkin was quite weak. By early 1966, Senator Fulbright, chairman of the Senate Committee on Foreign Relations, held a series of hearings to get to the bottom of what had happened there. Another incident that eroded the credibility of the president occurred in April 1965 when Johnson sent 23,000 marines to support the military dictatorship in the Dominican Republic. Though he claimed that this small country was under threat of a Communist and Castroist takeover, proof of that was flimsy at best and Johnson seems to have known that at the time. The press also judged Johnson's justification to be inaccurate. Congress members felt cheated yet again.[19]

With the Vietnam War costing $3.6 billion a year, the US's balance of payments crisis was getting worse. Foreign aid opponents therefore had the perfect pretext to call for reductions in all the plans that Kennedy had held in high esteem: direct loans and grants, food aid (a program also known as PL–480), and the Alliance for Progress. Cutting back on these programs seemed like the perfect way to get back at a president who had seemed to ignore Congress when making major foreign policy decisions.[20] Yet, Johnson was not offended by Congress's defiance. In fact, it merely served his purpose.

In 1965 Johnson decided to take control over food aid and ordered his secretary of agriculture not to sign any new agreements. Johnson instructed his administration that all further shipments of subsidized wheat would be made on the basis of short-term rollover contracts. All wheat shipments would be authorized by the president alone, and only after certain political and economic conditions had been met. From 1965 this policy was implemented with regard to India, Pakistan, Brazil, Colombia, Ghana, and Egypt. Johnson's advisers called it "the short tether."[21]

Despite the unpopularity of foreign aid in Congress, implementing the "short tether" was not always smooth sailing. The toughest case to sell was that of India, a country experiencing a severe drought and famine throughout 1965 and 1966. Johnson's argument against food aid for India was that its government messed up by investing too much in heavy industry and too little in agriculture. Until the Indian government mended its ways, maintained Johnson, the release of wheat installments would be done on a month-by-month basis. On other occasions, it seemed that something else was bothering him. After Indian Prime Minister Lal Bahadur Shastri called the situation in Vietnam "really depressing and dangerous," Johnson summoned the Indian ambassador, B.K. Nehru, in July 1965. Johnson told the ambassador that "there was no easy way to settle Vietnam, but constant Indian comments did not help the situation any. In effect, Shastri should keep quiet about Vietnam." Johnson informed the Indian ambassador that he had no intention of authorizing additional shipments of wheat, although he had the legal mandate to do so. Rather, he would put the matter before Congress, which would discuss it and decide. But Congress was in no mood to legislate new aid to India. Its war with Pakistan, which began in August, was used as proof of the wrongheaded agenda of the Indian government.[22]

India was hailed by the Eisenhower and Kennedy administrations as the best bulwark against Chinese domination of Asia, and American officials in the State Department, the NSC, and the Agency for International Development (AID) were applying pressure on Johnson to ignore Congress and feed the Subcontinent. But the president held firm. Talking on the phone with his ambassador to the UN, Arthur Goldberg, in September 1965, Johnson mused aloud: "I've got to make up my mind whether I'm going to send about $35 million a month in giveaway food to India ... I don't see any reason for doing it, although State Department and all the people want us to continue to give away ... They say if you don't, they'll go to Russia." Goldberg suggested an alternative: an oil embargo rather than a food aid cut-off; but Johnson ignored him: "I'm humane, but I don't have to feed the world ... I haven't got any inherent or constitutional requirement that I know of, to furnish it to them ad infinitum." Eventually, Johnson won the tussle with the State Department, and was proud of doing so.[23]

Meanwhile in Cairo, during the spring of 1965, Nasser responded to Johnson's pressure by being on his best behavior. Ten days after speaking with Zhou Enlai, the Chinese prime minister, Nasser leaked the contents of their conversation to Assistant Secretary of State Philip Talbot. Nasser explained to Talbot that China was eager to undermine the Soviet thesis of peaceful coexistence and draw the US into a protracted land war in Vietnam. Nasser recommended that the US declare a bombing pause and allow the Soviet Union to mediate. On the same occasion, Nasser indicated that he had ceased supplying aid to the rebels in the Congo and "stated that Arab water diversion works will not exceed, at least by much, Johnston Plan allocations." Nasser had also agreed to pay $500,000 to the US government to compensate for the damage caused to the American library in Cairo in November 1964. In June and August, Nasser offered himself as a mediator in the Vietnam conflict.[24]

In August, Nasser also reached an agreement with King Faisal of Saudi Arabia on a temporary truce in Yemen (which fizzled out in early 1966). He removed Ali Sabri, who was known to be friendly with the Russians, from the prime ministerial post and appointed the pro-Western Zakaria Mukhi al-Din in his place. Despite all these efforts, it took Johnson, who claimed to still be worried about the response in Congress, another two months to authorize the last shipment of the 1962 agreement. That gesture came with a caveat. The American ambassador was instructed to inform Nasser that any "untoward development" would jeopardize further food shipments. That was in June 1965. Although Robert Komer, still serving in the NSC, was eager to use the improvement in Nasser's behavior to conclude a new food aid agreement, Johnson was not enthusiastic. In October, Dr. Kaissouni, Nasser's economic adviser, traveled to Washington to assure the administration that Nasser wanted "to stabilize his relations with the West in a way that would permit long-term and regular assistance organized through the World Bank." Only then did Johnson allow negotiations with Egypt to be renewed. They were concluded in December in another food aid agreement. But Johnson kept the leash tight. Egypt requested a two-year deal to the tune of $300 million. Johnson authorized only a $55 million, six-month contract.[25]

That was the last hurrah of US–Egyptian relations under Johnson. What Nasser was really after was a long-term agreement such as that he had signed with Kennedy in 1962. He was willing to sign a short-term contract with Johnson in January 1966, but saw it only as a stopgap. In early 1966, the Egyptian government appealed for a one-year extension to the existing contract. Cairo knew that there was no point in asking for two years;

Congress had passed an amendment in late 1965 that specifically targeted Egypt and limited food aid contracts to a year only. The Egyptian government's attempt was rebuffed by the White House. The reason cited by administration officials was Nasser's decision to deepen his involvement in Yemen and his support to leftist opposition forces in Aden.

As for Nasser, he seemed to have realized that the game was no longer worth the candle. Eisenhower and Kennedy had allowed Egypt to pay for US wheat with its own currency, which it could print at will. Johnson, however, insisted on Egypt paying in dollars, which it lacked due to its severe economic situation. From 1962 the availability of cheap wheat had been factored into Egyptian economic planning. Johnson's short-tether policy, however, disrupted any attempt at long-term planning. What was once a steady supply stream became erratic: six months it was on, but in the next six months it was off. Nasser candidly relayed all these thoughts to a Canadian diplomat in December 1966, adding that it would be better for Egypt to avoid dependence on American wheat altogether; from that point on, he said, he would try to purchase wheat from the Soviet Union. (Nasser had already bought 300,000 tons from Moscow during 1965.)[26] It was the end of the affair. In the summer of 1967, when Washington wanted to induce Nasser to climb down from his high horse, it had no leverage. It could not threaten to suspend wheat shipments, because there were none.

On May 11, 1967, Donald Ness, who was in charge of the American embassy in Cairo, sent a colleague in the State Department the following observation:

> In brief, we now face all the dangers inevitably flowing from having pushed Nasser into a financial and food corner and from endeavoring to thwart him within his first two "concentric circles" [i.e. those of Africa and the Middle East]. Now we have the showdown I referred to last October.

Likewise, former Secretary of the Treasury Bob Anderson, who was used by the Johnson administration as an unofficial envoy to Nasser, underlined the link between the US's decision to stop supplying Egypt with subsidized wheat and the regional crisis in 1967. Talking with Walt Rostow on the day Nasser closed the Straits of Tiran, Anderson reported that "[the Egyptian] people are very close to starvation. A month ago when a food ship came into harbor, shopkeepers were instructed to put a sack of flour in front of their shops to prevent food riots. [Anderson] believes we made a serious mistake in cutting off Nasser without food as we did."[27]

15

ARMING THE MIDDLE EAST

IN EARLY 1965, the Johnson administration was groping for a cogent rationale that would explain the shifts in American policy toward the developing world. Walt Rostow was there to offer one. He had been aching to return to the limelight after Kennedy had sent him into exile a year after he had been appointed deputy national security advisor. Kennedy's intellectual romance with Rostow had ended when he discovered that Rostow's hobbyhorse was the Americanization of the conflict in Vietnam. Still convinced that the US should cure underdeveloped countries of the disease of Communism, Rostow authored a series of memos calling on Kennedy to bomb North Vietnam. With no intention of doing so, in November 1961 Kennedy kicked Rostow out of the White House and into Foggy Bottom to head the newly established Policy Planning Council.[1]

Kennedy's death changed Rostow's fortunes. Johnson liked Rostow and his bellicose views that matched his own. In November 1965 Johnson had already been thinking about bringing him back into the fold and appointing him as his national security advisor.[2] Six months earlier, Rostow had submitted to Rusk a proposal for what Rostow termed the "Johnson doctrine":

> It is our interest in each of the regions of the Free World to assist in the development of local arrangements which, while reducing their direct dependence on the United States, would leave the regions open to cooperative military, economic and political arrangements with the US. This requires of us a systematic policy designed to strengthen the hand of moderates in the regions and to reduce the power of extremists – whether those extremists are Communist or ambitious nationalists

anxious to take over and dominate their regions. We are for those who, while defending legitimate national and regional interests, respect the extraordinarily intimate interdependence of the modern world and pursue development and peace rather than aggrandizement.[3]

Two weeks later, talking with Harman, the Israeli ambassador, Rostow described Third World leaders such as Nasser, Sukarno, Ben Bella, and Nkrumah as "people who were making trouble by attempting to establish hegemony in their regions. [Rostow] referred to them as 'pocket Bismarcks' forcing on the US in each case a containment policy." Rostow agreed with Harman "that in each case, if the head would fall and be replaced by someone of the same views it would nonetheless be an advantage because it would remove a charismatic personality."[4]

This line of thinking also explains why Rostow, now serving as national security advisor to the president, was so pleased by Herzog's proposal on March 1967 that Israel would take the Federation of South Arabia under its wing. It meant that Israel was fulfilling exactly the kind of role that Rostow allotted to Washington's regional allies. Talking with Herzog, Rostow celebrated the fact that:

> When you look at the political developments of recent years, it turns out that there has been an "evaporation" of the Afro-Asian coalition as it was perceived by the world when this coalition was established, that is – a radical body which includes all developing countries. This is no longer the case. What we are witnessing in present times are the regional-coalitional unifications. There is an Asian unification, an African one and a Latin-American one. The radical Afro-Asian coalition ceased from representing the whole developing world. President Johnson fully supported the development of the regional coalition.[5]

Rostow believed that the moderates, whom he described in his memo to Rusk, would be able to confront regional extremists only if they were armed. So, while Lyndon Johnson tightened his grip over food aid shipments, he opened the doors of the American arms market to a select group of US regional allies: Malaysia, post-Sukarno Indonesia, South Vietnam, Turkey, Iran, Saudi Arabia, Jordan, and Israel. In March 1965, for instance, the Johnson administration signed two arms deals with Israel and Jordan. Israel bought 210 Patton tanks (for $32 million) while Jordan purchased 100 Patton tanks and 50 armored personnel carriers (APCs). In mid-1966 there was another round of sales to Israel and Jordan. The Jewish state bought forty-eight A-4 Skyhawk planes for $72 million, while Jordan purchased thirty-six second-hand F-104 jets.[6]

At the end of 1965 came Saudi Arabia's turn. The desert kingdom wanted to ensure that Egyptian MiGs, flying daily in Yemen's skies, would not be able to penetrate its airspace. King Faisal signed a joint contract with Britain and the US in December. It was a large arms deal in Middle Eastern terms: the king agreed to pay $400 million for ten batteries of Hawk missiles and three squadrons of a UK-made interceptor. In a subsequent meeting between Johnson and Faisal, which took place at the White House in June 1966, the president told the king that he was troubled by "How Moscow exploits local nationalists like Nasser." Johnson stressed that "we will not let Saudi-Arabia get swallowed up" and explained that he wanted to work with Faisal "to fill the gap the British will leave in South-Arabia and the Persian Gulf [when they leave Aden]." Three months later Johnson authorized an additional $100-million sale of military trucks and jeeps to Saudi Arabia.[7]

Johnson had no intention of leaving behind another loyal Persian Gulf ally who was fuming in the wings. The Shah had long been frustrated by Kennedy, who limited arms sales to Iran in order to pressure the Shah to spend more money on Iran's development and less on his army. However, during the mid-1960s, Iran was in the midst of an industrialization drive fueled by increased oil revenue. As a result, Iran was posting impressive annual growth rates – above 8 percent. In June 1964 Johnson claimed that "what was going on in Iran is about the best thing going on anywhere in the world." A month later the president authorized arms credit to Iran to the tune of $200 million. Since the Shah's appetite for new weapons was bottomless and he kept applying pressure on the US for more, in early August 1966 the president approved another $200 million in arms credit and agreed to sell the Shah thirty-two F-4 Phantom planes – the US's most advanced fighter-bomber.[8]

As president, Johnson turned Kennedy's Middle East policy upside down. While Kennedy shipped $413 million of subsidized wheat to Egypt following the signing of a three-year contract, Johnson gradually closed the spigot and authorized the sale of $800 million-worth of weapons to Middle Eastern countries. He was also the first president to sell Israel offensive weapons. While Johnson was considered by contemporaries as too preoccupied with Vietnam, he was personally involved in each of these arms deals. Quite often he had to fight against the resistance of Kennedy's holdovers (such as Rusk, McNamara, and Komer) who thought that Johnson was authorizing too many arms deals. Some senators criticized what Johnson was doing. Senator Fulbright argued in November 1966 that such sales were stoking an arms race in the Middle East. In April 1967 several congressmen and senators criticized American arms exports to conflict regions. As a result, the passage of the Military Aid bill was under threat. But Johnson, who readily cited resistance in Congress to explain his decision to halt food aid to India and Egypt, ignored such voices.[9]

In internal correspondence, Johnson's administration usually presented itself as a prisoner of circumstance. The 1965 arms deals with Jordan and Israel were vindicated by the fear that Jordan would purchase weapons from the Soviet Union. The king, at least, threatened more than once to do so. Once the administration decided that the arms deal with Jordan was inevitable, it had to contemplate the response of the Jewish lobby on Capitol Hill. To make sure that the deal with Amman would not be derailed in Congress, Johnson decided to authorize a parallel deal with Israel. Likewise, the arms deals with Saudi Arabia were intended to make sure that it would be strong enough to confront Nasser's encroachment in Yemen, and the one with Iran was needed to bolster Tehran's ability to withstand a Soviet invasion. Besides, like King Hussein, the Shah held a gun to Johnson's head: he threatened to buy weapons from the Soviets, and in January 1967 even signed a $110-million arms deal with Moscow.[10]

However, upon closer scrutiny, many of these arguments seem like pretexts. To begin with, the president had been little concerned when warned by the State Department and members of his staff that the refusal to supply aid assistance to Egypt and India would mean that they would strengthen their ties with Moscow. He ignored these warnings, although it was easy to see how India and Egypt, countries that had adopted central planning and nationalized large parts of their economies, could become close allies of the Soviet Union. Conversely, it was highly unlikely that the Jordanian and Iranian monarchies would ever allow themselves to become dependent on Moscow. King Hussein did threaten to buy planes and tanks from the Soviets but there was really no chance that the conservative monarch who ruled a divided and polarized society would allow Communist technicians into his country. Soviet instructors were bound to arrive, since Jordanian officers had trained with UK- and US-made weapons and had no experience in using Soviet equipment. The idea that Soviet officials would have direct access to Hussein's army – which was the best guarantee for the survival of the Jordanian monarch – must have sent shivers down Hussein's spine.[11]

Indeed, Israel itself complained that it was losing in the arms race to Egypt, but that was certainly not a matter of urgency as long as the best part of Nasser's army was wallowing in Yemen.[12] The Saudi army was a weak fighting force and it was doubtful that any arms deal, however large, would really make it a match for the Egyptian expeditionary forces. Indeed, in early 1967, when Faisal feared that Egyptian MiGs would attack Saudi Arabia, he doubted his air force so much that he resorted to asking Hussein to send him a squadron of the Jordanian Air Force.[13]

Finally, there was the Shah. The arms deal he signed with the Soviets had been concluded only *after* Johnson had authorized $400 million in military credits to Tehran. In any case, even then, the Shah had limited his shopping list to light weapons that would not put him in a position of technological dependence on Moscow. Like Hussein, the Shah had good reasons to fear close contact between his army and Communist advisers. Historian Andrew Jones, who studied the story in depth, concluded that "the Shah never had any real intention of vitiating or even seriously jeopardizing Iran's alliance with Washington." At the time, Rusk and McNamara advanced the argument that the real threat was not an Iranian defection to the Communist camp but rather instability in Iran due to the overinvestment of the Shah in military rather than civilian projects.[14]

A case was made at the time that with the US's deteriorating balance of payments, Washington could ill afford to lose lucrative export opportunities. For instance, when considering the Shah's request, Rostow wrote to Johnson: "Since he is determined to buy arms somewhere ... if we cannot dissuade him, no point in losing a good sale."[15] This argument made sense when it applied to states that had cash in hand, such as Saudi Arabia and Iran. But even when they did not, the Johnson administration found ways around it. Two other up-and-coming clients of American defense industries in the 1960s, Israel and South Vietnam, were far less endowed with natural riches. Thus, their expenses on weapons were partially waived via a presidential decree which determined that they were eligible for food aid (although according to the Food Aid law they were not considered poor enough). And so, while Israel paid the US $100 million for Patton tanks and Skyhawk jets, in 1964–67 it also received $100 million in subsidized wheat from the US to cover its military expenses. During the same years, South Vietnam received from the Johnson administration $350 million in subsidized wheat to cover its military purchases in the US.[16] Such arms deals – amounting to almost half a billion dollars – clearly could not improve the US's balance of payments.

An explanation of US arms policy in the Middle East during Johnson's presidency came in April 1966 when the Israeli ambassador, Avraham Harman, met with Stewart Symington, a Democratic senator from Missouri. Symington told the ambassador that the US should sell Israel whatever Israel needed to ensure its security but, while he understood why Israel requested economic aid, he could not be of assistance. In fact, Symington revealed that the previous year he had voted against the Foreign Aid bill as a whole. He

cited the American balance of payments crisis as the reason for his opposition.[17] Symington represented a state whose aerospace industry was the
main engine of its growth. More sales of American jets meant more jobs for
his voters, especially in the St. Louis area. He was only serving them well by
taking these positions. Symington was just one member of the southern–
western coalition that Johnson put together while he was a senator – the
coalition that brought him to power and supported him in the Senate. States
in these regions were dependent on military industries and thus could
benefit from widening opportunities for export.

In this way, Johnson's generosity toward Israel in the years leading up to
the Six-Day War was part of a general pattern. It is true that Johnson had
identified the Jews as a rising pressure group in the Democratic Party at an
early stage, and voted as congressman and senator for Jewish causes.[18] The
existence of a well-organized Jewish community definitely helped to
advance Israel's cause in Washington, but it was not the only reason that
Johnson made Israel the US's strategic ally in the Middle East. Johnson
exhibited the same kind of magnanimity toward Iran, Jordan, and Saudi
Arabia, which did not have a substantial ethnic lobby to support them.

As in the case of Iran, Johnson found the State Department and the
Pentagon to be in his way. They wanted to squeeze concessions out of Israel
in exchange for weapons, the most important being an Israeli agreement
to open the reactor in Dimona to regular American inspections. In order to
overcome these bureaucratic obstacles, Johnson created a backchannel to
the Israeli government that consisted of Jewish donors to the Democratic
Party, such as Abe Feinberg and Arthur Krim, which carried oral massages
from Johnson to Israeli diplomats. Two other Jewish officials, Arthur
Goldberg and Abe Fortas, were also used as errand boys. Thus, a dual-track
communications system existed between Washington and Jerusalem during
the Johnson years. The formal channel is documented in numerous State
Department telegrams and memos. The Jewish backchannel survives
mainly within dusty Foreign Ministry files in Israeli state archives.

The fact that Washington was talking to Israel out of both sides of its
mouth – one side issuing harsh utterances, the other more sympathetic –
created tensions in the Israeli elite during the weeks that preceded the
Six-Day War. Those who wanted to get the war going used messages that
arrived via the Jewish backchannel as proof that the White House had given
the green light to an attack against Egypt, while those who wanted to avoid
war clung to the correspondence with the State Department as proof that a
diplomatic solution could be found.

16

SECRET LIAISONS

On the Importance of Unuttered Words

IN JUNE 1964, Eshkol came to Washington for a fateful visit. He was worried that Johnson would bring up the tricky subject of the reactor in Dimona and demand that Israel allow American inspectors to visit it regularly. Other than that, Eshkol was eager to get an American commitment to supply Israel with offensive weapons, preferably tanks.

He worried needlessly. With the US elections on the horizon, the president had other things on his mind. Before Eshkol met with Johnson, Averell Harriman, under secretary for political affairs at the State Department, took aside Deputy Defense Minister Shimon Peres, a member of the Israeli delegation, for a talk. Harriman spoke first: "I am a politician, you are a politician. Let's talk as politicians do ... I want you to know that President Johnson has an interest that Mr. Eshkol would continue to serve as Prime Minister. We believe that Mr. Eshkol is interested that Mr. Johnson would continue to serve [as president]. One can presume that Mr. Johnson will remain in office for another eight years." Peres: "One can presume that Mr. Eshkol will remain in office for another five years." Harriman: "You will have nothing to worry about during this time ... Johnson's special relation with you ... is very clear. We have a few years ahead of us to do things together." In the subsequent talks Johnson raised the nuclear issue and suggested that Israel should allow inspection, but he did not press it.[1]

It turned out that Harriman delivered a crucial clue about the way Johnson would handle things. The content of his talk with Peres was suggestive rather than indicative. A political deal was implied but was not spelled out. Johnson was facing elections in November 1964. Eshkol's own elections were approaching in November 1965. Johnson needed Jewish votes to win. Eshkol needed the nuclear issue to be dormant. Rafi had already attacked him for allowing American inspectors one visit to the nuclear reactor at Dimona in December 1963. He did not want to relive the experience.[2]

Harriman's emphasis on the assumption that it was in both leaders' interests that the other would continue to serve in office seemed to allude to the political timetable. A bargain was implied: Jewish votes in exchange for quiet on the nuclear front. That was how Johnson did business with Israel. Words not uttered were more important than those that were.

In March 1965, for instance, negotiations between Israel and the US regarding a tank sale were approaching the home straight. Averell Harriman and Robert Komer came to Israel to iron out the final details. The State Department wanted to squeeze a string of concessions from Israel in return. One of them was that Israel should stop taking "premature preemptive action" against Syrian diversion works. State Department officials were convinced that Syria had neither the technical expertise nor the financial resources to follow up on its threats to implement the diversion project. The Israeli military, nevertheless, was adamant that it should take action. Rabin invited Komer and Harriman to join him on a helicopter flight above Syrian diversion sites. As they were hovering above the Syrian border, Rabin pointed out to the American officials that Israeli tanks stationed at the front could blow up Syrian tractors without crossing the border. Harriman and Komer listened with interest and said nothing. Rabin reported this back to Eshkol, who interpreted their silence as assent. In the following months, Eshkol's cabinet continued to approve operations against Syrian diversion sites.[3]

This was not the last time that the White House pointed Jerusalem toward Damascus. Washington encouraged Israeli operations against Syria after the Samu operation in November 1966. The Johnson administration reacted harshly to the Israeli raid on Jordan and threatened to cut the supply of weapons. At the same time, American officials expressed their amazement that Israel did not attack the Syrians instead. Unlike Jordan, a pro-Western monarchy, Syria was, in Rostow's parlance, a regional extremist, and thus fair game. Shortly after the Samu raid, Under Secretary of State Nicholas Katzenbach explained to Abba Eban the absurdity of Israel's decision to attack Jordan rather than Syria. It was, he said, as if he wanted to slap the Israeli ambassador but as he could not do so, smacked the ambassador's secretary instead.[4]

Four months later, in March 1967, a group of administration officials toured the northern front. Both Yariv and Rabin briefed them about Fatah attacks and made it clear that Israel was making preparations to retaliate soon. None of the Americans raised any objection. Moreover, one of them, Townsend Hoopes, a senior Defense Department official, told his hosts: "The Syrians are sons of bitches. Why the hell didn't you beat them over the head when it would have been the most natural thing to do?" At the end of that month, Harman talked with Eugene Rostow at the State Department. He claimed that Syria was becoming a Middle Eastern Cuba. Rostow's only response was to ask whether there had been a lot of incidents lately. Following this conversation Harman wrote Jerusalem that he was no longer opposed to a military operation against Syria as long as it would "come only after sustained and obvious provocation of a dramatic nature."[5]

These signals from Washington were well received by the Israeli General Staff. Three days after the massive air battle on April 7, 1967, Rabin told his generals: "There are some Jews [i.e. ministers] among us who think that they understand the Americans. The Americans could not tell us: 'go screw them' [i.e. the Syrians]. But when you screw [the Syrians] – they are happy even if they would not say that." One month later, Walt Rostow admitted that "A week ago, I would have counseled closing our eyes if Eshkol had decided to lash back at the Syrians. We just don't have an alternative way to handle these terrorist raids that are becoming more and more sophisticated. Unfortunately, however, [Eshkol's] own public threats seem to have deprived him of the flexibility to make a limited attack today."[6]

The White House vs. the State Department

It was thus from the very beginning. The White House and Congress were dependent on public support and therefore were more sensitive to the mood of the Jewish-American community. Those at the State Department and the Pentagon were appointed officials: they tended to think of state interests first and domestic constituents last. Except for a few sympathetic officials, these two departments saw Israel as a strategic pain in the neck rather than as a strategic asset.[7] This was something that Zionist diplomats were quick to discern, and the whole point of their activity in Washington following the end of World War II was to convince the American president, Harry Truman, to decide against the advice of the State Department and support the establishment of a Jewish state in Palestine. Running behind in the polls of 1948, desperate for votes and campaign contributions, this is exactly what Truman did.[8]

Likewise, Israeli diplomats during the 1960s were aware of the White House and the State Department's differences of opinion. During the

Johnson administration, the cause for disagreement was not just institutional but also biographical. In 1948, Senator Johnson worked behind the scenes to facilitate the flow of American weapons to the Israeli army. During the same year, Dean Rusk, as a mid-level official in the Department of State, fought against Truman's decision to support the creation of Israel. Two decades later, the former was president while the latter was his secretary of state. They saw most things eye to eye – for instance, they were both Cold War hawks – but they did not agree on the Israel issue.[9]

Israeli diplomats were well aware of that. In March 1966, Ephraim Evron, minister at the Israel embassy in Washington, complained to Harry McPherson, Johnson's speechwriter, that most State Department officials made their careers in Arab countries. As a result, they had pro-Arab views and took a hostile approach toward Israel. Recently, Evron claimed, while Secretary of Defense Robert McNamara was willing to move ahead with the Skyhawk deal, the State Department sought to delay and derail it. McPherson's response was typical. He said that if Evron was having trouble with State Department people, he could always approach him.[10]

In April 1967, Avraham Harman, the Israeli ambassador, observed that "it is true that today [Johnson] personally needs us very much . . . However, we must remember that the political and security elite which sets America's policy towards us does not take into account President Johnson's personal needs but the clear interests of the US alone, as they see them." Moshe Bitan, head of the North American desk at the Israeli Foreign Ministry, who received the letter from Harman, had his own theory:

> There is a self-sustaining mechanism here: Yisashar [Johnson's code-name in Israeli diplomatic correspondence] is the ultimate decider on all matters relating to Israel, even small ones. This infuriates officialdom, especially senior officials, in the Pentagon and the State Department. My opinion is that the almost total opposition to what we ask for is not the result of rational considerations but, most likely, a reaction to us going directly to Yisashar and Yisashar talking to us on these matters through his friends.[11]

State Department officials were well aware of what the Israelis were saying about them behind their backs. They claimed that Israeli diplomats were trying to create "a convenient fall guy" for their frustrations with American policy and hoped to "convince a few more Israelis that the Department of State is not a uniformly heinous institution." They noticed that the Israelis were "widely plugged into Washington" and used their direct access to the White House and Congress to bypass them.[12]

In February 1967, Walt Rostow wrote a memo to Johnson preparing him for a future meeting with Arthur Krim, a Jewish film producer who served as a go-between for Johnson and the Israeli embassy. Rostow's briefing was in his view "a neat and straightforward statement of what we've done for Israel and how our relationship has been pretty much a one-way street." These harsh words made little impression on Johnson. One month later, after a mundane meeting about the wage demands of train workers, Johnson pulled his interlocutor, lawyer David Ginsburg, aside. Ginsburg, a lifelong friend, often spent time at the White House although he had no official title. Johnson told Ginsburg that he had not forgotten that 95 percent of the Jewish community voted for him. Furthermore, "He [Johnson] remembers his friends well and they can rely on him. He would have liked Ginsburg to quickly come up with a detailed plan for him, containing things he can do, as the President of the United States, for Israel. The President then added that he assumes he will face objection from those 'sitting below' (meaning Walt Rostow and the State Department) and in the Congress. However, he is confident he can achieve his goals." Ginsburg, somewhat astounded, reported the president's message to Evron.[13]

A month later, Ginsburg came to the Oval Office with a list that the Israelis helped him to write. The main item was a request for the sale of 100 APCs (the Jordanians had received some in recent weeks and the Israelis wanted a counter-sale to balance that). Ginsburg described Johnson's response as warm and positive. The president promised he would start working immediately to get the process going. Johnson expected the State Department's and the Pentagon's response to be hostile. To prove his point he let Ginsburg read a memo submitted to him by Under Secretary of State Nicholas Katzenbach and McNamara, opining that a positive response to Israel's request would be "a serious mistake." Johnson did not despair, though, and told Ginsburg that "[we will] need to bypass them." It proved a difficult task.

A day after he met Ginsburg, Johnson talked with Abe Feinberg, a Jewish banker who also played a significant role in the backchannel arrangement. Johnson said that he had already received the comments of the State Department and the Pentagon in response to the Israeli memo. Unsurprisingly, they were against the sale. Johnson said that he did not know how to overcome McNamara's resistance. He would have to think of something. Most urgently, the president wanted to have the report of American inspectors who were to visit the reactor at Dimona the next day. Johnson said that if the report was positive it would be easier for him to overcome the State Department's resistance.[14] Dimona, of course, had been a contentious problem in Israeli–US relations since 1960. But Johnson had his own unique way of circumnavigating the issue.

Nuclear Compromise

When the matter was first brought up during the talks between Eshkol and Johnson in June 1964, Eshkol simply promised that Israel did not intend to produce nuclear weapons. Johnson on his part promised that he would work to arrange the sale of Patton tanks from West Germany to Israel. That would have enabled Johnson to overcome the State Department and Pentagon officials' traditional aversion to direct weapon sales to Israel. Thus, an informal agreement was struck between Johnson and Eshkol: American offensive weapons in exchange for Israeli agreement to remain a threshold state (a state that has the knowledge and capability of assembling a nuclear bomb but does not act on it). Johnson, for whom non-proliferation was far lower on the list of priorities than was the case with Kennedy, could live with that compromise.[15]

As was the case with the Shah and King Hussein, who agreed not to buy weapons from the Soviets – a step they had no intention of making – in exchange for American arms, Eshkol was also trading with something he did not really value. As minister of finance under Ben-Gurion, he had opposed the creation of the reactor in Dimona, and during several cabinet meetings had protested that the prohibitive costs of the project were diverting resources from social services such as education and healthcare. Eshkol even went as far as trying to convince Knesset members to vote against a special budget request to allocate funds for the reactor. When he became prime minister the reactor was an established fact. Shutting it down was a sure way to a confrontation with Ben-Gurion in the public arena where the Old Man would have the upper hand.[16]

Instead, Eshkol chose to slow down the race toward a bomb, and had started doing so even before he met with Johnson in June 1964. Already in July 1963, CIA Director John McCone asserted that the Israelis "have not shown much activity in the nuclear field recently." Four years later, in March 1967, the American ambassador to Jerusalem, Walworth Barbour, reported that "my own impression from such information as is available to us is that Dimona is not running at full blast." Moreover, Eshkol was thinking about using the reactor as a bargaining chip as early as September 1963. Talking with his senior security officials, Eshkol suggested that he would tell Kennedy, "If you want it, there will be no [nuclear weapons]. [But] give us something else which will deter [Arab countries from attacking Israel]."

And he elaborated: "That's why I say, [let's] exchange [nuclear] deterrence with [conventional] deterrence ... I do not destroy Dimona, I wait with Dimona" – that is, he would not move toward making a nuclear bomb in order to give the negotiations with Kennedy a chance: "... even if we lost a year [waiting for Kennedy to respond] it's worth it."[17]

The agreement between Johnson and Eshkol was formalized during the March 1965 talks over the tank sale. What brought these talks about was a leak in late 1964 that revealed the delivery of tanks from West Germany to Israel. The West Germans, worried about antagonizing their Arab customers, agreed to supply Israel with the tanks as long as this arrangement remained a secret. Once it was exposed, the German government stopped sending further shipments. Now the Israelis wanted the US to supply them directly. Johnson had to confront State Department and Pentagon resistance. Both demanded in exchange for the tanks Israel's agreement to international inspection of its nuclear facilities.

That was the demand that Komer and Harriman raised during the negotiations with Israel in March 1965. Eshkol did not budge as he knew that Johnson did not really support this position. The end result was a strengthening of the June 1964 understandings. Komer and Eshkol signed a memo that included the following clause: "the Government of Israel has reaffirmed that Israel will not be the first to introduce nuclear weapons into the Arab–Israel area." Eshkol later told the cabinet that he reached an oral understanding with Harriman before the memo was signed. According to Eshkol, Harriman had told him that "everything could be ready [in Dimona] up to the last pin, but you will not put that last pin in place." Johnson now could use the memo to prove to the State Department that he had got Israel to agree to an important concession. The tank sale went ahead.[18]

Following State Department pressure, Eshkol approved only four visits of American inspectors to the reactor in Dimona. Fearful of Rafi criticism, Eshkol dallied and haggled before each. The inspections were not really worthy of their name. The visits were scheduled months in advance, which allowed the Israelis to build ghost elevators and false corridors to hide sensitive parts of the Dimona complex from the inspectors. The visits took place always on Saturdays when all staff were off, so that the inspectors would not be able to talk with them. The inspectors were shown technical reports in Hebrew although they did not speak the language. They were also not allowed to take ground samples to measure radioactivity. And the CIA, which had superior knowledge about the current state of the Israeli project, refused to brief them. As a matter of fact, the inspections were a charade – and the inspectors knew it. Nevertheless, they dutifully carried out their role, writing detailed reports at the end of each visit which concluded that Israel was not pursuing the building of a bomb.[19]

Regardless, the visits became the sandbox in which the State Department, the White House, and the Israeli government frolicked. The State Department demanded the inspections, the Israeli government begrudgingly allowed them, and the White House used them to legitimize arms sales to Israel. The same thing happened in 1967. The American team that visited in April found no evidence of weapon-related activity at Dimona. Johnson used it to brush off Pentagon and State Department opposition, and in mid-May told Feinberg that Israel would get a $72 million aid package that would include the 100 APCs that Israel so desired.[20]

17

ABBA EBAN'S TIN EAR

ERUDITE, SUAVE, URBANE, eloquent. These were the words Abba Eban would have used to describe himself. His colleagues would have probably grasped for different adjectives: long-winded, verbose, vain, attention-seeking. For starters, sending Abba Eban to Washington was his idea. He raised it first on the morning of May 23 during a meeting with the Foreign Ministry staff. Moshe Bitan, head of the North American desk, remembered that Eban could offer no meaningful explanation as to why he had to go. To Bitan, Eban seemed panicky. The only rationale Eban put forward was that he had to talk with Western leaders – he was planning a stopover in Paris and London. Bitan was in the room before the cabinet meeting when Eban broached the idea with Eshkol. Eshkol shifted uneasily in his chair, saying that he could not decide at that moment – he would have to consult with other people. Then Eshkol suggested that someone else should travel to Washington. No names were mentioned, but it was clear he was thinking of Golda Meir, the former foreign minister. Meir's forceful personality and her strong connections to American Jewry could have served Israel much better in the negotiations with Johnson. "Maybe it is not a good idea for you to go," mused Eshkol aloud. "There will be government meetings and we'll have to consult with you." But Eban was adamant that he – and only he – should go to Washington. Otherwise, he would resign.[1]

The same conflict arose at the cabinet meeting. It was Abba Eban – not Eshkol – who raised the idea of sending himself to Washington. Eshkol countered that his preference was to send a letter to Johnson. But other ministers supported Eban's request to make the trip and Eshkol capitulated.[2] Nonetheless, Eshkol saw a silver lining in Eban's voyage. From an early stage of the crisis Eshkol had used the messages he received from the State Department to push back against the generals' pressure to start the war. These missives specifically requested that he avoid taking any military measures at this stage. Eshkol's argument, therefore, was that the Americans must be consulted before any decision could be made. Thus, Eban's trip to Washington should buy Eshkol precious time. Since it would be unseemly for the cabinet to make a decision while the foreign minister was talking to the Americans, everything had to be held in abeyance until Eban's return.[3]

There was something surprising about the emphasis Eban placed on his trip to Washington – rather than on his future meetings in Paris and London. Indeed, that was the true measure of the shift that Eshkol effected in Israeli foreign policy. The majority of the 1,300 tanks that the IDF had amassed by the eve of the Six-Day War had been manufactured in Western Europe: 650 were UK-made Centurions, and 150 were French-made AMXs. All of the Israeli Air Force's aircraft were manufactured in France. Ben-Gurion was not opposed to buying weapons from the US but he was leery of American non-proliferation policy. Becoming dependent on US-made weapons meant being exposed to incessant demands to open up Israeli nuclear facilities for inspection. That was something Ben-Gurion did not want to do. For that reason he and his allies in the security establishment, such as Shimon Peres, Moshe Dayan, and Ezer Weizman, worked tirelessly during the 1950s to build a strategic alliance with France. The Ben-Gurionists called the strategy of relying on France rather than the US "the rainy day option."[4]

The French, on their part, were still establishing their military industries and were eager for customers. They also worked hard to build an independent nuclear fighting force. Both the defeat of French forces in the battle of Dien Bien Phu in 1954 and the American ultimatum during the 1956 Suez Crisis suggested to the French that they needed to obtain nuclear weapons: otherwise, the superpowers would continue to push them around. Building nuclear capabilities was extremely expensive and selling nuclear equipment to the Israelis was a good way to offset the costs. The Israelis proved to be great customers. They paid in full, and their operations against Arab countries were like free advertising: they demonstrated how effective French weapons were. An Israeli newspaper reported that after the April 7 incident in which Israeli Mirages downed six MiGs, a French general called the Israeli military attaché to congratulate him.[5]

The French not only helped the Israelis build a nuclear reactor that could produce a bomb, they also supplied the Israelis with planes, such as the Mirage, and missiles that could carry a nuclear payload. Dayan and Peres saw the alliance with France as a guarantee of the development of an

Israeli nuclear strategy. For that reason, during 1964–65, when they served in Eshkol's government, Peres and Dayan opposed Eshkol's efforts to shift Israel's military purchases from European to American suppliers.[6] But by the summer of 1967, the pivot to the US was a *fait accompli*. The French and the British were esteemed *past* suppliers. The future of arms supply belonged to Washington. As importantly, neither France nor Britain had a power projection capability equivalent to the formidable Sixth Fleet – a US force that ruled the waves of the Mediterranean.

The Quest for a Security Guarantee

The American ability to intervene in any clash between Arabs and Jews was the main issue for Eshkol. It was not so for Eban and that was the main reason that Eshkol was reluctant to send him to Washington. Sure, Eshkol did not like Eban, and the feeling was probably mutual. Eshkol ridiculed Eban behind his back, calling him the "learned fool" and "Abuna" ("our father" in Arabic). But beyond the shared antipathy lay a real difference of opinion. Contrary to the image that Eban cultivated, he was not a moderate. At times he could be as hawkish as the generals in the General Staff. For instance, Eban supported wholeheartedly the raid on Samu in November 1966 and raised no significant objections when the matter was discussed in cabinet. Eban was for diplomacy, only as long as it put him in the limelight. For that reason he sought to take a leading role in the effort to open up the Straits of Tiran to Israeli navigation. Eban made his intentions clear during the cabinet discussion of May 23. The purpose of his trip, he told the ministers, was to convince Johnson to order American vessels to accompany the first Israeli ship to cross the Straits. The foreign minister asserted that this expression of American commitment would help break the Egyptian blockade.[7]

Eshkol wanted the crisis to be solved through diplomatic means but the closure of the Straits of Tiran to Israeli navigation was a side issue. Managing without the sea route to Africa and Asia was a nuisance but not an existential threat. Israel had had a fast growth rate between 1948 and 1956, the years in which Egypt had prevented Israeli ships from passing through the Straits as part of its policy of non-recognition of the State of Israel. When the Straits were opened to Israeli navigation in 1957, Israel at first was excited about the opportunity to increase its trade with Africa. Between 1958 and 1965, Israel, itself an aid recipient, disbursed no less than $199 million in loans and grants to African countries. However, by the summer of 1966 Eshkol had reached the conclusion that all that effort produced little in either political or economic terms. Israeli exports to Africa remained minuscule, and African countries supported several anti-Israeli decisions in the UN and in African conferences. As a result, Israel rapidly curtailed aid-giving to African countries. Likewise, Israel's trade with Asia was non-existent as it enjoyed no diplomatic relations with the giants of the continent, India and China. According to an Israeli Foreign Ministry memo written in May 1967, trade between Israel and Afro-Asia reached such a nadir that between 1965 and 1967 no Israeli ship had sailed through the Straits.[8]

A more substantive issue was Nasser's decision to cut off the route to Iran, from which Israel imported most of its oil. But it was a solvable problem. As Deputy Minister of Defense Zvi Dinstein told the cabinet on May 21, Israel was well stocked. Its oil reserves could serve for another four months. The oil from Iran could still reach Israel if the tankers circumnavigated Africa, though increased transportation costs would have pushed up the price of Iranian oil by 30 percent. Dinstein promised the government that oil could also be purchased from other suppliers such as Venezuela; however, again, higher transportation costs would have made Venezuelan oil more expensive for Israel. Minister of the Interior Shapira and Minister of Health Barzilay thought it wise to appeal to the US and ask for an aid package that would cover the costs of buying more expensive oil.[9]

Eshkol's mind was focused, then, not on the Straits but on getting a security guarantee from the US as a way to prevent a clash. Eshkol could have used the American promise of a security umbrella to counter the argument of the General Staff that launching a preemptive strike was best from a military perspective. Such a commitment would also have tied Israel's hands. It could not have acted freely if it was in treaty relations with the US.

Israel's quest for an American commitment to defend it were it to be attacked had been lengthy, beginning back in the 1950s. By December 1962, Israeli diplomacy achieved a certain measure of success when President Kennedy assured Foreign Minister Golda Meir "that in case of an invasion the United States would come to the support of Israel." Once Eshkol came into office, he evinced great interest in getting a more explicit commitment from Washington. Talking with an Israeli diplomat from the Washington embassy in August 1963, Eshkol wondered aloud whether he should tell the American president that "we have Dimona ... If you [the president] are opposed to that, what can you promise? If you can [give a security guarantee] please [tell us] how and why." In essence, Eshkol considered trading an Israeli promise to halt the nuclear project at Dimona for a US commitment in more robust language than that which Kennedy had used with Golda. "Suppose the President promised [to defend Israel if attacked]," mused Eshkol:

but then comes the moment when you need to go to war [i.e. send American troops to Israel] and then he says: "Wait a minute, I have to go to the Senate" [to get its approval] . . . Within a week the Arabs can win. And then, by the time [the Americans] arrive it is [too] late.[10]

Evidently, Eshkol sought a promise of immediate US assistance.

During their talks in June 1964, Eshkol had asked Johnson whether the US would come to Israel's help if it was attacked by all Arab countries. Johnson did not give a straight answer. But in November 1964 there was an American attempt to reassure the Israelis of the US's ability to take care of Israel's security. Rabin, Peres, and Weizman embarked on an American helicopter that took them aboard a Sixth Fleet aircraft carrier. Rabin was impressed. He was told that the Sixth Fleet had two of these vessels, each capable of carrying eighty planes. Rabin later wrote in his memoirs: "160 to 240 aircrafts, of the highest quality, of a type that no party to the conflict possessed, made it clear to us how powerful the US was and how significant was its presence in our area." Four months later Israel and the US signed the "Memorandum of Understanding," the first article of which stated that "the Government of the United States has reaffirmed its concern for the maintenance of Israel's security," and vowed to preserve "the independence and integrity of Israel." In April 1967, shortly before the crisis began, a news reporter asked Eshkol whether Israel would expect help from the US were it to be attacked by its neighbors. Eshkol replied in the affirmative, adding: "especially if I take into consideration all the solemn promises that have been made to Israel. We get these promises when we ask the United States for arms and are told: 'Don't spend your money. We are here. The Sixth Fleet is here.'"[11]

So it was no surprise that three days after Nasser sent his troops into Sinai, Eshkol wrote to Johnson with an urgent request "to reaffirm the American commitment to Israel's security with a view to its implementation should the need arise." Eshkol used the letter to remind Johnson of "the specific American commitment so often reiterated to us between May 1961 and August 1966." The next day Eshkol sent a similar letter to the French president, Charles de Gaulle, asking him to express France's willingness to support the sovereignty and territorial wholeness of Israel. Eshkol's request relied on the fact that, five years earlier, in March 1962, Israeli and French officers had signed a detailed memo specifying how French forces would come to fight alongside Israel if needed. The French representative's concluding words to the Israelis at the end of that meeting were: "We do not look forward to war, but if it happens, we will come to your aid wholeheartedly and willingly." Since then, de Gaulle had come to power and he had been more interested in building bridges with the Arab world. Relations with Israel cooled, and Eshkol's request for implementation of the French commitment received no meaningful response.[12]

Eshkol's position dovetailed with that of the General Staff. Yariv and Rabin also argued that the issue was not really the Straits but rather the Egyptian troop concentrations in Sinai. It would therefore be wrong of Eban to focus on opening the Straits. By May 25, the Egyptians moved their only armored division into Sinai, raising the overall number of Egyptian tanks at the front to 830. The Egyptian army augmented its forces in northern Sinai along the route that the IDF planned to use to invade Sinai. The southern route the Israeli army relied on also looked increasingly risky. As the Egyptian defensive alignment in Sinai amassed, the chances of a successful Israeli offensive dimmed.[13]

May 25 was the day on which Rabin awoke from the tranquilizing injection he had received from his doctor and resumed his activity. Rabin started his morning with a meeting with Weizman and Yariv in his home. Both wanted Rabin to meet with Eshkol and find out whether the IDF could get the go-ahead even before Eban's meeting with Johnson. Rabin was skeptical but said he was willing to try.[14] The three went to see Eshkol. Yariv spoke first, arguing that it was a mistake to send Eban abroad. It was just a waste of time. Rabin seconded Yariv: "We're getting close to the moment when everything will blow up." Rabin had a suggestion: telegraphing Eban to ask him to demand a clear-cut statement from the Americans affirming that any attack on Israel was tantamount to an attack on the US. Eshkol liked Rabin's proposal. He had been working to squeeze such a declaration out of Washington for the past four years. Eshkol decided not to let a good crisis go to waste and suggested sending a missive to Eban alleging that an all-Arab military assault was about to happen. Yariv and Adi Yaffe, Eshkol's adviser, were appointed to draft the telegram to Washington.[15]

The telegram instructed Eban to shift the focus of his talks with Johnson because "there has been a radical change in the Egyptian and Arab situation." The telegram alleged that "the problem is no longer the closure of the Straits but rather the very existence of Israel." Moving on to the envisioned Arab attack, the text of the telegram turned more speculative than certain: "Concentrations of Arab troops and the developing coordination between them *suggests the possibility* of an initiated Arab attack. Every passing hour strengthens [the Arabs'] appetite and defiance ... *which may lead* to a total military struggle [my emphasis]." Eban was told to ask the American president "what kind of practical (repeat: practical) steps he is willing to take to prevent the impending explosion."

The real intelligence assessment at the time told a different story. The worst that the Egyptians would do, according to military estimates, was mount a limited air attack on Israeli airfields. This was a reference to Amer's instructions to his pilots to plan an attack against Israeli airfields. Israeli intelligence services knew about it because since early 1967 they had been eavesdropping with some intensity on the Egyptian Air Force (EAF) as part of their planning toward a stealth attack on Egyptian airfields. Code-named "Project Senator," the close monitoring of the EAF involved creating a special unit that was devoted solely to listening in on EAF radio and building a nearby ops center where Israeli Air Force officers would be present to quickly translate raw data into orders for Israeli pilots.[16]

Indeed, it was this scenario which kept the military brass busy in the next hours. Rabin convened a meeting in the afternoon to discuss it. He started by admitting that there were no signs on the ground of an Egyptian initiative. Nevertheless, Motti Hod, commander of the Israeli Air Force, argued that the Egyptian Air Force might attack that night to forestall an Israeli air raid. Yariv speculated that Soviet intelligence services might have passed information to the Egyptians about Operation "Moked" and the Egyptians might want to act preemptively. He added that the fact that the Egyptian armored division had already entered Sinai might suggest that the air attack would be followed by a ground offensive.[17]

Did the Israeli Air Force really worry about an Egyptian air attack? Did the Egyptians have the capability to knock out the Israeli Air Force at the beginning of the war? These questions kept dogging senior IAF officers in the war's aftermath. In postwar interviews they gave decisive answers. "We thought that if they'd attack we would down them at the border," said Rafi Harlev, head of the operations branch at the IAF. He added: "in any battle in the sky, we were much better than them." Motti Hod sounded even more convinced: "Arab air-forces would not have been able to surprise us. No way would they have attacked first! . . . Every air-force commander in the world would have liked to have the same level of information about the enemy that I had in the Six Day War . . ."

Hod also explained why he had been so certain. In the weeks preceding the war, the IAF had been training all the time and was on high alert. Through "Project Senator" as well as its own radar system, the IAF monitored every movement of every officer and aircraft of the EAF. Most of the Egyptian planes were MiGs – fighter-interceptors that were ill-suited for bombing missions. The MiGs' range was limited; they were unable even to reach the IAF's main airfield in southern Israel. The IAF had other airfields farther away in central and northern Israel and it took care to disperse its aircrafts between all of them. The Egyptians had only two squadrons of heavy bombers, and they never trained for flying in radio silence mode – "So they could not have come at low-altitude," explained Hod; "they would have had to pull up and then we would have detected them." Hod also explained that the IAF was the only air force in the world that had well-protected underground hangars in which aircraft were sheltered from air raids. "We planned our air-fields according to what we wanted to do to Arab air-forces." Likewise, Weizman, who commanded the IAF before Hod, boasted in his memoirs that "our airfields are fortresses, far more protected than airfields anywhere in the world."[18]

Be that as it may, having spooked themselves into believing that an Arab air attack was imminent, at 6 p.m. Yariv and Rabin went to spook the prime minister. Rabin argued that if Eban's meeting with Johnson brought Johnson to commit forcefully to Israel's defense, then that would be reason enough to wait. But, mused Rabin, since the probability of that was virtually nil, "why are we waiting? Until when?" If the Arabs initiated the war, Israel would be in dire straits, warned Rabin. To appease the generals, Eshkol agreed that Rabin would help draft yet another telegram to Washington, this one to be addressed to Ambassador Harman. The telegram repeated the claim that Israel faced the danger of an imminent attack by Syria and Egypt and demanded that the American declaration of support "be followed by an order to US troops in the area to coordinate their actions with the IDF against any possible attack." Before the telegram was sent, Yariv was called to Eshkol's office. The prime minister asked him how the American intelligence community would respond to the claim that Arab armies were about to strike. "I told him that they would shrug it off as nonsense," recalled Yariv. The telegram was sent anyway. On one of the copies Eshkol wrote, as if to leave a clue for future historians, "anything to create an alibi."[19]

Seventy-Two Hectic Hours

If Eshkol did not want to send Eban to Washington, and mistrusted him, Johnson had no use for the voluble diplomat either. He urgently needed to communicate with the Israeli government. But not like this. Johnson's preferred method of delivering messages was through the informal Jewish backchannel, something that allowed him plausible deniability. But anything that the president might say to the Israeli foreign minister would be closely watched and recorded. Yariv shrewdly observed on May 25, when he and

Eshkol discussed the Eban mission, "Eban will not be able to collude [with the US government]." But Johnson could not ignore Eban. The American-Jewish community was terrified by Nasser's threat and feared nothing less than a second Holocaust. Jews all over the country were liquidating their assets and raiding their bank accounts, savings, and deposit boxes, and wiring the money to the "Israel Emergency Fund." Half a billion dollars was raised in humanitarian and economic aid for Israel in the weeks that preceded the war. Snubbing Eban meant insulting an ethnic group that had solidly supported Johnson in the last election.[20]

The initiatives that Eban wanted to discuss in Washington had proved stillborn even before he arrived. The option of a unilateral American operation to open the Straits was discussed on May 24 during an NSC meeting. Chairman of the Joint Chiefs of Staff General Earl Wheeler was far from enthusiastic. The Straits of Tiran formed a narrow waterway which the Egyptians secured using an artillery battery, neighboring airfields, and submarines patrolling the Red Sea. A ship entering these shallow waters was a sitting duck. Forcing Egypt to open the Straits would, therefore, necessitate bombing Egyptian airfields or sinking Egyptian submarines. In short, according to Wheeler, one could not simply open the Straits without starting a war. Wheeler's final conclusion was that an American operation in the Straits of Tiran was akin to kicking a hornets' nest "and that the Israelis can hold their own" without any American assistance. To ensure that the Israelis pulled it off, Wheeler recommended replenishing the stockpiles of the Israeli army.[21]

Not addressed by Wheeler or other participants was the question of whether Nasser would court disaster by sinking American vessels. After all, the Egyptian dictator was a gambler, not a lunatic. In any case, Johnson had little motivation to confront his generals. His administration was already embroiled in an ugly public clash with the Joint Chiefs of Staff (JCS) over the number of troops to be sent to Vietnam and on the bombing campaign against North Vietnam. The generals wanted more boots on the ground and an intensification of the air war against the north. Johnson and McNamara tried to curb their enthusiasm. The generals responded by appealing to Congress. During January 1967, McNamara and the generals aired their differences during several sessions of the Foreign Relations Committee of the Senate. Johnson, therefore, had little motivation to quarrel with the JCS on yet another issue.[22]

The second option that Eban wanted to explore in Washington was whether the US would cooperate with the UK in order to form an international armada that would open the Straits of Tiran. On May 25, George

Thompson, British minister of state for foreign affairs, was in Washington for talks with Rusk to discuss the matter. Once they got down to the nitty-gritty it turned out that the two countries had conflicting interests. Each wanted the other to lead the effort to recruit more countries to participate in the armada, as well as to supply most of the force's vessels. Johnson called the naval maneuver that the Brits proposed "idiotic." UK representatives thought the same about the American scheme. By the end of the day the idea of the armada was dead in the water.[23]

Nothing went according to plan for Eban. He had arrived in the American capital after a whirlwind tour of Paris and London. In London, Eban had heard British Prime Minister Harold Wilson promise that he would work to create an international armada that would allow Israel to use the Straits of Tiran. Eban had thought this was a good start. But in Paris de Gaulle had warned him that Israel should not start a war under any circumstances. As always, the old general was searching after France's lost grandeur. All problems should be solved by four-power talks, de Gaulle maintained – and he had no doubt that France was one of those powers. In the following days it became clear that de Gaulle's four-power scheme was going nowhere. Upon learning about it, Johnson mockingly queried: "Which are the other two?"

Eban was thoroughly disappointed to find the alarming telegrams authored by Yariv and Rabin. He quickly understood that the intelligence behind them was suspect and that they were part of Eshkol's effort to remote-control his mission.[24] He dutifully reported their content to Dean Rusk, but did not protest too much when Rusk told him that a US declaration along the lines of "an attack on you is an attack on us" was not realistic. Both Rusk and McNamara told Eban that their information totally contradicted the claim of an impending Syrian–Egyptian attack. The American intelligence community pointed out that the Egyptians were digging in – not preparing for an offensive. In any case, American intelligence agencies believed that Israel would be the winner, no matter who started the war. The embarrassed Eban responded by stating that "the telegram would not have been written as it was had he [Eban] been there."[25]

Both Rusk and McNamara explained that any American response could come only at the end of a long procedure involving deliberations at the UN and later a request for congressional approval. As Eban knew, this meant a lengthy process moving toward an unachievable outcome. Negotiations in the UN seemed deadlocked. In addition, Johnson's relations with the Senate and the public at large were poisoned by the war in Vietnam. He was accused of escalating the campaign there needlessly. Any initiative by Johnson to send troops abroad would be vigorously opposed. Indeed, White House consultations with Congress suggested resistance to a unilateral American operation in the Straits of Tiran.[26]

As diplomatic avenues were becoming clogged, parts of the administration – particularly the CIA, the Pentagon, and the White House – started signaling to Israel that the best solution would be if it dealt with the situation itself, a position that General Wheeler had already taken during the NSC discussion of May 24. On May 25, John Hadden, head of the CIA station in Israel, paid a visit to the home of his colleague, head of the Mossad, Meir Amit. Hadden, 40 years old, tall and thin, had been in Israel for several years by then and even knew a little Hebrew. Hadden wanted Israel to help the US support it by creating a justifiable pretext. In particular, Hadden wanted the Israelis to send a ship through the Straits of Tiran. If the Egyptians started shooting, Israel would have a good reason to launch an offensive. Hadden recalled that one of attendants in the meeting said, "But it doesn't matter. It's just cosmetic." "True," Hadden lectured his Israeli colleagues, "for you appearance and image do not matter but in our culture they are of utmost importance." Following his meeting with Hadden, Amit participated in a consultation at the prime minister's office. Amit quoted Hadden's proposal word for word, attributing it to the CIA. While the general director of the Foreign Ministry supported the idea, Yariv strongly opposed it. His argument was that Nasser would use the passage of the ship to launch an all-out war. This remained the generals' position in the following days. They simply refused to test the extent of Nasser's resolve to stop Israeli ships.[27]

The next day, May 26, the signals from Washington grew stronger. Yosef Geva, the military attaché in Washington, reported that American officers he talked to told him that the chances of mounting an American operation to open the Straits were declining by the day. These officers were not even sure the US would come to Israel's aid if it was attacked. His report quoted General Wheeler's assertion that Israel would win even if it absorbed the first blow. Geva maintained that the Pentagon had immense trust in Israel's military capabilities but only one worry: Israel must find a convincing pretext before launching its offensive. The same day, Israeli intelligence intercepted a communication between the Egyptian embassy in Washington and the Foreign Ministry in Cairo. According to the Egyptian report, a State Department official told an Egyptian diplomat that the US would not use military means to open the Straits.[28]

After reading these reports the head of the superpowers desk at military intelligence came to Yariv's office. "Commander," said Avraham Liff:

we, in Branch 3, have gathered together reports [from the last two days] and opened a file which we named "Greenlight." These reports prove that, essentially, the Americans have given us a green light to start the war. They do not understand why we are hoping that they would organize an armada that would open up the Straits; they do not understand why we are pressing them to get an authorization to launch our offensive. The Americans do not want in any way to be seen as if they are pushing us to war or colluding with us against Egypt . . . The American assessment is that we will defeat the Egyptians and [the Americans] wonder why we hesitate.

Yariv told Liff to distribute a memo on the topic and to be on the lookout for additional information that could substantiate his thesis.[29]

Liff's intervention was part of a wider effort by a frustrated General Staff to pressure the government to make a decision. The government convened yet another meeting on Friday, May 26, to discuss the situation. Mid-meeting, a report about Egyptian penetration into Israeli airspace arrived. Four MiG-21s had entered the Negev area flying at high altitude above Dimona and the IDF's deployment area. They were evidently taking photos. Weizman and Rabin pulled Eshkol out of the meeting for a discussion in the corridor. Rabin claimed the flight over Dimona might be the first step toward an attack on the reactor, although he admitted that Egyptian ground forces were not prepared for an offensive. Weizman was more confident: "All the signs point to an attack on Dimona, probably today. The Egyptians would send at least 40 planes to attack Dimona." Eshkol: "Can I understand from this that you want to attack today?"

Weizman and Rabin knew the government had to wait until Eban met with Johnson. Pressing for an attack now meant Rabin and Weizman would have to take responsibility for a crisis in Israeli–US relations. Beyond that was the knowledge, shared by Rabin and Weizman, that the chances of a successful Egyptian attack were slim indeed. The reactor was defended by several Hawk batteries and the full might of the IAF. Like any reactor, it was covered by a massive steel-reinforced concrete dome that could withstand even a direct hit. Rabin said it was better to wait until after the meeting at the White House. Weizman begrudgingly concurred, muttering that an Israeli attack should be launched "tomorrow morning" at the latest.[30]

Meanwhile the president kept delaying his meeting with Eban. Eban was showered with telegrams from Jerusalem urging him to come back as the government was on the verge of a momentous decision. Nervous, Eban called Rusk, telling him he intended to leave Washington that night. He could not allow himself to stay on any longer as the cabinet was about to decide whether to go to war. It was the first time since he reached the capital that Eban sounded angry and assertive. "I got it," answered a surprised Rusk, and hung up the phone. Not even that outburst, though, helped Eban get an audience with the president. Time was running out. It was already mid-afternoon. On the verge of desperation, Eban sent Ephraim Evron to the White House. Evron, the Number 2 in the Israeli embassy, had more influence than his title suggested. He was the man with the magic touch. Ever since he reached the American capital he had shown an incredible talent for networking. One of his colleagues recalled that he could get American officials to meet with him at 2 a.m. But his biggest prize was his friendship with Johnson; they even played golf together. If anyone could open the gates to the Oval Office, it was Evron.[31]

Evron arrived at 1600 Pennsylvania Avenue to plead with Rostow to arrange a meeting. He got far more than even he had bargained for when the president called and asked that Evron come over. Evron recalled later: "It was quite irregular. I was merely a junior official. The deputy of the ambassador . . . It was clear to me that he was using me as a tool or a conduit to deliver a message that maybe he would not say with such clarity to the Foreign Minister, whom he was to meet forty-five minutes later." Indeed, unlike his talk with Eban, Johnson's conversation with Evron had no official transcriber. The only people to witness it were the two interlocutors. This is exactly how Johnson chose to deliver messages to Israel in the past.

Johnson reiterated some of the positions put forth by Rusk and McNamara, emphasizing the need for congressional authorization. "I am sure he had no doubt," explained Evron, "that such a resolution was unlikely. So, the first message he conveyed was that the US was unable, did not intend . . . to take a military action to open the straits." Then Johnson reached the main point: "Israel was a sovereign Government, and if it decided to act alone, it could of course do so; but in that case everything that happened before and afterwards would be its responsibility and the United States would have no obligation for any consequences that might ensue."[32] Was the president threatening Israel or encouraging it to act? Shortly before Evron arrived at the White House, Rusk submitted a memo to Johnson in which he debated what the president would say when he met Eban. The first option was "to let the Israelis decide how best to protect their own national interests . . . i.e., to 'unleash' them." Rusk wrote that he was strongly against this option. But that seemed to be exactly what Johnson was doing.[33]

Next came the meeting with Eban, again at the Oval Office. Eban and Johnson had known each other for quite a long time. They had first met in 1952 when Eban was Israel's ambassador both to Washington and the UN. Johnson came to Eban's Washington residence to learn in the briefest time possible everything he could about Israel. Eban certainly formed an initial impression: "His interrogation had been avid, detailed, implacable and seemingly free of sentiment. He had the air of a man parsimonious of time and jealous of every minute not devoted to a functional end." As soon as Eban entered the Oval Office at 7 p.m. he found that he was gripped with tension. Lyndon Johnson was known in the Senate for something called "the Johnson treatment." At the height of six foot four, the Texan cut a lanky figure. He could hover over most men, lean closely into his interlocutor's personal space, grab him by the lapels, and hurl forth a torrent of threats and inducements. Tough men, seasoned politicians, the shrewdest in the country, crumbled and capitulated under his pressure.[34]

Now Eban was about to experience the "Johnson treatment" himself: "the President of the United States was seated opposite me with his eyes very close to mine, staring gravely into my face." Eban insisted on this meeting because of his boundless, perhaps naive, belief in the power of oratory. International media had always hailed him as one of the best speakers in the English language. One of his first sentences to the president – "the country [i.e. Israel] is on the footing of expectancy" – was an example of the grandiloquent language he used in an effort to impress Johnson. But Johnson was a formidable negotiator. He stuck to his script, sometimes even reading from a written statement. The conversation focused on the issue of the international armada, as was Eban's fancy. The usual caveats were repeated: Johnson's need to exhaust the process at the UN before asking for congressional approval. Nevertheless Johnson promised to try to reach a diplomatic solution. He asked Israel to help him in that. He intimated that if Israel acted, the US would not be able to help it, by repeating the sentence "Israel will not be alone, unless it decides to go alone."[35] But as Johnson knew rather well, Israel would not need any help if it decided to act. His entire intelligence community was unanimous on that point.

Last of all, Eban raised the issue that preoccupied Eshkol the most: military coordination between the IDF and the Sixth Fleet. Eban argued that if the Americans were serious about coming to Israel's help were it to be attacked, then "surely there must be some planning, some joint link." Johnson repeated that as far as he knew no attack was imminent "and that, if there were, you would knock them out." But Harman, who was present at the meeting, insisted on getting an answer. Johnson asked McNamara to "look into this." The secretary of defense responded: "Yes. Military liaison or something like that, but of course it would have to be secret." Yet, in the following days the Pentagon refused to create such a liaison. Harman later summed up the encounter between Eban and Johnson as an Israeli failure: "Without any doubt, it was a dreadful conversation."[36]

Eban and Johnson emerged from their conversation with very different impressions. After Eban had left the room, Johnson chose that moment to imitate him, calling him "a miniature Winston Churchill." He believed (or hoped) that Eban had got the message. Johnson guessed that "they're going to hit. And there's nothing we can do about it." According to another version, the president said: "I failed. They'll go." Conversely, Eban's impression "was that a new potentiality was only now beginning to grow in American–Israeli relations, and that it would be worthwhile to give it time to reveal itself." Eban got one last chance to be disabused of that notion when he met Arthur Goldberg, the US ambassador to the UN and a Johnson confidant.[37]

Goldberg was the last official to see Eban before he took off for Israel. Eban's impression was that Goldberg had been fully briefed by the White House on the details of his meeting with the president. Like Johnson's conversation with Evron, the meeting between Goldberg and Eban was another opportunity for Johnson to deliver a message to Israel without an official transcript being taken. Goldberg talked tough. He pointed out that nothing would come of the proceedings in the Security Council and he was likewise skeptical about the feasibility of pulling together an international naval task force. According to Eban, who was accused after the fact by his cabinet colleagues of lying to them about the content of his Washington talks, Goldberg turned at the end of the conversation to the question of whether Eban was able to convince the president that Egypt was the culprit and Israel was innocent. Goldberg had an entirely different recollection of what he said to Eban: "You owe it to your government, because lives are going to be lost and your security is involved, to tell your cabinet that the President's statement means a joint resolution of Congress before coming to your aid, *and the President can't get such a resolution because of the Vietnam War* [my emphasis]."

Their talk concluded, Eban boarded a plane back to Israel. While he was in mid-air over the Atlantic, Johnson and Goldberg made one last attempt to ensure that Eshkol would get the right message ahead of the cabinet meeting on Saturday evening, May 27. Goldberg said to Evron that he had told the president "that Israel might act alone due to emotional reasons or because time was of the essence." Johnson replied "that Israel alone can judge what it should do and whether time is such a constraint." The usual caveat – that in that case, Israel would be alone – was dropped.[38]

Holding his cards close to his chest, Eban did not report the results of his talks back to Jerusalem, keeping his colleagues in suspense. Nevertheless,

based on the reports already in his possession, Yariv drew his own conclusions, which he presented at a meeting of the General Staff on May 27: "The
Americans see an action by us as likely, but they do not intend to intervene.
They would do so only if the tide was turning against us." At that time, military intelligence was making hay from Nasser's last speech in which he
declared, "If we should be attacked, this will mean war and our first aim
would be the annihilation of Israel." The "annihilation" part was emphasized a lot; less so, the fact that it was a conditional sentence. Yariv was also
the man who spoke first during the government meeting that took place in
the evening of that day. Yariv said that the Egyptian deployment in Sinai
was still shambolic but he warned that the passage of time would allow the
Egyptians to improve and strengthen their defenses. He continued
ominously: "we know for certain that [the Egyptian] decision is to start [the
war] by using their air force. It's clear what would be the consequence of
them using their air force before we activate ours." "The noose is closing
around our necks," added Rabin helpfully.[39]

At that point Eban walked in. Israel being a gossipy country, he had
found out about all the dramatic events that had occurred in his absence
was away – the political tensions, Rabin's collapse, the panic in the cabinet
– during the short transfer from the airport to the city. Eban quickly realized that the generals were succeeding in frightening the ministers. If he
was to prevail, he had to present an even bigger threat to the cabinet. Eban
was a better actor than Rabin. He started talking about his meeting with de
Gaulle. He claimed that the French president had told him that "a tragedy, a
tragedy would happen if you are the aggressors. Never be the aggressors.
You should fight only if others attack you. It is impossible to describe the
calamity that would happen to you if that principle is not honored." Then
Eban moved on to denounce the telegrams that were sent to him while he
was in Washington, calling them "cheap tricks." He ended with the positive
aspects of his visit to Washington. Johnson, Eban gushed, was "solid as a
rock" and would use the Sixth Fleet if he had to, to open up the Straits. The
process of getting a resolution out of Congress "has nearly ended." He
warned that Israel would be left on its own if it attacked first.[40]

Some ministers noticed that Johnson's stern advice was not accompanied by any threat. Nevertheless, Eban's summary of his talks in Washington
created the impression that a diplomatic solution, backed by the full might
of the United States, was just around the corner if the government was
willing to wait. There was no official vote at the end of the meeting but it
was clear that nine ministers, including Eshkol, wanted to authorize the
army to start the war, while nine were for waiting and giving the diplomatic

game some time. Eshkol could have easily broken the tie. Minister of Finance Pinhas Sapir, Eshkol's closest ally, was among the doves. Had Eshkol asked him to abstain, Sapir would have surely assented. But Eshkol did no such thing. It was already four in the morning. Cigarette smoke filled the air. The ministers were bleary-eyed and tired from arguing the same points over and over. Eshkol moved to adjourn the meeting until the next afternoon. Then he said to the ministers that maybe Minister of the Interior Shapira was right and it would be wrong to go to war so soon after Eban's return from Washington. After all, "I would not want to antagonize the American President." Eshkol, it seems, wanted to be seen as a hawk, but in his heart he was still a dove eager to play for time, hoping that somehow something would turn up.[41] Yet, Eshkol's decision not to push through a war resolution sealed his fate. Within the next seventy-two hours Eshkol would lose his position as minister of defense.

As dawn broke, the ministers rushed to their homes in a desperate attempt to get some much-needed sleep. Yariv, however, was at his desk. He was looking at the "Greenlight" memo, according to which, although the Americans were saying that they were working tirelessly to create an international naval task force, there were no signs of that on the ground. The French intelligence service, which still retained strong ties to its Israeli colleagues, maintained that it was unaware of any preparations to create such a force. The second memo that Yariv read that morning discussed the Egyptian forces in Sinai. Recently obtained reports showed that while morale was high, the Egyptian army was in a state of complete chaos. Divisions and brigades were broken up to create new units; commanders did not know how to navigate in Sinai and were left in the dark by headquarters as to the precise nature of their missions; and the soldiers lacked maps, uniforms, spare parts, and weapons. "All well and good," Yariv muttered to himself. "That would be the right time to hit them."[42]

18

ONE SOVIET FOREIGN POLICY OR TWO?

A Trip across the Golan Heights

O N JUNE 11, while Israel was celebrating its astounding victory over an
Arab military coalition, Avraham Ben-Tzur, member of Kibbutz
Lehavot Ha-Bashan in the upper Galilee, was bothered by something
completely different.[1] Being a socialist, he was interested in socialist movements in the Arab world and even published a book about the topic in 1965.
Although he found ample sources on socialism in Egypt, there were scant
materials about Syria. His thoughts turned to Quneitra, the capital city of
the Golan Heights area, now safely in Israeli hands. He had no doubt that
the Baath had offices there and that if he hurried he might find Baath-
related materials that would help him expand his book. Consumed by curiosity, he started hitchhiking his way along the rocky and desolate terrain,
now dotted here and there by smoldering tanks.

Once in Quneitra, he used his Arabic to ask the few locals who had not
fled about the location of the Baath headquarters. When he finally reached
his destination he was somewhat sorry he had not arrived earlier. There
were many files to be had, but the reserve soldier who had taken over the
place had already started using them as toilet paper. Excited, short of breath,
Ben-Tzur shoved whatever he could lay his hands on into a big sack. He
threw it over his shoulder, then started hitchhiking his way back to Lehavot
Ha-Bashan.

There in the privacy of his home he could scrutinize his loot. What he
found were issues of *al-Munadil* (The Fighter), the Baath Party's secret
monthly, stenciled copies of which were sent to party branches across Syria.
Only party members could read it and they could do it only in the party

branch. Members were warned against taking the leaflets home. Anyone who read a copy had to sign it.[2] Once Ben-Tzur started reading the issues he found two articles that made his eyes widen in amazement. They told the story of two different Baath delegations that arrived in Moscow in 1966 and 1967. In both cases the Syrians found that Soviet officials strongly disagreed with each other. While in official talks the Syrians were urged to avoid a conflict with Israel, in private conversation Soviet party leaders expressed support for the Syrian policy of aiding Fatah. Ben-Tzur was taken aback. He had never heard about conflicts in the Kremlin before and was surprised that they were discussed with foreign visitors. He devoted the next years to learning Russian and delving into obscure Arab, Russian, and East German newspapers, magazines, and periodicals. In 1970 he produced one of the most thorough analyses of decision-making in the Kremlin in the years that preceded the Six-Day War. The documents that were unearthed in East European archives following the fall of the Berlin Wall only validated Ben-Tzur's findings: the Kremlin in the 1960s was a house divided.

Collusions over Red Square

Nikita Khrushchev came to power in 1953, shortly after Stalin's death. For decades the Soviet population had been chafing under Stalin's tough rule. Workers toiled for long hours, received low pay, found little they could buy in the market other than basic foodstuffs, lived in overcrowded housing (it was fairly common for four families to share one apartment), and were exposed to intrusive surveillance. If there was one thing that all the players in the Soviet elite could agree on, it was that things had to change. The status quo was inherently unstable. Khrushchev was acutely aware of the fact that if Communism was to survive long-term it must offer the same consumerist choice and material benefits that capitalism delivered – hence his promise to his people that Communism would overtake capitalist econ-omies by the 1980s.[3] Both his foreign and domestic policies were aimed, first and foremost, at achieving this goal.

To do so, Khrushchev forged alliances with Third World regimes so that the Soviet Union would be able to export to their markets. The resulting trade surplus, Khrushchev thought, would cover for the deficit in trade with the West, from which he hoped to import industrial equipment to build a new car complex and establish high-tech chemical factories.[4] To improve the productivity of Soviet agriculture Khrushchev introduced corn to Soviet fields, sent Communist youth to plow the "virgin lands" in Kazakhstan, and ordered that farmers be paid realistic prices for their produce. Raising the ire of Soviet generals, Khrushchev cut defense spending and troop levels to invest more in the production of consumer goods. Well aware of the resentment toward him within the ranks, Khrushchev also ordered stricter party control over the military.[5] Finally, Khrushchev tried to decentralize economic planning by taking away powers from the ministries in Moscow and devolving them to regional planning committees.[6]

Economic historians agree that Khrushchev's reforms made sense. The fly in the ointment was that he worked without much orderly staff work, relied on gut feeling, dismissed the advice of experts, and lorded imperiously over a complex system with many competing interest groups. He ended up not only having many enemies but also alienating his supporters. When Khrushchev was deposed in October 1964, the army stood aside (it had supported him during the failed Kremlin coup of 1957) while the KGB actively helped to bring about the transition.[7]

Khrushchev was replaced by a triumvirate of leaders that included Leonid Brezhnev and Alexei Kosygin. The two men's career paths had been very different. Brezhnev, sunny and optimistic, was a consummate party apparatchik and was well versed in the old art of Kremlin scheming; indeed, at much personal danger to himself, he led the Politburo rebellion against Khrushchev. Kosygin, dour, taciturn, and to-the-point, was an engineer by profession who climbed slowly through the ranks of state agencies. Initially they cooperated in order to remove Khrushchev from power. But once Khrushchev was out of the picture, and his tasks were divided between Brezhnev, who became secretary general, and Kosygin, who became prime minister, each started pulling in opposite directions.[8]

The dynamics of the struggle may be familiar to anyone who followed the post-Stalin succession melee. The Soviet Communist Party being the most powerful organization in the Soviet Union, the institutional advantage was always with the politician who succeeded in gaining the trust and support of the party apparatus. Brezhnev was able to do that by aligning himself with the conservative Stalinist majority. Kosygin, on the other hand, took it upon himself to represent the managerial class in the governmental agencies.

Both Kosygin and Brezhnev had an agenda that was well suited to the interests of the power blocs they represented. Kosygin wanted to reform and liberalize the Soviet economy, seeking to introduce market mechanisms that would allow factories and stores to enter into direct negotiations over prices and production quotes. He tenaciously defended the autonomy of factory managers and vocally denigrated party officials for trying to

meddle in economic affairs. Likewise, he questioned the Stalinist ortho-
doxy of giving precedence to heavy industry. Kosygin, who made his career
in the light industry sector, argued that preference should be given to the
production of consumer goods and claimed that the revival of Communism
would be achieved through raising the standard of living of Soviet citizens.
Unlike Brezhnev, Kosygin was looking at the non-Communist world with
hope. He wanted to develop Soviet industry by encouraging trade with the
West and spurring export-led growth. In his public speeches, Kosygin
argued that international trade and economic interdependency encouraged
peaceful relations between nations.

Kosygin used foreign policy to promote his domestic agenda, seeking to
improve relations with the West and the non-Communist world at large. He
also tried to reduce international tensions by brokering peace between
Pakistan and India in 1965 and through his deep involvement in peace
negotiations between Washington and Hanoi in 1967. All these efforts were
aimed at creating a stable international environment within which his
domestic reforms could proceed and trade with the West could flourish.[9]
Unfortunately for Kosygin, much of this did not go according to plan. The
escalating war in Vietnam, and Chinese radicalism, made it harder for him
to improve relations with the US. And, of course, he was derailed by his
internal enemies, most notably Brezhnev.

For Brezhnev, Kosygin's loose talk about market-based reform and
improving the lot of the Soviet citizen seemed irresponsible and dangerous.
Speaking to party officials, Brezhnev emphasized that one could not
measure the standard of living by looking at individuals. The Soviet Union
was a welfare state and it was investing in its citizens collectively. The idea
that workers and factories would be better motivated if the rules of profit
and loss were implemented was preposterous. The Soviet worker, Brezhnev
maintained, was not motivated by profit but rather by the Communist
ideology, and therefore more party work should be done at the factories.
Speaking also for the generals and the military-industrial complex that
supported him, Brezhnev maintained that the Soviet Union was under
threat.

Unlike Kosygin, who sought ways to cut down the defense budget,
Brezhnev wanted to increase military spending, especially on conventional
weapons. He sought to undo Khrushchev's defense cuts and increase troop
levels. Brezhnev also expedited the building of ballistic missiles and
supported the strategic vision of the Soviet admiral, Sergey Groshkov, who
called for an increase in the global presence of the Soviet navy.[10] Although
Brezhnev certainly did not want even to get close to a clash with the US, as

he was gazing into the future all he could see were the dark clouds of a continued confrontation with the West. Naturally, he advocated the preference of heavy over light industry and was not enamored with the idea of increased trade with the West.

Kosygin opposed Brezhnev, but never aspired to take his position, nor did he have much of a chance to do so considering his lack of understanding or involvement in party affairs. Brezhnev, for his part, was a very careful and patient man. He was willing to wait until he felt that he was strong enough to act against Kosygin. In the meantime, he was slowly building his coalition and installing his cronies in key positions.

This multitude of conflicting tendencies manifested itself in the controversies which enveloped Soviet foreign policy toward Europe. When in 1965 Kosygin understood that the escalating conflict in Vietnam would make improved trade relations with the US impossible, he suggested an economic offensive toward West Europe as well as other non-Communist countries on the European periphery such as Turkey and Iran. Brezhnev, on the other hand, was never a big supporter of East–West trade and wanted to limit cooperation with West European countries to the realm of security arrangements. Most notably, Brezhnev wanted to leverage de Gaulle's defiant policy toward the US to promote a new framework for collective security in Europe. It was said in the past that NATO was established to keep the Americans in, the Soviets out, and the Germans down. Brezhnev thought he could coordinate a policy with Paris to take advantage of the growing neutralist tendencies among West European countries, fueled by increasing estrangement from American policies in Vietnam, to create a European order that would keep the Americans out, the Russians in, and the Germans down.[11] But in the meantime, Brezhnev allowed Kosygin to implement his strategy by pursuing better trade relations with Britain, Turkey, and Iran. In public appearances, Brezhnev took credit for Kosygin's success in promoting his goals and claimed that better trade relations with these countries were part of the all-out effort to destabilize NATO by political means.[12]

The struggle in the Kremlin also shaped Soviet policy toward the conflict in Vietnam. Both Kosygin and Brezhnev agreed that the North Vietnamese needed to give negotiations with the Americans a chance. But for Brezhnev, negotiations with the US were only a ruse to enable the liberation of Vietnam. What he wanted were negotiations that would expose the fact that the US was unwilling to withdraw all of its forces from the country. Nor was Brezhnev willing to accept the American demand for a complete ceasefire during negotiations.[13] Kosygin, however, was willing, as long as the

North Vietnamese agreed. Most probably, had his hands not been tied by Brezhnev, he would have applied pressure on the North Vietnamese to accept that condition.

Kosygin made his boldest attempt to facilitate a dialogue between Hanoi and Washington during his February 1967 visit to London. But it was never clear to what extent he was representing the Soviet government or merely expressing his own opinion. This ambiguity made it easier for the hawks in the Lyndon Johnson administration to rebuff Kosygin's proposals. Once Kosygin returned from London, he became the subject of public rebuke by Brezhnev, who mocked his naivety. Kosygin responded by giving his own speech in which he explained that, although he had failed, his attempts to broker peace were well worth the trouble. He also blamed the Americans for not seizing the opportunity.[14]

Coordination of their conflicting strategies also eluded Brezhnev and Kosygin when they approached the problems of the Middle East. The men could agree that a war between the Arabs and the Israelis would be detrimental to Soviet interests. But they could not agree on anything else. The roots of their divergences were connected to larger themes of Soviet foreign policy. Kosygin wanted to wean Third World radical regimes from their dependence on Soviet economic and military aid and move bilateral economic relations toward trade. He was, however, willing to grant aid to countries with mixed economies (i.e. those that included both state- and privately owned companies) such as Turkey, India, Pakistan, and Afghanistan. In contrast, Brezhnev promoted two lines of policy that not only contradicted Kosygin's but also destabilized the Middle East. The first, a gesture to the party hardliners, was a call to grant military aid to governments that adopted socialist domestic policies and movements that engaged in the struggle against colonialism. Brezhnev also supported his minister of defense's expansionist plans to create a permanent Soviet naval presence in Arab harbors as well as an airfield on Egyptian soil to allow Soviet aircraft to spy on the Sixth Fleet. These conflicting agendas created an inconsistent Soviet Middle East policy in the years 1965–67.

Second-guessing the Adventure in the Third World

Already during the Khrushchev era it was clear that the way the Soviet Union was dispensing its aid was amateurish. A prime example was Soviet aid to Guinea. William Atwood, American ambassador to Guinea in the early 1960s, noticed glaring inefficiency on the docks at Conakry's port:

Soviet and Chinese credits for commodity purchases brought a weird hodgepodge of articles into Conakry. Some were ordered by inexperienced clerks in the anarchic state trading organization: one, told to buy some corrugated iron sheets for new housing, ordered enough to roof over the entire population of Guinea. We found warehouses piled high with Chinese oriental rugs and embroidered handbags. Other warehouses contained innumerable toilet bowls – with no bathrooms to put them in – enough canned Russian crab meat to last fifty years and six tons of quill pens. Exotic-looking machinery rusted on the docks, and vacant lots were filled with broken-down and abandoned trucks and buses. The trucks were mostly Russian and the buses Hungarian. But they were turned over to Guinean drivers who had no notions of maintenance and in any case could probably not read the service manuals – even if they had been printed in French. When the vehicles ground to a stop for lack of lubrication or spare parts, the Guineans just shoved them into the ditch and complained that they were junk.[15]

Indeed, already under Khrushchev Soviet economists had started to rethink the faulty assumption behind Soviet aid policies. It was noticed that agreements signed with developing countries did not ensure that the Soviets would enjoy the fruits of their investments. Such was the case in India, which the Soviets assisted in finding oil but the actual concessions from which were delivered to American companies. Not enough was done to secure repayment by aid recipients or to plan investments in a way that would benefit the Soviet economy, claimed these economists. Their main recommendation was to use Third World markets as outlets for Soviet-made industrial machinery and to build factories in developing countries that could produce labor-intensive products that the Soviet consumer needed, especially textiles, footwear, and processed food. That way, reasoned Soviet academics, the Soviet Union would be able to take advantage of the low costs of labor in the developing world.[16]

During the years 1964–65, a spate of bad news reached Moscow regarding right-wing military coups in countries in which the Soviet Union had made a large financial and political investment: Indonesia, Congo, Algeria, and Ghana.[17] And so, by the time that Brezhnev and Kosygin took over, Khrushchev's Third World policy was under attack also because of its ephemeral political achievements. For instance, in the lead-up to the October 1964 Politburo meeting in which Khrushchev was deposed, Dmitry Polyanski, one of the plotters, prepared a list of Khrushchev's foreign policy errors. His conduct in the Third World received a thorough analysis. Polyanski judged the results of Khrushchev's efforts so "lamentable" that "the capitalists laugh at us, and they are right to laugh." Polyanski wrote that in several instances developing countries used aid offers from Moscow only to extract more generous aid from the West. He gave several examples of countries that received massive aid from the USSR yet showed no gratitude. Polyanski recounted how in 1962 Guinea refused to allow Soviet planes on their way to Cuba to stop for refueling at Conakry airport even though the Soviets had built it.[18]

The Soviet ambassador to Washington, Anatoly Dobrynin, believed that Moscow's radical allies were purposefully trying to undermine Soviet–American relations. Dobrynin claimed that in February 1965 the North Vietnamese were deliberately trying to damage Soviet–American relations by launching a major offensive against the Americans, without consulting with the Soviets, while Kosygin was in Hanoi. Their and the Cubans' behavior at the time, asserted Dobrynin, blocked any meaningful discussion of problems that were of key importance to the Soviets.[19]

Bobazhdan Gaforov, a Tajik orientalist who was employed by the Central Committee, emphasized that idea in a letter sent to Brezhnev in March 1966. Gaforov complained that despite the millions of roubles in arms and aid poured into Asia and Africa, the Soviet Union had failed to develop a viable Third World strategy. Gaforov claimed that Soviet diplomats were ignorant of Asian and African affairs and repeatedly misled Moscow with regard to the stability of the regimes the Soviet Union had been supporting in Iraq, Ghana, Indonesia, and elsewhere. Gaforov further argued that the Soviets had no control over the weapons they had been delivering to Third World countries. As a result, these were used in the service of policies to which the Soviets were actually opposed, such as exterminating Communists in Indonesia after the military coup there. Part of the problem, according to Gaforov, was that Soviet leaders had insufficient knowledge about the internal dynamics of Third World regimes, placing decision-makers at a tactical disadvantage. For these reasons Gaforov argued that the funds allocated to Third World countries might be better used in the Soviet Union to finance domestic development.[20]

Likewise, Polish Party Chairman Władysław Gomułka, complained in a Kremlin meeting with Kosygin and Brezhnev in October 1966 about the insufficient knowledge of Third World affairs of Soviet leaders, himself included. He predicted that there might be a hundred coups in Africa before that continent would be transformed into "a Marxist-Leninist force."[21] When meeting in May 1966 with his Soviet counterparts, Czechoslovak Deputy Foreign Minister Jan Pudlak attacked the same problem from a different angle, claiming that the Third World counter-coups pointed to the fact that the Soviet bloc had been spreading its resources too thin. It would be better, he advised, to concentrate Soviet efforts on a few major Third World countries.[22]

The Soviets took these suggestions to heart. Kosygin adopted a negative attitude to aid requests by radical Third World governments such as Uganda, Guinea, Burma, Algeria, and Egypt, and the net outflow of resources to developing countries fell from a peak of $290 million in 1964 to $125 million in 1967.[23] A foreign policy memo which Soviet Foreign Minister Andrei Gromyko submitted to the Politburo in January 1967 described the new Third World policy thus: "Considering the shortage of our reserves, we should focus on *economic cooperation* with the most progressive countries that have embarked on the road of non-capitalist development, such as Egypt, Syria, Algeria, Mali, Guinea, Burma, Congo, Tanzania, and countries of strategic importance to us (Afghanistan, Turkey, Pakistan, and Iran)." Relations with other Third World countries, the memo maintained, should be built on mutually beneficial trade ties rather than loans or grants.[24]

The reduction of funds devoted to aid radical Third World regimes was only one facet of the new Soviet Third World policy. Another was an effort to ensure that these regimes would not embroil the Soviet Union in regional conflicts that might escalate into outright war with the US. Though this was never stated, it seems that the bitter lessons of the Cuban missile crisis were looming in the background. Indeed, Gromyko's foreign policy memo argued that, "on the whole, international tension does not suit the state interests of the Soviet Union and its friends. The construction of socialism and the development of the economy call for the maintenance of peace." Gromyko's January 1967 memo also maintained that "Considering the experiences of Vietnam and the Middle East, we should take timely measures to relax tension in the ganglions in the three continents where sharp conflicts are possible which, in turn, can combine to lead to an 'acute situation.'" Gromyko therefore recommended supplying Cuba and Vietnam with defensive weapons systems only. Indeed, a recent study of Soviet military aid to North Vietnam in the years 1965 to 1967 found that Moscow's main concern was to help Hanoi establish air defense complexes consisting of surface-to-air missiles, jet fighters, and anti-aircraft guns.[25]

RESTRAINING DAMASCUS, DISCIPLINING CAIRO

Relations in Decline

NASSER TOOK THE news of Khrushchev's ouster pretty hard. "It is a catas-
trophe for us," he said, according to an unnamed CIA source. He was
even more worried two days later when he again addressed the subject. "If
they do this to Khrushchev, what will they do to us?" he opined. The source
reported that he had never seen Nasser so distressed and unhappy. Nasser's
working assumption was that Khrushchev had been defenestrated due to his
generosity toward developing countries. He started going over all the promises that Khrushchev had made during his May 1964 visit: postponement of
payments on Soviet loans, new loans to construct a major new steel plant
that could produce up to a million tons a year, and new arms deals. Nasser
said he had already been making preparations to send Amer to Moscow to
sign the deal. "Now all is gone," Nasser said sadly. Although Ambassador
Yerefeyev promised him that no change would take place in Moscow's
policy toward Egypt, Nasser did not believe him. The Soviets "were saying
good words to everyone," he claimed. Nasser was reluctant to write a letter
congratulating the new leaders in the Kremlin, but Murad Ghaleb, his ambassador to Moscow, nagged him, so in the end he did.[1]

Soon enough it transpired that Nasser's fears were well founded.
Egyptian hopes that Soviet generosity would continue under the new leadership in Moscow had already been dashed during Nasser's visit to the
Soviet Union in September 1965. New credits were not being offered and
Anastas Mikoyan, chairman of the Presidium of the Supreme Soviet,
advised Nasser in a public speech to reform the Egyptian economy and
base his relations with the Soviet Union on trade. According to an East

German report, the Soviets explained to Nasser that they also faced economic difficulties so they could not continue furnishing loans as before. The importance of debt repayment was underlined, and the Soviets expressed their hopes of receiving timely shipments of Egyptian cotton (the Egyptians made payments mainly in kind).[2]

At the same time, the Egyptians' refusal to allow the Soviet navy greater access to their harbors brought negotiations over new arms deals to a standstill. During his visit Nasser had been so frustrated by the Soviet attitude that in a closed meeting with members of his entourage he promised to eliminate Soviet influence in Egypt once the Aswan high dam had been completed. Eventually, however, Nasser relented. Egypt's economic situation was dire and his relations with the Johnson administration had already taken a turn for the worse. Since Nasser had no place to go for aid other than the USSR, he agreed to allow irregular visits of the Soviet navy in two specified Egyptian ports. As a result, he was able to secure a moratorium on $500 million of Egyptian debt and was granted permission to buy some naval equipment at what to Egyptian admirals were steep prices.[3]

Soviet pressure to allow its navy and air force even greater access to Egyptian military bases would persist throughout 1966 and 1967. In those years, the Soviet navy considered the creation of a counter-force to the Sixth Fleet's presence in the Mediterranean to be an absolute necessity, and the permission to use local harbors the best means to implement that plan. Soviet admirals were also interested in establishing an airfield in Egypt to allow their planes to monitor Sixth Fleet vessels. In order to make that demand more palatable to the Egyptian leadership, the Soviet navy tried to bribe the Egyptians by offering discounted naval equipment. While Nasser was willing throughout this period to consider a growing number of irregular visits of Soviet ships to Egyptian ports, ultimately he refused to allow the Soviets to establish a permanent presence in Egyptian air and naval facilities.[4]

Improved – But Not by Much

During the early 1960s, relations between the Soviet Union and Israel remained minimal and strained. The primary reason, it seems, was commercial. One clue was provided by the Soviet ambassador to Israel, Mikhail Bodrov. When Eshkol asked Bodrov in 1963 why there was no meaningful trade between Israel and the Soviet Union, Bodrov said that the Soviet Ministry of Foreign Trade was not keen to increase trade with Israel and no one higher up had an interest in changing that policy. A memo prepared in the East German Foreign Ministry that year explained in greater detail why foreign trade officials in the Communist bloc did not want to expand trade with Israel: "It is undesirable that the effort to create political ties with Israel will disturb the good relations with the Arab countries ... This does not concern only diplomatic links in the political sphere, but is associated equally with foreign trade. Except for a cheap supply of citrus and a few chemical products, for East Germany, Israel is no substitute for Arab markets."[5]

In a memo submitted by Bulgarian Foreign Minister Ivan Bashev to the Politburo in 1965, he elaborated on why Communist countries preferred to trade with the Arab world rather than Israel:

> Political and economic interests of our country in the Arab world require Bulgaria to define the relations with Israel within a framework that would not affect the economic cooperation with the Arab countries. This line is dictated by the fact that the economic, technological and scientific cooperation of Bulgaria with the Arab countries is *significant and has endless opportunities*, while with Israel this *cooperation is minor and with insignificant perspectives for development*. Arab countries are a big prospective market for our goods for export, especially for the production of our developing industry. During 1964 our country exported to Arab countries goods worth $21,340,000 ...

In comparison, exports to Israel during the same year were a paltry $2.76 million. Bashev further noted that Bulgaria could not have it both ways. Trade with Israel and the Arab world was mutually exclusive because of the Arab boycott. Arab countries blacklisted and boycotted companies and countries that traded directly with Israel: "In such cases, as the practice demonstrated, small countries [such] as Bulgaria with whom [the Arabs] do not risk major economic interests are a preferred victim."[6]

One of the most profitable ventures for the Soviet bloc was to sell their weapons in the Middle East. The Soviets usually sold the obsolete weapons that were about to be phased out as part of the modernization of Soviet armed forces. Thus, in terms of aircraft, Egypt received from the Soviet Union relatively old models of MiG-15s, MiG-17s, and certain models of the MiG-19. The Soviet Union sold about $2.7 billion worth of weapons to countries in the Middle East ($1.5 billion to Egypt alone) during the years 1955–67. Though the terms were lenient – repayments were spread over ten to twelve years with 2.5 percent interest – Moscow's customers had to pay eventually, usually in the form of raw materials shipments. Thus, these arms deals ensured the Soviet bloc had a steady supply of raw materials which it could either process or sell to Western countries to gain hard currency. And it was not just the Soviet Union that was eager to sell weapons in the area. Its satellites in Bulgaria and East Germany also wanted to increase their share of arms exports to underdeveloped countries, seeing it as a welcome source of revenue.[7]

Eshkol was nonetheless hoping that with the help of the US an arrangement could be found that would freeze the superpower's deliveries of weapons to the area. At the end of 1964, an Israeli diplomat, Mordehai Gazit, was making inquiries in Washington, talking both to Soviet and American officials about Eshkol's initiative. The Americans explained to Gazit that it was highly unlikely that the Soviets would give up a tool that had helped them gain influence in the area. Soviet diplomats told Gazit that tensions between the superpowers were too high because of the Vietnam War, and therefore an agreement along the lines suggested by Eshkol was impossible. Another Soviet diplomat said that in the Middle East the interests of the two superpowers did not overlap. The senior counselor in the Soviet embassy in Washington, Alexander I. Zinchuk, maintained that such an arrangement might be reached only after a marked improvement in Israeli–Arab relations as well as US–USSR relations. In October 1965, Dean Rusk proposed an agreement to Gromyko to put an end to the arms race in the Middle East, to which the Soviet foreign minister replied, "This thing is not practical."[8]

So, the Soviet Union did not want to trade with Israel and did want to sell weapons to its enemies. At the same time, there were officials in the USSR's government who were worried about the prospect of war in the Middle East and sought to prevent it. This position was expressed in response to a crisis in the Israeli Communist Party. The question of whether Eshkol would take a new line in Israeli foreign policy, one that would allow Soviet–Israeli relations to improve, had vexed the Soviets. In 1965 it also tore the tiny Israeli Communist Party into two opposing groups: a pro-Eshkol group headed by Moshe Sneh and Shmuel Mikunis, and an anti-Eshkol group. Early in 1966, representatives of the two opposing factions of the Israeli Communist Party went to Moscow to seek support from the Soviet Communist Party. In a meeting that included both splinter groups, the anti-Eshkol group had to sit silently while Boris Ponomarev, head of the international department at the Central Committee, and Mikhail Suslov, Politburo member, argued for a nuanced approach to Israeli politics.

Suslov said that it was necessary to distinguish between different elements in the Israeli leadership. His government favored a peaceful solution of Middle Eastern problems and urged Arab leaders, such as Nasser or Iraqi President Abd al-Rahman Aref, to avoid war with Israel. Moreover, stressed Suslov, his government had nothing in common with Mao Zedong's radical politics which called for such a war. Immediately afterward, Ponomarev read a letter prepared in advance by party authorities emphasizing that the party opposed any anti-Israeli chauvinism, especially in the Arab world. The Communists, the letter said, must not be indifferent to liberal tendencies in the Israeli government, thus stressing Soviet support for the pro-Eshkol group. Both Ponomarev and Suslov talked openly about the difference of opinion between the international department and the Soviet Foreign Ministry with regard to Israel. The Soviet Foreign Ministry, they claimed, was trying to stifle any pro-Israeli pronouncement lest the Arab ambassadors loudly protest as they had done in the past. However, when Mikunis suggested that the Soviet Union should initiate actions toward bettering Soviet–Israeli relations, Ponomarev and Suslov demurred, saying that they preferred to wait for more encouraging signals from Jerusalem. The contents of this meeting were dutifully reported by Sneh and Mikunis to the Israeli government.[9]

It was not the last time that an insider recommended that the Soviet government initiate a thaw with Tel Aviv. Dmitri Chuvakhin, Soviet ambassador to Tel Aviv, adopted wholeheartedly the Mikunis–Sneh view of the Eshkol government. At that time, he was already an experienced diplomat who had served in the US, Albania, and Canada. Michael Haddow, the British ambassador to Israel, who had a long talk with Chuvakhin in mid-1966, went as far as describing the Soviet diplomat as "Pro-Israeli." In an interview, Chuvakhin said that international conflicts should be resolved peacefully. The Soviet Union, he opined, should intervene to stop either Israeli or Arab aggression.[10]

In the long memo Chuvakhin sent to the Soviet Foreign Ministry in March 1966 he argued that the Soviet Union must take advantage of a rare opportunity made possible by Eshkol's rise to power and the unique set of circumstances in which Israel found itself in the mid-1960s. He claimed that it was finally dawning on the Israelis that they could no longer afford to be in constant conflict with the Arab world. The Soviet Union, recommended Chuvakhin, should leverage its influence in the Arab world to improve its relations with Israel and persuade it to jettison its pro-Western stance in favor of a neutralist foreign policy. Specifically, he advised the Soviet Union to adopt its own peace initiative. Although he did not believe it was possible to solve the conflict at the time, Chuvakhin thought that several security-building measures could be taken. The Soviet Union should work "In the Arab countries – against radical anti-Israeli tendencies, their preparations for war and physical elimination of Israel and [work] for a recognition in principle of Israel's right to exist." Chuvakhin argued that, in return, Israel would agree to join a declaration calling for the establishment of a nuclear-free zone in the Middle East.[11] This was not speculation: Chuvakhin's conclusion was based on his conversations with Eshkol and Eshkol's emissary, Eliezer Livneh.

Chuvakhin and Ivan Dedyulya, the KGB resident in Tel Aviv, made the mistake during March 1966 of talking publicly of their hope that the Soviet Union would take a more active role in mediating between the Arabs and the Jews. Arab ambassadors in Moscow immediately sought audiences with Soviet officials to complain, thus affirming Suslov's and Ponomarev's depiction of the dangers inherent in a pro-Israeli line. Chuvakhin and perhaps even Dedyulya were reprimanded.[12] In short, the Arabs made it clear to the Soviet Union that it could be either with them or against them. The gains of a pro-Israeli policy always in doubt, the Soviets decided not to be too vocal about their difference of opinion with the Arabs, although they probably thought that the Arab ambassadors were overreacting.

Amid all of this, Moshe Sneh reported to Chuvakhin that an Eshkol adviser had told him that Israel was working to develop an atomic bomb. Chuvakhin was instructed to feed to Sneh the following message from Moscow: the Soviet Union would view any Israeli step toward a nuclear bomb most unfavorably. However, Israel should know that the Soviet Union would work to maintain peace in the region and had suggested the establishment of a nuclear-free zone in the Middle East.[13] Most likely, the Soviets were trying to make it clear to Israel that cooperating with the Soviet Union could bring about the same outcome that the nuclear project set out to achieve: a secure Israel. The dialogue, however, was discontinued at that point due to dramatic events in Damascus.

With Friends Like These

A military coup in Syria which took place on February 23, 1966 had nipped Soviet–Israeli rapprochement in the bud. The tension between Soviet aims and Syrian ones was not evident in the first few months following the coup and, in fact, Syrian–Soviet relations enjoyed a sort of a honeymoon during that time – one that angered and frustrated Jerusalem.[14] At the outset, what really caught the attention of the international department of the Communist Party of the Soviet Union was the extraordinary treatment that the Syrian Communists had received from the new government. While in other parts of the Arab world (including Nasser's Egypt) Communists were persecuted, the military Baath regime released Communists from jail, allowed their exiled leader, Khaled Bakdash, to return to Syria, and included a minister with ties to the Communist Party in the new government.[15]

In response, the Soviet government decided to invite a high-level Syrian delegation to Moscow in April. For the Syrians, the crowning achievement of that visit was the Soviet decision to give Syria a generous loan to finance the building of a major dam over the Euphrates. By taking on the financing of the dam, the Soviet Union was changing its position: Syria's request for a loan from the Soviet government in August 1964, when Khrushchev was still in power, had been refused.[16] Behind this shift was Brezhnev. It dovetailed with his policy of helping radical Third World regimes.

By that stage it was already known that the new Baath faction in power was more radical than the one that had preceded it. The new leaders had already made harsh anti-Western and anti-Israel declarations and expressed their support for North Vietnam's struggle against "world imperialism." Arab countries should support Fatah, so the new regime in Damascus said, in the same way that the North Vietnamese supported the Vietcong.[17] Rather than recoil, Brezhnev sought to bring the new Syrian government closer to Moscow. He insisted on meeting the Syrian delegation. That was highly unusual, given the fact that foreign policy was considered to be Kosygin's purview, but Brezhnev drew attention to the head of the Syrian delegation, Yusuf Zuayn, being leader of the Baath Party just as he was leader of the Soviet Communist Party.

The Syrian delegation's two meetings in Moscow – one with Kosygin and the other with Brezhnev – produced two different communiqués. The Syrians were not entirely silent about the divisions they discerned within the Soviet elite and they elucidated them in an article that appeared in *al-Munadil* one month after their return from the Russian capital. The article started with a discussion of the first communiqué, which appeared after the delegation's meeting with Kosygin. The first paragraph, by way of apology, explained that such communiqués were the result of a compromise rather than a full expression of the opinion of the Baath Party. Indeed, the communiqué made no mention of Soviet military support to Syria nor the topic that was so near and dear to the hearts of Baathists: Fatah's popular war of liberation. The communiqué spoke at length about the need to put a stop to the arms race in the region and discussed in great detail Syria's economic development. In reality, although Minister of Defense Assad was a member of the Syrian delegation, he never got to meet his Soviet counterpart. Nor did he have any meeting with other military officials. Kosygin and his men chose to avoid the issue of military aid altogether.[18]

What irked the Syrians even more was the rather moderate reference to the plight of the Palestinian refugees that appeared only at the end of a long paragraph discussing the urgent need to solve international conflicts peacefully. "With regard to the Palestine issue," wrote the anonymous author in *al-Munadil*, "the comrades should understand, that the wording which appeared in the joint communiqué was the maximum that Soviet officials could agree upon." The Syrian article mentioned that delegations from Egypt and Algeria had also had to agree to a rather innocuous formula on Palestine and that, comparatively, the Syrian–Soviet communiqué's phrasing was preferable to that in other Soviet–Arab declarations. The Arabs, reasoned the writer, would have to do a lot more explaining to convince socialist countries to take a principled rather than an opportunistic position on the Palestine question. Nevertheless, the writer complained, "this [Palestine] clause [in the communiqué] is inadequate and we have to push the socialist countries . . . This change will not come by itself."[19]

One thing that gave the Baathists hope was that the Soviets were far from united. While in the formal negotiations the Syrians were forced to moderate their position on Palestine, they found that:

> there are many within the Politburo, the Central Committee and the government in the Soviet Union (and Bulgaria) that admitted to us during chance encounters and informal talks that they think that our views on the Palestine question are correct but they still cannot turn this position into a formal policy. It was implied that there was a need to push the others through our principled position regarding our main national problem of Palestine in order that their private opinion would become the official policy of their government . . .[20]

Like the Israeli diplomats in Washington, the Syrians found out that the superpower they were dealing with was speaking with two voices. If in Washington it was the White House against the State Department, in Moscow it was the party, led by Brezhnev, against the government, led by Kosygin. Indeed, the article in *al-Munadil* praised the communiqué published after the meeting between Brezhnev and the Syrian delegation, and added that during the talks with Brezhnev the Syrians felt that they "were no longer confined by the narrow governmental framework."[21]

The rather ambiguous message the Syrians heard in the Soviet capital, and the intensifying conflict between Jadid and Assad that flared up after the latter returned from Moscow, created a real problem for Soviet diplomacy. The main goal of the Soviet Foreign Ministry was to prevent an Arab–Israeli war. Since the Syrians constantly claimed that Israel was about to attack them, something had to be done about it. What happened in mid-May

1966 was a case in point. When Syrian Foreign Minister Ibrahim Makhus met with the Soviet ambassador to Damascus, Anatoli Barkovski, he spoke of the Syrian government's worries that imperialist countries and Arab reactionary states were increasing their attempts to undermine the Baath regime. Proof of that could be found in Israeli and Jordanian troop concentrations on the Syrian border.[22] The Soviets cooperated and delivered warnings to Israel and Jordan not to interfere in internal Syrian affairs – a step that Makhus in his conversation with Barkovski had explicitly requested.[23]

Still, it did not take much longer for Soviet diplomats to become disenchanted by the behavior of their Syrian ally. In August 1966, Soviet diplomats in Washington told State Department officials that Syria was unstable and its regime unpredictable. One could not tell, complained the Soviets, who was giving orders to whom or decipher how Syrian bureaucracy worked.[24] Moreover, from September onward, the Israeli Foreign Ministry received reports from Paris and Bonn according to which Syrian–Soviet relations had deteriorated and the Soviets were slowing down their preparations to make the Euphrates dam loan available. There were also rumors, later proven correct, that the Soviets were delaying their arms shipments to Syria. Indeed, in the period between 1965 and 1967, the Syrians received almost no major items of weaponry from the Soviet Union.[25]

Pushing Nasser into the Baath's Arms

One of the main aims of Kosygin's visit to Egypt in May 1966 was to solve the Syrian problem. Due to Brezhnev's intervention the Soviet Union shackled itself to an unpredictable and unreliable ally. Kosygin wanted to remedy the situation by encouraging Egypt to create an alliance with Syria. In such a framework, Nasser's level-headedness would temper Syrian radicalism. Therefore, during their talks, Kosygin asked Nasser to improve his relations with Syria and expounded on the need to create a united front of Arab progressive countries.[26]

That was all very well, but the Egyptians were waiting for Kosygin to offer new funds to support their country's increasingly failing economy. No money was promised, though Kosygin probably agreed to ease some of the credit terms of Egypt's previous loans. Shortly after Kosygin's visit, a Soviet diplomat in Cairo confessed to his French colleague that with regard to financial matters, Egypt was a bottomless pit that swallowed roubles without delivering results.[27] Presumably this reasoning was the driving force behind the Soviets' tight-purse policy toward Egypt. Later that year, Kosygin also claimed that during his Cairo visit Nasser had asked for his help with economic planning. Tellingly, the reform-minded Kosygin responded by sending Yevsei Liberman – a Soviet economist, who, like Kosygin, supported the introduction of market-based methods into the Soviet economy – to Egypt.[28] This was probably Kosygin's way of further pressuring Nasser to reform the Egyptian economy instead of asking for more loans.

In August 1966, the State Department, following various talks with the Soviets, had informed the Israelis that the Soviets insisted on being paid for the arms they had delivered to Arab countries.[29] A French journalist claimed at the time that the Soviet Union was so insistent that past debts must be settled that Soviet ships carrying equipment for the Aswan project had refused to unload their cargo in Alexandria unless stacks of cotton – Egypt's main payment in kind – were visible at the docks. According to the journalist, Soviet advisers were visiting the offices of the Suez Canal Company regularly to monitor its efficiency.[30] Later on, even during the state of emergency caused by the entrance of the Egyptian army into Sinai on May 15, 1967, Dmitri Pozhedaev, Soviet ambassador in Cairo, saw fit to question Amer four days later about why Egyptian cotton was being delivered to the Soviet Union at such a slow pace. Pozhedaev hinted that Egypt should think about how to solve this problem if it wanted to continue to purchase weapons from the Soviet Union.[31] In other words, even in the thick of the May 1967 international crisis, the Soviets were still insisting on implementing a strict policy of debt repayment. Nor did the Soviet Union show much enthusiasm for replacing the US as Egypt's main grain supplier. Although the Johnson administration's refusal to continue to supply Egypt with discounted wheat created an opportunity, at various points in 1966 the Soviets informed the Czechoslovaks, the Americans, and the French that they did not consider themselves capable of solving Egypt's food problems.[32]

Syria, Fatah, and the Specter of Chinese "Adventurism"

Gravely concerned about recent Israeli–Syrian clashes on the border, on October 11, 1966 Chuvakhin sent a telegram from Tel Aviv which explained that Palestinian guerrilla operations were playing into the hands of the hawks in Israel who were interested in launching an attack against the Baath regime. Chuvakhin argued that the Syrian media's support for these acts was making things worse. He recommended approaching the Syrian government and asking it to distance itself from these operations.[33]

That same day, Chuvakhin was instructed by the Soviet Foreign Ministry to visit the Israeli foreign minister and inform him that the Soviet Union had received reports of Israeli troop concentrations on the Syrian border which were part of preparations for a large air and land attack against Syria. The Soviet Union, Chuvakhin had been ordered to say, was closely following events in the region. Since the Syrians considered the Jordanians to be their arch-enemies in the Arab world, Jordan also received a note of warning from the Soviet Union. At the same time, the Soviets sent a notice to Egypt presenting the warnings to Jordan and Israel as proof of Soviet support for Egypt and Syria. Two days later, on October 13, Anatoli Barkovski, the Soviet ambassador in Damascus, met with Syrian Foreign Minister Ibrahim Makhus and updated him on his country's diplomatic activity on behalf of Syria. Makhus was pleased, and thanked the Soviets.[34] But did the Soviets really believe that the Syrian report was genuine?

While Soviet ambassadors in the region were delivering their threats, Syrian Minister of Defense Hafez al-Assad met with senior officers in his office. He told them that the Soviets had made it clear over a series of meetings that while they were willing to help the Syrian army by supplying it with weapons, they did not want to be dragged into a superpower confrontation in the Middle East along the lines of the Cuban Missile Crisis.[35] Four days later, on October 15, Soviet Deputy Foreign Minister Victor Semyonov met with the Syrian ambassador in Moscow. He told him that his government had no information regarding Israeli aggressive intentions against Syria and advised the Syrians to cool their emotions.[36]

Reporting to the Politburo in the second half of November, Gromyko claimed that Barkovski had met with Syrian Prime Minister Yusuf Zuayn and told him that the Palestinian sabotage activity against Israel could create serious complications in the Middle East. The Palestinian organizations, Gromyko added, had influential supporters in high places in Syria, Jordan, and Iraq. Worse, these organizations seemed poised to commit even more serious acts of sabotage. Tellingly, the memo claimed that the Chinese were behind all of this. By training the "Palestinian partisans" and their cadres, the Chinese were trying to create "a second Vietnam" in the Middle East. Summarizing the events of October, Gromyko wrote that the Soviet Foreign Ministry was adopting a two-pronged approach to the problem. On the one hand, a warning was sent to the Israeli government demanding that it cease its aggressive policy toward the Arab countries. On the other hand, a note was sent to the governments of Iraq, Jordan, and Syria, informing them that a warning had been sent to Israel, but also explaining that the Soviet government held a negative view of Chinese activity in the Middle East and the irresponsible behavior of the Palestinian guerrilla organizations.[37]

No doubt, the Chinese were in contact with the Palestinian Fatah movement. They also supplied weapons to that organization and allowed its members to be trained in China. Furthermore, the Chinese conducted several propaganda campaigns in the Middle East calling for Arab resistance against imperialism.[38] Indeed, the loaded term "a second Vietnam" appears in inverted commas in Gromyko's memo, signaling that he was quoting Chinese propaganda, or at least thought he was. However, the notion of the Chinese being behind Palestinian guerrilla operations seems rather to highlight the fact that the Soviets had their own "bogeyman" theories, conjured from past experiences in other regions rather than from the contemporary realities of the Middle East.

To be sure, during 1965–66 the Chinese were the Soviets' *bête noire* in Vietnam, where the considerable aid China was sending to North Vietnam gave it more influence over Hanoi than the Soviets.[39] But interpreting the Syrian situation through the analogy of Vietnam made little sense. While Vietnam was in China's backyard, Syria was a distant territory in which Chinese aid could never match that supplied by the Soviets. A Czechoslovak report on Chinese activity in Syria from February 1967 concluded that while the Syrians, due to their "petit-bourgeoisie radicalism," were amenable to Chinese propaganda, in truth Chinese influence on Syria was negligible. It also claimed the Syrians were well aware that Soviet-bloc aid to Syria was vital for the country's economic development, while all the Chinese had to offer were slogans and declarations.[40]

Another memo submitted by Gromyko to the Politburo two months later indicated that the Soviets were still worried. The January 1967 report referred to Vietnam and the Middle East as two flashpoints where tensions must be relaxed to avoid an "acute situation." "In this connection," argued Gromyko, "we should, while supporting the Arab countries in their struggle against Israel's expansionist policy, flexibly dampen the extremist trends in the policy of certain Arab states, e.g., Syria, orienting them toward domestic consolidation."[41]

Amer and Jadid in Moscow

Another low point in Soviet–Egyptian relations was reached during Abd al-Hakim Amer's visit to Moscow in late November 1966. The first sign that the negotiations with the Soviets would not go well came at the end of October. With an inkling of things to come, Egyptian army representatives approached the Czechoslovak embassy in Cairo to ask whether Amer could visit Czechoslovakia if the Soviet Union would not satisfy his demands for weapons. The Soviets, on their part, told the Czechoslovaks that they were going to refuse some of Amer's requests.[42] Still, Amer and his colleagues went to Moscow at the end of November with high hopes. Earlier that month, Cairo had concluded a defense treaty with Syria – something that the Soviets had encouraged the Egyptians to do ever since Kosygin's May visit – and they were under the impression that as a result the Soviet Union would be much more accommodating to Egyptian requests.[43] The visit, however, turned out to be a huge disappointment.

Amer's request for more tanks was refused by Defense Minister Marshal Andrei Grechko, who was the chief negotiator. Egyptian demands for the latest models minted by the Soviet arms industry, such as the MiG-25, were not only rejected but also made the butt of Brezhnev's taunting; during a speech he gave at a formal dinner (attended by Amer), he likened the Egyptians to a child who asks for sophisticated toys without having the slightest idea as to what to do with them. Amer was so enraged by these remarks that he almost got up and left. The Egyptians' claims that these planes, as well as other advanced air-defense systems, were needed to confront Israel's strong air force were rebuffed. Grechko explained to the Egyptians that the MiG-25 was not even sold to Warsaw Pact allies and claimed that the air-defense systems they requested required special technical skills that the Egyptians did not possess.

To add injury to insult, the Soviets agreed to deliver only part of the 400,000 tons of flour that Amer had requested. Moreover, a personal appeal to Kosygin, whom Amer had met with no less than four times during his stay in Moscow, to allow Egypt to further spread its payments was answered by another exhortation on the need to reform the Egyptian economy. This time Kosygin castigated the Egyptian custom of appointing ex-officers to management positions in the state-owned industry. Civilians, claimed Kosygin, could do a better job. Despite disappointing the Egyptians in more ways than one, the Soviets did not shy away from demanding yet again greater access to Egyptian naval and air facilities. The Egyptians agreed to allow the Soviets to store fuel in their naval facilities but said they needed more time to consider permitting access to their airfields, from where the Soviets wanted to conduct reconnaissance flights. Later, Amer would openly admit that he was offended by the treatment he had received in Moscow during his November visit.[44]

Two months later, another Syrian delegation arrived in Moscow. This group, which stayed in the Soviet capital through January 20–26, 1967, was led by Salah Jadid, the assistant secretary of the Baath Party and for all practical purposes Syria's strongman. It was received rather coolly. This time Brezhnev did not meet with the Syrian visitors. In general, there were almost no reports on the Syrian delegation in the Soviet press and the

Soviets only sent low-ranking party officials to the meetings with the Syrians, much to Jadid's anger. There was no agreement on the text of the final communiqué that was issued, quite unusually, only four weeks after the delegation returned to Damascus. The Syrians wanted the Baath acknowledged in the communiqué as the most progressive, anti-imperialist element in the Arab world. The Soviets answered that the Baath was only one of a group of other equally progressive Arab parties, such as those in Egypt and Algeria. The Syrians also wanted their cooperation with other left-leaning parties in Syria to be extolled. The Soviets answered that lately the Baath regime had treated the Syrian Communists harshly. The Soviets were equally inflexible when the Syrians tried to insert a paragraph calling for the liquidation of Israel. The Czechoslovak report on the visit concluded triumphantly that:

> As a result of the visit, certain elements in the Baath Party learned that Soviet support to the progressive Syrian regime does not mean unconditional support for any step which the regime might take without weighing whether the action is taken on the basis of a realistic assessment of the situation and whether it would lead to negative results.[45]

Jadid came back to Damascus in a foul mood and rumors started spreading that the regime was planning a wave of arrests against the Communists. When one of Jadid's minions, Khaled al-Jundi, head of the Trade Union Federation, was asked about the results of Jadid's visit to Moscow, he retorted: "To hell with the Soviets. They will pay for this."[46] The Soviets were equally angry with Jadid. While talking with the British ambassador in Damascus shortly after the delegation returned, Barkovski said that "if Jadid stopped meddling with everything, it would surely improve Syria's sorry state."[47]

To complement their efforts to restrain the Syrians, the Soviets approached both Cairo and Jerusalem. The head of the Middle Eastern Department at the Soviet Foreign Ministry, Alexei Shchiborin, met twice with Israeli diplomats in March and April 1967. In both meetings he stressed that the Soviet Union acknowledged Israel's right to exist, was interested in peace and stability in the region, and actively tried to convince the Arabs to relinquish any thoughts of attacking Israel. At the same time, admitted Shchiborin, Soviet influence on the Arabs and especially Syria was limited. The most important thing, he pleaded, was that Israel should not do anything to aggravate an already combustible situation.[48]

The Soviet Union and the Yemen War

In March 1967, Gromyko arrived in Cairo for a state visit. It had been initi-ated by the Soviets and was announced to the Egyptians only shortly before Gromyko's arrival, creating a sense of anticipation as to what would be on the agenda.[49] Hints were provided by leaks from knowledgeable sources claiming that Egypt's involvement in Yemen would be at the center of the Nasser–Gromyko talks.[50]

The Soviet government had already expressed its displeasure with Nasser's Yemen policy. It had insisted on the need to secure the peace in Yemen being inserted into the communiqué following Nasser's September 1965 visit. The Soviets had also made it known to Nasser that they supported his attempts to reach a truce with Faisal, and assured the French and the Americans that they were not encouraging Nasser's aspirations in Yemen. According to some reports, the Soviets found Nasser's interventions particularly regrettable because the human and financial costs were eroding the Egyptian leader's popularity at home. They had therefore advised Nasser to scale back his commitments in Yemen and focus on mending the Egyptian economy. The fact that Nasser had asked Kosygin in 1966 to foot the bill for his South Arabian escapade did little to enhance Soviet enthusiasm; indeed, Soviet officials told Egyptian diplomats in early 1967 that the Soviet Union would not be able to continue financing the Egyptian intervention in Yemen.[51]

This was yet another sign of the radical shift in Soviet foreign policy. In 1962, when Nasser lacked the means to send urgent assistance to the Yemeni republican forces in the remote south, he had appealed to the Soviet Union for help. Although Khrushchev was then preoccupied with the Cuban missile crisis, he reacted with gusto, ordering a fleet of Antonov An-12 transport planes, manned by Soviet pilots, to help Egypt dispatch its troops to Yemen. A few weeks later, Tupolev Tu-16 bombers with mixed Soviet–Egyptian crews carried out bombing missions over Yemen.[52]

However, by the mid-1960s the situation had changed, and avoiding a confrontation with the US seemed to trump all other policy objectives. Shortly before and after Gromyko's visit to the UAR, Cuba received threat-ening telegrams from Moscow which emphasized that Havana should cease its support for Latin American guerrilla movements working against American interests in the continent. Should Cuban support for these move-ments involve it in a war with the US, warned the Soviet telegrams – which were sent personally to Castro both at the end of 1966 and in the spring of 1967 – the Cubans would have to face the Yankees alone: Moscow would not lift a finger to help them.[53]

However, while the Soviets were trying to extinguish the flames in Latin America, Nasser was threatening to ignite a conflagration at the other end of the world. A month before Gromyko's arrival in Cairo, Nasser gave a major speech in which he talked vehemently about Egypt's intention to continue its involvement in Yemen. A reference to the British troops stationed in Aden was interpreted by the Quai d'Orsay as a veiled threat to intervene militarily there.[54] However, any trouble in Yemen could have had a very destabilizing effect on superpower relations in the Middle East. There were not only British forces in Yemen, but also American troops stationed in Saudi Arabia. One could predict that, were hostilities between British and Egyptian forces to occur, the US would support the British and the Soviets would be compelled to back the Egyptians. In short, the Soviets could see how Nasser's devotion to the revolution in Yemen could turn this desolate corner of the world into another Cold War hotspot. Sources close to the Egyptian embassy in Moscow claimed that Gromyko would ask Nasser "not to take actions that might embroil other countries in the tense situation in the Middle East."[55]

These leaks only angered Nasser and as a result the Gromyko–Nasser meeting went just as badly as other Soviet–Egyptian summits in those years. Although Yemen was not the only topic discussed by the two men – Nasser was none too pleased with the Soviet Union's burgeoning relations with the Iranian Shah and improved rapport with the US – it dominated the conversation. Nasser brought up the pre-visit leaks and portrayed them as a Soviet attempt to dictate his policy in Yemen. In fact, he felt that Soviet official ideology should have compelled the Soviets to support him. He therefore demanded a clear answer from Gromyko: was the Soviet Union with him or against him with regard to Yemen? Although Gromyko tried to reassure Nasser that the USSR still considered Egypt a strategic ally, as far as Yemen was concerned, he had no kind words to offer.[56]

Provoked by an American diplomat at the end of April, an Egyptian counselor at Egypt's embassy in Moscow admitted that Yemen was discussed during Gromyko's visit to Cairo but that no decisions had been reached. He added – with evident irritation – that what went on in the Red Sea area was none of the Soviets' concern. The Egyptian counselor also claimed that the Soviets had learned long ago that when talking to Egypt, they could only advise, not instruct. When asked what the Soviet attitude would be if Egyptian troops occupied Aden after the British pulled out, he stated that the Soviets would strongly oppose such a move.[57]

20

A SOVIET HALL OF MIRRORS

B Y MAY 14, 1967, Moscow already felt it had lost control over events in the Middle East. Meeting with Ghaleb on that day, Semyonov used sharp words to describe local agents of Red China who were trying to turn the struggle with Israel into another Vietnam; Ghaleb had no doubt he was referring to Syrians.[1] Eight days later, Semyonov met with the Syrian ambassador, and urged Syria not to do anything to provoke an Israeli or Western attack.[2]

Official Soviet media received with stunned silence Nasser's decision to close the Straits of Tiran on May 21 and to ignore a well-known Israeli *casus belli*. One day after the closing of the Straits, a Soviet diplomat confided in a French colleague that although Moscow understood Cairo's desire to maintain its prestige in the Arab world, it believed that Egypt had gone too far. The Soviets, he said, did not consider the Arabs capable of winning a war against Israel. Bilateral consultations were not going smoothly. He underlined the need for both parties to remain calm and said that the Soviet Union was trying to convince Egypt to do just that. The Soviet diplomat also claimed that if Israel made concessions, Egypt would reciprocate.[3]

But yet again, while Soviet diplomacy was trying to calm the waters, others in Moscow were making sure the crisis would not die down. The tension became visible when Nasser decided to embroil the Soviet Union still further in the crisis. The first step in this elaborate dance was taken by Foreign Minister Mahmud Riad and Amer, who on May 16 separately met with the Soviet ambassador, Dmitri Pozhedaev. They asked him for further clarification on the information the Soviet Union had given Egypt regarding Israeli troop concentrations on the Syrian border. (It was of little importance then, as Egyptian forces were already in Sinai.) On May 20 the Politburo authorized Pozhedaev to meet with Riad and Minister of War Shams Badran to tell them more about what the Soviets knew. The most important part of the updated Soviet assessment was the claim that Israel had only postponed its operation against Syria, but had not canceled it. This piece of evidence seemed to justify the permanent presence of Egyptian troops in Sinai. The Soviets also claimed that Israel had deployed two contingents near the Syrian border, each comprising four brigades, one to the north and one to the south of the Sea of Galilee. Aided by an aerial attack, Israeli forces were to destroy and occupy Syrian positions on the Golan Heights within thirty-six hours and withdraw only after the creation of a UN force that would be permanently placed along the Syrian–Israeli border.[4]

By that time there should have been enough evidence to disprove the original intelligence report that started the crisis. Soviet military intelligence could have consulted their 400 military advisers embedded among Syrian troops at the front. But who in Moscow was eager to stoke Egyptian fears? One important clue is supplied by the Egyptian ambassador in Moscow, Murad Ghaleb, who recalled that "when I informed [Marshal Andrei] Grechko [the Soviet minister of defense] about the results of the Fawzi trip he was surprised and said that he knew for sure that there are Israeli concentrations on the Syrian border and that the Soviets know not only the names of the senior Israel commanders [of the troops] but even the names of the battalion commanders."[5] Grechko, a brash Soviet general and a political ally of Brezhnev, would become in the days ahead a key figure in the story. More than any other institution in the Soviet Union, it was the army that could gain from the crisis and it is clear that what it sought was a way of using the situation to gain naval access to Egyptian facilities, this time on a permanent basis.

Nasser Closes the Offensive Window

The closure of the Straits of Tiran to Israeli navigation was a momentous step for Egypt and it increased the chances of war considerably. The high-stakes atmosphere also increased the friction between Nasser and Amer. Amer was still considering limited offensive operations that would either respond to an Israeli offensive or would be used to trigger an Israeli campaign. At this stage high command did not envisage an all-out Israeli offensive against Egypt, but rather believed that the Israelis would launch an operation focusing on Sharm al-Sheikh. Amer was still contemplating a response in the form of an air and land attack on Eilat or on Israeli settlements bordering Gaza. But Nasser, who was more attuned to the tenor of international public opinion and was in contact with the superpowers, wanted nothing of the kind. His assessment was that he had already won a major political victory over his enemies in the Arab world. For years Jordan and Saudi Arabia had taunted him for hiding behind the apron of the UN emergency forces in Sinai. Now he had proved them wrong. Moreover, he had demonstrated that he could limit Israel's freedom of action. By doing so he renewed the pre-1956 status quo. That was enough for Nasser, and he was willing to quit while he was ahead.

Nasser was concerned by Eban's visit to Europe and Washington as well as by news that the Americans were evacuating their citizens from Egypt. He assumed that Israel was conspiring with the UK and the US behind Egypt's back. If that was not enough to worry him, then an intelligence memo of May 25 surely clarified that Nasser was playing a high-stakes game. According to the report, General Odd Bull, commander of UN troops in the area, had told his officers in Gaza during a closed meeting that "the military establishment in Israel – especially the military intelligence – is yearning for war right now." Bull said he had never seen Israel in such a state of high alert before, and advised his officers to be ready. Like Amer, Nasser assumed that Israel would attack Sharm al-Sheikh, an assault that would involve American forces in the Mediterranean.[6]

Nevertheless, Nasser hoped that this scenario was avoidable. He took several steps to prevent the tense situation from exploding. He sent a letter to the Syrians, ordering them to cease Fatah activity at once, and sat down with Ahmad Shukeiri, head of the PLO, for a long talk. Nasser told Shukeiri that "We are not ready for the liberation campaign. The liberation of Palestine may happen only in the far future." Nasser asked Shukeiri to use his contacts in Damascus to make sure that Fatah stopped its guerrilla warfare against Israel. The same day, May 26, Nasser contacted the US through an emissary, confirmed that he had no intention of attacking Israel, and asked Washington not to intervene militarily in the dispute.[7]

Most important was his intervention in General Staff discussions at main headquarters. While participating in a military conference on May 25, Nasser realized that Amer was still considering offensive operations. Nasser pointed out during the meeting that he doubted whether Egypt would gain anything from launching a limited local attack of the sort Amer was discussing. After the conference, Nasser took Amer aside. Emerging from that private consultation, Amer canceled his order to the air force to be ready to commence Operation "Assad" – an air raid on southern Israel – in the early morning of May 27. Mohamed Fawzi, the chief of staff and Amer's enemy, wrote wryly that Amer's cancelation of that order came exactly two hours after he had issued it. The following day, May 26, Nasser received a telegram from Washington detailing what Abba Eban had told the Americans. Eban's claim that Egypt and Syria were on the verge of launching an all-out attack on Israel worried Nasser. He started suspecting that Amer's offensive plans had been leaked to the Israelis, something that would surely strengthen the war hawks in Eshkol's cabinet.[8]

Another military conference took place the day after, around 9 p.m. To his surprise, Nasser found that Amer was still discussing offensive operations with the generals. This time the emphasis was on Operation "Fajer" – a ground operation to take the Israeli city of Eilat. Nasser said nothing during the meeting itself but afterwards sat down with Amer once again to try to impress upon the marshal the error of his views. Nasser claimed that all the talk of offensive plans only confused the troops on the ground and the officers. As far as world opinion was concerned, Egypt made the first aggressive step when it sent its forces into Sinai and closed the Straits. Nasser then told Amer: "If we take another step now, we would create the situation which Johnson and Israel hope for. A great part of world opinion would support Johnson if he gave the Sixth Fleet the order ... to move against us. We will not be able to deal with that during the crisis." He added:

> My main objective in managing this crisis is that we would end it in peace and without war and although the probability of a war erupting has gone up to 60 percent ... I still trust that the effort done by many ... would be able to buy time ... To come now and say that we would strike the first blow is an irresponsible thing to do.

Finally, Amer was convinced. At a late hour, he called the head of the operations branch to ask him to cancel all the previous instructions regarding offensive operations and to instruct the forces to prepare for "active defense."[9]

Shams Badran Goes to Moscow

Shams Badran bore the title Minister of War. In practical terms, he was Amer's right-hand man, and Amer made him responsible for appointments and promotions. Badran was the person most involved in creating and maintaining the networks of patronage within the army which owed loyalty to Amer. Amer trusted him completely, but that did not necessarily qualify Badran to be either a commander or a diplomat. Nevertheless, he was the one chosen by the regime to travel to Moscow to conduct high-level talks on the eve of war. According to his own testimony, Badran's mission came about as a result of a chance encounter with Nasser at headquarters. It was late at night when Nasser pulled him aside and told him, "Prepare yourself, you are traveling tomorrow to Russia." Badran was surprised. "How come?" he asked. Nasser answered: "It's a public relations affair so that people would say the Minister of War went and met the Russian Defense Minister . . . it is going to have an effect." Badran could not have been Nasser's first choice as envoy. It was probably Amer who pressed for it and Nasser acquiesced.[10]

At that time, the situation of the Egyptian army at the front seemed dire. Equipping tens of thousands of reserve soldiers emptied Egyptian arsenals. Amer was increasingly worried about it, and already on May 19 had asked the Soviet ambassador for an expedited shipment of 40 MiG-21s and 100–150 armored troop carriers. This request had been approved by the Soviets but Amer wanted much more: an urgent shipment of light weapons and ammunition – all of them in short supply on the front lines in Sinai – as well as all the weapons the Soviets had committed to deliver to Egypt in 1968. Amer's anxieties compelled him to do something he had not done before: allow the Soviet navy to establish its own airfield in Alexandria which it could use to spy on the Sixth Fleet.[11] For years, the Soviet navy had been promising Egypt an abundant supply of weapons in exchange for unlimited access to Egyptian naval and air facilities.[12] Now Badran was instructed to propose that that deal be consummated.

A description of the different factions in the Kremlin written by Nasser's confidant, Mohamed Hassanein Heikal, suggests that Badran went to Moscow with a firm grasp of the main players he would meet:

> Kosygin and Brezhnev were talking three different languages. Brezhnev was enthusiastic and oratorical, Kosygin was wary and calculating . . . As for the military, they were even more complicated. Given the importance of the military supply relationship and the prominence of the military leaders in the power structure, their words carried particular weight with the Egyptians, but it often appeared that the circuit was closed. Grechko, a ground forces officer, liked the atmosphere of crisis, while Rodenko, the Air Marshal, was taken by the good flying weather all year long [in Egypt], while Admiral Gorshakov had eyes only for straits and gulfs connected with the three colored seas: the Black, the White [Mediterranean] and the Red.[13]

Badran arrived in Moscow on May 25. His first meeting was at 5 p.m. with Grechko. Grechko's message was clear: Egypt had gained a good deal so far. It had Moscow's support. But now was not the time to start a conflict with the imperialists. Egypt should make sure it was not being dragged into a war. In this context, Grechko shared with Badran his worries about the Syrians who were, according to him, "flying in the air." They might attack Israel, speculated Grechko, and the result would be a "political defeat."

Grechko would have known more than most about the efforts made by the Soviets over the past decade to train and equip the Egyptian army – for mainly defensive purposes. The same sort of initiative was evident in Moscow's policy regarding aircraft sales to Egypt. The Soviets were willing to provide the Egyptian Air Force mostly with fighter-interceptors such as the MiGs. But only fifteen SU-7s, heavy bombers of the kind that would allow long-range incursions, were supplied to Egypt before the war (and this was why Hod, commander of the Israeli Air Force, knew that the Egyptians could not really perform a successful stealth air raid). The Egyptian admirals who negotiated with the Soviets over naval arms deals also had the impression that the Soviets were intent on selling them only defensive weapons such as anti-ship missiles. Moreover, Soviet advisers were heavily involved in writing the "Qaher" plan, which was a defensive maneuver.[14]

Badran and his delegation met with Gromyko at 10 p.m., five hours after their appointment with Grechko. Gromyko said he knew that Egypt took only defensive measures "and had no intention of blowing up the situation." The Soviet foreign minister added that the Soviet Union had a mighty fleet in the area. Indeed, on the eve of war, June 1, there were thirty Soviet warships and ten submarines in the Mediterranean, the greatest number of vessels the USSR had ever assembled in the area.[15]

The next day, Badran's chief interlocutor was Kosygin. With very few pleasantries exchanged, their 9.30 a.m. meeting turned almost immediately to the specifics of the crisis. Badran made it clear that the reason for his presence was to request an immediate airlift of weapons to Cairo due to the dire state of Egyptian supplies: a quick mobilization had emptied Egyptian depots. He submitted a long list of items to Kosygin, explaining that Egypt had no intention of attacking Israel but needed the weapons to deter it from initiating a pre-emptive attack. If deterrence failed, said Badran, then the Egyptian army would use the weapons to defend itself.[16]

Badran also elaborated on the rules of engagement surrounding the Straits of Tiran. Despite the rumors, he assured Kosygin that Egypt had not mined the area. The only ships Egyptian forces were instructed to apprehend were those carrying the Israeli flag, and oil tankers. Any other ship, even coming out of Eilat, would be allowed to pass. Israeli ships accompanied by an American vessel would also be allowed through; as Badran explained, this would expose the alliance between Israel and American imperialism. If the Israelis tried to break the blockade by force, Egypt would fight back. Badran also discussed other war scenarios. He said that if Israel attacked Gaza, Egyptian troops would attack elsewhere. He believed that Israel still needed time to complete its mobilization and therefore would not strike in the coming week. After that, an Israeli attack was possible, provided Washington approved of it. Israel, the confident Badran prophesied, would receive a mighty blow if it did so. Moreover, if the Americans joined the Israeli attack, Egypt would fight them until its last drop of blood. Badran was especially pleased that "reactionary regimes" such as Jordan and Saudi Arabia had had to express their support for Egypt's leadership.

Cairo was also interested in receiving information from Moscow about the movements of the Sixth Fleet, especially its aircraft, Badran said. He claimed that in the last few days American planes had constantly entered Egyptian airspace, carrying electronic equipment to detect Egyptian radar systems and obstruct the operation of surface-to-air batteries. Badran was also interested in getting intelligence on the movements of British naval forces. Rather melodramatically, Badran announced that Amer had instructed him not to come back to Egypt empty-handed. If he did so, he would be hanged.[17]

All this talk of war – even if only in response to an Israeli attack – was rather disconcerting for a politician like Kosygin. He said that all the information available to the Soviets pointed to Israel being ready to attack by the end of May. Kosygin observed that so far the Egyptians have achieved a political and military victory: the UN forces were gone and the Egyptian army was in Sharm al-Sheikh and Gaza. Pointedly, he asked Badran whether the Egyptians wanted anything else. Badran responded in the negative. If that was the case, said Kosygin, then the Egyptians must have a peace plan, and soon they should lay a proposal on the table. Kosygin stated that if the Egyptians accepted his view, then they and the Soviets were on the same page; but if they refused to follow his recommendation, then he wished to be notified in advance.[18]

Finally, addressing Badran's main request, Kosygin said he would submit the list of weapons to the minister of defense and a reply would be given the next day. However, Kosygin emphasized, the weapons must not be used to start a war: "a war is not in your interest or the interests of the progressive forces." Badran quizzed Kosygin on what the Soviets knew about the decision-making process in Tel Aviv. He replied, "we know that the military and the right-wing elements are putting pressure on the [Israeli] government to start a war ... They think that any delay is dangerous and it seems that they have a prior understanding with the US. The Israeli propaganda is working overtime to convince the people that they must fight for their survival." Kosygin ended the meeting by telling Badran that the Politburo would convene that night to discuss his request, and he would be in touch the next day.[19] A strange chain of events then began to unfold.

While waiting for the Soviets to formulate an answer, General Hilal Abdullah Hilal, a member of Badran's delegation, went to the Ministry of Defense and handed a detailed list of weapons to Marshal Ivan Yakubovsky, commander of the Warsaw Pact Joint Command and first deputy to the minister of defense. The two agreed that Hilal would wait for a phone call from Yakubovsky informing him how things went at the Politburo meeting.[20] One may wonder about the promise of a real-time update by Yakubovsky – after all, Kosygin had promised to give Badran an answer the next morning. But the Ministry of Defense clearly had a vested interest in having the deal offered by Badran – permanent Soviet access to an Egyptian airfield in exchange for expedited arms supplies – approved by the Politburo.

The Politburo meeting went on late, well past midnight, which should be taken as evidence of the fierce debate within the Kremlin. As the Politburo was deliberating, the phone rang at the residence of the Egyptian delegation. Yakubovsky was on the line and he wanted talk to Badran. The Politburo discussion, he said, was going in the wrong direction and Egypt might end up getting less than it was hoping for. He recommended that Badran call Cairo and ask Nasser to apply pressure on the Politburo through the Soviet ambassador there. Badran phoned Cairo and spoke to Abd al-Hakim Amer, giving him the code-word they had agreed on prior to Badran's departure to signal that his mission was in trouble. That night, both Amer and Nasser met with Dmitri Pozhedaev, the Soviet ambassador, and implored him to send an urgent telegram to Brezhnev himself, asking for the immediate supply of all the items on the Egyptians' list.[21]

The Politburo meeting eventually ended in an intricate compromise between hawks and doves. Amer's original request for the delivery of 40 MiGs and 100 APCs was reconfirmed. The Ministry of Defense received an order to extract from its own depots light weapons and ammunition which would be instantly delivered to Egypt. But the shipment of other items on Badran's list was postponed; as Kosygin informed Badran the following day, the weapons that were to be delivered in 1968 could not be supplied until July or August. Yet the doves also had their way. The Politburo decided that urgent telegrams would be sent at once to the leaders of Egypt and Israel calling upon them to take measures to avoid war. The ambassadors in Tel Aviv and Cairo were instructed to immediately deliver letters signed by Kosygin.[22]

And so it was that at 3 a.m., Dmitri Chuvakhin in Tel Aviv and Dmitri Pozhedaev in Cairo got into their cars to convey their missives to the respective heads of state. Chuvakhin found Eshkol at Tel Aviv's Dan Hotel where he was staying the night, probably to be closer to military headquarters. Eshkol, flustered and still in his pajamas, let the ambassador in. Chuvakhin read out Kosygin's letter. In it, Kosygin noted that currently the Israelis seemed to be forming an opinion that "there was no other way than to take military measures." He desired to see "serious political wisdom" prevail over "the warmongers," and ended by expressing his hope that Israel would do everything it could to avoid war. Chuvakhin, probably following instructions, asked Eshkol four times whether he could report back that Israel would not be the one to start a war. Eshkol evaded each time but he did put forward a constructive proposal: he asked that a senior Soviet representative come to talks in Jerusalem, or, alternatively, he would be willing to go to Moscow. Years later, Chuvakhin recalled recommending that Eshkol be invited to Moscow; had Eshkol and Kosygin met, he thought, war would have been avoided.[23]

At about the same time, Pozhedaev knocked on the door of Nasser's private residence. Nasser hastily threw on a robe, slid his feet into slippers and scurried downstairs to where Pozhedaev was waiting for him. The message stated that Kosygin had recently been contacted by the American president who claimed that Egypt was preparing an attack against Israel. As usual, Nasser said that Egypt had no intention of launching an offensive, but rather would respond if attacked. Pozhedaev informed Nasser that, at that moment, the Soviet ambassador in Tel Aviv was delivering a much harsher message to Levi Eshkol. The Soviet Union, explained Pozhedaev, was appealing to both sides in order to leave nothing to chance.[24]

Kosygin was indeed taking no chances. A few hours later he sent a letter to Lyndon Johnson, restating his analysis of Israeli politics that he had outlined in his talks with Badran and his letter to Eshkol. "Israeli militant circles," Kosygin maintained, "are attempting to impose upon their Government, their country and their people an 'adventurist' action for the purpose of resolving all problems by military means ... If there will be no encouragement on the part of the US," Kosygin intoned, "then Israel will not dare step over the line." The letter ended with an appeal to Johnson "to take all necessary measures to prevent an armed conflict." Similar letters were sent to Harold Wilson and Charles de Gaulle.[25]

The next day, May 27, at 2 p.m., Kosygin touched base with Badran. He knew that news of the delay of some military items might disappoint the Egyptian minister, and used his dry humor to soften the blow, telling Badran that he and his Politburo colleagues had been up the whole night making sure that Badran would not be hanged. Giving a run-down of the items available immediately and those postposed for later, he explained that the weapons came as a loan carrying 2 percent interest, but there would be a 50 percent reduction on the cost.[26]

Though Kosygin did not ask, Badran reiterated Egypt's stance on the Straits of Tiran and maintained that a concession on that point would be a setback for Egypt. (Apparently the question had been raised by Soviet officials between Badran's two meetings with Kosygin.) Badran well understood that what spooked the Soviets the most was a scenario in which the US was fighting side by side with Israel. He therefore tried to convince Kosygin that Egypt could deter the US from doing so:

> In that sense we see ourselves as the first line of defense for the whole of the Third World. If there is a war against the Americans, there will be a conflagration in the whole region. World opinion would be against them and the workers of the region would sabotage all oil-related infrastructure ... I think it implausible [that under these terms] the Americans will intervene.[27]

Kosygin then moved to update Badran on the results of the talks between Eshkol and the Soviet ambassador. According to Kosygin, Eshkol had said that Israel was not interested in war, and had asked the Soviet ambassador "How can we prove it to you [that we don't want war]? We want a continuation of the status quo."[28]

As if to drive home this message to Nasser, Victor Semyonov invited Egyptian Deputy Minister of Foreign Affairs Ahmed Fiqi, a member of the Egyptian delegation, to a private pre-departure meal at his dacha. Over the dinner table, with only his wife present, Semyonov discussed issues that, he told Fiqi, the Soviets were uncomfortable referring to in their formal negotiations with Badran. It had taken the Soviet economy a long time to get to the point where Soviet citizens could enjoy a degree of material comfort; we the Soviets, emphasized Semyonov, do not want to lose it for the sake of an unnecessary conflict. The US was a strong adversary and the Soviet government had no interest in starting a war with it. Nasser should give some thought to the idea of opening the Straits.[29] Tellingly, Semyonov was echoing Kosygin's vision, which CIA analysts described as "Cooperation Abroad, Reform at Home": a vision that emphasized the relaxation of international tensions and the revitalization of Communism through improvement of the average citizen's standard of living.[30]

Still, the Soviet army had one last chance to sway things its way. On the day Badran was to leave Moscow, Grechko escorted him to the airport. Like

American officials, Soviet bigwigs also preferred to use informal venues to deliver highly sensitive information. Just as Johnson had sent Eban messages he preferred not to utter in recorded official talks by way of his chat with Evron and Eban's meeting with Goldberg, so Grechko now engaged Badran in the classic institution of a conversation on the tarmac. (The event that had ignited this whole crisis was, after all, Sadat's informal talk with Semyonov just before he departed for Egypt.) Minutes before Badran boarded his plane, Grechko told him:

> I want to make it clear to you that if America entered the war, we will fight by your side – do you understand what I am saying? . . . Our navy in the Mediterranean is now close to your shores, and it includes destroyers and submarines armed with weapons you do not know about . . . if something happens and you need us, just send us a signal and we will come immediately to Port Said, or to any other place.

When Badran tried to shake Grechko's hand goodbye, the Soviet general seized him in a bear hug. Not long after, Grechko attempted to distance himself from this chat, telling the Egyptian ambassador to Moscow that he was only giving Badran "one for the road." It was, nonetheless, a dangerous lie. The Soviet *Eskadra* in the Mediterranean was no match for the Sixth Fleet.[31]

That clumsy attempt to use the crisis in the Middle East to augment the presence of the Soviet navy in Egyptian harbors was the postscript to a letter, addressed to the Egyptian and the Syrian governments and written at the navy's headquarters on May 24, suggesting that the Soviet navy would be dropping in on both countries. Alexandria, Port Said, and Latakia were specifically mentioned as venues to which a detachment would be sent which would include "a cruiser, an escort vessel, one to two submarines and a tanker." Another draft letter from the same day, addressed to Nasser from Brezhnev, revolved around Soviet willingness to transfer an air force unit to an Egyptian airfield as a show of solidarity. Brezhnev, it should be mentioned, was the man who had called for the removal of the Sixth Fleet from the Mediterranean only six weeks earlier during a conference of Communist leaders at Karlovy Vary, Czechoslovakia.[32]

Repercussions of the Badran Mission

Badran insisted on meeting Nasser as soon as he returned to Cairo in order to give the president an oral report. As with Eban, Badran put a rosy spin on the results of his mission. According to Badran the Soviet Union was standing four-square behind Egypt. Moreover, to show their support, the Soviets had agreed to supply Egypt with forty MiGs and to equip an infantry brigade and mechanized brigade. Badran added that Moscow had also expressed its commitment to use its navy to defend Egypt. The Soviet Union accepted Cairo's request not to invite Eshkol to Moscow (something the Israeli premier had asked for during his talk with the Soviet ambassador on May 27).[33] If Nasser had any misgivings about Egypt's ongoing closure of the Straits of Tiran, they were gone. In the days leading up to the Six-Day War, Nasser insisted that the blockade against the shipment of oil to Israel would be maintained, giving Eshkol no room to maneuver.[34]

Another result of Badran's trip to Moscow was a letter that Johnson sent to Eshkol on the morning of May 28. The president had to respond Kosygin's letter of the 27th calling on him to take measures to restrain Israel. In response, the State Department drafted a letter warning Israel not to take "preemptive military action." Johnson had to sign it – otherwise, he would be seen as pushing Israel toward war. Nevertheless, the president moderated the language of the letter by striking out the sentence "Preemptive actions by Israel would make it impossible for the friends of Israel to stand at your side." Rusk was overjoyed. He and other officials in the State Department still believed that they could cobble together an international armada that would open the Straits. Celebrating his victory, Rusk added an instruction to the US ambassador to update Eshkol orally about the Canadian and the Dutch having already agreed to join the armada. That piece of information strengthened the impression that Eban was right and the US was serious about tackling the closure of the Straits. Rusk, as a *coup de grâce*, ended his oral message on a menacing note: "unilateral action on the part of Israel would be irresponsible and catastrophic."[35]

It was all very confusing. Washington was talking to Israel in two voices. There were formal messages calling on Israel to wait. And then there were oral missives from the president that suggested that he would *not* punish Israel if it decided to act alone. The Jewish backchannel that carried these missives had always proven reliable. But Eshkol wanted to avoid war. He decided to heed Rusk's warning.

The Israeli government convened in the afternoon of May 28. Eban supported Eshkol enthusiastically, and claimed that in his conversation with Johnson the president had committed himself to open the Straits even if it meant the US having to act alone. (Johnson, of course, made no such promise.) Rabin resisted, urging the ministers to strike now. In three weeks' time, argued Rabin, it would be even harder to attack the Egyptian army.

Eshkol, this time, was resolute. He reproached Rabin and asked whether he was willing to disobey the President of the United States of America. "Even if you say 'yes,' I am not interested [in listening]!' the prime minister yelled.

The cabinet decided to allow diplomacy another three weeks.[36] But the army was unwilling to wait that long. An impatient General Staff joined hands with various civilian partners that wanted to see Eshkol gone. And Washington, with a wink and a nod, prodded Eshkol into going to war.

21

A VERY ISRAELI PUTSCH?

Dayan Ascendant

O N MAY 20, war was in the air. Eighty thousand men had already been recruited, while more Egyptian units were making their way into Sinai. Diplomatic activity bore no fruit, and the Israeli public started to suspect that the government had no idea what to do. At 7 p.m., Moshe Dayan, former chief of staff and a Rafi Knesset member, called Eshkol's office. He sought permission to tour the southern front and visit the troops. Yisrael Lior, Eshkol's adjutant, could see nothing innocent about that request. Dayan was only interested in capturing the media's attention and creating an opportunity to stage a comeback after several years in the political wilderness.[1]

Dayan was not used to being idle. Up to 1958 he had enjoyed a rapid promotion through the ranks. To outside observers it was slightly perplexing. Unlike Allon, Dayan never commanded large units in complex battles during the war of 1948. He led a commando battalion and later served in staff positions. But it was of no matter to Ben-Gurion. Dayan was one of the few officers in the IDF who was not part of the Palmach tribe and therefore he could rely on him. Besides, Dayan had the famous eyepatch, a souvenir from a 1941 battle against Vichy forces in Syria. The bullet had smashed the bones around Dayan's eye and made it impossible for the doctors to fit a glass prosthesis. The only solution was a prominent patch befitting a pirate. Dayan hated it. The air behind it would heat up, causing him severe headaches.[2] It made him into a short-tempered and irascible man. But to the rest of the world, the patch was a mark of valor.

In 1953, Ben-Gurion made the 38-year-old Dayan chief of staff. As a result, Dayan was the one who led the troops in the 1956 campaign. He was also the architect of the alliance with France that enabled Israel to start the war. But he did not excel at controlling the army once the action was underway. After consulting with the French, Dayan devised an elaborate plan, the main aim of which was to give the French and the British an excuse to attack Egypt. Israeli paratroopers were to land deep behind enemy lines, close to the Suez Canal. The soldiers' mission was to engage an Egyptian force, which the IDF would publicize. France and Britain would then issue an ultimatum calling both sides to withdraw 10 kilometers from the Canal. Egypt was bound to reject this demand and would therefore supply Britain and France with the perfect pretext to intervene in the crisis. On paper, the plan looked great. The problem was that Dayan did not update his generals on this, as he deemed his tacit understandings with France and Britain to be too sensitive. Failing to understand the logic of Dayan's plan, the commander of the southern front sent his tanks ahead of time into Sinai. Dayan had to spend the rest of the war chasing his troops around the desert trying to figure out where they were.[3] Nothing of that became known to the public, who continued to worship Dayan as a war hero.

In 1958 Dayan shed his uniform and became a civilian. The following years were not as golden as those in the army. His term as minister of agriculture (1959–64) was marred by his decision to instruct all farmers to stop growing the local variety of tomatoes and instead sow only the "money-maker" strain, a more hardened and round tomato beloved by housewives in the UK. Dayan thought his plan would give a boost to agricultural exports. Instead, he angered Israeli housewives who became irritated when they could not find the juicy flat tomato they were used to. Along the way he earned the moniker "General Moneymaker."[4]

His family life was not going well either. Shortly after the 1956 campaign, his wife, Ruth, discovered his infidelity with numerous lovers. Most of them were short-term affairs but there was a more constant relationship with Rachel Rabinowitz, a lawyer's wife, whom Dayan had met on a transatlantic flight. According to journalist Uri Avnery (who should know, given he dated Dayan's underage daughter, Yael, for a while), the family home in Tel Aviv was more akin to a federation of rooms than a normal household. Each family member locked the door to his or her room. An old maid acted as a go-between.[5]

When Ben-Gurion resigned from the government in June 1963, Dayan resigned as well out of loyalty. Most likely, Dayan was frustrated that Eshkol had taken the defense portfolio for himself rather than appointing him. Dayan agreed to stay on after Eshkol, and Sapir promised him that several governmental agencies would be added to his portfolio. Nothing came of that, though, and by the end of 1964 Dayan felt that he was marginalized within the government. Reluctantly, Dayan resigned in November 1964. He joined Rafi even more reluctantly in 1965. Dayan did not believe that a splinter party headed by Ben-Gurion would get more than a few seats in the Knesset. His and Peres's preference was to stay within the party and lead its "youngsters" wing. Hopefully this could be leveraged to squeeze concessions out of Eshkol. But Ben-Gurion forced Dayan and Peres to join him at Rafi. After Rafi failed at the ballot box, Dayan became the Knesset member of a small and uninfluential party. He was a man of action and was not cut out for parliamentary life. Increasingly bored, he begged Eshkol to let him run a government-owned fishing company. Other than that, he devoted most of his time to writing *The Diary of the Sinai Campaign*, which was published in 1965 and further helped solidify his image as a security expert.[6]

Although a member of the Knesset (MK), Dayan was rarely present. In 1966, he left the life of a backbencher to travel to Asia. Collecting a writer's fee from *Maariv* and the *Washington Post*, Dayan embedded himself with American troops in Vietnam. War excited him and, although he was 51, he marched with infantry units into the jungles, bathed in rivers, and endured both oppressive heat and torrential rain. It was there that Dayan became enthusiastic about the massive use of technology to fight a counter-insurgency campaign. He believed that this was the way of the future.[7]

No wonder his nostrils flared in May 1967 as the whiff of war intensified. War made Dayan, and Dayan made wars. If there was one soul he was really attached to, it was his daughter, Yael, who was living at the time in Greece with the film director Michael Cacoyannis. He telegraphed her to return to Israel quickly, assuming that she would want what he wanted: to be on the front line as history unfolded. Forty-eight hours later the good daughter was back home. Dayan treated her to a "festive" four-course dinner in a restaurant to celebrate the coming war. Looking at her father, Yael saw that something had changed:

> I couldn't take my eyes off him, and was fascinated by the changing expressions on his face rather than what he told me . . . his face lit up, as if transformed chemically from the inside, when he spoke of the troops, of the commanders he knew . . . all the camaraderie this man could summon glittered in his one eye. When he spoke of the diplomatic efforts to attain American consent and guarantee for free passage in the Gulf of Suez, or the negotiations with the UN and with the European heads of state, his face showed dismay if not contempt.[8]

When Lior told Eshkol about Dayan's request to tour the front, the prime minister merely smiled and gave his permission. Eshkol could read Dayan's intention as much as Lior, but he probably thought that by giving Dayan something to do, he could keep him under control. In retrospect, Eshkol was too sanguine. Unwittingly, he gave Dayan the launching pad from which he would catapult himself into the Ministry of Defense. Yariv, the commander of military intelligence, was asked to contact Dayan with regard to his request. Yariv was also aware that Dayan's appearance at the front was a sensitive matter and tried to play for time, telling him that maybe it was better for him to postpone his tour for a week or two. But Dayan was having none of that. He wanted to strike while the iron was hot. It was agreed that he would get uniforms, an army-owned car, a driver, and an assistant with the rank of colonel.[9]

While touring the southern front in the last week of May 1967, Dayan shared his views – which were the complete opposite of Rabin's – with senior commanders. Whilst Rabin tried to rein in his General Staff and limit the confrontation with Egypt, Dayan was itching for the fight. It was not just a matter of temperament. Dayan's theory of the Arab world was different from that of Rabin and Yariv. They distinguished between moderate Arab states (Egypt and Jordan) and radical ones (Syria). Dayan's theory envisioned strong Arab states (Egypt) and weak ones (Syria and Jordan). Dayan criticized Rabin and Eshkol for investing too much time and effort in battling Syria and Fatah. Speaking in the Knesset on October 17, 1966, Dayan had said: "If I thought for a moment that our reprisal or military activity will drag us into a war . . . I would say that Fatah operations do not justify that even if we will have to bear a heavier burden of terror and sabotage attacks than we currently suffer."[10]

In March 1966, Dayan called on the government to demand the evacuation of UNEF from Sharm al-Sheikh and the Gaza Strip. In Dayan's view, this would force Egypt to decide whether Israel was friend or foe, and whether to shoot at Israeli ships passing through the Straits of Tiran. When Dayan wrote an op-ed in the summer restating this position, Abba Eban responded in cabinet that such a policy recommendation reminded him of a man shooting himself in the head because he was curious to know whether the gun was loaded.[11]

While Yariv and Rabin cared about the frontier settlements and created a security doctrine with them at its core, Dayan was a classic creature of the military establishment. For him, state interests came first and the needs of the kibbutzim came later. Dayan averred that there was no Arab country Israel could work with and he discerned no "Arab Realism." Every Arab country was an enemy country and those that were strongest had to be confronted. A more sinister interpretation of Dayan's outlook would be that his approach sought to perpetuate the conflict between Israel and the Arab world.

In his visits to the various fronts, Dayan delivered the same message again and again. The IDF could win. It needed a strong leader (the implication being that Dayan was that person). Dayan explained that he favored a short campaign – he assessed that the superpowers would bring the fighting to an end within seventy-two hours – focused on northern Sinai. Territory, he said, mattered less. The main thing was to annihilate Egyptian troops in Sinai. He hoped that the IDF would have enough time to destroy hundreds of tanks. He also had other aspirations. While dining with his daughter he had met Uzi Narkiss, commander of the central front. Dayan told him that if the Jordanians attacked, Israel must take parts of Jerusalem and never let go of them.[12]

Dayan's tours in the south were avidly covered by the press, and the public was taking notice. When walking through the streets of Beersheba, the capital of the Negev, young people congregated to call out "Moshe Dayan! Moshe Dayan!" Restaurant owners declined to take money for the meals they served him, one of them explaining: "Just be healthy and bring us victory." Dayan encountered similar scenes at cafés and gas stations. His impression was that the "simple folks" (Dayan's expression) wanted to see him at the helm, preferably as minister of defense. On May 27, Yisrael Shenkar, a textile magnate, came to meet Dayan. Shenkar told him that he should become the minister of defense. "How do we do this?" Shenkar asked. Dayan, pessimistic as always, said he did not know whether it was possible. Shenkar promised to try to muster support from the industrial lobby to make it happen.[13] The conversation with Shenkar provides a vital clue to the riddle of Eshkol's political demise. The army was definitely interested in forcing the government to launch an attack, but it also found several willing civilian partners.

Mafdal and the War Coalition

At the forefront of the efforts to replace Eshkol at the Ministry of Defense was Mafdal (the National Religious Party). Its leader, Haim-Moshe Shapira, was responsible for uniting all the streams of religious Jewry in one party (ultra-orthodox Jews had their own separate parties). In essence, Mafdal functioned as a pressure group that ensured that the state would take responsibility for religious services and appoint Mafdal-affiliated rabbis to key positions. There were also Mafdal-affiliated schools and kibbutzim and even a university – all of which required state funding, which there was no shortage of thanks to Mafdal's continuous presence in the Israeli government ever since the founding of the state.[14]

Mafdal felt like the odd-man-out in Eshkol's socialist coalition where the workers' parties held strong secular beliefs. As early as 1965, there were calls within Mafdal to bring into the coalition other parties, such as Ben-Gurion's Rafi, that had a more accommodating approach to Mafdal's demands. Gachal, the main opposition party, was another element that Mafdal wanted to see inside the coalition. Menachem Begin, Gachal's leader, had hawkish views, calling for a tough stance against the Arabs and fiercely backing the estab-lishment of the Greater Land of Israel on both banks of the Jordan River. Begin wrapped his political philosophy and Jewish religious values together. Many in Mafdal believed that their party could be more influential with Rafi and Gachal within the government. For that reason, there had been strong calls within the party to form a national unity government from late 1966, when the recession began to bite into Israeli incomes. The argument that Mafdal made back then was that the harsh economic climate necessitated a broad coalition. In this, Mafdal was not alone. Even members of Mapai and op-ed writers from the privately owned media took the same position.[15]

It did not take Shapira long to understand that the national security crisis that began on May 23 was a golden opportunity for him to achieve a goal that Mafdal had been pursuing over the last six months. On May 24, representatives of Mafdal, Gachal, and Rafi decided to work together to make Ben-Gurion the next prime minister and convince Eshkol to serve under him as minister of defense. This explains why Shapira's meeting with Rabin that day – the one that according to Rabin hastened his mental collapse – was so stormy. Shapira was not merely presenting dovish views: he was reiterating word-for-word Ben-Gurion's position. Ben-Gurion, still living the crisis of 1956, was arguing at the time that Israel should "dig-in" and wait until it received from the superpowers a firm commitment to support it militarily. On the day Shapira hectored Rabin, Eshkol met with Begin and rejected out of hand the proposal that he and Ben-Gurion serve in the same government. "These two horses shall never again pull the same cart," Eshkol said.[16]

"Come to Ben-Gurion. He loves you."

The next day, May 25, Shapira met with Eshkol to make a slightly different offer: Eshkol would remain as prime minister and Ben-Gurion would serve as minister of defense. Eshkol flatly rejected that proposal as well. Before the May crisis, Shapira was one of the most dovish ministers in Eshkol's cabinet. His attempts to get Rafi into the government were suspect in the eyes of Eshkol. Trying to make Shapira feel awkward about what he was doing, Eshkol asked him: "Why do the doves [Mafdal] want the hawks [Rafi] to join the government?" Meanwhile, a group of Rafi MKs convened to discuss the state of play. One of them suggested appealing to the press for their help in fostering an atmosphere conducive to the creation of a national unity government. In fact, that was already happening. On May 22, Ben-Gurion had met with the editorial board of *Haaretz*. Peres, who was leading the Rafi faction in the Knesset, was close friends with *Haaretz*'s economics editor, Avraham Schweitzer, and briefed him regularly on Rafi's positions. *Yediot Ahronot* and *Maariv*, two other privately owned newspapers, joined the fray. Likewise, senior officers contacted military correspondents and guided them on what they needed to write.[17]

In addition, the private sector, which owned these newspapers, identified an opportunity to weaken the grip of the socialist Mapai over the economy. As a member of *Haaretz*'s editorial board, Amnon Rubinstein, later explained:

> Other than personal admiration [for Dayan among *Haaretz* journalists], there was another matter: the hope that Dayan would bring about a total change of a social system that all the members of *Haaretz*'s editorial board believed was harmful for the national economy ... We have to remember that Israel at the time had an *etatist* and centralized economy – *Haaretz* called it Bolshevist – which was partially nationalized. There was no free competition or equal access to credit ... So, [Gershom] Shocken [*Haaretz*'s publisher], [Walter] Gross [a columnist] and myself sought to liberate Israel from an economic policy that did not efficiently employ the Jewish genius in Israel ...[18]

It was only reasonable that factory owners such as Shenkar and all the liberal parties that represented business owners would take the same position. Both the Independent Liberals, who were part of Eshkol's coalition, and the Liberal Party, which was part of the Gachal bloc, supported the appointment of Dayan as minister of defense and lobbied for it.[19]

On May 23 the editor of *Yediot Ahronot* wrote that the Eshkol government was capitulating to aggression and demanded the establishment of a unity government. The next day, *Maariv*'s editorial recommended a war cabinet that would be composed of personalities rather than parties and would function in parallel with the "civilian government." On the same day, Zeev Schiff, the military correspondent of *Haaretz*, argued that "Neither the British nor the Sixth Fleet would open the blockade for us. The blockade is like a rotten tooth that needs to be pulled. Otherwise, the whole body will rot."[20]

Many within Rafi and Mafdal believed that the only obstacle in their path was the strong-minded general secretary of Mapai, Golda Meir. Meir, 69 at the time, was considered one of the hardest-working politicians in Israel. A strict routine of long working hours, black coffee, and chain-smoking made her increasingly ill in the early 1960s and the public got used to hearing about her hospital admissions. In early 1966 she relinquished her position as foreign minister and focused her attention on Mapai. She remained the iron lady of Israeli politics and her control over the party apparatus was legendary.[21]

At the height of crisis, Meir had Eshkol's back. Eshkol admired her skill as a political operator and called her *die Malke* (the queen). They were long-time political partners, though never close friends. Meir had to deal with the fact that several sections of the party had begun to accept the idea of Eshkol's removal from his ministerial post. First were the young back-benchers, who well understood that Eshkol, the man who unleashed a harsh recession, would be an electoral liability in the next election cycle. Second was the Haifa branch, which was controlled by Ben-Gurion disciples. Meir parried the pressures within the party and outside it. She was especially set against any inclusion of Rafi in the governing coalition. Meir had a partic-ular dislike of Shimon Peres, who as deputy minister of defense had under-mined her more than once, and Moshe Dayan, who in his speeches constantly denigrated the old and stale leadership of Mapai (i.e. Golda and her friends). Discussing the possibility that Gachal and Rafi would join the government, she quipped: "We won't be the first socialist party to let fascists rise to power without a fight."[22]

But by May 27, even Meir understood that something had to be done. She met with Eshkol and recommended that he appoint Allon as minister of defense. Eshkol again refused. There was a logic behind his stubbornness. Eshkol devoted all his energy to avoiding war. It was one thing to let *die Kinderlach* (the boys) from the General Staff have a go at the Syrians, espe-cially when he was seeing his popularity dip. War was a different issue alto-gether. It would cost Israel dearly. When asked by a prominent journalist why he was hesitating to give the marching orders, Eshkol simply said in Yiddish, "Blood would run like water." As far as Eshkol was concerned there was still time to pursue other avenues. Further, Allon wanted to start the war immediately. He had returned from a state visit to Russia on May 24. After talking with Rabin and other generals, Allon had recommended attack. He did not even want to wait until Eban came back from America. Allon suggested cabling Eban a "cover story" that would allege that it was Egypt that had begun the war. And for that reason, Eshkol did not want him as minister of defense.[23]

On May 27, representatives of Gachal, led by Menachem Begin, came to meet with Ben-Gurion at his home. At that point, Gachal was seriously considering supporting Ben-Gurion's candidacy to the premiership even though he was already turning 80. Pola, Ben-Gurion's wife, sensed acutely what this would mean. She well understood that the May crisis was the last opportunity for her husband to return to power. Pola called one of her friends, a known socialite, to ask for help: "It's Saturday," she said, "all the stores are closed. Bring me some delicatessen from your house." When the friend came over with a basket of goods, Pola told her, speaking in her unique blend of English, Yiddish, and Hebrew, that Begin was coming to visit and she wanted him to have a good time. Pola's friend was perplexed. Begin had led the main opposition party since 1948. Ben-Gurion and Begin had been saying the most awful things about each other – including "the H word" (Hitler) – for fifteen years. And now Pola was happy to have him as a guest? But Pola knew that politicians, like states, have no constant hatreds or friendships; only interests. A few days earlier she had even telephoned Golda Meir, the arch-enemy, telling her: "Come to Ben-Gurion. He loves you." Pola cheerfully suggested that her friend help her drag a sofa into the living room so Begin would really feel at home.[24]

Alas, all of Pola's efforts came to naught. Ben-Gurion told Begin that he supported an operation that would be focused on the Straits alone. Ben-Gurion also argued that Israel must wait another week or two until it convinced the world of the legitimacy of its actions. But Begin did not want to wait. He wanted to expand Israel's borders and thought the crisis was a good opportunity to do so. And thus Ben-Gurion failed Begin's audition. But the efforts to defenestrate Eshkol did not stop, not even momentarily. In a nearby restaurant, Peres and Begin reached an agreement. The minimum goal from that point on would be to make Dayan minister of defense. The agreed line of action was that Gachal rather than Rafi would promote this initiative.[25]

The Stutter

Within twenty-four hours the generals were defeated twice. The first came at 4 a.m. on May 28, when the ministers refused to yield to the military's pressure and authorize a strike. Rabin and Weizman were bitter. At the end of the meeting Rabin grumbled, "If the state of Israel thinks that its existence is dependent on an American commitment – then I have nothing to add." Weizman told the ministers, "You commit an injustice – born perhaps out of ignorance – when you fail to believe in our strength." The second defeat occurred during the government meeting that afternoon, when Johnson's letter convinced the cabinet to wait for another three weeks. That morning, Zeev Schiff, the General Staff's mouthpiece, published an op-ed in *Haaretz* equating Nasser with Hitler and Israel's current predicament with the Holocaust. Schiff claimed that Israel had arrived at a moment when excessive wallowing in the diplomatic mud was harmful to the national interest. If Israel did not attack, warned Schiff, Nasser would.[26]

As the afternoon's meeting closed, Rabin warned Eshkol that the generals would be livid. He suggested that Eshkol attend a meeting of the General Staff and explain the cabinet's decision. Eshkol agreed. Meanwhile, the prime minister had other business to attend to. His office had arranged for a recording of a speech to the nation to be broadcast at 8.30 p.m. Technicians from *The Voice of Israel* arrived at 7 p.m., but Eshkol and his people were taking their time to write the speech and review it. Minutes ticked by. The speech had to be recorded and then edited to erase pauses, coughs, background noise and the like. The radio crew argued that there was no time left to do that now, and the prime minister should postpone.

But Eshkol insisted on his speech going out at half past eight precisely. This was a prime-time slot and therefore an excellent occasion for him to pre-empt the torrent of criticism that would be unleashed in tomorrow's newspapers. And so it was decided that Eshkol would read his speech live. The prime minister reached the studio in Tel Aviv with a text full of crossings-out and scribbled adjustments. It was late and he had not slept properly the night before due to a cabinet meeting that went on until the early hours of dawn. If that were not enough, he had also undergone cataract surgery a few days earlier. Given the cue, Eshkol started reading his statement. He had an authoritative bass voice, but when speaking in public was prone to a monotonous delivery. This time he also sounded quite tired. At one point he reached a word that seemed to him out of place. He stopped, turned to his assistants, and whispered to them. He was born at the end of the nineteenth century: the idea of live broadcast was foreign to him. After he corrected the errant word, Eshkol continued reading.[27]

Everybody had tuned in to listen the dramatic announcement. There were no TV broadcasts at the time in Israel. Radio was the most instantaneous means to deliver news and since May 23 the transistors had been blaring in every household non-stop. Eshkol's wife Miriam was on her way from Jerusalem to Tel Aviv and was listening in. She understood immediately that something had gone awry. Pinhas Sapir, Eshkol's loyal minister of finance, was listening to his friend in his office. He went red in the face. "He seemed to be on the verge of a heart-attack," recalled Moshe Zandberg, his adviser. "I did not know how to calm him down." Yariv, Gavish, and other generals listened to the speech as well. They all were appalled. "I instantly grasped that Eshkol had made a mistake, perhaps a fatal mistake," wrote his adjutant, Lior. At the Knesset, the Gachal faction was having a heated discussion. Suddenly an MK came in. She said: "Something terrible has happened. Eshkol talked for five minutes. Then he began to stammer. He was probably tired. One couldn't understand what he was saying."[28]

In small settings, Eshkol could be a charming conversationalist.[29] But he was never considered a great speaker: he was inarticulate and would easily lose his train of thought. In normal times, people would have shrugged off his momentary confusion as Eshkol being Eshkol. But with newspaper headlines describing Israel as being under dire threat, military correspondents writing apocalyptically about a second Holocaust, and Knesset members intensely busy with internal scheming, nothing was normal. Eshkol's slip would soon be magnified and used against him. Both Sapir and Miriam Eshkol later wondered why the speech was not postponed and why Eshkol was not prepared properly.[30] But that was beside the point. Eshkol's rivals were able to paint him into a corner and under pressure, like most people, he made mistakes. He was 72 at the time and suffered from a heart condition. Usually he kept to a leisurely schedule. Even as prime minister, he found time to bathe in the sea or catch an afternoon nap. But since May 15 he had found no respite. He was harried, running from one meeting to the other. And such was his fate also on that evening. For immediately after he delivered that unfortunate speech, he had to go to the meeting with the General Staff where he suffered yet more ignominy.

Eshkol, Allon, and Lior reached the famous "pit" – the IDF's underground command center in central Tel Aviv – around 9 p.m. "The neon lamps," wrote Lior, "projected a pale, ominous light onto the generals," their faces heavy with tension. Rabin decided not to speak. He had already been defeated once when he tried to rein in his generals; this time he decided not to get in their way. The military men reiterated the same position they had put forward over the last ten days: Israel must attack first. An attack now would be cheaper in human lives than an attack later, because the enemy would use the time to entrench himself in Sinai. Israel was eroding its deterrence by not responding to Egyptian defiance. The troops were impatient, especially the young officers and soldiers. They were chomping at the bit and raking the ground with their boots: it would be hard to hold them for long. The generals were also exaggerating for effect. The head of logistics, Major General Matti Peled, went as far as saying that "every passing hour might bring about the destruction of the Third Temple." Yet, shortly after Eshkol left the pit, both Rabin and Narkiss admitted that they did not believe that the Arabs would attack.[31]

With his back to the wall, Eshkol responded with a defiant speech. He started by reminding the generals that Israel had got along pretty well up to 1956 without using the Straits. He challenged their recommendation of a preemptive strike: "I don't accept the logic that says that the presence of the Egyptian army in Sinai means war. There is no reason for that. Why didn't we do it two or three months ago [when the Egyptian army augmented its presence in Sinai following the air battle of April 7]?" Eshkol maintained that "the Jew in Kibbutz Gadot [in the upper Galilee] doesn't care about Sharm al-Sheikh . . ."[32] This was an oblique reference to Eshkol's decision to go along with Rabin's preference and take a tough line against Syria. The implication of what Eshkol was saying was that the purpose of all the activity in the demilitarized zones was to defend kibbutzim in the north, not to unleash a war against Egypt. Indeed, Eshkol was promised several times by Rabin and Yariv that Egypt would not intervene.

Eshkol believed there was an unwritten pact between himself and the generals: he would deliver the weapons they wanted and the generals would be obedient. As they seemed not to fulfill their end of the bargain, Eshkol decided to spell out the deal: "[You] needed more weapons? OK. You wanted 100 planes? You got it. You got tanks as well." However, Eshkol insisted, "You did not receive all of these [weapons] so that one day we sit and say: 'Now we can annihilate the Egyptian army.'"[33] But that was exactly why the General Staff had demanded that Eshkol buy all these weapons during the previous years. They were purchased to build an offensive army that was capable of expanding Israel's borders. The military had been working on that plan for over a decade. Now they had a chance to implement it and the prime minister was in their way. And thus the debate ended with heated emotions on both sides after a young colonel heckled the prime minister.[34]

Unsurprisingly, the next day's headlines were critical of Eshkol's speech. *Haaretz* wrote that Eshkol "is not the person that should be Prime-Minister and Minister of Defense at this time. The coalition in its current composition cannot lead the country in this hour and it must be replaced by a new leadership. Time is of the essence." *Haaretz* thought it "wise" that a new coalition should be formed in which Ben-Gurion would serve as prime minister, Dayan as minister of defense, and Eshkol "would deal with civilian affairs."[35]

The next day, May 30, Eshkol's troubles doubled when King Hussein climbed aboard his plane and took off for Cairo.

The Jordanian–Egyptian Pact

Within a span of hours, Hussein had concluded and signed a military treaty with Egypt. He was in such haste that he asked Nasser to root out the text of the military treaty that Egypt had signed with Syria and simply replace the word "Syria" with "Jordan."

There was something genuinely baffling about Hussein's decision, especially for the Israelis who were following events from up close. Hussein's Jordan and Nasser's Egypt had been enemies for years. Hussein had given aid and help to the rebels in Yemen. At the height of their rivalry Nasser had called Hussein a "whore."[36] Hussein responded by describing Nasser as a coward hiding behind the apron of UNEF. What brought the king to fall into the arms of his worst enemy?

After the war, King Hussein claimed that he had no choice. He believed that the Samu operation had proved that the Israelis were untrustworthy. While lulling him with claims that they wished to pursue cooperation, they were planning a major raid on his country. Hussein inferred from Samu that what the Israelis were really after was the West Bank. Moreover, Jordanian public opinion strongly supported Nasser and his defiance of Israel. Had Hussein not agreed to join the Arab war effort, he believed, "the country would tear itself apart . . ."[37] The actual story, however, was slightly more complicated than the king cared to admit. As a result of Hussein's conservative policies over the previous decade, large sectors of Jordanian society supported Nasser more than they supported the monarchy. That was Hussein's central problem, and that was the main reason he had to go to Canossa and acknowledge the hegemony of his rival.

The Jordanian monarchy was established after World War I as an explicit pact between the court and the Bedouin tribes of the Jordan River's East Bank. It promised the Bedouin tribes employment and access to education in exchange for their willingness to serve as the king's Praetorian Guard. A similar arrangement was achieved with the Trans-Jordanian merchant elite, concentrated in Amman. It gave financial services to the royal family and in exchange was allowed to hold a monopolistic position in the Jordanian economy. The court also granted the Amman merchants privileged access to state tenders. This arrangement was put in place by King Abdullah in the interwar years, but it outlasted him. When Jordan was able to take over the West Bank during the 1948 war, a new, threatening element entered into the equation. The Palestinians were now the majority population of Jordan (900,000 out of 1.3 million). They were more radicalized than the Bedouin tribes, and Nasser's persona held wide appeal for them since they believed only he could unite the Arab nation and, thereafter, liberate Palestine for them. The Palestinians were reluctant to be ruled by the Hashemite monarchy (and it was symbolically fitting that King Abdullah's assassination in 1951 was at the hands of a Palestinian). King Hussein chose to leave in place the pact that his grandfather had created. The army was used as a tool to repress the Palestinians and it remained the most powerful institution in the Jordanian state. Between 1955 and 1960, military spending was increased by 74 percent. Most of the money went into expanding the size of the army rather than new weapons purchases. By 1965 the proportion of Jordan's population employed by the military was the highest in the Arab world. Meanwhile, even aid received from multilateral aid agencies specifically to alleviate the plight of Palestinian refugees was siphoned off to East Bank projects rather than the West Bank where the Palestinians resided.[38]

In the mid-1960s Hussein started having second thoughts about the dominance of Bedouin officers in his army. They might have been loyal but they were also corrupt and inefficient. Many of them were busier smuggling weapons and drugs into the kingdom than running the army. The Bedouin officers were turning the army into a source of revenue and the king felt his control over the armed forces slipping through his fingers. Hussein there-fore decided to allow a group of talented Palestinian officers to take up the reins of power. They were led by Brigadier Amer Khammash whose family hailed from Nablus. In May 1965, Khammash, backed by Hussein, was appointed chief of staff and went on to infiltrate his supporters into key positions. A British diplomat noted that Hussein "was alienating the very forces that he had traditionally and historically relied upon." Indeed, Hussein was taking an awesome gamble, the significance and the importance of which became clear only as the Six-Day War grew nearer.[39]

Just as the Israelis had been preparing since the 1950s to conquer the West Bank, the Jordanians had been racking their brains to find ways to defend it. The old guard – the Bedouin officers Hussein jettisoned – planned for a campaign in which Jordan would fight alone. They well understood that the minuscule Jordanian army would not be able to hold out for long against the full might of the Israeli war machine. At the center of the old defense plan was Operation "Tareq." It was a bold maneuver akin to a Hail Mary pass. The Jordanian army was to concentrate most of its troops in the environs of Jerusalem, then, once the campaign had begun, to conquer the Jewish sector of the city as quickly as possible and hold on to it until a ceasefire was established. Knowing how near and dear Jerusalem was to Jewish hearts, the Jordanians planned to use their conquest as a bargaining chip: the Jews could have western Jerusalem back if they withdrew from whatever part of the West Bank they had been able to take.[40]

The new defense plan, the one that Amer Khammash envisioned, started off with the opposite premise: that trying to fight the Israelis alone would be suicidal. Jordan must join forces with Arab countries and coordinate its military policy with them. The aim was to force Israel to fight a war on three fronts. If Jordan faced only a third of the IDF, it would have a fighting chance. Rather than concentrate Jordanian forces in one place, the Khammash plan envisioned a deployment throughout the West Bank.[41]

After the reorganization of the army was completed in 1965, a British official remarked that the question remained "whether this future army, officered by younger and even more professionally qualified men, will provide the same sort of prop for the Hashemite regime that the army has done in the past." The answer came soon enough. After the Samu raid, the West Bank erupted. Violent demonstrations involving thousands of people broke out in all of the main cities, from Jerusalem (the eastern area of which was held by Jordan) to Nablus and Hebron. The demonstrators demanded that the government provide them with weapons to defend themselves. At first the police were used, but when they proved unable to contain the resentment, the army was sent in. The Palestinian officers were angry that they had to point their guns at their brothers rather than at the Israelis. CIA reports from Amman in late 1966 and early 1967 described widespread discontent within the ranks and plots to overthrow the king.[42]

Ali Sabri, Nasser's right-hand man, elucidated to the East German ambassador the reasons for Hussein's hasty arrival in Cairo on May 30. He maintained that Hussein was "still acting like a paid agent of the USA, but was forced to go down on his knees, since the public sentiment in Jordan is against him." Moreover, "the army – which is controlled by officers who are ashamed of Hussein's position – had already been prepared to overthrow him." Indeed, the steps Nasser took inflamed the imagination of the Palestinian masses. Radio broadcasts from Damascus and Cairo declaring the coming end to Israeli aggression could be heard from radio transistors throughout the West Bank. Stormy demonstrations erupted yet again and Chief of Staff Khammash and other senior officers warned the king "that they could not hold their men in check for much longer and that there would be a serious crisis if Jordan failed to act."[43]

Hussein arrived in Cairo accompanied by Khammash, and it was clear that the latter wanted the king to close the deal on the spot. Khammash had arrived in Cairo a week earlier and had tried to coordinate a joint defense arrangement with Egypt, but had been rebuffed. On May 30 the monarch convinced the Egyptians to take Khammash seriously. Khammash was in the room when Hussein negotiated the military pact with Nasser. He volunteered the information that Jordanian troops were mobilized and ready. The king spoke after him and expressed his agreement to something he had always opposed: the entrance of Iraqi troops into Jordan. But Nasser was in for an even bigger surprise. Hussein asked that an Egyptian officer take over the command of the Jordanian army. While Nasser was thinking the matter through, the king turned to Amer and suggested Lieutenant General Abd al-Munim Riad. Hussein picked Riad because he was the commander of the United Arab Command – the military arm of the Arab League – and was therefore the very embodiment of Jordan's Pan-Arab security doctrine. Hussein and Khammash probably hoped that the mere presence of Riad in Amman would ensure that other Arab armies would fight shoulder-to-shoulder with the Jordanian army and thereby relieve the pressure from the eastern front.[44]

Actually, it was Nasser who hesitated and was unsure as to how to respond. He well knew that Israel had declared in the past that if foreign troops entered Jordan or the Jordanian army came under the control of another state, this would be a cause for war. Nasser was also worried that any Egyptian commander arriving in Jordan would have minimal influence on the conduct of the battle. Nonetheless, after his frequent exhortations about Arab unity, Nasser could hardly ignore Hussein's request. As soon as he had expressed his assent, Hussein asked that Riad join him on his plane and go with him to Amman so that he would have enough time to acquaint himself with the deployment of Jordanian troops in the West Bank.[45]

Eshkol Beleaguered

At about 2 p.m., the transistor in the Knesset's lobby started announcing the news of the Egyptian–Jordanian treaty. The MKs' faces fell, and they became serious and grave. The chairman of the Knesset's security and foreign affairs committee, David Ha-Cohen, from Mapai, started yelling: "We have to change . . . I don't give a damn about the opposition . . . If it's Dayan – so be it . . ." But Ha-Cohen did not broadcast his secret: the night before, his son-in-law, the commander of the central front, General Uzi Narkiss, paid him a visit and instructed him to lobby for changes in the government.[46]

At 6 p.m., the Mapai faction in the Knesset convened. Eshkol did not want to come but he was present; the party whip, Moshe Baram, had called and beseeched him: "Eshkol, you must be there. Otherwise, there'll be a rebellion." Baram opened the meeting and asked Eshkol to give those present a *tour d'horizon*. But Eshkol refused. Exuding self-confidence, he asked the faction members to speak their minds. The first was Akiva Govrin, a veteran MK. Govrin maintained that since Rafi and Gachal had asked to join the coalition, Mapai must invite them. "The people demand it," claimed Govrin. Eshkol interjected: "How do you know what the people want?" "I know how to listen to the people," insisted Govrin.[47] Actually, the prime minister's question was to the point. Everybody in the Knesset and the media made the same argument. Every journalist and politician seemed to know what the people wanted: national unity government and Dayan as minister of defense. Except that the people were not asked. The last time that the electorate had expressed its opinion was in the 1965 elections, when it had voted Eshkol in and Rafi out. Had its opinion changed all that much since then?

A poll by the Communication Institute at the Hebrew University of Jerusalem conducted on June 4, one day before the Six-Day War started, found that only 25 percent thought that Israel should have responded to Egypt's unilateral action by going to war. That number rose to 50 percent during the war and 72 percent only after the war had ended. Many of the respondents who at first had not supported the war claimed after the fact that they were for it. Even those who wanted war sooner were pleased by the way the government was handling the crisis. On the very eve of war, 75 percent of those polled expected that the civilian population would be bombed by Arab planes and 50 percent believed towns would be hit by Arab artillery. Nevertheless, most of them were confident that Israel would be able to emerge victorious.[48]

In retrospect, it seems that journalists and politicians who opposed Eshkol were able to convince themselves that they were representing a silent majority. But there was little evidence of that. The only moment there was any sign of popular resentment came on June 1, when a hundred women demonstrated in front of Mapai's headquarters carrying banners calling for Dayan's appointment as minister of defense. It was later revealed that all of them were Rafi activists. A day earlier, a group of senior officers' wives started writing a petition calling for Dayan's appointment. Nothing came of that effort.[49]

In any case, on May 30, during the Mapai faction meeting, none of that mattered. Most Mapai MKs wanted Eshkol to appoint another person at the Ministry of Defense, preferably Dayan. Eshkol left the faction meeting, slamming the door behind him. And the next day brought more misery for Eshkol. Mafdal was threatening to cede from the government if Dayan was not appointed. Without Mafdal, Eshkol would only have a one-vote majority in the Knesset. But the worst for Eshkol's policy of restraint was yet to come.[50]

The Evaporation of the American Commitment

Since Eban's return from Washington on May 27, Eshkol's trump card had been the American commitment to open up the Straits. He used that assurance to convince his cabinet to adopt a three-week wait-and-see period. He made further use of the American promise during the stormy discussions between himself and the generals on May 28. Between the 29th and the 31st, under Eshkol's personal instruction, Israeli emissaries were sent to seek ways to solidify the vague promise given by McNamara to "look into" the issue of joint military planning. The military attaché, Yosef Geva, talked with a Pentagon official and raised the possibility of "combined contingency planning" for "a situation in which Hussein might be overthrown or for some other reason the US would consider it necessary to intervene with military forces." Ephraim Evron, a minister at the Israeli embassy in Washington, met with Walt Rostow and let him know that there was a letter from Eshkol to Johnson in the pipeline that was "likely to express to you his 'disappointment' that [the Americans] had not picked up the suggestion of Eban for some sort of military liaison." In both cases, Israeli probing was met with an evasive response.[51]

At the same time, reports coming from Washington indicated that Johnson's commitment was not as strong as Eban portrayed it. Arthur Goldberg, the American ambassador to the UN, talked with his counterpart, Gideon Raphael, and told him he could not take it upon himself to advise the Israeli government when to act: that should be Israel's decision. Goldberg said he had read Eban's report on his meeting with the president and he would like to repeat what he said to Eban on the night of his departure to Israel: was he certain that he had received Johnson's "defined assurance"? Evron reported that during his talk with Rostow on May 30, the national security advisor sounded pessimistic. Rostow said he did not see a way out from the current crisis. But the real bombshell fell when Eshkol sent his letter to Johnson in which he repeated his request for close military liaisons. Rostow summoned Evron to tell him that the president was disturbed by one particular passage in the letter: "I welcome the assurance that the US will take any and all measures to open the Straits of Tiran to international shipping." The president, intoned Rostow, was not authorized to make this commitment and this was not what he had said to Eban. Evron was aghast. What the president just said, explained Evron, would disappoint many in Israel and would probably push the Israeli cabinet toward unilateral action. In response, Rostow only reiterated that the president simply could not give an assurance of this kind.[52]

Eshkol learned about Johnson's message only the next day, June 1, sometime in the early afternoon. Eshkol was shocked, as was Rabin when Eshkol updated him at 2 p.m. Why did we wait so long, Eshkol wondered aloud, if an American commitment to open the Straits never existed? Rabin's conclusion was that Eban had lied about the content of his talks. It was at this point that Eshkol decided to throw in the towel. He called his wife and asked her to come to his office at military headquarters in Tel Aviv. Miriam arrived shortly before 4 p.m. Eshkol told her that he was giving up: he was going to appoint Dayan as minister of defense. Afterward, Eshkol instructed his secretaries to locate Dayan and summon him urgently. (Tellingly, they phoned Dayan's mistress rather than his wife: Rachel knew where to find him.) Unbeknownst to Eshkol, Dayan was actually sitting in a nearby office receiving an intelligence briefing from the deputy commander of military intelligence, Dudik Carmon.

While Dayan was making his way down the neon-lit corridors of general headquarters, Ezer Weizman barged into Eshkol's office.[53] Ever since his ill-fated decision on May 24 to order Israeli troops to prepare for an attack without securing approval from the prime minister, Weizman's standing had gone from bad to worse. He had been punished by Rabin and Eshkol: Haim Bar-Lev, his rival, was recalled from Paris to take his place as deputy chief of staff. Weizman talked Shapira into lobbying for him on his behalf, telling him that Bar-Lev was unpopular with the General Staff, which was not true, and feeding Shapira secret information that he was not supposed to know. It got to the point where Shapira called Eshkol's office several times a day to try to convince the prime minister not to dismiss Weizman. These efforts failed and by June 1 it was clear that due to Rabin's unstable condition, Bar-Lev would be the person who would run the war.

Weizman described himself in those days as being "in the mood of a beat-up dog." He had no idea that the political maneuvering to remove Eshkol was about to end successfully. On June 1, vexed that Operation "Moked," which as commander of the IAF he had nurtured for many years, would never see the light of day, Weizman lost it. He broke down crying in front of a stunned Eshkol, yelling: "The state is ruined! Everything is ruined! Eshkol, give the order and the IDF would go to war. Why do you need Dayan? Why would you need Allon? We have a strong army and it only awaits your order. Give us an order and we will win. You will be a victorious Prime Minister." And then he left.[54]

There was something infantile about the whole scene. In any case, it did not matter all that much: Eshkol had already made his decision by the time Weizman entered the room. There were many vectors pushing the prime minister to yield: the incessant pressure of the military, the fractures in his coalition, the rebellion by backbenchers in his own party, and the hoots of derision from the press. But the immediate trigger was his reckoning that the diplomatic road out of the crisis was blocked: Washington was unable or unwilling to open the Straits and there was no point in waiting for it. Israel could have lived without access to Iranian oil; Eshkol himself had reminded the generals that Israel had survived without the Straits up until 1956. But the military establishment was unwilling to listen. Letting go of the plan to launch an attack against the Egyptian army involved much more than a loss of face. It involved a wholesale examination of the way Israeli officers had been thinking about war ever since 1948. If the offensive methods that the General Staff supported meant that Israel would be involved in a regional war every decade or so, was it not better to reconsider?

Not according to Dayan. As he argued in an article written in April 1967:

> although the Israeli army's official title is "the Israeli Defense Forces," it is not a defensive force ... the most visual manifestation of the new approach ... is the lack of fortifications and fences along the borders ... simply put, Israeli Defense Forces are an aggressive offensive-minded fighting force. The Israeli military implements this approach in its thinking, planning and *Modus Operandi*. [The offensive values] run in [the military's] DNA and [are] inscribed in the marrow of its bones.[55]

Although on a personal level the ex-Palmach officers in the General Staff did not like Dayan – relations between Dayan and Rabin, for instance, were always strained – they spoke a common language. And as military men they shared a worldview according to which military force was the best means of solving international disputes.

Shaping the Military Campaign

The one-eyed ex-general entered Eshkol's office at 4.15 p.m. Eshkol offered him the position of defense minister and Dayan instantly accepted. This was the beginning of the end of the fierce jockeying that had gone on over the past week. Dayan's appointment was the final piece in the political jigsaw. In the previous days Rafi had demanded this appointment, while Gachal refused to join without Rafi. Now it was clear that both parties would join the government. Thus, by appointing Dayan, Eshkol was inviting not just one but three hawks into his cabinet (one minister for Rafi, which had ten seats in the Knesset, and two for Gachal, which had twenty-six). The cabinet's balance of hawks and doves was about to change decisively in favor of the former.

Back at military headquarters, Yariv summoned his senior officers for a meeting. "Guys," he exclaimed, barely holding back his enthusiasm, "two hours ago Eshkol appointed Moshe Dayan as minister of defense. We need to be ready for the onset of hostilities starting from tomorrow night . . ." The government convened with the new ministers later that evening. Although Rabin admitted that the Egyptian army was still deployed to defend Sinai, Dayan argued that time was running short. The Arabs, he said, would assume that with Begin and him now in the cabinet, the Israeli attack would come soon – and they would therefore try to pre-empt it.[56]

22

LAST DAYS

THE CONFLICT BETWEEN Nasser and Amer continued to bear down on Egypt's preparations for the confrontation with Israel. On June 2, the day after Dayan had joined Israel's government, Nasser convened a meeting of all the senior commanders of the Egyptian army on the sixth floor of military headquarters in the Madinet Nasr neighborhood of Cairo. Chief of Staff Mohamed Fawzi believed it was "the most important meeting that took place in Amer's office." Nasser opened the meeting with a broad survey of the international and regional situation, then turned to an analysis of military and political developments in Israel. Finally, Nasser suggested that Israel was about to complete its preparations for war and would attack Egypt either on the 4th or the 5th; he later became more categorical that Israel's opening offensive would be an aerial attack on June 5. The Egyptian president explained that this analysis was based on his experience of Israel's decision-making process in 1956. But seven days later, during a secret meeting of the heads of the Warsaw Pact, Soviet Party Chairman Leonid Brezhnev made a stunning assertion: Nasser was not guessing. He *knew*. The source of the information, claimed Brezhnev, was an official at the American embassy in Cairo, who approached Nasser a few days prior to the war and supplied him with the exact and correct date on which the Israelis would start their offensive.[1]

This was not a speech for propaganda purposes. No one asked Brezhnev whether Nasser had foreknowledge of the Israeli attack; he simply volunteered the information. And, on closer examination, Brezhnev's claim looks less improbable. There is evidence that by June 4 information about the Israeli attack had leaked. Abe Feinberg, the Jewish philanthropist, claimed that on that day, during a fundraiser, he had leaned over and whispered in Johnson's ear: "Mr. President, it can't be held any longer. It's going to be within the next twenty-four hours." Jack O'Connell, head of the CIA station in Amman, recalled that on the evening of June 4 the assistant military attaché entered his office to discuss some unrelated issue. O'Connell noticed that the young officer was uneasy and nervous. After questioning, the officer opened up and said that he had received unofficial information from the military attaché's office in Tel Aviv that Israel would launch an attack the next day. Israel wanted to surprise the Egyptian Air Force and bomb it while its planes were on the ground, leaving Egypt open to invasion.[2]

At the time, the Israelis discovered that the American embassy had a great interest in troop movements, and its diplomats were dispersed all over Israel making observations and filing reports. Their findings greatly increased the anxiety of Walworth Barbour, the American ambassador, who feared that the window of opportunity to find a peaceful solution was closing. On June 1, Yeshayahu Bareket, head of the Israeli Air Force intelligence branch, complained to Yariv that the US military attaché, Colonel Anthony J. Perna, was driving him crazy. Perna was calling all the time interrogating Bareket about Israel's next move. Bareket said that Perna was so insistent that he was worried the secret of Israel's air attack would become known to the Egyptians. Perna, described by a colleague as an "eager beaver" and a "capable officer," had been serving in Tel Aviv since 1965 and had good contacts in Israel's security establishment.[3] So the US military attaché's office in Tel Aviv could have been the source of the leak that reached Nasser's ears. Then again, the evidence suggests that Perna figured out the Israeli ploy on June 4. Fawzi, though, maintained that the crucial meeting with Nasser took place two days earlier. It makes even more sense to suspect that the source of the leak was none other than the head of the Mossad, Meir Amit.

The Amit Mission

The Amit mission was born of a brainstorming session in Eshkol's office on May 29. Yariv was there and he presented his "Greenlight" thesis according to which the Americans had already signaled their consent to an Israeli attack on Egypt. Eshkol was still skeptical and said he preferred to wait. Yariv turned to Amit. He recalled that Amit was a close friend of CIA Director Richard Helms. Yariv suggested that Amit go to Washington and meet with him. The purpose of that talk, advised Yariv, should be to find out whether the Americans were serious about opening the Straits and what their position might be if Israel commenced its military campaign. Eshkol nodded approvingly in what was yet another vote of no confidence in Eban, who had been to the American capital and asked the same questions. Amit left Israel on May 31 when there was still some ambiguity about the administration's position.[4] He decided that he would not try to figure out whether the Americans would turn a blind eye to an Israeli initiative, but rather sell them the war and create a shared understanding as to what the US should do for Israel once the tanks started rolling.

Amit cherry-picked the agencies he talked to. It was already known in Israel that the CIA and the Pentagon were amenable to an Israeli strike, and accordingly, Amit met with McNamara and Helms. He did not talk with State Department people, who were still working frantically to find a peaceful solution. Amit told both McNamara and Helms that Israel would go to war soon and that he, Amit, would support it. In doing so, he saved Helms and McNamara the trouble of formulating a response. It was clear to all three men that silence equaled acquiescence. Indeed, McNamara and Helms said nothing in support of or against Amit's statement. The formula from Eban's visit – "Israel would not be alone, unless it decided to go alone" – was not repeated by either American. Amit told them Israel could fight and win the war alone. The most important thing that the US could do during the fighting was to deter the Soviet Union from intervening militarily on the side of the Arabs. Knowing something about Washington's Cold War mentality, Amit warped his sales pitch with a domino theory: if Nasser got away with it, the whole of the Middle East, including Iran and Turkey, would fall under Egyptian–Soviet domination. (Amit did not explain what made this scenario plausible, nor was he asked to.)[5]

One could almost say that Amit perfected the art of colluding without being seen to be doing so. Almost. Because after he left McNamara's office accompanied by Deputy Director of the CIA Rufus Taylor, Amit wondered aloud whether it was a good idea for him to meet the president before he left Washington. Taylor was horrified: the whole point was that Amit would *not* meet the president. Plausible deniability was the name of the game. Taylor spoke in a way that even this uncouth Israeli official would understand. "I told him such a move would be entirely out of the question, totally inappropriate," Taylor wrote in his report. Incredibly, Amit still did not get it; he "wondered whether he should stay around town a little longer to see what happens." Taylor was dumbfounded by how dim Amit could be. Just moments ago "the Secretary of Defense had . . . indicated this would serve no purpose." Taylor decided to be as clear as he could: "I urged him to get a night's sleep and go back to Israel as soon as possible because he would be needed more there than here."[6]

Amit got up the next morning, June 2, in a chatty mood. The man responsible for keeping Israel's secrets secret was not very discreet. He told a senior CIA officer that he and Harman had just received telegrams urgently summoning them to return to Jerusalem. As if the CIA officer might have had trouble figuring out the implication, Amit decided to make it crystal clear. He explained that "he felt that must mean the time of decision had come to the Israeli government. He stated there would have to be a decision in a matter of days." He then decided to share another piece of information: "Israel had lost 'the moment of surprise' by its failure to strike early last week. He indicated that this was a very important element, implying that the Israelis may engage in some kind of deception to lull the Arabs."[7] Did someone at CIA HQ decide to deliver the knowledge gleaned from Amit's loose talk to Cairo? The dates, at least, suggest so. Nasser convened his senior commanders on the very day that Amit revealed to the Americans the Israeli plans.

Of course, without further documentation it is hard to know for certain. But what this sequence of events confirms is that information on the timing of the Israeli assault started leaking in the two days that preceded the Six-Day War. It had reached Nasser but he was careful not to reveal his source; the Egyptian dictator presented his scoop as emanating from a historic and geostrategic analysis. Whatever its origin, this foreknowledge should have been a godsend for the Egyptian armed forces, allowing them to ready themselves for Israel's surprise. Indeed, that was Nasser's explicit order to his generals: to be on high alert so that the Egyptian forces in Sinai would be able to blunt Israel's attack. But the troublesome nature of civil–military relations in Egypt got in the way. Amer did not take Nasser seriously enough.

Following the meeting with Nasser, Amer warned Gamal Afifi, deputy commander of air defense, that Egypt would be the victim of an Israeli attack. He also issued a general order to the armed forces in which he assessed that "the establishment of an emergency cabinet in Israel in which extreme war-mongers participate" meant that "Israel would attack Egypt soon." However, Amer did not cancel his plans to tour the Sinai front on June 5, and he did not argue much with Sidqi Mahmud, commander of the air force, when the latter told him he was unable to move squadrons from Sinai, where they would be exposed to Israeli bombing, to airfields around Cairo and Alexandria. Mahmud argued that taking such a step would lower the morale of the pilots. Amer, who knew that keeping more planes in Sinai would make it easier to launch a surprise attack on Israel, told Mahmud that for the time being he could do as he pleased. The matter, said Amer, would be discussed again on June 5.[8]

Shaping Israel's Campaign

While Nasser was consulting with his senior commanders about how to prepare for Israel's assault, the Israeli political elite was completing the final discussions of how and when to attack. On the morning of June 2, at 8.30 a.m., there was a joint meeting of the General Staff and the new cabinet. It revolved around the by-now familiar positions: the generals wanted to strike at once; Eshkol argued for waiting for a clearer signal from Washington. The generals implied that Eshkol did not understand anything about military affairs, while the prime minister told them they underestimated the importance of diplomacy. Rabin admitted once again that the Egyptians were still deployed in a defensive alignment, but Dayan, who spoke after him, emphasized that Israel must respond to the Egyptian presence in Sinai by attacking, and the longer Israel waited, the harder it would be to launch a successful offensive. This discussion ended inconclusively.[9]

Yet, after the ministers and the generals left, Eshkol convened a more intimate forum that included himself, Allon, Dayan, Eban, and Rabin. "This was the most important meeting I had participated in yet," Dayan confided in his memoirs. Eshkol indicated that the purpose of the meeting was to establish an agreed position that would be presented to the cabinet, which was due to convene again on Sunday morning, June 4. Dayan felt that Eshkol wanted him to be the one to propose going to war. The beleaguered prime minister simply could not get the words out of his mouth. So Dayan did. He sketched a timeline: the decision would be made on June 4 and the IDF would commence its attack on June 5. No one opposed him, not even Eban. Eshkol nodded approvingly. The die had been cast. Eshkol told Lior at the end of the meeting, "Actually we have exhausted diplomatic activity. We cannot wait any longer."[10]

That evening, at 8.30 p.m., there was another important meeting at military headquarters. Up to that point the debate over Israel's aims in the coming military campaign had been left undecided. There were two proposals. Plan A resembled Rabin's Atzmon plan: it was focused on conquering the Gaza Strip and using it as a bargaining chip in the negotiations that would take place after the war. Plan B was more ambitious: it included an offensive along the Gaza–al-Arish axis as well as the movement of two divisions toward central Sinai. The first division would focus on taking the large military compound in Abu-Ageila that controlled the road to Ismailia; the second would take advantage of the battle at Abu-Ageila to move through the battle zone in order to hit the road toward central Sinai and the passes. Plan B was to allow the IDF to reach the passes before most of the Egyptian contingency force was able to escape. Having encircled the

Egyptian troops by completing a pincer movement – one arm of which would move through the coastal area in the north while the other passed through central Sinai – the IDF intended to annihilate the Egyptian army.[11]

Dayan was aware of the fierce debate that took place surrounding this question. His source of information was Major General Ariel Sharon. Sharon was the strongest advocate of the plan to exterminate the Egyptian forces. During that morning's tense meeting between the generals and the ministers, Sharon had made it clear that in his view the main aim of the coming war "should be nothing less than a total destruction of the Egyptian forces . . . our aim is to take care that for the next ten to twenty years or for a generation or two, the Egyptians would not want to fight us . . ." During the debate in cabinet, Sharon passed a handwritten note to Dayan: "Moshe, we should only approve a plan that brings about the annihilation of the main force [of the Egyptian army]. (Gaza, in my opinion, should not be our target). I think that the current plan envisions fighting in stages, Arik." Dayan scribbled back: "I asked Yizchak [Rabin] to have a meeting today over the plans." Sharon had a personal interest in all of this. He wanted to command the division that would wage the crucial battle at Abu-Ageila. In Sharon's mind's eye, personal glory and Israel's redemption were intertwined. Sharon also knew that the campaign had a good chance of succeeding. Two days earlier, an Egyptian jeep carrying three officers and two soldiers mistakenly drove across the border. Sharon's troops took the Egyptians prisoner. Sharon interrogated the soldiers personally. They told him they came from a village in the Nile Delta. To Sharon's trained eye they seemed frightened. They did not know how to find their way across the desert and seemed out of place. Their morale was low.[12]

So, when Dayan walked into the pit that evening, he knew exactly what was going on. Cocksure, Dayan turned to Rabin and thundered: "Please, present your plan. If you don't have one, I have one of my own!" Rabin was not in a position to argue or resist. He had still not recovered from his nervous breakdown. Before coming to this meeting, Rabin had visited military airfields to learn about their preparations for Operation "Moked." The initiative came from Motti Hod, who recalled: "Rabin's mood was horrible. I told myself I must encourage him: he should come and see the pilots." When the pilots saw their chief of staff at the Tel Nof base they could not believe their eyes. "Rabin was sleepless," wrote one of them shortly after the event. "His eyes were red and the burning cigarette between his fingers kept quivering." One commander asked his pilots to congregate in their club to hear Rabin give a short speech. Nothing went as planned. "I felt really weird," the commander recalled, "not just me but all the officers. This man was not able to utter one word. He was confused. All he was able to say to the fifty or so officers was: 'You will succeed . . . Good luck.' He stood there with his quivering cigarette between his trembling fingers. 'Goodbye,' he said. Then he turned around and left."[13]

Dayan was waiting for an answer. Gavish, the commander of the southern front, leaned toward Rabin and asked: "What plan shall I present? The large one or the small one?" Rabin knew what Dayan wanted to hear and said: "The big plan." And that was that. The decision to annihilate the Egyptian army was made. The attempt to limit the campaign against Egypt was dead and buried. Dayan well understood how crucial was his contribution to the decision-making process. Years later, Dayan said:

> If Dayan and Begin had not entered the government and a national unity coalition had not been formed, things would have developed along these lines: A war would have started, because Israel could not have lived without the straits. But the army would then have implemented its plan to conquer the Gaza strip. Then we would have haggled with the Egyptians [and said]: "Open the straits, let the UN forces back and you will get Gaza in return." And then, we would have returned to the status quo that had existed before the Six-Day War.[14]

When Amit returned from Washington on Saturday, June 3, there was little that was new that he could tell those who awaited him. That day, even before Eshkol met Amit, he told his adjutant, Lior: "There's no point in waiting further. [The Americans] cannot help us. We have to go to war as early as tomorrow morning." The most interesting aspect of Eshkol's inner circle's discussion that evening was the resurfacing of the proposal to test Egyptian resolve by sending an Israeli ship through the Straits of Tiran. Amit suggested the idea: he was certain that the Egyptians would shoot at it and give Israel a pretext to start the war. Eshkol was willing to support him: for the prime minister, it was a pretext to postpone the conflict. It would have taken a ship between seven and nine days to reach the Straits, and Eshkol must have pondered the many developments that could occur in the interim. But Dayan was there to nix that idea. Every delay, he warned, would come at the cost of thousands of casualties. Dayan expected the war to go smoothly: "Within an hour or two we will have a substantial achievement in the air war . . . within two days we could start driving toward the [Suez] Canal." Eshkol let go.[15]

The cabinet meeting on Sunday morning, June 4, was pro forma. The hawks had the majority and the prime minister supported them. Eshkol

stated candidly that had the US sent Sixth Fleet ships into the eastern
Mediterranean, indicating that they might act to break the blockade, he
would have recommended waiting a week. But they did not do so, and
Eshkol was therefore for the war.

At this point Eban read the ministers a personal message just received
from Lyndon Johnson. Most of the letter was a restatement of the American
commitment to solve the crisis by peaceful means. But it also contained a
sentence that Johnson had insisted on inserting into the text: "We have
completely and fully exchanged views with General Amit." It was another
wink, another nod, but it was lost on most of the ministers who were not
aware of the Amit mission. At the end of the meeting, all ministers, except
two who chose to abstain, voted for a resolution to instruct the IDF to
"liberate Israel from the tightening military noose around it." The prime
minister and the minister of defense were authorized to launch an attack at
a time of their own choosing.

In the last forty-eight hours, the General Staff, aware of the changing
political and international circumstances, completed its final preparations
for the war. At 7.45 a.m., Monday, June 5, with the onset of the air offensive,
General Rehavam Zeevi called the deputy commander of the southern
front and gave the agreed-upon code-word: "*Nachshonim*, good luck,
activate!" The war machine began to roll forward.[16]

SIX DAYS AND AFTER

THE KEY TO the Israeli victory in the war was long-term planning. Every maneuver, every battle plan had been drilled and re-drilled for years. Intelligence had been gathered on the routine activity of Arab armies for over a decade. And Israeli planners used this information to good effect, building a strategy and war machine that could exploit the weaknesses on the other side of the border. Their achievements enabled Israel to defeat armies much larger than the IDF. There was no equivalent degree of preparation and planning in Arab countries, the primary reason for which was the differing relations that the militaries in Israel and in the Arab countries had with their respective governments. First and foremost, Arab armies were built to ensure the survival of the regime. They were better suited to serve as internal police than as a fighting force. The regimes that sustained these armies held loyalty in higher esteem than efficiency or battle readiness.

The constant purges of officers – to deter coups – prevented the development of capable cadres. In the Syrian army, for instance, 2,000 officers and 4,000 non-commissioned officers had been purged from the ranks since 1966. That was also the reason why the Egyptian and Syrian armies could not make efficient use of the military technology they had received from the Soviets.[1] In Israel, though party affiliation did play a role in appointments within the IDF, in general officers were promoted according to their abilities and skills. Ezer Weizman, for example, had reached the rank of major general and was appointed deputy chief of staff despite being known to be a supporter of the main opposition party, Herut.[2] The Israeli army had no other function but to prepare for the next war.

The IDF achieved all its aims in June 1967. After cracking open the Arab lines of defense, Israeli formations pushed forward at a surprising speed. As Arab generals tried to take back control of the situation, they discovered that the Israelis had already moved deep into their territory. Since the Arab armies were needed at home to ensure that the regimes would survive the humiliation of defeat, Arab leaders in Amman, Cairo, and Damascus were quick to order a hurried retreat after just a few days' fighting. They were unwilling to sacrifice their armies to halt the Israeli ground forces. Whenever regime survival was in conflict with state interests, Arab governments chose the former. Arab regimes preferred to cede territory in order to save what was left of their Praetorian Guard.

"Moked"

The commander of the Egyptian Air Force, Lieutenant General Sidqi Mahmud, had known for two years that Egyptian radar systems were unable to detect planes flying at low altitude (500 meters and below). Mahmud was part of Amer's loyal guard and he had been serving as commander of the air force for over a decade. Despite the fact that in 1956 British bombers had destroyed 200 Egyptian planes while they were on the ground, Mahmud remained in office, protected from Nasser's rage by Amer, who valued loyalty above all else. Under Mahmud, the air force did nothing more than appeal to the Soviets for more advanced radars. No attempt was made to create a doctrine that would address this chink in Egypt's armor.[3]

Conversely, the IAF built its entire war plan around Egypt's Achilles heel. For countless hours Israeli pilots trained to fly in full radio silence at low altitude. Nothing was left to chance. Numerous experiments were made in order to reach the conclusion that the best way to shut down Egyptian airfields would be to bomb runways first and planes only later. Each Israeli bomber was loaded with special bombs, purposely designed to explode after being dropped at low altitude. Various scenarios for the attack were run through a computer no less than 1,500 times, accurately predicting that at least 10 percent of Israeli aircraft would not make it back.[4]

On the morning of June 5, two Israeli Votour planes flew at high altitude through the Sinai sky, carrying devices whose electronic signals suppressed the activity of the Soviet-made SA-2 missiles and jammed Soviet-made radar systems. Egyptian radar operators were aghast as that morning their screens went blank. Reports from Egypt also claim that on that day the Bedouin, who had been on the Israeli intelligence's payroll, used special electronic equipment to jam radio communications between Egyptian land forces in Sinai and headquarters in Cairo. The giant military force that Amer had so painstakingly created in the desert lost its nerve system in the first hours of the war.[5]

The Israeli air attack went smoothly and Egyptian losses were considerable: 286 out of 420 Egyptian aircraft were destroyed. After smashing the Egyptian Air Force to pieces, the IAF went ahead and did the same to the Jordanian, Syrian, and Iraqi air forces. Weizman, who was in the pit when it all happened, called his wife and declared triumphantly: "We won the war!" Reuma responded: "Ezer, have you gone insane? At 10 a.m. you finished the war?!" Weizman was partially right: the IAF performed magnificently in the first hours of the campaign and Israel did go on to win the war. Coincidence, however, does not equal causation. Fighting the IDF without air cover was certainly a major handicap for Arab armies, but had they stood their ground, they could have halted the onslaught of Israeli ground troops. Despite the looming presence of Israeli aircraft, Arab armies could move forces by night, unmolested. Israeli ground forces, wary of being hit by friendly fire, preferred that Israeli aircraft attack the rear area of the front rather than the main battle zones. As it was, the most decisive land battles on the Sinai and West Bank fronts were won by Israeli land forces in the first twenty-four hours of the war while Israeli planes were busy achieving air superiority.[6]

Abu-Ageila

A prime example of a skirmish won without air support was the battle of Abu-Ageila, which was fought during the first night of the war. For the Israeli army, everything was at stake. First was the need to penetrate the Egyptian defense line. This task was made easier thanks to an Israeli deception plan and Nasser's and Amer's intervention. In the tense ten days that preceded the war, the two armies had been watching each other through binoculars and conducting reconnaissance flights. The Egyptians shadowed the Israelis. They responded to any change in Israeli redeployment with a shift of their own troops. If the Israelis augmented their presence in the northern Negev, the Egyptians assumed that the Israelis would invade from that direction and moved more tanks to northern Sinai. The Israelis took advantage of that and launched Operation "Red Tongue." Two transport planes, four or five lorries that shifted position, and several chatty soldiers who talked on the radio all the time simulated the movement of a full division to the southern Negev. They were able to fool the Jordanian and Egyptian intelligence services: the Jordanians even claimed that they witnessed the movement of 500 lorries in the direction of Eilat. The success of "Red Tongue" was impressive. On May 25, the Egyptians had positioned 663 tanks along the northern and central axis of Sinai through which the IDF planned to invade. By June 4, the Egyptians deployed only 404 tanks along these routes. While on May 25 there were only 35 tanks along the southern axis of Sinai, by June 4 there were 397 tanks.[7]

But the fatal shift of troops to the southern axis – where they were of little use once the invasion was underway – can only partly be credited to Israeli acumen. Amer sent reinforcements to the southern axis also because he had not relinquished his plan to attack Eilat. He pushed forward units to positions by the border so they would be available for offensive operations. Nasser had also intervened in this debate on May 25 by insisting that the loss of Gaza would be harmful to Egypt's prestige. Gaza was predominantly populated by Palestinians, explained Nasser, and if Israel conquered that territory it would seem that Egypt was not loyal to the Palestinian cause. The defense force at Sharm al-Sheikh, Nasser said, also needed to be forti-fied. The end result of that debate was that more troops were sent to Gaza and Sharm al-Sheikh.[8]

As a result of all these changes, the "Qaher" (Arabic for conqueror) plan became disorderly. This elaborate defense plan devised by Soviet advisers was hollowed out. The third line of defense at the passes was thinned down to four battalions of reserve soldiers who were inexperienced in fighting. Brigades that should have been in the second line of defense were pushed forward to the first defense line, which now stretched a further 100 kilome-ters. The Egyptian army simply did not have enough troops to man the full length of the front and empty spaces were opened up along the border. The role of the first line of defense, according to the "Qaher" plan, was to blunt Israel's attack. Then, units in the second line of defense were to launch a counter-offensive and wipe out the enemy. As things stood in early June, too many brigades were located in areas that were far away from the main roads in Sinai and were therefore unable to stop the advance of Israeli forces. There were not enough brigades in the second line of defense to mount counter-offensives. If the Israelis broke through the first line of defense, the road to Suez would lie open. Um-Katef, overlooking the road to Ismailia, was a prime location to target.[9] But there was another reason to strike at Abu-Ageila: namely, the aspiration to envelop and annihilate the Egyptian army. The Egyptian compound controlled one of the shortest routes to the passes; blocking them was a key element in the annihilation plan. Arriving there before the Egyptian brigades were able to escape would be crucial.

The battle at Abu-Ageila was Ariel Sharon's brainchild. General head-quarters wanted to avoid a frontal attack on the most heavily fortified compound in Sinai. But Sharon insisted. He lobbied aggressively, as only he could, to attack along this route and demanded enough troops to carry out the mission. Sharon's division was strengthened with forces belonging to Major General Avraham Yoffe, commander of the 31st Brigade, who was more passive. Sharon knew everything about the compound. The painstaking efforts of Israeli intelligence services to collect every morsel of information on enemy fortifications, and the numerous reconnaissance flights flown by the IAF planes over Sinai, had paid off. Sharon knew the compound so well that he was able to build a small-scale model of it. Abu-Ageila was what the Romans called *pars pro toto* – a part representing the whole. It was basically a miniature version of the "Qaher" plan, with three consecutive lines of trenches that were dug into the slopes of a ridge. The trenches were manned by a 16,000-strong infantry brigade. In the rear was an 87-gun artillery battalion which was fortified by 83 tanks. In the front there was a 4 kilometer-long strip strewn with mines and barbed wire. Even before the invading force reached that strip it would have to deal with further outposts and three smaller compounds at the rear. Both flanks of the rear were surrounded by two seemingly impassable terrains: one mountainous, the other consisting of treacherous dunes. Impregnable? Not for Sharon.[10]

Israeli generals identified the key weakness of the Soviet doctrine as practiced by Arab armies: it made troops static. The best way to deal with these formidable fortifications was to attack them from the rear and to outflank them. Sharon also planned to attack by night to use darkness as another element of surprise. Both Rabin and Gavish asked Sharon to wait until early light so that the IAF could soften the area with massive bombing, but Sharon was so confident that he declined. Besides, waiting the night meant giving the enemy a chance to escape, and Sharon would have none of that.

As early as the afternoon of the 5th, an infantry brigade was ordered to start marching 15 kilometers over the dunes in order to reach their marked position by nightfall. Their mission was to attack Egyptian infantry in the trenches, and it was their actions that would decide the fate of the battle. Israeli infantry carried stick lights with them so they would not be hit in the dark by friendly fire. The enemy's artillery battalion was to be neutralized by an airborne attack by paratroopers. A battalion of Centurion tanks was to complete a deep maneuver in the northwest and end by attacking Egyptian cavalry from the rear. Another attack was to commence from the front by Sherman tanks, but only as a deception.

At 10 p.m. Sharon told his artillery officer: "let the ground tremble." "It will tremble alright," said Yaacov Aknin. Within twenty minutes, 6,000 shells fell on the compound. Sharon was pleased. "This is hellfire," he appreciatively remarked to Aknin. "I've never seen such an inferno." An Egyptian officer caught in the midst of it all was interrogated after the battle and described it as "like being enveloped by a snake of fire." Then all of Sharon's forces attacked from all directions. There was one moment of panic when the Centurion tanks were held up by a minefield. Combat engineers kneeled down and plucked mines out of the ground with their bare hands as if harvesting potatoes. Within half an hour, the tanks could break through. By dawn the battle was winding down, and Yoffe's brigade could pass through on the Ismailia road.[11]

Withdrawal

Sometime in the afternoon of June 6, the second day of the war, Abd al-Hakim Amer made the decision that sealed its fate. At this stage the Egyptian Air Force had been destroyed and the first line of defense had been breached. But the majority of Amer's troops were yet to see a fight, including three brigades and two mechanized divisions. Amer could have pulled his troops from southern Sinai and had them regroup by the passes to stop the IDF from advancing. When Stalin found himself in a similar situation in the summer of 1941 he gave his troops a simple order that considerably slowed the advance of the German army: "Not a step back." Anyone who dared to retreat was shot by a firing squad. The Man of Steel was willing to shed the blood of millions of Red Army soldiers to buy precious time. Then again, the Red Army was not the only source of his power: Stalin had the party, the NKVD, and the heavy industry lobby at his side. Amer, though, was nothing without his army, especially his officers, who were not simply military men; Amer was their patron and they were his clients. Without them, Amer was a Samson shorn. To sacrifice them for the sake of "Egypt" would simply mean that, immediately after Egypt's defeat, Nasser would make Amer the scapegoat and finally get rid of him (as indeed happened). To survive politically, Amer had to bring his officers back.[12]

In his memoirs, Fawzi – who was the chief of staff, and bore at least some of the responsibility – chose to describe Amer as suffering a mental meltdown, thus laying the blame squarely on his superior. Yet, in retrospect, Amer was simply a very political general. When he discovered, on the morning of June 5, that the pilot of his plane was flying him back to Cairo instead of landing him in Sinai, Amer suspected he was the victim of a plot. The onset of the war was far from his mind: Amer's attention was completely devoted to political intrigue.

Further, Amer had the past in his rearview mirror, not the future. And in the past – in 1956, to be exact – Nasser and Amer had given the Egyptian army the order to beat a hasty retreat, which had meant that most of the troops returned to the Suez Canal's western bank unscathed. In popular memory this came to be seen as an Egyptian Dunkirk. But there was one big difference between 1956 and 1967. Then, the Israelis wanted the Egyptians to escape and focused instead on taking territory. Now, the Israelis had no intention of letting the Egyptian soldiers slip away. When Amer made his decision, he did not know that.

But that was part of the problem. There was an asymmetry of knowledge on the level of command between the Israelis and Arabs. For instance, Sharon knew everything about the Abu-Ageila compound, while the Egyptian commander, Major General Sadi Nagib, had no clue as to how the Israeli attack would unfold. Israeli intelligence services were busy spying on the Arabs; Arab intelligence services were busy spying on their citizens and on each other. Israeli pilots on the morning of June 5 knew every last detail about the airfields they bombed, while all their counterparts had were aerial photos from 1948. Israel had invested millions of dollars in the years that preceded the war to create a special commando unit – Sayeret Matkal – whose main role was to attach bugging devices to telephone lines in Lebanon, Syria, and Sinai.[13] And Israeli intelligence had at least two high-level spies working inside Damascus and Cairo. Elie Cohen and Wolfgang Lutz arrived at the Syrian and Egyptian capitals, respectively, between 1960 and 1961. Thanks to lavish funding from the Mossad, they hobnobbed with the political and military elite. Up to their capture in 1965 both were able to send back top-drawer information about political and military affairs. Their reports painted a picture of a political elite too busy with petty corruption to prepare efficiently for war. In 1961, Lutz had a frank talk with Egyptian General Abd al-Salam Suleiman. Drunk on whisky, Suleiman offered an assessment of Egypt's armed forces that proved prescient:

> We [in Egypt] have enough military equipment to conquer the whole Middle East, but equipment isn't everything. The army right now – in terms of training, military competence, and logistics – will not be able to win a battle against a fart in a paper bag ... the trouble is that Gamal [Abd al-Nasser] and the Marshal [Abd al-Hakim Amer], together with the other generals ... are rejoicing in the new equipment – the new Russian aircraft and tanks – like a bunch of kids with a new football. But the best ball ain't worth a damn thing if you don't know how to kick it.[14]

Most Egyptian and Israeli generals agree that had Amer decided to fight until the last bullet, the war would have ended differently. Protracted land warfare would have developed in the desert. The Israelis would have conquered part of Sinai but not the whole of it. Then a UN-sanctioned ceasefire would have been imposed. The Israelis might have been more cautious in the West Bank, biting off chunks of territory in the environs of Jerusalem. With fierce fighting still going on in Sinai, Israel would not have dared to start a campaign to take the Golan Heights.

But none of these things happened, because in the afternoon of June 6 Amer gave Fawzi a categorical order to retreat from Sinai within one night. Troops were to grab their personal weapons and flee. What increased the confusion and chaos still further was that the order was not reported in an orderly manner. Operations branch distorted what Amer said and reported that a retreat was to take place within three nights. Then it was amended to two. Different units heard different versions of the order at different times. For this reason some units fell apart while others continued to fight. On top of it all, Amer contacted his favorite officers and encouraged them to hop on a vehicle and rush back to Cairo. A young Egyptian officer described accurately what happened to the troops on the third day of the war as a result of Amer's order: "Everyone lost their heads ... It was a massacre, a disaster. Israel never would have achieved a quarter of its victory if not for the confusion and chaos."[15]

Annihilation

On the third day of the war, June 7, Israeli brigades conducted a frantic race against time to reach the passes before Egyptian units got there. The convoys of Israeli and Egyptian troops sped down the roads shoulder-to-shoulder and sometimes it was hard to tell which was which. Whenever possible, Israeli aircraft strafed and bombed Egyptian convoys trying to escape. The IAF had a special routine to ensure the lethality of its attacks. Aircraft would make one sortie over the convoy to assess its size and speed. In the second sortie, Israeli planes would make sure that they were bombing the head of the column to stop the movement of the whole convoy. Then they would drop napalm bombs on the vehicles. Egyptian tanks and lorries caught fire and black smoke filled the sky.[16]

Finally, in the late afternoon, an Israeli cavalry battalion was able to reach the Mitla Pass and assume position on the slopes. As night was falling, the soldiers decided to set a lorry on fire to supply some light. Suddenly they realized that a long Egyptian column – three Egyptian divisions, totaling more than 30,000 men – was moving toward them and the Canal, trying to escape. The Israelis charged their cannon and did not stop firing until dawn broke. Another major annihilation battle took place the next day when 6th Armored Division tried to escape westwards from the south. Sharon, leading the forces of 38th Division, laid an ambush at the Nakhal oasis. The forces opened fire on the retreating Egyptians, blowing up 70 tanks and 400 lorries and killing about 1,000 Egyptians. The stench of burning bodies filled the air. At 2 p.m. Sharon could proudly report to Gavish: "We have finished off an enemy brigade ... The enemy was totally annihilated. It's an unusual scene. I would urge you to come and see."[17]

The desire to wipe out Nasser's army was not confined to Dayan or Sharon. It percolated down to the lower echelons. A week before the war, Colonel Shmuel Gorodish, commander of 7th Armored Brigade, gave a speech before his soldiers in which he explained that "Nasser wants to annihilate us. We should therefore annihilate him ... Do not waste cannon shells on [Egyptian] infantry! Run over them wherever they are. Kill, kill the enemy. We will not repeat the mistakes of [the 1956] Sinai [campaign], when we did not run over them." This was something that Yael, Dayan's daughter, who was embedded with Sharon's division as a journalist and witnessed the battle of Abu-Ageila, also recognized:

> now we were to destroy enemy forces wherever they were – another carrier, another tank, another company. An unpleasant task, perhaps, but a preventive one. Eleven years ago we were in this area and the enemy was defeated rather than fully destroyed. This time we had to ensure maximal destruction.

As one Israeli reserve corporal wrote in his diary on the third day of the war: "There's nothing to worry. The sky is clear. The Egyptians are running toward the [Suez] canal. [We] don't let them. [We] want to annihilate them." Another wrote to his girlfriend: "We have turned the Sinai peninsula into a charnel house, into one big cemetery. People without weapons, who raise their hands [to surrender], are shot despite the orders ... I saw so many instances of murder that I can no longer cry."[18] There were 100,000 Egyptian soldiers and officers in Sinai when the IDF began its campaign; by the end of it, 10,000 of them had been killed. One in ten Egyptians who had crossed the Suez Canal in mid-May 1967 lay dead at the war's end.[19]

Jerusalem

Israel's central command was at a disadvantage in the beginning of the campaign, as most of the IDF's brigades were in the south. Thanks to the rapid disintegration of the Egyptian army, the southern command could let central command use some of its forces, especially Motta Gur's paratroopers brigade. The Israelis thus reached parity with the Jordanians, with both sides commanding 56,000 troops.[20]

What played into the hands of the Israelis was King Hussein's decision to appoint a foreign officer, Egyptian General Abd al-Munim Riad, as commander of the Jordanian army. On the opening morning of the war, Eshkol wrote a letter to Hussein urging him to sit out the fight. For Hussein, it was too late: he was no longer in command of his troops. As the war started in the south, the Jordanian army launched its weapons from all its positions in Jerusalem. Its Long Tom gunners opened fire on Tel Aviv (although most of the shells landed in the sea). In the afternoon Jordanian troops entered the UN compound in Jerusalem at Jabel Mukaber. It was a reckless move that played right into the hands of the hawks in Israel. Dayan used Riad's orders to convince Eshkol to authorize two attacks that would kick off the campaign to conquer the West Bank: one in Jenin, and the other in the environs of Jerusalem.[21]

What made matters worse conflict that Riad conducted the war according to Egyptian interests. As the old guard in the Jordanian army knew, their best chance was to concentrate troops around Jerusalem and try to encircle the Jewish part of the town in order to hold it to ransom. Instead, Riad ordered Jordanian troops to deploy in the southern areas of the West Bank in expectation of an Egyptian attack on the Negev. Jordanian troops were supposed to complete a pincer movement that would cut off the southern Negev. But the Egyptian attack on the Negev never happened. Instead, this move threw the north and center of the West Bank open to Israeli attacks in Jenin and Latron. One of the veteran Bedouin officers threw down his *kafiyah* (a headscarf) in despair after seeing how clueless Riad was in directing the war.

By the second day of the conflict, the IDF was able to encircle Jerusalem and invade deeper into the West Bank. Inside the city, secured in their trenches and positions, Jordanian soldiers fought bravely, giving as much as they got. The Israelis were at a disadvantage here, as they dared not call in the IAF for fear of destroying holy sites. However, supplies of ammunition could not get through to the Jordanian forces and little by little the Israelis wore them down. By midday on June 6, the IDF had conquered the whole of Jerusalem except the Old City. Elsewhere, the Jordanians fared even worse, losing all key tank battles in which they engaged. When they tried to transfer their troops from the south of the West Bank to the Jerusalem area, the IAF strafed and bombed them. As with the Egyptians, the Jordanians panicked too soon. In the morning of the second day of fighting, Riad warned Hussein that "If we don't decide within the next 24 hours, you can kiss your army and all of Jordan good-bye!" The claim was exaggerated. Hussein had enough troops to delay Israeli advances until the UN imposed a ceasefire. But, just like Amer, King Hussein was nothing without his army. Its annihilation would spell the downfall of his monarchy.[22]

At this point, Hussein decided upon a desperate course of action: he tried to offer a ceasefire. This could have been an opportunity for Israel to avoid having to conquer the West Bank, with the hundreds of thousands of Palestinians living in it. At that time, Dayan was insisting that Israel had to conquer the West Bank in order to bring about the fall of Jerusalem. In retrospect, this was not the case: Israel could have destroyed the annoying Long Tom cannon, whose shells reached the Tel Aviv neighborhood of Zahala, in which most senior officers resided, by bombing it from the air, and conquered Jerusalem without taking over the whole of the West Bank. Yet, Narkiss and other senior commanders had been dreaming of and planning for that goal for such a long time. Although in the first hours of the war central command did not believe that the West Bank could be taken in this round of hostilities, the plans were in place and the circumstances were propitious: an accommodating minister of defense; a hawkish cabinet now dominated by Dayan, Begin, and Allon; and a king careless enough to give Israel a perfect pretext. Israel effectively turned down Hussein's proposal for a ceasefire. Dayan was most resolute in his opposition, telling Rabin: "First we finish the work he [Hussein] imposed on us, then we'll send him an appropriate reply."[23]

By noon the next day, Motta Gur's paratroopers were able to enter the Old City and reach the Western Wall. Lior called central command asking whether Eshkol would be able to come and make a special announcement. He was told that it would be unsafe as there were still Jordanian snipers lurking around. At about the same time, Dayan, accompanied by Narkiss and Rabin, entered Jerusalem through the Lions' Gate and headed toward the Western Wall. Dayan, with his distinctive talent for public relations, had made sure that a gaggle of reporters and photographers accompanied his arrival at the Old City.

As in 1956, Dayan's ability to control his troops was limited: Gaza was taken on the first day of the war despite his instructions not to waste men on that mission, and over the next two days IDF forces advanced in Sinai up to the eastern bank of the Suez Canal despite Dayan's explicit order not to head there. But his ability to control the PR machine was unmatched. An iconic photo was taken documenting the three conquistadors – Dayan,

Narkiss, and Rabin – marching side by side through the gate. Narkiss and Rabin were in uniform, of course. But so was Dayan. Since May 23, a uniform and helmet had accompanied him everywhere, even after he had become minister of defense. The picture of the three generals entering the old city symbolized where power lay in those days. It was the generals' war, and they had won it. At the Western Wall Dayan declared: "we have reunited the city, the capital of Israel, never to part it again." The paratroopers cried, ultra-Orthodox Jews danced. It was all so moving. Except for Eshkol, who sat frowning in his office. He visited the Western Wall the next day and made an anodyne speech. This event drew far less attention.[24]

The Heights

For four years, Syria had been the heart of the problem. It was unstable, and it spread its instability across the region. Its proclamations of its intentions to divert the waters of the Jordan River and the help it provided to Fatah units played into the hands of the hawks in Israel and embarrassed the doves in the Arab world. It would be wrong to suggest that the Syrians were sitting idly by, but they had not pulled out all the stops to help their Arab brothers. Syria tried to launch an offensive from the Golan Heights on the morning of the second day of the war. But its efforts in that field proved pathetic.

The Syrian attack, planned by Soviet advisers, was code-named Operation "Nasser" (victory). There was a considerable disparity between the operation's promising name and its actual implementation. As in Egypt, the doctrine of the Syrian army was defensive. Syrian troops were trained to defend the Golan Heights. Although there had been planning for offensive operations, a drill to acquaint officers and soldiers with how to mount an attack never took place. As in Egypt, the Soviets took care to supply the Syrian army with defensive weapons and helped them build massive fortifications. Syria's high command held little esteem for the professional abilities of its officers and did not believe Syria could emerge victorious should it launch an offensive against Israel.[25]

A diversionary attack on the kibbutzim in the Galilee on June 6 was repulsed by groups of Israeli reserve soldiers, pensioners, and high-school students. Meanwhile, three Syrian brigades prepared for a major offensive that would begin with crossing the Jordan River and end in the Israeli city of Safad, about 20 kilometers west of the Israeli–Syrian border. Incredibly, it was at that moment that commanders of the brigades found out that their tanks were too wide to pass over the bridges. Other units that were to participate stayed in their camps and refused to leave. Accurate hits by Israeli artillery and one sortie by Israeli bombers was enough to convince Syria's high command to order a withdrawal. Fifty-one Syrians were killed during Operation "Nasser." After this ignominious failure, Syrian military headquarters did not try their luck again, other than to bomb nearby Jewish settlements the next morning.[26]

Dado, the commander of the northern front, continuously lobbied for permission to start activating the "Makevet" plan. Even before the beginning of the war, Dado had met with Allon and promised him that not only would he be able to break through the Syrians' fortified positions on the Golan Heights, but he was certain he would be able to reach Damascus. Allon tried to cool the enthusiasm of his young protégé and told him that aiming for the Syrian capital was too much. On June 7, the third day of the war, Dado had secured permission to start a limited offensive but cloudy skies, which precluded air support, and the fact that two brigades that had been promised by general headquarters had failed to materialize, made him hesitate. He decided to postpone the attack until the next day – but then it transpired that Moshe Dayan was opposed. The minister of defense supported the war of annihilation in the south and the conquests in the east, but he could live with letting Syria emerge from the war unscathed. He had little sympathy for the settlers in the north: they never supported Dayan or Rafi anyway.

Angry, Dado took a helicopter to Tel Aviv to plead his case with the prime minister.[27] Talking to Eshkol, it quickly became clear to Dado that he was preaching to the converted. The matter, however, would have to go before cabinet. For some reason, the only one manning the phones in Eshkol's office that day was his wife, Miriam; perhaps the other secretaries needed a rest. Dado chatted with her about his predicament on his way out. Miriam tried to encourage him: "Look, I have a birthday soon and I want the Banias [River, which runs through the Heights] as a birthday present." Dado smiled. "Miriam, I'll do everything to make that happen but you should work for it too."

The cabinet convened that night to discuss whether to authorize Dado's request. Eshkol resolved that he too could be as hawkish as Dayan, and embraced the cause of the kibbutzim. To embarrass Dayan, Eshkol permitted representatives of the kibbutzim to enter the cabinet meeting and lobby for the attack on the Golan – something not done before or since. Years later, Dayan claimed that when those settlers entered the room, he could see the lust for land on their faces. Most of the ministers were for the Golan campaign. It simply seemed improbable to them that the Syrians, who did so much to destabilize the Middle East, should emerge from this war unpunished. But Dayan fought like a lion. He warned the ministers that the Soviet Union would react harshly to an attack on Syria. A more reasonable course of action would therefore be to move the settlers 10 or even 20 kilometers from the border. Dayan's prestige was such that even though he was in the minority, the cabinet decided not to venture into the Golan Heights – a decision that effectively ended the war, as the fighting on all the other fronts had already died down.[28]

Dado was informed of the outcome, and he went to bed gloomy and depressed. In fact almost all the protagonists – Eshkol, Rabin, Allon, and Begin – retired for the night; as far as they were concerned, the war was over. But one man could not sleep. At about 6 a.m., Dayan's assistant entered the pit and asked that the ops room be prepared for the arrival of the minister of defense. "I thought he was kidding," recalled one of the officers in the room. He was not. Tormented by his own self-doubt, Dayan entered the ops room. An officer told him there was evidence to suggest that the Syrians were deserting their fortifications and retreating. Restless, Dayan started poking around the intelligence tray.[29] He spied a translated telegram from Nasser to the Syrian president recommending that he immediately accept a proposal for a ceasefire to save the Syrian army. There was also an aerial photograph which showed that the bases around Quneitra, the only city on the Heights, were empty – though there was no way of knowing whether that was because all the troops had withdrawn to Damascus or because they had all advanced to the front. The intelligence memo attached to the aerial photograph, written by analyst Elie Weisbrot, nevertheless claimed that this was proof that the Syrian army on the Golan Heights was retreating. The end of the memo was also highly unusual: "It is unclear," Weisbrot wrote, "if such a situation would happen again." That was not a professional but a political assertion.

Yariv had seen the memo before it went out. Yariv was certainly for taking the Golan. He, Rabin, and Dado had been waiting for the right opportunity for years; it is just that he was not sure that what Weisbrot wrote was true. "Elie, are you certain that the Syrian army is 'collapsing'?" an incredulous Yariv had asked Weisbrot. Regardless, Yariv let the memo be distributed with Weisbrot's unorthodox comments in it.[30]

Dayan, for whom Weisbrot's memo had really been written, decided that this was incontrovertible proof that the Syrian army was collapsing. Later, Dayan confessed that this was simply a pretext. "I capitulated," he admitted. He did not want to bear the sole responsibility for not having conquered the Heights. Like Rabin and Eshkol, Dayan, the tough and cunning general, succumbed to the pressure of the generals–settlers coalition. At 7 a.m., without consulting anyone else, Dayan called the ops room at northern command. Bewildered, shirtless, and half-naked, Dado ran to the phone. "Dado, can you attack?" asked Dayan. "I can attack immediately," replied Dado. "Then attack," said Dayan. The minister of defense tried to explain that the Syrian army was falling apart but Dado cut him short: "I don't know if it's collapsing or not. It doesn't matter. We are attacking. Thank you very much." Dado hung up the phone and yelled: "They will not stop me now!"[31]

In the following two days the Israeli attack on the Golan Heights gathered pace. With warfare on the other fronts settled, all the might of the IDF was turned on the 50,000 or so Syrian soldiers and officers locked in their fortresses upon the mountain. At the start of the Six-Day War, Dado had only one infantry brigade and one armored brigade under his command. Following the end of hostilities on the West Bank, three armored brigades and two infantry brigades were sent by the General Staff to the northern front. On the eve of the Golan offensive, Dado had at his disposal 30,000 men and 500 tanks. Moreover, the IAF had no other business to attend to other than helping to ensure the success of the Golan campaign. Dado had asked Hod to slam everything he had into the Golan and Hod complied. In four hours, the IAF made 300 sorties over the Heights, dropping no less than 400 bombs. Clouds mushroomed over the land, gray from the napalm bombs and black from the regular ones. A Syrian officer in the 12th Brigade reported fifty-two dead, eighty injured, and six missing. The military hospital in Quneitra was a mess. It quickly filled up with casualties with napalm burns.[32]

Dado's forces proceeded to use the tried-and-true methods of the Israeli doctrine, driving tanks through impassable terrain and attacking Syrian compounds from their rear or flanks. The fighting in the first twenty-four hours of the campaign was intense and bloody. As it turned out, Dayan was wrong: the Syrian army was not collapsing – yet; it was fighting back.[33] Also contrary to expectations, the Syrians did not send their best units to the front. The ones that were considered the most effective and loyal, like the 70th Brigade, which was equipped with the sturdy T-54 and T-55 tanks, were retained near the capital to keep the Baath regime safe from its internal enemies. All in all, three of the best brigades in the Syrian army – two armored and one mechanized – were camped near Damascus, the troops being used to secure the party's headquarters, as well as the TV and radio stations. Even at this point, the regime feared its internal enemies more than it feared its Israeli foe. Thus, units considered less loyal, such as the ones manned by Druze soldiers, were sent to the front. In the Zaura and

Ein-Fit outposts, Alawite soldiers suspected the Druze of delivering secret information to the enemy and, in retribution, they tied up Druze soldiers outside the trenches, where they were exposed to Israeli bombing. "Die at the hands of your masters!" the Alawites shouted at their victims.[34]

Soon the Syrian forces in the Golan began to disintegrate under the weight of the formidable Israeli war machine. Troops on the Golan Heights suffered from low morale before the war had even started. The regime made sure to transfer families of Alawite Baath members from the front to the Damascus area. Hundreds of trucks were used for this purpose while the troops at the front were having serious trouble with logistics. When non-Alawites turned to the local governor and asked to be evacuated from the Quneitra area as well, he refused their request and threatened them with execution. Such behavior inflamed the hatred between Alawites and non-Alawites.[35]

Despite orders by Syria's high command to shoot anyone who tried to retreat, on the evening of June 8 commanders of first-line units were no longer certain that headquarters was determined to hold the line. Rumors started spreading about a retreat order that had already been given. Baathist senior officers received an invitation to come to an urgent party meeting in Damascus: they took that as a coded message that allowed them to retreat. Colonel Ahmed al-Mir, commander of the Golan front, left his headquarters at Quneitra on the back of a donkey, because he was worried that if he used a military vehicle Israeli planes would spot and strafe him. When officers called on regional headquarters at Quneitra and found that it was empty, they took that as permission to flee.[36]

While rear units withdrew, front-line troops were cut off, unaware that the regime had deserted them. They discovered they were fighting alone only on June 9, the first day of fighting on the Golan. Some of these units fought bravely that day and Israeli ground forces were able to advance no more than 13 kilometers along an 8-kilometer front. Nevertheless, on the night of June 9–10, Syrian soldiers and officers retreated under cover of darkness, mostly from the northern and central Golan, where the bloodiest battles of the previous days had taken place.

Colonel Izzat Jadid's story is illustrative of that time. He commanded the 44th Armored Brigade that was equipped with T-54 tanks, which Syrian officers considered superior to the Israeli Sherman and Patton tanks. On June 9, Deputy Chief of Staff Major General Awad Bar gave Izzat an order to move his brigade to the front line during the night and launch a counter-offensive on the morning of the 10th. Darkness should have helped the tanks of the 44th to redeploy without fear of the marauding Israeli planes.

Instead of obeying, Izzat contacted his powerful cousin and Syrian strongman, Salah Jadid, and told him he was afraid that Bar would court-marshal him for disobedience. Salah promised to protect Izzat. As a result, on the night during which the 44th was supposed to drive to the front, it retreated to Damascus.[37]

The retreat of army units occurred amid a broader civilian flight. On June 10, tens of thousands of people, both civilians and soldiers, were attempting to flee from the Golan. As in Sinai, the conceit of the General Staff had led to the transfer of second-line units to the first line of defense in preparation for the attack on Israel that failed miserably on the second day of the war. Syrian General Staff failed to order troops to move back to man the second line of defense. The result was that once the first line had disintegrated, there was nothing to stop the Israelis from rolling forward to Damascus.[38]

This is precisely what Syria's high command believed that the IDF wanted to do on the morning of June 10, the last day of the war. The fear of Israel's military prowess was now considerable. The Syrians knew they were fighting an army that had already chewed up the Jordanian and Egyptian forces and had conquered Sinai and the West Bank in a mere four days. Fear of an Israeli conquest of Damascus was so great that the central bank, the archives of the secret services, and Syria's foreign currency and gold reserves were hurriedly evacuated from Damascus to northern Syria under heavy security. In these circumstances, it made more sense to pull units away from the front in order to make a last-ditch effort to defend the capital. As in Sinai, the order to withdraw was given in a haphazard manner, which led to a loss of faith in the high command.[39]

In the early morning, observers in Quneitra erroneously identified a Syrian battalion as an Israeli force that had breached the city's defenses. (At that point, the Israelis were still four hours away.) At 8.30 a.m. Radio Damascus was ordered by the regime to announce that the Israelis had taken Quneitra. At 11 a.m. Syrian high command realized that they had made a mistake and Radio Damascus aired a correction, but it was far too late to have any effect. Syrian soldiers were already running away. Front-line desertion turned into a rout.[40]

At around the same time as the mistaken message was broadcast, units in the southern Golan, yet to see any major battle, were given orders to withdraw. The officers drove along the road connecting the trenches and called out to the soldiers to take their personal weapons and leave. They were to go on foot up to the village of Hital and launch a counter-offensive from there.

Instead, the soldiers preferred to cross the border and flee to Jordan. The same thing happened in the central area of the front. A retreat order was given at 8.15 a.m., but the chaotic flight from front-line positions preceded the order by two hours. The first to flee were the senior officers, then the junior ones. Finally, the soldiers took off. Just as in Sinai, any attempt to conduct an orderly withdrawal failed. The Syrian General Staff was receiving partial and mostly unreliable reports from front-line units and therefore could not monitor their movements. The Israeli war machine was moving too fast and the generals in Damascus were too slow in responding.[41]

As in Sinai, the Israelis knew everything about the Syrian positions: their size, location, structure, the type of weapons that were installed, and the number of troops in each position. Information was collected using agents, observations, and reconnaissance flights. Conversely, the Syrians, in the words of the Soviet advisers who were embedded in the Syrian army, "had zero intelligence on their enemy." As in Sinai, the first priority of the Baath regime was to save its own neck. Preserving the Golan was a secondary issue. Doubtless, Minister of Defense Assad and Chief of Staff Ahmed Sawidani were thinking about the following day. Sawidani commanded the loyalty of the ground forces, and Assad those of the air force. Neither could afford to sacrifice his troops or pilots: they would be needed for the internal battle that was bound to follow the defeat. Thus, because of the internal rivalries at the top, the Syrian front line in the Golan had crumbled. The speed at which that happened explains the low number of casualties among the Syrian troops: only 450 out of 50,000 were killed.[42]

The Superpower Moment

The road to Damascus was now clear. The only thing the Syrians could do was to call on their Soviet patrons and cry for help. On the last day of the war, at 7.30 a.m., the hotline teletype at the White House started ticking a threatening telegram from Soviet Prime Minister Kosygin: if the Israeli assault did not cease, the Soviet Union would sanction all measures, including military.

In fact, there was a fierce debate going on in the Kremlin as to what to do. Nikolai Yegorychev, then head of the Moscow City Committee of the Communist Party, recalled that when he had called Brezhnev's office sometime during the Six-Day War, he heard in the background a stormy debate in which Kosygin was shouting: "And what if they use atomic bombs against us? Is it worth it?" According to another report, Kosygin and Gromyko squared off with Grechko and Yuri Andropov, head of the KGB, when

Andropov and Grechko pushed for involving Soviet units in the war by landing a force on the shores of Sinai.[43] During the war itself, Soviet units received conflicting orders. For example, the Soviet navy in the Mediterranean was given an order to prepare for landing on the Israeli coast, followed by another order rescinding it. Soviet pilots in airfields in the proximity of the Middle East also recalled sitting in their cockpits after the hostilities had started and receiving contradictory orders from Moscow. In each case, however, the final order given by the Kremlin was to avoid any involvement in the June 1967 war.[44]

There was far less ambiguity in Washington. When Meir Amit was in the American capital on June 1, James Jesus Angleton, head of counter-intelligence at the CIA, was quite enthusiastic about the bright future awaiting the Middle East after Israel's military campaign. Angleton prophesized that the coming war would solve the region's problems and make it safer for American investment. Walt Rostow, the president's national security adviser, also believed that the war would create a more prosperous Middle East. In a long memo that Rostow submitted to Johnson on June 4, he argued that Nasser's regional influence was already on the wane. Arab Socialism did not work well as an economic system and Nasser's foreign policy adventures had ended in failure. "Just beneath the surface," claimed Rostow, "is the potentiality for a new phase in the Middle East of moderation; a focusing on economic development; regional collaboration; and an acceptance of Israel as part of the Middle East . . . But all this depends on Nasser's being cut down to size."[45]

The Israelis never believed they would have more than forty-eight to seventy-two hours to conduct their campaign. They thought that Johnson would react in the same way Eisenhower had when he found out, at the end of October 1956, that the Israelis were invading Sinai. Eisenhower was furious and told his aides, "We're going to apply sanctions, we're going to the United Nations the first thing in the morning. When the doors open. Before the USSR gets there."[46] Johnson did no such thing. When on the second day of the war Hussein begged Washington to help him convince Israel to agree to a ceasefire, the Johnson administration's reply was as cold as ice: as long as the Jordanian army was commanded by an Egyptian officer, Washington would do nothing to stop the Israelis.[47]

Two days later, when it seemed that the Syrians might get away with it, McGeorge Bundy, a member of an inter-agency team that had followed the war from the White House, asked Abba Eban about the state of play on the northern front. Bundy argued that it would be unfortunate if Syria, which more than any other Arab state was responsible for the regional instability, emerged from the war unpunished and free to start the "whole deadly sequence again." Eban's conclusion was that the White House would welcome an Israeli campaign against Syria. Meir Amit, who had his own sources in the CIA, got the same impression.[48]

Arthur Goldberg, Johnson's ambassador to the UN, carefully coordinated his positions with the Israeli delegation, whose instruction from Jerusalem was simple: play for time. Goldberg insisted on a ceasefire resolution that called on the warring parties to simply stop the fighting. Arab diplomats were against it: they wanted the warring countries to withdraw to the pre-war lines. By the time Arab diplomats understood that this issue could not be haggled over, it was already too late. Egypt agreed to a ceasefire only after it had lost Sinai, Jordan after it had lost the West Bank, and Syria after it had lost the Golan Heights.[49]

Even the SS *Liberty* incident on the fourth day of the war, when Israeli planes had strafed the American surveillance vessel and Israeli ships had torpedoed it, had not effected a change in American policy toward the war. Some of Johnson's closest advisers, such as Dean Rusk and Clark Clifford, suspected that the Israeli version – that the incident was a classic case of friendly fire – was untrue and that the Israelis had their own nefarious reasons to attack the ship. Although these suspicions were never proved, the fact that they existed at all made America's steadfast support of the Israeli case all the more remarkable.[50]

On the second day of the war Eshkol delivered a secret message to Johnson in which he reiterated Amit's request for the US to prevent the Soviets from intervening in the fighting. After the White House had received the threatening telegram from Kosygin on the last day of the war, the Johnson administration responded according to Jerusalem's request. Sixth Fleet ships were given orders to sail instantly to the eastern Mediterranean. Yet Washington's verbal response to Kosygin's telegram was measured and calm: it called on both sides to restrain their proxies in order to achieve peace.

Eventually, superpower conflict was averted. A ceasefire came into effect on June 10 at 6 p.m. Israel took the Golan Heights but resisted the temptation to march on Damascus (although it probably could have). War was over. Only six tumultuous days had passed, but the Middle East would never be the same.[51] Israel won a resounding victory, but no peace had ensued. This was just the end of another round of fighting.

Civil–Military Relations and the War's Aftermath

Arguably, civil–military relations can also explain the fact that no settlement followed the end of the Six-Day War. The army had been a central institution of Israeli society before the war and it became even more so after the decisive victory.[52] As a consequence of the war, Israeli generals now had the defense lines they had always dreamed of. The military establishment, led by Defense Minister Moshe Dayan, advanced quickly to create the institutions and the arrangements that would turn the occupation into a low-cost, permanent condition. Thus, officers rushed to establish military rule in the occupied territories, and helped groups of settlers to establish "facts on the ground" in the Golan Heights and in the West Bank.[53]

Dayan himself became the architect of Israel's policy toward the Palestinians in Gaza and the West Bank. At first, Dayan held to the illusion that treating the Palestinians harshly would convince many to leave of their own volition. As Dayan explained at a party meeting in September 1967, "Let's tell [the Palestinians]: 'we have no solution [for you] and you will continue to live like dogs.' Those who want to leave – will leave. We will see what this process would yield ... in five years 200,000 [Palestinians] may leave and that would be a great thing."[54] But after a while Dayan realized these were but pipe dreams. The Palestinians had no intention of leaving and nowhere else to go. Dayan had fathered a policy that combined liberal treatment of the Palestinian population at large with tough measures toward those who dared to challenge the Israeli occupation; for instance, he authorized the demolition of saboteurs' homes. The "open bridges" policy Dayan adopted allowed farmers in the West Bank to move to Jordan and market their fruits and vegetables there; that way, agricultural products from the West Bank did not compete with the crops of Jewish farmers in the Israeli market. At the same time, the "open bridges" policy created an incentive among Palestinian farmers not to engage in demonstrations or guerrilla acts, as their livelihood was dependent on the permission – issued by Israeli officials – to cross the border into Jordan.[55]

Back in the winter of 1966 Eshkol had abolished military rule over the Arab citizens of Israel. For as long as it had been in effect, the military had wielded a powerful tool in the form of the work permits it issued to Arab workers. Naturally, the military establishment resented Eshkol's decision. However, military rule over the West Bank and the Gaza Strip proved to be even more beneficial to the IDF's interests. Up to 1966, the IDF had governed the lives of about 400,000 Arab citizens; after June 1967 it ruled over more than a million Palestinians. The IDF used this immense power to buy the support of the strongest pressure group in Israeli society: the Histadrut. The military supplied Histadrut factories with new sources of revenue by helping them market their products in the West Bank and Gaza. It also delivered cheap Palestinian labor to Histadrut factories and signed an agreement that allowed the Histadrut to tax the salaries of Palestinian workers and shift the revenue into Histadrut-owned pension funds. This truce between the two most powerful institutions of Israeli society ensured the flow of cheap labor into the Israeli economy, fueling a post-war boom.[56] Obviously, this made the post-1967 borders ever more popular.

Unbeknownst to the General Staff, the Israeli government did adopt a resolution immediately after the end of the war, offering to trade the new territories for peace agreements and security arrangements with Egypt and Syria. (A majority in the cabinet declined to make the same offer to Jordan.) In truth, the government's willingness to compromise was born out of fear, not a desire for peace. Eshkol and his ministers worried that the US would put pressure on Israel to withdraw immediately from all the occupied territories – just as President Eisenhower had, back in 1956, when the Israelis captured Sinai for the first time.[57] Once it had been revealed that Lyndon Johnson would do no such thing, the cabinet slowly backtracked on its initial offer.

While the Israelis were winning in the Middle East, Johnson was losing both the war in Vietnam and his battle for re-election. It was clear that his sympathies lay with Israel and not with Nasser or Syria. In a telephone conversation with Arthur Goldberg, his UN ambassador, in March 1968, Johnson fully identified with the Israelis: "They're in about the same shape I am ... Because I got a bunch of Arabs after me – about a hundred million of 'em and there's just two million of us," Johnson chuckled, as did Goldberg. Johnson also confided that "I just want to be damn sure that I don't end up here getting in the shape Eisenhower did [in 1956, during the Suez Crisis] where I want to put sanctions on 'em." One of his last acts in office was to authorize the sale of the Phantom fighter-bomber – one of the most advanced weapons in the US arsenal – to Israel. This assured the Israelis that they would be able to maintain an advantage over their adversaries and, therefore, hold the post-1967 lines.[58]

On the other side of the hill, civil–military relations were even edgier. Both in Syria and in Egypt, war was followed by domestic battles between civilians and the military, each trying to place the onus of the blame onto the other. In Egypt, Nasser took the power struggle between himself and Abd al-Hakim Amer, who commanded the Egyptian army during the war, to the streets by announcing his resignation on June 9. The clandestine organizations of the ruling party, the Arab Socialist Union (ASU), had been groomed for this very moment for years. In an interview that was published three weeks before the crisis in the Middle East began, Ali Sabri, general secretary of the ASU, said he could put 20,000 people on the streets in eight hours, and 50,000 in ten hours. It was blackout time in Cairo, around 8 p.m., by the time Nasser ended his speech announcing his resignation. Nevertheless, observers throughout that city and in Alexandria saw the same scene repeating itself: trucks and buses full of noisy youths arriving at key locations, carrying banners, and chanting "Nasser, Nasser!" and "We want Nasser!"[59]

Meanwhile, Amer was on his way to the radio station to tell the people his version of the story. He was about to accuse Nasser of denying him the opportunity of executing offensive operations that could have changed Egypt's fortunes on the battlefield for the better. However, Nasser's men prevented Amer from entering the building. The demonstrations calling on Nasser to rescind his resignation continued throughout the night and spilled into the next day. ASU activists from the far corners of Egypt were brought into the capital during the night and morning. Nasser was scheduled to give a speech in the National Assembly and members of the ASU's youth organization were ordered to seal the building and prevent Nasser from leaving until he withdrew his resignation.

There was no need for that, however. Less than twenty-four hours after he announced his resignation, Nasser rescinded it. The next day, June 11, Nasser asked that units of the Revolutionary Guard, which up to that point had been stationed in the Canal area, be sent quickly to Cairo. Nasser deposed Amer and appointed a loyalist, Mohamed Fawzi, in his stead. He then proceeded to purge Amer supporters from the ranks. A tense stalemate followed as the officers, whom Amer had helped to escape from Sinai, armed themselves and surrounded their former commander's villa. However, by September Nasser's security services had lured Amer from his hideout and taken him under arrest. Amer died on the 14th: his detainers had probably poisoned him, although the regime claimed that the marshal had taken his own life. Yet Nasser's troubles did not end even then. Up until his death in 1970, his leadership of Egypt was increasingly challenged by students who demonstrated for more democracy. In response, Nasser dug in his heels and declared that Egypt could not afford to waste time and energy on internal reforms while it was still at war with Israel. War, rather than negotiations, had become the Egyptian regime's source of legitimacy.[60]

In Syria, a similar clash took place between Salah Jadid, who headed the Baath Party, and Hafez al-Assad, the minister of defense. Both factions had loyal units within the ranks, but Assad's supporters were more numerous. Since Jadid and his men had run the show before the war, it was easy to pin the blame on them. So, while in Egypt the party won the contest with the army, in Syria the army vanquished the party.[61]

Obviously, with politics being so polarized in both countries, no leader could have taken on the contentious task of negotiating a peace-for-territory exchange with Israel. Furthermore, the Soviet Union was all too willing to help mitigate its Arab allies' losses by supplying them with military and financial aid. This, however, came at a cost: the Soviets demanded that Soviet military advisers would be embedded in every unit of both the Syrian and the Egyptian armies, thereby increasing Soviet control over Arab forces. Their aim was to ensure that never again would the Arabs initiate military maneuvers without Moscow's consent. The Soviets also asked for, and received, permission to build their own naval installations in the ports of Alexandria and Latakia.[62]

Ostensibly, the Soviet Union was merely pursuing its age-old goal of augmenting its naval presence in the Mediterranean. In truth, it was Leonid Brezhnev, together with the military, who pushed forward a scheme that did great damage to the Soviet Union both at home and abroad. Indeed, the Soviet policy of propping up its Arab allies following their defeat was vehemently opposed by other Soviet satellites. Debates about the crisis in the Middle East exposed fracture lines in the Communist alliance. While Yugoslavia and East Germany applauded the efforts to resuscitate Arab resistance, others, such as Czechoslovakia, Poland, and Hungary, suggested that the Communist bloc was throwing good money after bad. Romania used the events in the Middle East to assert its independence and refused to sever its relations with Israel, as other satellites had done. In short, the gains in the Middle East came at the cost of weakening the cohesion of the Warsaw Pact, something that became all too clear during the Prague Spring.[63]

The defeat of Moscow's allies in the Middle East was also used by the young guard at the Kremlin to paint Brezhnev as an incompetent guardian of Soviet security. The interpretation of many in the Communist bloc was that the war in the Middle East had proved that Western weapons were better than Soviet ones. French-made Mirages and Vautours easily fooled the Soviet-made radar systems that the Arabs had used. This was all the more worrisome because the Soviet Union took a large gamble on air defense and invested huge sums in deploying surface-to-air missiles around Moscow. Security usually fell within the portfolio of the party chairman: Brezhnev. On June 20, during a Central Committee meeting, the head of the Communist Party in the Moscow region, Nikolai Yegorychev, accused Brezhnev of failing to modernize Moscow's obsolete air defense system. Yegorychev went on to argue that Moscow was completely exposed to air raids.[64] In East Germany, at the end of August 1967, Stasi agents were instructed to find out whether NATO and West German armed forces shared the same capacities in electronic warfare as the IDF.[65] Two months later, a Bulgarian General Staff study, prompted by the events in the Middle East, concluded that the Bulgarian army would fail just as miserably as the Egyptians in forestalling a surprise attack by the Greek and Turkish armies.[66]

The Six-Day War increased Jewish solidarity with Israel, and the rise of Jewish nationalism in the Soviet Union threatened to confer legitimacy on other national movements in the world's last multi-ethnic empire. The Soviet decision to take a unilateral position toward the Arab–Israeli conflict meant that the regime was at loggerheads with a million of its citizens. They were helped by an international campaign, orchestrated by Israel, under the slogan "Let my people go!" Israeli diplomacy also strove to exclude the Soviets from any involvement in Israeli–Arab negotiations. Both outcomes proved costly to the Soviet Union.[67] The refusal to allow the free emigration of Jews derailed Soviet efforts to reach a détente with the US in the 1970s. Lack of diplomatic relations with Israel was the reason the Soviet Union was not party to the Camp David accords in 1979. Some decision-makers grasped the deleterious ramifications of Soviet policy in the Middle East early on. Back in June 1967, Prime Minister Alexei Kosygin, a moderate, and Foreign Minister Andrei Gromyko thought it would be a mistake to sever relations with Israel, yet they had to take that decision when confronted with the hawks at the Politburo – chief among them the militant minister of defense, Marshal Andrei Grechko.[68]

These were the reasons that a settlement had not materialized at the end of the Six-Day War. In Israel, the army used its prestige and institutional power to press the government not to withdraw. It was helped by a friendly White House, which did not put pressure on Israel to soften its positions, and which also decided to pursue additional arms deals with the Jewish state. In Syria and Egypt, civilian leaders decided against negotiating with Israel due to the fierce tussle with the military. This inflexible response was supported by the Soviet Union, which used the war to augment its military presence in the Middle East. In exchange, it increased its arms sales to its allies and supplied them with ample aid.

Repercussions and Consequences

The tense status quo created following the war – also known as a no war, no peace situation – was merely the prelude to another two rounds of conflict. The euphoria that had swept Israel after June 1967 would slowly dissipate. Rather than being a decisive move to resolve the Arab–Israeli conflict, the Six-Day War reinforced regional tensions. A series of sporadic confrontations by the Suez Canal had escalated into a continuous exchange of fire between 1969 and 1970. Meanwhile, in the east, the Palestinians, now based in Jordan, had renewed their guerrilla operations, this time deadlier than before.

In 1973, the Syrians and the Egyptians pulled the same trick which had been used so skillfully by the Israeli army in June 1967: they launched a joint surprise attack which shattered Israel's superiority complex. In 1973, the Arabs were also able to implement another plan they had failed to enact in 1967: the use of an oil embargo as a political weapon. The energy crisis that ensued forced the US to take Arab grievances more seriously. The Israeli–Egyptian peace treaty, signed in 1979, was one consequence of that change. Jordan and Israel, always the best of enemies, found their way to peace in 1994, after King Hussein had relinquished his claim on the West Bank.

Other consequences of the war did not prove as reversible. The occupation of the West Bank and the Gaza Strip brought Arabs and Jews, hitherto separated by the pre-June 1967 borders, into direct contact. In 1987, after twenty years of Israeli military rule, the Palestinian Intifada (Arabic for "popular uprising") had erupted, starting a national conflict that continues to this day. The religious and messianic fervor of Israeli society in the aftermath of the Six-Day War spawned a settlement movement in the West Bank, which in turn established an enduring reality: 650,000 Jewish settlers residing among 2.7 million disgruntled and increasingly desperate Palestinians. Israel still controls the Golan Heights, which it captured from Syria during the Six-Day War. The Syrians never forgave, or forgot, which explains their support of the Lebanese Shia guerrilla group, Hezbollah. This organization has been involved in a low-intensity conflict with Israel since the 1980s.

The civil war so prevalent in 1960s Syria has been quiescent for forty years. Once Hafez al-Assad took over from Jadid in 1970, he created a repressive national security state that held ethnic tensions and class conflict in check for over four decades. The most direct challenge to Assad's rule came from Hama, the city that had been at the epicenter of the Muslim Brotherhood-led uprising against the Baath in 1964. A campaign of guerrilla warfare and terror by members of the Syrian Muslim Brotherhood, which started in 1976, culminated in a general uprising in Hama in 1982. The Assad regime lost control over the city for a few days and Muslim Brotherhood fighters executed scores of policemen and Baath officials. Assad brought even greater devastation on the old city of Hama, where Muslim Brotherhood fighters entrenched themselves, bombing it from the air and killing an even larger number of people – about 20,000 – than the

Baath regime had in 1964. Though the Assad regime prevailed and Syria was relatively stable for another thirty years, it has recently disintegrated into its various ethnic, religious, and geographical components.

The success of the Israeli offensive in 1967 made an indelible impression on the minds of Israeli officers. Blind faith in the efficacy of an offensive doctrine was a direct consequence. The final tally of the costs, though, should have given Israeli decision-makers pause. Victory in the war itself came relatively cheaply: only 679 Israeli soldiers were killed. But in the wars that followed the Six-Day War, and which were the direct result of it, many more Israelis died. Whereas between 1965 and 1967 there were 125 Fatah attacks killing 11 Israelis, in the three years following the Six-Day War there were 5,840 Fatah operations against Israel killing 141 Israeli civilians and military personnel. This time, these operations were supported by a vengeful Jordan, and some of the perpetrators were among the 250,000 Palestinians who had fled there from the West Bank during the war. The Jordan River, ostensibly a natural defense line according to pre-1967 IDF planning papers, proved far more volatile than the meandering border established in 1948. So too, in the south, the War of Attrition with Egypt (1967–70) caused the deaths of 367 Israeli soldiers and officers. And in the October 1973 war, when Syria and Egypt tried to take back by force the territories that Israel had taken from them, 2,222 Israeli soldiers and officers lost their lives.[69]

Before the Six-Day War, Israel's General Staff cited cost as a reason not to use defensive methods. At that time, the maximal assessment of building a defense perimeter equipped with sophisticated electronic sensors was $400 million. The total cost of the Six-Day War to the Israeli taxpayers, according to Finance Minister Pinhas Sapir, was $1 billion. Moreover, after the Six-Day War, Israel's defense expenses ballooned. From a defense budget of $241 million, or 6.4 percent of GDP, in 1966, by 1970 it had grown five-fold to $1.3 billion, or 24.7 of GDP. Most of the money went on purchasing Skyhawk and Phantom planes from the US. Israel purchased American military equipment to the tune of $308 million in 1968. In 1970 that sum grew to $736 million. Israel slowed down the rate of its purchases in the next two years, but in 1972 it still spent $507 million on American weapons. The defense budget for that year was $1.6 billion, or 17.9 percent of Israel's GDP. Some of these outlays were covered by US military aid, which increased from $95 million in 1968 to $714 million in 1972.[70]

The IDF perceived the growth in its budget as the reward for its success in the Six-Day War. However, for the Israeli taxpayer, the payoff was far from impressive. The economic costs of the 1973 Yom Kippur War were higher than the 1967 conflict, the death toll was heavier, and the military outcome inconclusive. In part, this was a consequence of an embarrassing error in the IDF planning department's assessments. In the decade that preceded the Six-Day War, that department insisted, along with the Israeli General Staff, that Israel would be safer within borders that included the West Bank, Sinai, and the Golan Heights. These were deemed Israel's "natural borders" since they included natural obstacles such as the Jordan River and the Suez Canal. But there had never been any serious work done on calculating the amount of manpower needed to defend the new borders. It was only after the Six-Day War had ended that the General Staff pondered that question.

By the time the Yom-Kippur War rolled around, it turned out that regular IDF forces were too few to hold the line in Sinai, from Kantara in the north to Sharm al-Sheikh in the south, against an all-out Egyptian attack. Israel invested a lot in trying to mitigate this limitation: it extended the compulsory military service by six months (to three years), quadrupled the size of the armored divisions, and committed two-thirds of its tanks to the Suez front. It did not help. The Israelis were still vastly outgunned. Slightly fewer than 300 Israeli tanks deployed in Sinai were supposed to halt the crossing of an army of half a million Egyptians. Moreover, they were supposed to deter the Egyptians from attacking. Unlike the pre-1967 situation, when the Egyptian army had to drive through the length of Sinai to reach the Israeli border, post-1967 there was a distance of only 200–500 meters between Israeli and Egyptian positions. The Egyptians could mount an offensive at short notice and catch the Israelis by surprise. The same situation existed on the Golan Heights, where 60–80 Israeli tanks were supposed to stop an attack of 600 Syrian tanks. In both cases, Israeli regular forces were instructed to hold their position for forty-eight hours until the reserve units arrived.[71]

From a military standpoint it was clear that this was no solution at all. Israeli regular forces would be overtaken once the Syrians and the Egyptians started their attack. Instead of confronting this uncomfortable truth, Israel's generals became addicted to magical thinking. Several assumptions were developed during the years 1967–73 to explain how Israeli forces would be able to halt an all-out Egyptian or Syrian attack, despite the glaring numerical inferiority: that Arab soldiers were inherently bad soldiers; that military intelligence would be able to give ample warning before the Arabs attacked; and that the IAF would serve as a flying artillery that would quickly break the Arab onslaught. All of these assumptions crumbled on October 6, 1973, when Syria and Egypt mounted a joint attack.[72] Would Israel have started the Six-Day War if the true costs of holding on to the "natural borders" had been tallied in advance? Perhaps.

But it seems that, prior to the Six-Day War, Israeli generals preferred not to contemplate the future consequences.

Since the Yom Kippur War, Israel's army has conducted innumerable raids and mini-wars, each bringing diminishing returns. Yet the Israeli cult of the offensive, born of the Six-Day War, still holds strong and the IDF remains the most powerful institution in Israeli society. The same can be said about the Arab countries that Israel fought against in 1967. The military regimes then controlling Damascus, Amman, and Cairo are still with us today, despite the many trials and tribulations over recent years. Like other parts of the late developing world, the Middle East remains in the grip of generals. Perhaps that is the reason why there the sound of gunfire never quite dies down.

ENDNOTES

Introduction: From the Local to the Global

1. The literature on various aspects of the war is vast but three monographs have emerged as authoritative accounts: Michael R. Oren, *Six Days of War: June 1967 and the Making of the Modern Middle East* (New York: Ballantine Books, 2002); Jeremy Bowen, *Six Days: How the 1967 War Shaped the Middle East* (New York: Simon & Schuster, 2003); Tom Segev, *1967: Ve-Ha-Aretz Shinta Panyeh* [The Land has Changed] (Jerusalem: Keter, 2005). An English edition of Segev's book was published in 2007. For an excellent edited volume on the topic see: Wm. Roger Louis and Avi Shlaim, eds, *The 1967 Arab-Israeli War: Origins and Consequences* (Cambridge: Cambridge University Press, 2012). For first-hand accounts published immediately after the end of the war see: Randolph Churchill, *The Six Day War* (London: Heinemann, 1967); Walter Laqueur, *The Road to Jerusalem: The Origins of the Arab-Israeli conflict, 1967* (London: Macmillan, 1968); Michael Bar Zohar, *Embassies in Crisis: Diplomats and Demagogues behind the Six-Day War* (Englewood Cliffs, NJ: Prentice-Hall, 1970); Edgar O'Ballance, *The Third Arab-Israeli War* (London: Faber & Faber, 1972).

2. Hazem Kandil, *Soldiers, Spies and Statesmen: Egypt's Road to Revolt* (New York: Verso, 2012), pp. 43–98.

3. The literature on this topic is vast and no attempt will be made here to include the ocean of publications on this topic. The foundational works on civil–military relations remain: Samuel P. Huntington, *The Soldier and the State: The Theory and Politics of Civil–Military Relations* (Cambridge, MA: Belknap Press, 1957) and Morris Janowitz, *The Military in the Political Development of New Nations* (Chicago: Chicago University Press, 1964). Recent studies which criticize and develop this earlier literature include: Jack Snyder, "Civil–Military Relations and the Cult of the Offensive, 1914 and 1984," *International Security*, Vol. 9, No. 1 (Summer 1984); Peter D. Feaver, "The Civil–Military Problematique: Huntington, Janowitz, and the Question of Civilian Control," *Armed Forces & Society*, Vol. 23, No. 2 (Winter 1996); Michael C. Desch, *Civilian Control of the Military: The Changing Security Environment* (Baltimore, MD: Johns Hopkins University Press, 1999); James Burk, "Theories of Democratic Civil–Military Relations," *Armed Forces & Society*, Vol. 29, No. 1 (Fall 2002). For literature on civil–military relations in developing countries see: Amos Perlmutter, "The Praetorian State and the Praetorian Army: Toward a Taxonomy of Civil–Military Relations in Developing Polities," *Comparative Politics*, Vol. 1, No. 3 (April 1969); A.R. Luckham, "A Comparative Typology of Civil–Military Relations," *Government and Opposition*, Vol. 6, Issue 01 (January 1971); Joel Migdal,

Strong Societies and Weak States (Princeton, NJ: Princeton University Press, 1988). For Middle Eastern case studies see: Keith Krause, "Insecurity and State Formation in the Global Military Order: The Middle Eastern Case," *European Journal of International Relations*, Vol. 2. No. 3 (1996); Mehran Kamrava, "Military Professionalization and Civil–Military Relations in the Middle East," *Political Science Quarterly*, Vol. 115, No. 1 (Spring 2000).

4. Steven Heydemann, *Authoritarianism in Syria: Institutions and Social Conflict* (Ithaca, NY: Cornell University Press, 1999), pp. 142–161.

5. Jeffry Frieden, *Global Capitalism: Its Fall and Rise in the Twentieth Century* (New York: Norton, 2007), pp. 278–330.

6. Barry Eichengreen, *Globalizing Capital: A History of the International Monetary System* (Princeton, NJ: Princeton University Press, 2008), pp. 118–125.

7. Harry G. Johnson, "A Theoretical Model of Economic Nationalism in New and Developing States," *Political Science Quarterly*, Vol. 80, No. 2 (June 1965); Frieden, *Global Capitalism*, pp. 351–355; Vijay Prashad, *The Darker Nations: A People's History of the Third World* (New York: The New Press, 2008), p. 73.

8. Frieden, *Global Capitalism*, p. 353; Sebastian Edwards and Julio A. Santaella, "Devaluation Controversies in the Developing Countries: Lessons from the Bretton Woods Era," in Michael D. Bordo and Barry Eichengreen, eds, *A Retrospective on the Bretton Woods System: Lessons for International Monetary Reform* (Chicago: University of Chicago Press, 1993), p. 440.

9. Michael Brecher, "India's Devaluation of 1966: Linkage Politics and Crisis Decision-Making," *British Journal of International Studies*, Vol. 3, No. 1 (April 1977); Habibur Rahman, "India's Liberation of Goa and the Anglo-American Stand," *South Asia: Journal of South Asian Studies*, Vol. 19, No. 1 (1996); John W. Graver, "China's Decision for War with India in 1962," in Robert S. Ross and Alastair Iain Johnston, eds, *New Approaches to the Study of Chinese Foreign Policy* (Stanford, CA: Stanford University Press, 2006); Srinath Raghavan, "Sino-Indian Boundary Dispute, 1948–60: A Reappraisal," *Economic and Political Weekly*, Vol. 41, No. 36 (2006); Srinath Raghavan, "Civil–Military Relations in India: The China Crisis and After," *Journal of Strategic Studies*, Vol. 32, No. 1 (2009); Rudra Chaudhuri, "The Limits of Executive Power: Domestic Politics and Alliance Behaviour in Nehru's India," *India Review*, Vol. 11, No. 2 (2012); Lorenz Luthi, "Sino-Indian Relations, 1954–1962," *Eurasian Border Review* (2012).

10. Daniel S. Lev, "The Political Role of the Army in Indonesia," *Pacific Affairs*, Vol. 36, No. 4 (Winter 1963–64); Donald Hindley, "Indonesia's Confrontation with Malaysia: A Search for Motives," *Asian Survey*, Vol. 4, No. 6 (June 1964); Harold Crouch, "Patrimonialism and Military Rule in Indonesia," *World Politics*, Vol. 31, No. 4 (July 1979); Bradley R. Simpson, *Economists with Guns: Authoritarian Development and U.S.–Indonesian Relations, 1960–1968* (Stanford, CA: Stanford University Press, 2008); William A. Redfern, *Sukarno's Guided Democracy and the Takeovers of Foreign Companies in Indonesia in the 1960s* (PhD dissertation, University of Michigan, 2010), pp. 182–204; Robert B. Rakove, *Kennedy, Johnson, and the Nonaligned World* (New York: Cambridge University Press, 2012), p. 151.

11. The critical literature on the role of modernization theory in the Cold War is vast. See in particular: Nils Gilman, *Mandarins of the Future: Modernization Theory in Cold War America* (Baltimore, MD: Johns Hopkins University Press, 2004); David C. Engerman et al., *Staging Growth: Modernization, Development, and the Global Cold War* (Amherst, MA: University of Massachusetts Press, 2003); Odd Arne Westad, *The Global Cold War: Third World Interventions and the Making of Our Times* (Cambridge: Cambridge University Press, 2005); David Ekbladh, *The Great American Mission: Modernization and the Construction of an American World Order* (Princeton, NJ: Princeton University Press, 2009); Nick Cullather, *The Hungry World: America's Cold War Battle against Poverty in Asia* (Cambridge, MA: Harvard University Press, 2010); Michael E. Latham, *The Right Kind of Revolution: Modernization, Development, and U.S. Foreign Policy from the Cold War to the Present* (Ithaca, NY: Cornell University Press, 2011). See also a special issue of *Dilpomatic History*, Vol. 33, No. 3 (June 2009), edited by David C. Egerman and Corinna R. Unger.

12. G.H. Jansen, *Afro-Asia and Non-Alignment* (London: Faber & Faber, 1966); David Kimche, *The Afro-Asian Movement* (Jerusalem: Israel Universities Press, 1973); Natasa Miskovic, Harald Fischer-Tiné and Nada Boskovska, eds, *The Non-Aligned Movement and the Cold War* (New York: Routledge, 2014).

13. Rakove, *Kennedy, Johnson*, p. 205; Guy Laron, "Stepping Back from the Third World: Soviet Policy toward the United Arab Republic, 1965–1967," *Journal of Cold War Studies*, Vol. 12, No. 4 (Fall 2010).

14. Amman to Department of State, May 31, 1967, DDRS, Doc. No. CK3100501438.

15. I am relying here mainly on: Snyder, "Civil–Military Relations"; Stephen Van Evera, "The Cult of the Offensive and the Origins of the First World War," *International Security*, Vol. 9, No. 1 (Summer 1984); Volker R. Berghahn, "Origins," in Jay Winter, ed., *The Cambridge History of World War I*, Vol. 1 (Cambridge: Cambridge University Press, 2014). Defensive realism theory also has a strong technological component known as "the defense–offense balance." I found it less relevant to my discussion.

16. Christopher Clark, *The Sleepwalkers: How Europe Went to War in 1914* (New York: HarperCollins, 2014), pp. 3–64, 242–313.

17. Dan Reiter, "Exploding the Powder Keg Myth: Pre-emptive Wars Almost Never Happen," *International Security*, Vol. 20, No. 2 (Fall 1995); Risa Brooks, *Shaping Strategy: The Civil–Military Politics of Strategic Assessment* (Princeton, NJ: Princeton University Press, 2008).

18. On the usefulness of inferring generalizable knowledge from historical case studies see: Alexander L. George and Andrew Bennett, *Case Studies and Theory Development in the Social Sciences* (Cambridge, MA: MIT Press, 2004), pp. 3–36.

Chapter 1: The Article

1. Raphael Lefevre, *Ashes of Hama: The Muslim Brotherhood in Syria* (New York: Oxford University Press, 2013), pp. 46–47.

2. Yaacov Bar-Siman-Tov, *Linkage Politics in the Middle East: Syria between Domestic and External Conflict, 1961–1970* (Boulder, CO: Westview Press, 1983), p. 158; Damascus to Department of State [hereafter DOS], Incoming Telegram, May 5, 1967, Central Policy Files [hereafter CPF], 1964–1966, POL 23 SYR, RG 59, NARA.

3. *al-Hayat*, May 6, 1967; Bar-Siman-Tov, *Linkage Politics*, pp. 158–159.

4. *al-Hayat*, May 7, 1967; Thomas Pierret, *Religion and State in Syria: The Sunni Ulama from Coup to Revolution* (Cambridge: Cambridge University Press, 2013), pp. 44–45.

5. *al-Hayat*, May 7 and 9, 1967; Damascus to Foreign Ministry, Incoming Telegram 4883, May 10, 1967, A MZV.

6. *al-Hayat*, May 9, 1967; Damascus to DOS, Incoming Telegram, May 9, 1967, CPF, 1964–1966, POL 23 SYR, RG 59, NARA.

7. Ibid.

8. Patrick Seale, *Asad of Syria: The Struggle for the Middle East* (London: I.B. Tauris, 1988), pp. 44–46.

9. Amos Perlmutter, "From Obscurity to Rule: The Syrian Army and the Ba'th Party," *The Western Political Quarterly*, Vol. 22, No. 4 (December 1969), p. 828; Raymond A. Hinnebusch, *Authoritarian Power and State Formation in Ba'thist Syria: Army, Party and Peasant* (Boulder, CO: Westview Press, 1990), pp. 20–48; Nikolaos Van Dam, *The Struggle for Power in Syria: Politics and Society under Asad and the Ba'th Party* (London: I.B. Tauris, 1996), pp. 1–14.

10. John F. Devlin, *The Ba'th Party: A History from Its Origins to 1966* (Stanford, CA: Hoover Institution Press, 1976), pp. 23–46; Hinnebusch, *Authoritarian Power*, pp. 86–89, 91; Van Dam, *The Struggle for Power*, p. 17.

11. Itamar Rabinovich, *Syria under the Ba'th, 1963–66: The Army–Party Symbiosis* (Jerusalem: Israel Universities Press, 1972), pp. 6–8; Hinnebusch, *Authoritarian Power*, pp. 93–94, 106; Malik Mufti, *Sovereign Creations: Pan-Arabism and Political Order in Syria and Iraq* (Ithaca, NY: Cornell University Press, 1996), p. 48.

12. Hinnebusch, *Authoritarian Power*, pp. 87–88, 101–103; Mufti, *Sovereign Creations*, p. 88.

13. Hinnebusch, *Authoritarian Power*, pp. 81–82, 97; Van Dam, *The Struggle for Power*, pp. 26–29. On that period see also: Gordon H. Torrey, *Syrian Politics and the Military, 1945–1958* (Columbus, OH: Ohio State University Press, 1964); Patrick Seale, *The Struggle for Syria: A Study of Post-War Arab Politics 1945–1958* (London: Oxford University Press, 1965); Eliezer Beeri, *Ha-Ktzuna Ve-ha-Shilton Ba-Olam Ha-Aravi* [The Officer Class in Politics and Society of the Arab East] (Tel Aviv: Sifriat Poalim, 1966), pp. 48–62, 104–107, 114–119, 358–361.

14. Perlmutter, "From Obscurity to Rule," pp. 830–831, 834; Hinnebusch, *Authoritarian Power*, pp. 82–83; Steven Heydemann, *Authoritarianism in Syria: Institutions and Social Conflict, 1946–1970* (Ithaca, NY: Cornell University Press, 1999), p. 107.

15. Daniel Lerner, *The Passing of Traditional Society: Modernizing the Middle East* (New York: Free Press, 1958), p. 297; Perlmutter, "From Obscurity to Rule," pp. 829–832; Hinnebusch, *Authoritarian Power*, pp. 81–85; Mufti, *Sovereign Creations*, pp. 55–56; Pesach Melubani, *Mi-Tzafon Tipatach Ha-Raa: Tzva Surya, Alilotav Ve-Milchamotav, Mabat Mi-Damesek* [Out of the North an Evil Shall Break Forth: The History of the Syrian Army] (Tel Aviv: Contento de Semrik, 2014), pp. 90–95; Hinnebusch, *Authoritarian Power*, p. 107.

16. Hinnebusch, *Authoritarian Power*, pp. 106–110; David W. Lesch, *Syria and the United States: Eisenhower's Cold War in the Middle East* (Boulder, CO: Westview Press, 1992); Mufti, *Sovereign Creations*, pp. 87–88; Salim Yaqub, *Containing Arab Nationalism: The Eisenhower Doctrine and the Middle East* (Chapel Hill, NC: North Carolina University Press, 2004), pp. 147–185.

17. Mufti, *Sovereign Creations*, pp. 91–93 (quoting Aflaq); Heydemann, *Authoritarianism in Syria*, pp. 82, 84.

18. Perlmutter, "From Obscurity to Rule," p. 836; Hinnebusch, *Authoritarian Power*, p. 111; Mufti, *Sovereign Creations*, pp. 93–98, 122–124, 133; Samuel Segev, *Boded Be-Damesek* [Alone in Damascus: The Life and Death of Eli Cohen] (Jerusalem: Keter, 2013), p. 85; Melubani, *Mi-Tzafon Tipatach*, pp. 123–124.

19. Rabinovich, *Syria Under the Ba'th*, p. 21; Hinnebusch, *Authoritarian Power*, pp. 85, 112; Mufti, *Sovereign Creations*, pp. 132–135; Van Dam, *The Struggle for Power*, p. 29; Elie Podeh, *The Decline of Arab Unity: The Rise and Fall of the United Arab Republic* (Brighton: Sussex Academic Press, 1999), pp. 142, 149, 151; Heydemann, *Authoritarianism In Syria*, pp. 126–133; Lefevre, *Ashes of Hama*, p. 87.

20. Eliyahu Kanovsky, *The Economic Development of Syria* (Tel Aviv: University Publishing Projects, 1977), pp. 55, 58; Hinnebusch, *Authoritarian Power*, p. 113; Mufti, *Sovereign Creations*, p. 136; Heydemann, *Authoritarianism in Syria*, pp. 142–145.

21. Hinnebusch, *Authoritarian Power*, p. 113; Heydemann, *Authoritarianism in Syria*, pp. 154–155.

22. Mufti, *Sovereign Creations*, pp. 137–138; Heydemann, *Authoritarianism In Syria*, p. 155; Van Dam, *The Struggle for Power*, pp. 30–31.

Chapter 2: The Baath in Power, 1963–66

1. Seale, *Asad*, pp. 72, 76; Rabinovich, *Syria under the Ba'th*, p. 49; Heydemann, *Authoritarianism In Syria*, pp. 156–162.

2. Rabinovich, *Syria under the Ba'th*, pp. 81–96; Hinnebusch, *Authoritarian Power*, pp. 124–127; Heydemann, *Authoritarianism in Syria*, pp. 181–183.

3. Rabinovich, *Syria Under the Ba'th*, pp. 114–115, 141; Hinnebusch, *Authoritarian Power*, p. 136; Heydemann, *Authoritarianism in Syria*, pp. 183, 174.

4. Seale, *Asad*, p. 93; Mufti, *Sovereign Creations*, p. 173; Heydemann, *Authoritarianism in Syria*, p. 185; Lefevre, *Ashes of Hama*, pp. 45–46.

5. Seale, *Asad*, p. 97; Heydemann, *Authoritarianism in Syria*, pp. 174, 177, 186–187.

6. Damascus (Grunert) to Berlin, February 27, 1966, File C 1368\75, RG MFAA, PAAA; Damascus to DOS, March 5, 1966, CPF, 1964–1966, POL 23–9 SYR, RG 59, NARA.

7. Rabinovich, *Syria under the Ba'th*, pp. 76, 118; Hinnebusch, *Authoritarian Power*, pp. 114–115.

8. Avraham Ben-Tzur, "The Neo-Ba'th Party of Syria," *Journal of Contemporary History*, Vol. 3, No. 3 (July 1968); Rabinovich, *Syria under the Ba'th*, pp. 22, 36–43; Hinnebusch, *Authoritarian Power*, pp. 115–116, 122–123.

9. Rabinovich, *Syria under the Ba'th*, pp. 24, 46, 57; Seale, *Asad*, pp. 63–65, 98; Hinnebusch, *Authoritarian Power*, p. 120; Van Dam, *The Struggle for Power*, pp. 31–47; Mufti, *Sovereign Creations*, p. 159; Melubani, *Mi-Tzafon Tipatach*, p. 121.

10. Rabinovich, *Syria under the Ba'th*, pp. 180–208; Seale, *Asad*, p. 85; Hinnebusch, *Authoritarian Power*, pp. 117, 121–122; Mufti, *Sovereign Creations*, p. 175.

11. Stasi report, Berlin, April 1, 1966, File MfS Hauptverwaltung Aufklärung Nr. 216, BStU; Damascus (Stupka) to Foreign Ministry, "The Current Situation in Syria, Political Report no. 66\7," July 13, 1966, Folder 13 (116\311), Box 2, RG TO-T, Syrie, 1965–69, A MZV.

12. Fred H. Lawson, *Why Syria Goes to War: Thirty Years of Confrontation* (Ithaca, NY: Cornell University Press, 1996), pp. 34–41; *al-Hayat*, October 16, 1966.

13. Hinnebusch, *Authoritarian Power*, p. 134; Stasi report, April 1, 1966, File MfS Hauptverwaltung Aufklärung Nr. 216, BstU; *al-Hayat*, June 29 and September 8, 1966; Damascus (Stupka) to Foreign Ministry, "The Current Situation in Syria," July 13, 1966, Folder 13 (116\311), Box 2, RG TO-T, Syrie, 1965–69, A MZV.

14. "The Situation in the Syrian Arab Republic and the Relations between the GDR and the SAR," October 26, 1966, File DY 30/J IV2/2J/1807, SAPMO, BA; Aleppo to DOS, "Year End Situation in Aleppo – Syrian Arab Republic," December 6, 1966, Airgram A–71, POL 2, Gen. Reports and Stat., RG 59, NARA.

15. Pierret, *Religion and State in Syria*, p. 159; *al-Hayat*, April 28 and November 8, 1966; Rami Ginat, "The Soviet Union and the Syrian Ba'th Regime: From Hesitation to Rapprochement," *Middle Eastern Studies*, Vol. 36, No. 2 (2000), pp. 160–161.

16. *al-Hayat*, May 10 and June 8, 1966.

17. *al-Hayat*, October 4, 1966, April 21, 1967; Damascus (Marter) to Foreign Ministry, June 12, 1966, File C 489/73, RG MFAA, PAAA; Damascus to Foreign Ministry, Incoming Telegram 1341, February 7, 1967, A MZV; Damascus to Foreign Ministry, Incoming Telegram 1713, February 16, 1967, A MZV.

18. *al-Hayat*, June 8 and July 18, 1966.

19. *al-Hayat*, July 31 and September 6, 1966; Van-Dam, *The Struggle for Power*, pp. 48–55.

20. *al-Hayat*, September 7–10 and October 6, 1966; Van-Dam, *The Struggle for Power*, p. 56; Melubani, *Mi-Tzafon Tipatach*, p. 156.

21. *al-Hayat*, September 17, 19 and 21, and October 14, 1966.

22. *al-Hayat*, October 8, 14 and 19, and November 9, 1966; April 7, 1967; Rabinovich, *Syria under the Ba'th*, p. 68.

Chapter 3: Playing the Israel Card

1. A. Abir, "Ha-Ezorim Ha-Mefurazim" [The Demilitarized Zones], *Maarachot*, 182 (March 1967); Yigal Kipnis, *Ha-Har Shehaya Ke-Mifletzet: Ha-Golan Beyn Surya Le-Yisrael* [The Mountain That Was a Monster: The Golan between Syria and Israel] (Jerusalem: Magnes, 2009), p. 39; Melubani, *Mi-Tzafon Tipatach*, pp. 130–132.

2. Ehud Yaari, *Fatah* (Tel Aviv: Levin-Epstein, 1970), p. 32; Moshe Shemesh, "Prelude to the Six-Day War: The Arab–Israeli Struggle over the Water Resources," *Israel Studies*, Vol. 9, No. 3 (Fall 2004), p. 9.

3. Rabinovich, *Syria under the Ba'th*, p. 35; Andrew Rathmell, "Brotherly Enemies: The Rise and Fall of the Syrian–Egyptian Intelligence Axis, 1954–1967," *Intelligence and National Security*, Vol. 13, No. 1 (1998), pp. 239–240; Segev, *Boded Be-Damesek*, p. 124; Podeh, *Decline of Arab Unity*, p. 169.

4. Bar-Siman-Tov, *Linkage Politics*, p. 107.

5. Rabinovich, *Syria under the Ba'th*, pp. 49–50; Bar-Siman-Tov, *Linkage Politics*, pp. 122–125; Mufti, *Sovereign Creations*, pp. 149–153.

6. Seale, *Asad*, p. 83; Mufti, *Sovereign Creations*, pp. 153–157.

7. Rabinovich, *Syria under the Ba'th*, pp. 56–57, 72; Bar-Siman-Tov, *Linkage Politics*, pp. 126–128; Segev, *Boded Be-Damesek*, p. 220.

8. Segev, *Boded Be-Damesek*, p. 241.
9. Malcolm Kerr, *The Arab Cold War: Gamal Abd al-Nasir and his Rivals, 1958–1970* (London: Oxford University Press, 1971), p. 101; Bar-Siman-Tov, *Linkage Politics*, pp. 134–140, 153.
10. Shemesh, "Prelude to the Six-Day War," p. 31; Kipnis, *Ha-Har Shehaya*, p. 55; Avshalom Rubin, *The Limits of the Land: Israel, Jordan, the United States, and the Fate of the West Bank* (PhD dissertation, University of Chicago, 2010), pp. 136–145.
11. Yoram Nimrod, *Mey Meriva: Ha-Mahloket Al Mey Ha-Yraden* [Angry Waters: Controversy Over the Jordan River] (Givat Chaviva: Ha-Merkaz Le-Limudim Arviyim Ve-Afro-Asyaniyim, 1966), p. 110; Yoram Nimrod, *Ha-Neshek Lo Shavat: Gormey Metihut Bi-Gvul Yisrael Surya* [The Armistice that Never Was: Origins of Syrian–Israeli Tensions] (Givat Chaviva: Ha-Merkaz Le-Limudim Arviyim Ve-Afro-Asyaniyim, 1967), p. 16; Bar-Siman-Tov, *Linkage Politics*, pp. 106–107, 134–140; Segev, *Boded Be-Damesek*, pp. 244–245; Kipnis, *Ha-Har Shehaya*, p. 55; Melubani, *Mi-Tzafon Tipatach*, 157–160.
12. Yaari, *Fatah*, pp. 51–52; Moshe Shemesh, *The Palestinian Entity, 1959–1974: Arab Politics and the PLO* (London: Frank Cass, 1988), pp. 62–66; Segev, *Boded Be-Damesek*, p. 247; Yezid Sayegh, *Armed Struggle and the Search for a State: The Palestinian National Movement, 1949–1993* (Oxford: Clarendon Press, 1997), p. 93; Melubani, *Mi-Tzafon Tipatach*, pp. 128, 160–161.
13. Yaari, *Fatah*, pp. 10–19, 31–32, 41, 43, 46; Sayegh, *Armed Struggle*, pp. 67, 81, 104, 106, 123.
14. Yaari, *Fatah*, p. 25; Sayegh, *Armed Struggle*, pp. 88, 91, 119–121.
15. Benny Morris, *The Birth of the Palestinian Refugee Problem Revisited* (Cambridge: Cambridge University Press, 2004).
16. Sayegh, *Armed Struggle*, pp. 46–54.
17. Yaari, *Fatah*, pp. 48, 62, 75; Sayegh, *Armed Struggle*, pp. 95–100, 135–142; Memo of Conversation between D.S. Nikiforov, the Soviet ambassador to Lebanon and the Chairman of the Organization for the Liberation of Palestine, Ahmad Shukeiri, August 9, 1965, in V.V. Naumkin et al., eds, *Blizhnevostochnyi Konflikt, 1957–1967: Iz Dokumentov Arkhiva Vneshnei Politiki Rossiskoi Federatsi* (Moscow: Mezhdunarodnyi Fond Demokratiya, 2003), Vol. 2, pp. 482–484.
18. Bar-Siman-Tov, *Linkage Politics*, p. 153; Wendy Pearlman, "The Palestinian National Movement," in Louis and Shlaim, eds, *The 1967 Arab–Israeli War*, p. 132.
19. Yaari, *Fatah*, pp. 53, 59. Sayegh, *Armed Struggle*, pp. 67, 107, 119, 126–128. Some of the weapons supplied to the Fatah arrived from the Syrian National Guard, Algeria, and China.
20. Yaari, *Fatah*, pp. 39, 78–79; Segev, *Boded Be-Damesek*, pp. 168–171.
21. Yaari, *Fatah*, pp. 58–61; Seale, *Asad*, p. 125; Shemesh, *The Palestinian Entity*, p. 65; Sayegh, *Armed Struggle*, pp. 94, 104, 124–128; Melubani, *Mi-Tzafon Tipatach*, p. 162.
22. Bar-Siman-Tov, *Linkage Politics*, pp. 102–105; Melubani, *Mi-Tzafon Tipatach*, p. 160.
23. *al-Hayat*, September 27 and October 16, 20 and 29, 1966.
24. Akram Hourani, *Mudhakirat Akram Hourani* [Memoirs of Akram Hourani] (Cairo: Maktabat Madbuli, 2000), Vol. 4, p. 3404; Avraham Ben Tzur, *Gormim Sovyetyim Ve-Milchemet Sheshet Ha-Yamim: Maavakim Ba-Kremel Ve-Hashpaatam Be-Ezurenu* [Soviet Factors and the Six-Day War: The Influence of Power Struggles in the Kremlin on Our Region] (Tel Aviv: Sifriyat Hapoalim, 1975), pp. 127, 149; "Regarding the Conspiracy against the Party and the Revolution," April 20, 1967, Box "Miscellaneous, no. 21–45," Special Ba'ath Collection, Moshe Dayan Center archive, Tel Aviv University; *al-Hayat*, June 9, 1966; Ahmad al-Shukeiri, *al-Hazima al-Kubra* [The Terrible Defeat] (Beirut: Dar al-Awda, 1973), Vol. 1, pp. 52–57.
25. *al-Hayat*, April 13, 1967.
26. "Regarding the Conspiracy against the Party and the Revolution," April 20, 1967, Box "Miscellaneous, no. 21–45," Special Ba'ath Collection, Moshe Dayan Center archive, Tel Aviv University; Incoming Telegram 4381, Damascus to Foreign Ministry, April 25, 1967, A MZV.
27. *al-Thawara* [an official Syrian daily], May 12, 1967; C. Ernest Dawn, "The Egyptian Remilitarization of Sinai, May 1967," *Journal of Contemporary History*, Vol. 3, No. 3 (July 1968), p. 210; Richard B. Parker, *The Politics of Miscalculation in the Middle East*

(Bloomington, IN: Indiana University Press, 1993), pp. 41–42; Georgy Kornienko, *Cholodnaya Voina: Svidetelstvo yeyo Uchastnika* [The Cold War: Testimony of a Participant] (Moscow: Ulma Press, 2001), p. 168.

Chapter 4: The Spy Who Came Back from the Cold

1. Mohamed Hassanein Heikal, *1967: al-Infijar* [1967: The Explosion] (Cairo: Markaz al-Aharam, 1990), pp. 441–442.
2. "The Problem of Arab Unity, Political Report no. 7," Damascus (Kroselt) to Foreign Ministry, April 12, 1967, RG TO-T, Syrie, 1965–69, Box 2, Folder 13 (116\311), A MZV; Shimshon Yitzhaki, *Be-Eyney Ha-Aravim: Milchemet Sheshet Ha-Yamim U-Leahreya* [Through Arab Eyes: The Six-Day War and After] (Tel Aviv: Misrad Habitachon, 1969), p. 82; Moshe Shemesh, *Me-Ha-Nakba La-Naksa: Darko shel Nasser Le-Milchemet Sheshet Ha-Yamim* [From Nakba to Naksa: Nasser's Path to the Six Day War] (Beersheba: Ben-Gurion University Press, 2004), p. 180.
3. Heikal, *1967*, pp. 433–434.
4. Arriving Telegram 4230, Damascus (Pishtor) to Foreign Ministry, A MZV; Ami Gluska, *Eshkol, Ten Pkuda!* [Eshkol, Give the Order!] (Tel Aviv: Maarachot, 2004), pp. 196–197; *al-Hayat*, April 21 and 23, 1967.
5. Heikal, *1967*, pp. 442–443.
6. Yossi Melman, "Ha-Ish Shelanu Ba-KaGeBe" [Our Man at the KGB], *Haaretz*, September 20, 2006, available at: www.haaretz.co.il/misc/1.1139332 (accessed October 6, 2016).
7. Yossi Melman, "Yesh Eyzeshu Neum Shel Khrushchev Me-Ha-Veida" [The Khrushchev Speech], *Haaretz*, March 7, 2006, available at: www.haaretz.co.il/misc/1.1089815 (accessed October 6, 2016).
8. Ibid.
9. Shlomo Shpiro, "KGB Human Intelligence Operations in Israel 1948–73," *Intelligence and National Security*, Vol. 26, No. 6 (2011), pp. 864–885.
10. Melman, "Ha-Ish Shelanu Ba-KaGeBe."
11. Ibid.
12. Yossi Goldstein, *Eshkol: Biyografia* [Eshkol: Biography] (Jerusalem: Keter, 2003), pp. 536–537 (Goldstein's source is the protocol of the cabinet meeting which was since re-classified); Amos Gilboa, *Mar Modiin, Ahrale Yariv* [Mr Intelligence, Ahrale Yariv] (Tel Aviv: Yidiot Ahronot, 2013), p. 219; Moshe Gilboa, *Shesh Shanim, Shisha Yamim: Mekoroteyah Vw-Korotyeh Shel Milchemet Sheshet Ha-Yamim* [Six Years, Six Days: The Origins and the History of the Six Day War] (Tel Aviv: Am Oved, 1969), p. 82.
13. Ibid.; Ahmed Hamrush, *Qisat Thawrat Yuliyu: Kharif Abd al-Nasser* [The Story of the July Revolution: Abd al-Nasser's Autumn] (Beirut: al-Mua'sasa al-Arabia lil-Dirasat wa-al-Nasher, 1978), Vol. 5, p. 114; Roland Popp "Stumbling Decidedly into the Six-Day War," *Middle East Journal*, Vol. 60, No. 2 (Spring 2006), p. 287. Segev, *1967*, pp. 233–235; Gluska, *Eshkol*, pp. 198–199; Parker, *The Politics of Miscalculation*, p. 13.
14. Segev, *1967*, pp. 233–235; Parker, *Politics of Miscalculation*, pp. 16–17.
15. Boris Morozov "The Outbreak of the June 1967 War in Light of Soviet Documentation," in Yaacov Ro'i and Boris Morozov, eds, *The Soviet Union and the June 1967 Six Day War* (Washington, DC and Stanford, CA: Woodrow Wilson Center Press and Stanford University Press, 2008), p. 56.
16. Kornienko, *Cholodnaya Voina*, p. 169; Murad Ghaleb, *Maa Abd al-Nasser Wa-al-Sadat* (Cairo: Markaz al-Aharam, 2001), p. 124.
17. Parker, *Politics of Miscalculation*, pp. 18–19; Gilboa, *Mar Modiin*, p. 219; Shimon Shamir, "Mekora shel Ha-Haslama Be-May 1967: Tanat Ha-Iyum Ha-Yisraeli," in Asher Susser, ed., *Shisha Yamim, Shloshim Shana: Mabat Chdash al Milchemet Sheshet Ha-Yamim* [Six Days, Thirty Years: New Perspectives on the Six Day War] (Tel Aviv: Am Oved, 1999), pp. 66–75.
18. Eytan Haber, *Hayom Tifrots Milchama: Zichronotav shel Tat-Aluf Yisrael Lior, Hamazkir Ha-Tsvai shel Rashey Ha-Memshala Levi Eshkol Ve-Golda Meir* [There Will Be a War

Today: Memoirs of Brigadier-General Yisrael Lior, Military Secretary of Prime Ministers Levi Eshkol and Golda Meir] (Tel Aviv: Idanim, 1987), p. 131.

19. Memo of conversation between Jospeh Tkoa and Dmitri Chuvakhin, June 29, 1966, File MFA 4048/24, ISA; Parker, *Politics of Miscalculation*, pp. 9–10; Yossi Melman and Dan Raviv, *Shutafim Le-Dvar Maase: Betochechey Ha-Brit Ha-Yisraelit-Americanit* [Friends in Deed: Inside the US–Israel Alliance] (Tel Aviv: Maariv, 1994), p. 116.

20. Melman, "Ha-Ish Shelanu Ba-KaGeBe."

21. Morozov "The Outbreak of the June 1967 War," pp. 46–47.

22. "A Report by the Commander of Reconnaissance Operations in the Intelligence Branch at the South-Western Command (Qunetra)," March 22, 1966, Vol. 4, "Syria – Intelligence," RG Six-Day War, 1967, Captured Documents Collection, Intelligence and Terrorism Center, Glilot, Israel; "Summary of Daily Reports made by Syrian Intelligence Unit 211 up to June 4, 1967," ibid.

23. Memo of conversation between Gromyko and Sadat, May 13, 1967 in Naumkin et al., eds, *Blizhnevostochnyi Konflikt*, Vol. 2, pp. 551–553.

24. Heikal, *1967*, pp. 444–445.

25. Kornienko, *Cholodnaya Voina*, pp. 169–170; Murad Ghaleb, *Maa Abd al-Nasser*, p. 121; "Soviet Policy and the 1967 Arab–Israeli War," March 16, 1970, CIA, Directorate of Intelligence (Caesar XXXVIII), available at: www.foia.cia.gov/sites/default/files/document_conversions/14/caesar-50.pdf (accessed September 23, 2015); Indar Jit Rikhye, *The Sinai Blunder* (London: Frank Cass, 1980), p. 11.

26. Shaul Shay, "The Israeli Evaluation of the Soviet Position on the Eve of the Six Day War," in Ro'i and Morozov, eds, *The Soviet Union*, pp. 123–124; "Regarding the Imperialist-Zionist-Reactionary Conspiracy, the Zionist Threats, and the Tasks of the Party Apparatus," May 19, 1967, a secret Baath memo to the party apparatus, Document 69, Box 'Miscellaneous no. 21–45,' Special Baath Collection, Dayan Center Archive, Tel Aviv University; Abd al-Adhim Ramadn, *Tahtim al-Aliha*, p. 41, Gilboa, *Mar Modiin*, p. 232.

27. Abd al-Muhsen Murtagi, *Al-Fariq Murtagi Yurawi al-Haqaiq* [Lieutenant General Murtagi Reveals the Truth] (Cairo: Dar al-Watan al-Arabi, 1976) p. 49; Mohamed Abdel Ghani El-Gamasy, *The October War* (Cairo: American University in Cairo Press, 1989), p. 21; Haber, *Hayom*, p. 151.

Chapter 5: The Corruption of the Revolution

1. Discussion of Nasser's early years in power is based on: Guy Laron, *Origins of the Suez Crisis: Postwar Development Diplomacy and the Struggle over Third World Industrialization, 1945–1956* (Washington DC and Baltimore, MD: Woodrow Wilson Center Press and Johns Hopkins University Press, 2013), pp. 13–84.

2. Ibid.

3. Ibid.

4. Robert Mabro, "Egypt's Economic Relations with the Socialist Countries," *World Development*, Vol. 3, No. 5 (1975), p. 310; Kirk J. Beattie, *Egypt During the Nasser Years: Ideology, Politics and Civil Society* (Boulder, CO: Westview Press, 1994), pp. 192–193.

5. Malcolm Kerr, *The Arab Cold War: Gamal Abd al-Nasir and his Rivals, 1958–1970* (London: Oxford University Press, 1971); Salim Yaqub, *Containing Arab Nationalism: The Eisenhower Doctrine and the Middle East* (Chapel Hill, NC: North Carolina University Press, 2004).

6. *Quarterly Economic Review of Egypt, Sudan, Libya* [a publication of *The Economist* Intelligence Unit] (November 1956), p. 1; Muhammad Faiq, *Abd al-Nasser wa-al-Thawara al-Afriqiya* [Abd al-Nasser and the African Revolution] (Beirut: Dar al-Wahda, 1980), p. 53.

7. Podeh, *The Decline of Arab Unity*, pp. 68, 133–134; Charles Issawi, *Egypt in Revolution* (London: Oxford University Press, 1963), p. 309.

8. Heydemann, *Authoritarianism in Syria*, pp. 86–105; Podeh, *The Decline of Arab Unity*, p. 152; Eliyahu Kanovsky, *The Economic Development of Syria* (Tel Aviv: University Publishing Projects, 1977), p. 56.

9. Alfred G. Mursey, *An Arab Common Market: A Study in Inter-Arab Trade Relations* (New York: Praeger, 1969), pp. 107–115; *Quarterly Economic Review of Egypt, Sudan, Libya* (October 1964), p. 1; Zach Levey, "Israel's Strategy in Africa 1961–67," *International Journal of Middle East Studies*, Vol. 36, No. 1 (February 2004), p. 72; Anwar Zaqlama, *Nihna wa-Afriqya* (Cairo: Maktabat al-Angelo al-Misriya, 1965), pp. 112–113, 147–148; African Desk to Lagos (Hanan Yavor), "Train Conference in Africa," January 1, 1963, File MFA 306\19, ISA.

10. "An Afro-Asian Economic Conference in Cairo," December 21, 1959, Research Desk Background Paper, File MFA 291\7, ISA; Director of the Afro-Asian Desk to various embassies, "AAPSO Conference," December 15, 1959, File MFA 291\7, ISA; "AAPSO Conference – Meeting of the Executive Committee," November 22, 1960, Research Desk Background Paper, File MFA 1028\7, ISA; "Toward the Preparatory Meeting of the 'Non-aligned' Countries in Cairo," June 2, 1961, Research Desk Background Paper, File MFA 918\15, ISA; G.H. Jansen, *Afro-Asia and Non-Alignment* (London: Faber & Faber, 1966), p. 257; Alba Ogunsanwo, *China's Policy in Africa, 1958–71* (Cambridge: Cambridge University Press, 1974), pp. 41–44; Tareq Ismael, *The UAR in Africa: Egypt's Policy under Nasser* (Evanston, IL: Northwestern University Press, 1971), p. 59; Vijay Pashad, *The Darker Nations: A People's History of the Third World* (New York: Free Press, 2008), p. 100; G. Afroka Nweke, *Harmonization of African Foreign Policies, 1955–1975* (Boston, MA: African Studies Center, 1980), pp. 95–97.

11. Jesse Ferris, *Nasser's Gamble: How Intervention in Yemen Caused the Six-Day War and the Decline of Egyptian Power* (Princeton, NJ: Princeton University Press, 2013), p. 196; Mufti, *Sovereign Creations*, pp. 82–98; David M. Witty, "A Regular Army in Counterinsurgency Operations: Egypt in North Yemen, 1962–1967," *Journal of Military History*, 65 (2001), pp. 401–439; Laura James, *Nasser at War: Arab Images of the Enemy* (London: Palgrave Macmillan, 2006), pp. 51–78.

12. James, *Nasser at War*, p. 76.

13. "Supply Problems in Egypt," November 8, 1963, MFA Research Desk, File MFA 746\4, ISA; "Presidential elections in Egypt," January 17, 1965, MFA Research Desk, ISA; Translation of "On the Internal Situation in Egypt," September 11, 1965, *al-Hayat*, in File MFA 746\5, ISA; Cairo to Canberra, "Current Situation in the U.A.R.," February 2, 1966, [an Australian memo given to British diplomats], File FO 371/190186, BNA.

14. Translation of "Rise in Prices and Bad Quality of Goods," October 23, 1963, *Akhar Saah*, File MFA 746\4, ISA.

15. Middle Eastern Desk to all the embassies, "Egypt," December 8, 1963, File MFA 746\4, ISA; Ferris, *Nasser's Gamble*, p. 190; Oren, *Six Days*, p. 305.

16. "Professor Morrow Berger's Impressions from his Trip to Egypt," March 10, 1964, File MFA 3567\17, ISA; Translation of "On the internal Situation in Egypt," September 11, 1965, *al-Hayat*, in File MFA 746\5, ibid.

17. "Nasser's Speech to the National Council," November 15, 1963, Research Desk, File MFA 746\4, ISA; Middle Eastern Desk to all the embassies, "Egypt," December 8, 1963, ISA; Cairo to Foreign Ministry, "Speech by President Nasser," November 14, 1963, File FO 371\178580, BNA; "Haikal Argues UAR Policy is Worth More Than It Costs," translation of Heikal's article from December 31, 1965 in CPF, 1964–1966, POL 1 Gen. Policy Background UAR, Cairo (Richard B. Parker) to State Dept., Airgram A–572, RG 59, NARA.

18. "Nasser's Speech to the National Council," November 15, 1963, Research Desk, File MFA 746\4, ISA; IMF report on the state of the Egyptian economy, February 2, 1967, File FCO 39/291; Letter from William R. Polk to Lucius Battler, November 16, 1965, Doc. No. CK 31000619523, Declassified Documents Reference System [hereafter DDRS]; Beattie, *Egypt*, pp. 190–193; Hazem Kandil, *Soldiers, Spies, and Statesmen: Egypt's Road to Revolt* (New York: Verso, 2012), pp. 63–64; John Waterbury, *The Egypt of Nasser and Sadat: The Political Economy of Two Regimes* (Princeton, NJ: Princeton University Press, 1983), pp. 83–84, 241–242.

19. "The Economic Crisis in Egypt," November 17, 1963, File MFA 746\4, ISA; "Wilbur Ira Wright, American labor attaché in Egypt," March 10, 1966, Zeev Levin to Moshe Bitan, File MFA 4041\3, ISA; Kandil, *Soldiers*, p. 64.

20. Alfred G. Mursey, *An Arab Common Market: A Study in Inter-Arab Trade Relations* (New York: Praeger, 1969), pp. 107, 119–121; George Khalil Kardouche, *The U.A.R. in Development: A Study in Expansionary Finance* (New York: Praeger, 1966), p. 18; Memo of a Tito–Nasser Conversation, May 13, 1963, KPR, File I-3-a/121-30, Arhiv Jugoslavije [Archive of Yugoslavia, Belgrade; hereafter AJ]; Sh. Siton, Economic Advisor, Washington Embassy to M. Gazit Deputy Director MFA, July 15, 1966, File MFA 7029/4, ISA.

21. "Egypt's Economy," August 30, 1964, MFA Research Desk to London, File MFA 746/4, ISA; "Egypt and the President of the World Bank," September 24, 1964, MFA Middle East Desk, ISA; "UAR – Quarterly Economic and Commercial Report" for December 31, 1963, March 31, 1965, August 3, 1965 in File FO 371/183915, BNA; Cairo to Foreign Ministry, May 5, 1965, File FO 371/183883, BNA; "President Nasser's Speech at Minia," May 15, 1965, File FO 371/183883, BNA; Cairo to Foreign Ministry, November 29, 1965, File FO 371/183916, BNA.

22. "Nasser's Speech to the National Council," November 15, 1963, Research Desk Memo, File MFA 746\4, ISA; Sh. Siton, Economic Advisor, Washington Embassy to M. Gazit, Deputy Director MFA, July 15, 1966, File MFA 7029\4, ISA; MFA Research Desk to various embassies, August 3, 1966, File MFA 6592\22, ISA; London (Tagar) to Research Desk, September 14, 1966, ibid.; Research Desk Memo, June 29, 1966, File MFA 1389\7, ISA; Cairo to Foreign Ministry, October 28, 1965, File FO 371/183916, BNA; Cairo to Foreign Ministry, December 23, 1965, ibid.; Cairo to Foreign Ministry, "U.A.R. Government Changes," September 19, 1966, File FO 371/190188, BNA; Cairo to Foreign Ministry, "U.A.R. Internal Situation," June 6, 1966, File FO 371/190187, BNA; "Planning Realist Loser in Cairo Cabinet Shift," *Washington Post*, September 15, 1966; Beattie, *Egypt*, pp. 193–194; Ferris, *Nasser's Gamble*, p. 208.

23. Ferris, *Nasser's Gamble*, p. 140; "U.A.R. Relations with the I.M.F. and the U.S.," January 16, 1967, FCO 39/287, BNA; *Daver*, March 1, 1967, p. 1; Waterbury, *The Egypt*, pp. 97–98.

24. "Professor Morrow Berger's Impressions from his Trip to Egypt," March 10, 1964, File MFA 3567\17, ISA; Middle Eastern Desk to all the embassies, "Egypt," December 8, 1963, File MFA 746\4, ISA; "The Farmers under Nasser," January 26, 1965, Research Desk Memo, File MFA 746\5, ISA; Sh. Siton, Economic Advisor, Washington Embassy to M. Gazit Deputy Director MFA, July 15, 1966, File MFA 7029\4, ISA; Memorandum from the President's Special Assistant (Rostow) to President Johnson, February 14, 1967, Doc. No. 390, Vol. 18, Foreign Relations of the United States (FRUS), 1964–1968; Beattie, *Egypt*, pp. 193–194; Kandil, *Soldiers*, p. 44.

25. Cairo to Foreign Ministry, "Moslem Brothers' Plot," August 8, 1965, File FO 371/183884, BNA; "The Trials of the Muslim Brothers in the U.A.R.," January 9, 1967, File FO 371/190189, BNA; Waterbury, *The Egypt*, p. 328.

26. "Ferment in Egypt," Research Desk Memo, August 29, 1965, File MFA 746\5, ISA; Beattie, *Egypt*, pp. 192–193; Waterbury, *The Egypt*, p. 86.

27. "Class warfare in Egypt," Research Desk Memo, May 8, 1966, File MFA 6592\22, ISA; Kandil, *Soldiers*, pp. 68–69.

28. Ghaleb, *Maa Abd al-Nasser*, p. 97.

29. Salah Nasr, *Mudhakirat Salah Nasr* (Cairo: Dar al-Khiyal, 1999), Vol. 1, p. 240; Aryeh Shalev's lecture at the Conference of Intelligence officers at Tel Aviv, November 22, 1956, File 2004\535\543, IDFA; Vol. 14, FRUS, 1955–1957, pp. 398–399, 404, 437–438; Kandil, *Soldiers*, p. 44.

30. Kandil, *Soldiers*, p. 48.

31. Wajih Abu Dhikri, *Madhbahat al-Abriya* [Massacre of the Innocents] (Cairo: al-Maktab al-Misri al-Hadith, 1988), pp. 71–74, 79; Paris (Y. Hadas) to Foreign Ministry, "Amer talks in Paris," November 3, 1965, File 7230/5–A, ISA; Mohamed Fawzi, *Harb al-Thlath Sawat, 1967–1970* [The Three Years War, 1967–1970] (Beirut: Dar al-Wahda, 1983), pp. 40–41.

32. Dhikri, *Madhbahat*, p. 72; Ghaleb, *Maa Abd al-Nasser*, p. 97; Kandil, *Soldiers*, pp. 50–51.

33. Beattie, *Egypt*, p. 159; Kandil, *Soldiers*, p. 53.

34. Beattie, *Egypt*, p. 160; Kandil, *Soldiers*, p. 54; Ghaleb, *Maa Abd al-Nasser*, p. 98.

35. Beattie, *Egypt*, p. 161; Kandil, *Soldiers*, p. 54; Ferris, *Nasser's Gamble*, pp. 66–67.

36. Ferris, *Nasser's Gamble*, p. 139; Yitzhaki, *Be-Eyney Ha-Aravim*, p. 15.
37. Patrick Seale, "Rumours of Unrest in Nasser's Army," *Scotsman*, May 5, 1966; Ferris, *Nasser's Gamble*, pp. 199–205; Kandil, *Soldiers*, p. 51.
38. James, *Nasser at War*, pp. 69–70; Heikal, *1967*, pp. 62–63; Memo of conversation between Soviet ambassador to the UAR, V.Y. Yerofeev and Vice President of the UAR, February 23, 1965, in Naumkin et al., eds, *Blizhnevostochnyi Konflikt*, Vol. 2, pp. 458–462.
39. al-Fariq Salah al-Din al-Hadidi, *Shahid Ala Harb 67* [A Witness to the 1967 War] (Beirut: Dar al-Sharuq, 1974), p. 76; Abu Dhikri, *Madhbahat*, p. 99; Waterbury, *The Egypt*, p. 339–342.
40. Zeev Levin to Moshe Bitan, "Wilbur Ira Wright, American labor attaché in Egypt," March 10, 1966, File MFA 4041/3, ISA.
41. Abu Dhikri, *Madhbahat*, pp. 105–107; "Political Analysis of the UAR Leadership," May 26, 1966, Folder 4, TO–T SAR 196569, Box 1, A MZV; Cairo to Foreign Ministry, incoming telegrams, Telegram 2785, March 16, 1967, MZV; "Report on a meeting with A. Sabri, general secretary of ASU," May 3, 1967, Folder 10, RG To–T SAR, Box 2, MZV.
42. Cairo to Foreign Ministry, November 2, 1965, File FO 371\183884, BNA; Cairo to Foreign Ministry, November 30, 1965, ibid.; Cairo to Foreign Ministry, "About a conversation with the employee of the Soviet embassy, Gudjow," March 27, 1966, File DY 30 IV A2\20\833, SAPMO, BA; "Political Analysis of the UAR Leadership," May 26, 1966, Folder 4, TO–T SAR 1965–69, Box 1, A MZV; *al-Hayat*, August 22, 1966; Kandil, *Soldiers*, pp. 57–61.
43. "Political report on the visit of the of the USSR delegation in the UAR," April 29, 1967, Folder 2, Box 3, RG TO–T, SAR 1965–1969, A MZV.
44. Beattie, *Egypt*, pp. 179–186; Kandil, *Soldiers*, p. 59.

Chapter 6: Sliding into War

1. Nimrod, *Mey Meriva*, pp. 97–98.
2. Letter from Paris (Yochanan Maroz) to the US Desk MFA (Shimshon Arad), March 9, 1964, File MFA 3567\17, ISA; "Professor Morrow Berger's Impressions from his Trip to Egypt," March 10, 1964, ibid.
3. Report on the conference of Arab leaders in Alexandria, September 5–11, 1964, Folder 1, Box 1, TO–T SAR 1960–64, A MZV; Yitzhaki, *Be-Eyney Ha-Aravim*, p. 39; Gilboa, *Shesh Shanim*, p. 37; Avi Shlaim, *Lion of Jordan: The Life of King Hussein in War and Peace* (New York: Knopf, 2008), p. 222.
4. Moshe Gilboa, *Shesh Shanim*, p. 48; MFA Research Desk Memo, August 29, 1965, File MFA 746\5, ISA; Zaki Shalom, *Diplomatya Be-Tzel Milhama* [Diplomacy in the Shadow of War: Myth and Reality in Advance of the Six Day War] (Tel Aviv: Misrad Habitahon, 2007), p. 148; Heikal, *1967*, p. 67; James, *Nasser at War*, p. 100.
5. MFA Research Desk Memo, July 26, 1964, File MFA 746/4, ISA; Paris (Y. Hadas) to Foreign Ministry, "Amer talks in Paris," November 3, 1965, File A 7230/5, ISA.
6. Yaari, *Fatah*, pp. 37–38.
7. Samir A. Mutawi, *Jordan in the 1967 War* (Cambridge: Cambridge University Press, 1987), pp. 67–68; Conversation between Minister Winzer and Comrade Gromyko, June 7, 1966, File A 001165, RG MFAA, PA AA; June 11, 1966, *al-Hayat*.
8. Akram Hourani, *Mudhakarat Akram Hourani* [Memoirs of Akram Hourani] (Cairo: Maktabat Madbuli, 2000), Vol. 4, p. 3388.
9. Heikal, *1967*, pp. 363–367.
10. Ibid.
11. Hamrush, *Qisat Thawrat Yuliyu*, p. 95; Yitzhaki, *Be-Eyney Ha-Aravim*, p. 77.
12. Hamrush, *Qisat Thawrat Yuliyu*, pp. 96–97.
13. Shemesh, *Me-Ha-Nakba*, pp. 293–295.
14. Shemesh, *Me-Ha-Nakba*, pp. 292–297; Yaari, *Fatah*, pp. 66–74; al-Shukeiri, *al-Hazima*, Vol. 1, pp. 52–53.
15. Gilboa, *Shesh Shanim*, p. 23; Avi Cohen, *Ha-Hagana Al Mekorot Ha-Maym: Medinyut Hafalt Chayl Ha-Avir Le-Tkifa Bi-Gvol Yisrael-Surya, 1956–1967* [Defending Water

Resources: The Policy of Using Air Raids on the Israel–Syria Border, 1956–1967] (Tel Aviv: Misrad Ha-Bitahon, 1992), p. 19.

16. Fawzi, *Harb*, p. 73; Heikal, *1967,* pp. 367–370.

17. Rikhye, *The Sinai Blunder*, pp. 71–72; Heikal, *1967,* pp. 1073–1074.

18. Fawzi, *Harb*, p. 70.

19. Kandil, *Soldiers*, p. 58.

20. Memo of conversation between Nasser and William Polk, in Polk Telegram to Rostow, February 5, 1963, Folder UAR 1\63–11\63 [Folder 4 of 4], Box 446, National Security Files [NSC], John F. Kennedy Library, Boston, MA, USA. (I am grateful to Nathan Citino who passed this document to me.)

21. Hadidi, *Shahid*, pp. 13–14, 31, 61, 72; Fawzi, *Harb*, pp. 60–61; El-Gamasy, *The October War*, pp. 25, 37–38, 40.

22. Hadidi, *Shahid*, p. 158; Yitzhaki, *Be-Eyney Ha-Aravim*, p. 75; Research Desk Memo, January 19, 1967, File MFA 1389\7, ISA.

23. Parker, *Politics of Miscalculation*, pp. 64–65; Sami Sharaf *Snawat wa-Ayam ma'a Gamal Abd al-Nasser* [Years and Days with Gamal Abd al-Nasser] (Cairo: Dar al-Fursan, 2005), Vol. 1, pp. 297–298.

24. Murtagi, *Al-Fariq Murtagi Yurawi*, p. 53; Abd Allah Imam, *al-Fariq Muhamad Fawzi: al-Naksa, al-Istinzaf, al-Sijen* [General Mohamed Fawzi: Defeat, Attrition, Jail](Cairo: Dal al-Khyial, 2001), pp. 89–91; Heikal, *1967,* p. 455.

25. Murtagi, *Al-Fariq Murtagi Yurawi*, pp. 53–56, 64; Fawzi, *Harb*, pp. 71–72; al-Shukeiri, *al-Hazima*, Vol. 1, pp. 58–59; Hadidi, *Shahid*, p. 150; Memo of Conversation between the Soviet Ambassador in the UAR Pozhedaev with Egyptian Minister of War Shams Badran, May 16, 1967, in Naumkin et al., eds, *Blizhnevostochnyi Konflikt*, Vol. 2, pp. 554–555; Cairo to Foreign Ministry, May 17, 1967, Arriving Telegram 5207, A MZV.

26. Hadidi, *Shahid*, pp. 152–155; El-Gamasy, *The October War*, pp. 39–40; Memo of Conversation between the Soviet ambassador in the UAR Pozhedaev with Egyptian Minister of War Shams Badran, May 16, 1967, in Naumkin et al., eds, *Blizhnevostochnyi Konflikt*, pp. 554–555.

27. Rikhye, *The Sinai Blunder*, pp. 16–57; Heikal, *1967,* pp. 464–465; Shemesh, *Me-Ha-Nakba*, p. 587.

28. Gluska, *Eshkol*, p. 238.

29. Heikal, *1967,* pp. 514–517; Murtagi, *Al-Fariq Murtagi Yurawi*, pp. 67–68; El-Gamasy, *The October War*, p. 39.

30. Fawzi, *Harb*, pp. 74–75; Hadidi, *Shahid*, p. 164.

31. Imam, *al-Fariq Muhammad Fawzi*, pp. 89–91; Heikal, *1967,* pp. 518, 1074; Murtagi, *Al-Fariq Murtagi Yurawi*, pp. 66–67; Hadidi, *Shahid*, pp. 152–153, 163–167; El-Gamasy, *The October War*, p. 41.

32. Shemesh, *Me-Ha-Nakba*, pp. 593–594.

33. Hamrush, *Qisat Thawrat Yuliyu*, p. 115; Cairo (Nes) to DOS, May 20, 1967, CPF, 1967–1969, Folder POL – POLITICAL AFFAIRS & REL ARAB-ISR, RG 59, NARA; Cairo to DOS, May 21, 1967, Doc. No. 28, Vol. 19, FRUS, 1964–1968; Paris to DOS, May 23, 1967, CPF, 1967–1969, Folder POLITICAL AFFAIRS & REL ARAB-ISR, RG 59, NARA.

34. Memo of Conversation between Pozhedaev and Nasser, May 22, 1967, in Naumkin et al., eds, *Blizhnevostochnyi Konflikt*, Vol. 2, pp. 561–563; Heikal, *1967,* pp. 522–526.

Chapter 7: The Phone Call

1. Shlomo Nakdimon, *Likrat Shat Ha-Efes* [Towards Zero Hour] (Tel Aviv: Ramador, 1968), p. 15; Michael Bar-Zohar, *Ha-Chodesh Ha-Aroch Be-Yoter* [The Longest Month] (Tel Aviv: Levin-Epshtein, 1970), p. 20.

2. Gilboa, *Mar Modiin*, pp. 129, 144, 232–233.

3. Gilboa, *Mar Modiin*, pp. 233–236; Haber, *Hayom*, pp. 147–148.

4. Nakdimon, *Likrat*, p. 15; Bar Zohar, *Ha-Chodesh*, p. 27; Gilboa, *Mar Modiin*, pp. 233–236; Yitzhak Rabin, *Pinkas Sherut* [Report on my Service] (Tel Aviv: Maariv, 1979), p. 134.

5. Gilboa, *Mar Modiin*, p. 236; Yeshayahu Gavish, *Sadin Adom: Sipur Hayay Me-Ha-Palmah Ve-Ad Beyt Ha-Palmah* ["Red Sheet": The Story of My Life] (Or Yehuda: Zabam, 2016), p. 98.
6. Bar-Zohar, *Ha-Chodesh*, p. 30; Haber, *Hayom*, p. 149; Rabin, *Pinkas*, p. 134.
7. Arnold Krammer, *The Forgotten Friendship: Israel and the Soviet Bloc 1947–53* (Urbana, IL: University of Illinois Press, 1974); Yoseph Heller, *Yisrael Ve-Ha-Milhama Ha-Kara* [Israel and the Cold War] (Beersheba: Ben-Gurion University Press, 2010), pp. 31–60.
8. Moshe Zak, *40 Shnot Siyach Im Moskva* [40 Years of Communication with Moscow] (Tel Aviv: Maariv, 1988), pp. 310–311.
9. Rubin, *The Limits of the Land*, pp. 162, 173–174; Protocol of a Meeting between Eshkol and Golda Meir, August 4, 1964, File A 7933\7, ISA; M. Gazit (Counselor) to A. Harman (Ambassador), "The Arms Race in the Middle East," December 28, 1963, File MFA 4301\4, ibid.
10. Abba Eban, *An Autobiography* (New York: Random House, 1977), p. 298; Protocol of a Meeting between Eshkol and Golda Meir, August 4, 1964, File A 7933\7, ISA; Report on an Eban – Rusk Meeting, December 7, 1964, File MFA 4327\21, ISA; Report on an Eban – Gromyko Meeting, December 19, 1964, File MFA 3573\24, ISA.
11. "The Prime Minister's Declaration on the Oder–Neisse line," August 20, 1964, File A 7936\1, ISA.
12. Memo of conversation between Eshkol and the Soviet Ambassador, Sergei Bodrov, September 23, 1963, File A 7936\1, ISA; Memo of conversation between Eshkol and Soviet Ambassador, Dmitri Chuvakhin, April 20, 1966, File MFA 4048/28, ISA.
13. Protocol of a meeting between Eshkol and Golda Meir, August 4, 1964, File A 7933\7, ISA.
14. Protocol of a meeting of Mapai ministers, October 31, 1963, File A 7921/9, ISA; Protocol of a meeting on Soviet Jewry, November 8, 1963, File A 7938\5, ISA.
15. Memo of conversation between Dmitri Chuvachin and Abba Eban, January 4, 1966 in Naumkin et al., eds, *Blizhnevostochnyi Konflikt*, Vol. 2, pp. 485–487.
16. Memo of conversation between Aliezer Livneh and A.S. Lichachuv (Counselor at the Soviet Embassy in Israel), December 26, 1963, File A 7936\1, ISA; Protocol of a meeting between Eshkol and Golda Meir, August 4, 1964, File A 7933\7, ISA; Eshkol's letter to Alexei Kosygin, undated, File MFA 4048/28, ISA; Memo of conversation between Abba Eban and Dmitri Chuvakhin, January 19, 1966, File MFA 4048/28, ISA; "Brief Prepared by the Middle Eastern Department at the Soviet Foreign Ministry regarding Israeli Intentions to Obtain Nuclear Weapons," February 23, 1966, in Naumkin et al., eds, *Blizhnevostochnyi Konflikt*, Vol. 2, pp. 487–489; Adam Raz, *Ha-Maavak al Ha-Ptzatza* [The Struggle over the Bomb] (Jerusalem: Carmel, 2015), p. 492.
17. Michael Bar-Zohar, *Hayav U-Moto shel Nasich Yehudi: Dr Yaacov Herzof, Ha-Biografia* [The Life and Times of a Jewish Prince: A Biography of Yaacov Herzog] (Tel Aviv: Yediot Ahronot, 2003) p. 208; Shlaim, *Lion*, p. 179; Clea Lutz Hupp, *The United States and Jordan: Middle East Diplomacy during the Cold War* (London: I.B. Tauris, 2014), p. 78.
18. Hupp, *The United States*, pp. 82, 87; Rubin, *The Limits of the Land*, pp. 83–133, 186.
19. Anne Mariel Peters and Pete W. Moore, "Beyond Boom and Bust: External Rents, Durable Authoritarianism, and Institutional Adaptation in the Hashemite Kingdom of Jordan," *Studies in Comparative International Development*, Vol. 44, No. 3 (September 2009), pp. 268–269; Shlaim, *Lion*, p. 195.
20. Bar Zohar, *Hayav*, pp. 210–212; Shlaim, *Lion*, pp. 200–201.
21. Bar Zohar, *Hayav*, pp. 213, 223.
22. Bar-Zohar, *Hayav*, pp. 225–229, 232–234; Shlaim, *Lion*, pp. 209–211, 214–216; Rubin, *The Limits of the Land*, pp. 136–145.
23. Rubin, *The Limits* of the Land, pp. 206–215.
24. Meir Amit, *Rosh Be-Rosh: Mabat Ishi al Aeyroim Gdolim U-Parshiyut Alumot* [Head to Head: A Personal Reflection on Historical Events and Confidential Affairs] (Or Yehuda: Head Artzi, 1999), pp. 204–208.
25. Ibid., p. 211.
26. Ibid., pp. 215–219.

27. Ibid., pp. 219–225.
28. Ibid., p. 225.
29. Zaki Shalom, "Hizdamnut She-Huhmetza? Hanisayon Litzur Magaim Yeshirim Beyn Yisrael U-Mitzrayim Arev Milchemet Sheshet Hayammim" [A Missed Opportunity? The Efforts to Open Direct Channels between Israel and Egypt on the Eve of the Six Day War], *Ha-Ziyonot* (2001), pp. 321–353; "Egypt," January 17, 1967, File MFA 4092\7, ISA.
30. Yemima Rosenthal et al., eds, *Levi Eshkol, Rosh Ha-Memeshala Ha-Shlishi: Mivhar Teudut Me-Pirkey Hayav* [Levi Eshkol, the Third Prime Minister: Selected Documents] (Jerusalem: Israeli State Archive, 2002), p. 479; Gilboa, *Mar Modiin*, p. 186; "Arab Realism," November 17, 1965, MFA memo, File A 7936\6, ISA; Memo of conversation between M. Gazit and Dmitri Chuvakhin, December 14, 1966, File MFA 314\5.
31. Rosenthal et al., eds, *Levi Eshkol*, pp. 403–408, 482, 510.

Chapter 8: Defying Israel's Founding Father

1. Yonathan Shapiro, *The Formative Years of the Israeli Labour Party, 1919–1930* (London: Sage, 1976), pp. 180–253.
2. Peter Y. Medding, *Mapai in Israel* (Cambridge: Cambridge University Press, 1972), pp. 146–153, 214–215.
3. Michael Shalev, "Labor, State, and Crisis: An Israeli Case Study," *Industrial Relations*, Vol. 23, No. 3 (Fall 1984), pp. 369–371; Lev Luis Grinberg, *Ha-Histadrut Maal Ha-Kol* [The Histadrut above Everything] (Jerusalem: Nevo, 1993), pp. 20–24.
4. Grinberg, *Ha-Histadrut*, p. 41.
5. Ibid., p. 77.
6. Ibid., pp. 73–77; Zaki Shalom, *Ke-Esh Be-Atzmotav: Ben-Gurion Ve-Hamaavak al Dmut Ha-Hmedina, 1963–1967* [Like Fire in his Bones: Ben-Gurion's Struggles, 1963–1967] (Beersheba: Ben-Gurion University Press, 2004), p. 47; Rosenthal et al., eds, *Levi Eshkol*, pp. 330–332; Asher Yadlin, *Edut* [Testimony] (Jerusalem: Idanim, 1980), pp. 102–105.
7. Grinberg, *Ha-Histadrut*, p. 79; Rosenthal et al., eds, *Levi Eshkol*, p. 333.
8. Shabtai Teveth, *Ben-Gurion's Spy: The Story of the Political Scandal That Shaped Modern Israel* (New York: Columbia University Press, 1996).
9. Eyal Kafkafi, "Moshe Sharett Ve-Parashat Lavon: Sipora shel Hatzata Mauheret" [Moshe Sharett and the Lavon Affair: A Story of Delayed Comprehension], *Ha-Tziyonot* (2003), pp. 339–344.
10. Moshe Sharett, *Yoman Ishi* [Personal Diary] (Tel Aviv: Maariv, 1978), pp. 561–562, 666, 672, 705–706, 709, 711, 715–716, 720–723, 730–738; Kafkafi, "Moshe Sharett," p. 346.
11. Benny Morris, *Israel's Border Wars, 1949–1956: Arab Infiltration, Israeli Retaliation, and the Countdown to the Suez War* (Oxford: Clarendon Press, 1993), pp. 306–339; Kafkafi, "Moshe Sharett," p. 346.
12. Grinberg, *Ha-Histadrut*, pp. 44–80.
13. Ibid., p. 97; Shalom, *Ke-Esh*, p. 55.
14. Grinberg, *Ha-Histadrut*, p. 101; Rosenthal et al., eds, *Levi Eshkol*, pp. 349–350.
15. Grinberg, *Ha-Histadrut*, p. 98, 101–104; Rosenthal et al., eds, *Levi Eshkol*, p. 351.
16. Grinberg, *Ha-Histadrut*, p. 99; Kafkafi, "Moshe Sharett," p. 349.
17. Avner Yaniv, *Deterrence Without the Bomb: The Politics of Israel's Strategy* (Lexington, MA: Lexington Books, 1987), pp. 77–79; Avner Yaniv, *Politika Ve-Estrategya Be-Yisrael* [Politics and Strategy in Israel] (Tel Aviv: Sifriyat Poalim, 1994), p. 146; Avner Cohen, *Israel and the Bomb* (New York: Columbia University Press, 1998), p. 367; Raz, *Ha-Maavak*, pp. 110–111; Grinberg, *Ha-Histadrut*, p. 164; *Maariv*, May 12, 1967.
18. Grinberg, *Ha-Histadrut*, p. 94; Rosenthal et al., eds, *Levi Eshkol*, p. 351; Yemima Rosenthal, *Yitzhak Rabin, Rosh Memshelet Yisrael: Mivhar Teudot* [Yitzhak Rabin, Israeli Prime Minister: A Selection of Documents] (Jerusalem: Israeli State Archive, 2005), p. 305; Gilboa, *Mar Modiin*, pp. 119–120.
19. Rosenthal et al., eds, *Levi Eshkol*, p. 440.
20. Ibid., p. 416.

21. Gabriel Sheffer, *Moshe Sharett: Biography of a Political Moderate* (Oxford: Oxford University Press), pp. 959–976; Kafkafi, "Moshe Sharett," pp. 351–352; Rosenthal et al., eds, *Levi Eshkol*, pp. 453–455.
22. Shalom, *Ke-Esh*, pp. 67–68.
23. Rabin, *Pinkas*, p. 149; Yadlin, *Edut*, pp. 124–125; Shalom, *Ke-Esh*, pp. 66–67, 113–114; Yitzhak Grinberg, *Pinhas Sapir: Biographia Kalkalit Politit, 1949–1975* [Pinhas Sapir: A Political Biography] (Tel Aviv: Resling, 2011), pp. 246–247.
24. Grinberg, *Sapir*, p. 249.
25. Shalom, *Ke-Esh*, pp. 74–75.
26. Rosenthal et al., eds, *Levi Eshkol*, p. 479; Shalom, *Ke-Esh*, pp. 120–155.

Chapter 9: Expanding Israel's Borders

1. Gluska, *Eshkol*, pp. 50–54; Rosenthal, *Yitzhak Rabin*, pp. 318–321.
2. Michael Bar-Zohar, *Ben-Gurion* (Tel Aviv: Am Oved, 1977), pp. 825–826, 858–860; Dov Tamari, *Ha-Uma Ha-Hamush: Aliyata U-Shkiata shel Tofaat Ha-Miluiam Be-Yisrael* [The Armed Nation: The Rise and Decline of the Israeli Reserve System] (Tel Aviv: Maarachot, 2012), p. 215.
3. Cabinet Minutes, October 19, 1953, ISA; Sharett, *Yoman Ishi*, p. 1021; Stuart Cohen, *Supreme Command* (New York: The Free Press, 2002), pp. 162–163; Morris, *Israel's Border Wars*, p. 242; Avi Shlaim, *The Iron Wall: Israel and the Arab World* (London: Penguin, 2000), pp. 66, 100; Zaki Shalom, "Amadot Be-Hanhagat Ha-Medina Be-Sugiyat Ha-Status Quo Ha-Teritoriali Ba-Shanim Ha-Rishonot She-Lahar Milhemet Ha-Atzmaot: Bhina Mehudeshet" [Positions of Israeli Leaders Regarding the Territorial Status Quo during the Years that Followed the 1948 War], *Iyunim*, Vol. 8 (1998), pp. 113–115.
4. Tamari, *Ha-Uma*, pp. 214–223; Shimon Golan, *Gvul Ham, Milhama Kara: Hitgabshut Mediniyut Ha-Bitahun shel Yisrael, 1949–1953* [Hot Border, Cold War: The Evolution of Israel's Security Policy] (Tel Aviv: Maarahot, 2000), pp. 216–243.
5. General Staff meeting, October 26, 1955, Israel Defense Forces Archive, Ramat Efal, Israel [hereafter IDFA], File 1962\847\63.
6. Moshe Dayan, *Story of My Life* (New York: Warner Books, 1977), pp. 238, 269.
7. Rosenthal, *Yitzhak Rabin*, pp. 218–219, 224.
8. Tamari, *Ha-Uma*, pp. 311–318; Gluska, *Eshkol*, pp. 256–260.
9. Nigel Ashton, *King Hussein of Jordan: A Political Life* (New Haven, CT: Yale University Press, 2008), p. 95; Moshe Elad, *Im Tirtzu – Zu Ha-Gada: Ha-Mimshal Ha-Yisraeli Ba-Gada Ha-Maarvit Ba-Asor Ha-Rishon, 1967–1976* [This is the West Bank – If You Want It: the Israeli Rule over the West Bank in its First Decade] (Haifa: Pardes, 2015), pp. 56–57, 70–75; Meir Shamgar, *Pirkei Haim* [Chapters from my Life] (Tel Aviv: Yidiot Ahronot, 2015), pp. 74–89.
10. Segev, *1967*, pp. 480–485; Elad, *Im Tirzu*, pp. 75–76.
11. Uri Ben-Eliezer, *The Making of Israeli Militarism* (Bloomington, IN: Indiana University Press, 1998); Anita Shapira, *Land and Power: The Zionist Resort to Force, 1881–1948* (Stanford, CA: Stanford University Press, 1999), pp. 219–252.
12. Gluska, *Eshkol*, pp. 35–39.
13. Ben Eliezer, *The Making*, pp. 51–64; Gavish, *Sadin*, pp. 17–20.
14. Segev, *1967*, p. 92.
15. Zeev Drory, "Societal Values: Impact on Israel Security – The Kibbutz Movement as a Mobilized Elite," *Israel Studies*, Vol. 19, No. 1 (Spring 2014), p. 167.
16. Segev, *1967*, p. 97; Drory, "Societal Values," pp. 167, 175.
17. Yigal Allon, *My Father's House* (New York: Norton, 1975); Anita Shapira, *Yigal Allon, Native Son* (Philadelphia, PA: University of Pennsylvania Press, 2007).
18. Yigal Allon, *Masah Shel Hul: Yisrael Ve-Arav Beyn Milhama Leshalom* [A Curtain of Sand: Israel and the Arab World between War and Peace] (Tel Aviv: Ha-kibbutz Ha-Meuchad, 1959), pp. 239–263; Drory, "Societal Values," pp. 171–173.
19. Gluska, *Eshkol*, pp. 82–84.
20. Rabin, *Pinkas*, pp. 84–87; Rosenthal et al., eds, *Levi Eshkol*, p. 416; Yossi Goldstein, *Rabin: Byografia* [Rabin: The Biography] (Tel Aviv: Shocken, 2006), pp. 43–73; Shaul Veber,

Rabin: Tzmihatu shel Manhig [Rabin: The Growth of a Leader] (Tel Aviv: Maariv, 2009), p. 207.

21. Rabin, *Pinkas*, p. 97; Zaki Shalom, *Diplomatya Be-Tzel Milhama: Illutzim, Dimuyim U-Mavayim Ba-Derech Le-Milhemet Sheshet Ha-Yamim* [Diplomacy in the Shadow of War: Myth and Reality on the Road to the Six-Day War] (Tel Aviv: Misrad Ha-Bitahon, 2007), p. 60; Segev, *1967*, p. 209.

22. Nimrod, *Ha-Neshek*, pp. 13–14; Rosenthal, *Yitzhak Rabin*, pp. 206–207, 213, 215, 217.

23. Tamari, *Ha-Uma*, p. 315.

24. Rosenthal, *Yitzhak Rabin*, p. 334; Rosenthal et al., eds, *Levi Eshkol*, p. 416; Gluska, *Eshkol*, pp. 29–31; Drori, "Social Values," p. 170.

25. Chanoch Bartov, *Daddo: 48 Shana Ve-Od 20 Yom* [Dado: 48 Years and 20 Days] (Or Yehuda: Dvir, 2002), pp. 37–76.

26. Bartov, *Daddo*, pp. 100–106.

27. Ibid., pp. 107–120; Moshe Bril, "Ha-Shiryon Be-Havkaat Maarahim Mevutsarim" [How the Cavalry Will Break Through Fortified Positions], *Maarahot*, Issue 172 (January 1966).

Chapter 10: Confronting Syria

1. Memo of Conversation between Eshkol, Rabin, and Bar-Lev, August 12, 1964, A 7933\7, ISA; Gluska, *Eshkol*, p. 87.

2. Bartov, *Daddo*, pp. 124–125; Gluska, *Eshkol*, p. 90.

3. Gluska, *Eshkol*, pp. 90–92.

4. Ibid., p. 93.

5. Bartov, *Daddo*, pp. 127–128.

6. Ibid., pp. 134, 141.

7. Ibid., p. 132.

8. Moshe Shemesh, "Prelude to the Six-Day War: The Arab–Israeli Struggle over Water Resources," *Israel Studies*, Vol. 9, No. 3 (Fall 2004) pp. 3–5, 19.

9. Miriam R. Lowi, *Water and Power: The Politics of a Scarce Resource in the Jordan River Basin* (Cambridge: Cambridge University Press, 1993), pp. 79–114.

10. Nimrod, *Ha-Neshek*, p. 16; Shemesh, "Prelude to the Six-Day War," pp. 18–19.

11. Nathan J. Citino, "The Ghosts of Development: The United States and Jordan's East Ghor Canal," *Journal of Cold War Studies*, Vol. 16, No. 4 (Fall 2014), pp. 181–183; Eban, *An Autobiography*, p. 312; "Lebanon's Position on the Question of Palestinian Refugees," March 24, 1964, in Naumkin et al., eds, *Blizhnevostochnyi Konflikt*, Vol. 2, pp. 420–421; *New York Times*, September 7 and 6, 1964, and September 16, 1965; *Davar*, January 29, 1965; *Herut*, June 29, 1965.

12. *Davar*, January 29, 1965; *Maariv*, August 5, 1965; Rosenthal, *Yitzhak Rabin*, p. 383; Gadi Heimann, *Sofa Shel Yedidut Muflaa: Yahasey Yisrael-Tsarfat Be-Tkufat Nesiutu shel De-Gaulle* [The End of a Beautiful Friendship: French–Israeli Relations under de Gaulle] (Jerusalem: Magnes, 2015), p. 162.

13. *Davar*, January 29 and February 12, 1965, and January 3, 1966.

14. *Davar*, April 16 and June 11, 1965.

15. *New York Times*, January 13, 1964; *Herut*, March 15, 1964; *Davar*, January 17, 1965; Gluska, *Eshkol*, p. 98.

16. *Davar*, November 6, 1963, and April 16, 1965; Gluska, *Eshkol*, pp. 99–105.

17. Cohen, *Ha-Hagana*, pp. 123–128; Gluska, *Eshkol*, pp. 107, 112.

18. Gilboa, *Mar Modiin*, p. 175; Rosenthal, et al., eds, *Levi Eshkol*, pp. 472–473.

19. Rosenthal et al., eds, *Levi Eshkol*, p. 490; Nimrod, *Ha-Neshek*, p. 37; Gluska, *Eshkol*, pp. 112, 120–123.

Chapter 11: The Self-Inflicted Recession

1. Rachel Michaeli, *Hatum al Ha-Shtar: Moshe Zanbar, Kalkelan Be-Olam Politi* [Signed on the Bill: Moshe Zanbar, an Economist in a Political World] (Tel Aviv: Yediot Ahronot, 2010), pp. 67–68; Shalev, "Labor," pp. 364–372.

2. Miryam Bihem and Aharon Kleiman, "Mechiro Shel Mitun" [The Price of Recession], *Rivon Le-Bankaut*, Vol. 8, No. 29 (June 1968), p. 32; Rosenthal et al., eds, *Levi Eshkol*, p. 373.

3. *Herut*, March 25, 1963, March 3, 1965; *Davar*, May 26 and July 25, 1963, and July 17, 1964; *Maariv*, August 9, 1966; Shalev, "Labor," p. 378; Yadlin, *Edut*, pp. 116–117.

4. Grinberg, *Ha-Histadrut*, pp. 113–118; Segev, *1967*, p. 51.

5. Minutes of the Ministerial Committee for Economic Affairs, October 13, 1964 and October 18, 1964, in file G 16700/8, ISA; Michaeli, *Hatum*, pp. 68–69.

6. Rosenthal et al., eds, *Levi Eshkol*, p. 499; Arnon Lammfromm, *Levi Eshkol: Biographia Politit* [Levi Eshkol: A Political Biography] (Tel Aviv: Resling, 2014), pp. 449–450; Segev, *1967*, p. 50.

7. Ronen Mandelkern, "The February 1962 New Economic Policy: How Israeli Economists Almost Changed the Israeli Economy," *Israel Studies Review*, Vol. 31, No. 2 (Winter 2016); Government Minutes, September 11, 1966, ISA; Shalev, "Labor," p. 379; Lammfromm, *Levi Eshkol*, p. 456.

8. Shalev, "Labor," p. 380; Yigal Allon brought up the problem of Arab-Jews in development towns on March 13, 1966 in the Ministerial Committee for Economic Affairs in file G 10345\4, ISA; Rosenthal et al., eds, *Levi Eshkol*, p. 499.

9. *Maariv*, May 2, 1966; *Davar*, August 17, 1966; *Davar*, December 15, 1966; *Maariv*, December 27, 1966; *Davar*, March 5, 1967; *Maariv*, March 30, 1967; *Maariv*, April 4, 1967; Rosenthal et al., eds, *Levi Eshkol*, p. 499.

10. Lammfromm, *Levi Eshkol*, p. 456; *Maariv*, December 25, 1966; *Davar*, May 8, 1967; Segev, *1967*, pp. 53–56.

11. Segev, *1967*, p. 104; Lammfromm, *Levi Eshkol*, p. 468; Meir Hazan, "Meoravoto shel Iton Haaretz Ba-Maaraha Ha-Politit Be-Tkofat Ha-Hamatna" [The Involvement of Haaretz Newspaper During the Waiting Period], *Yisrael*, Vol. 10 (2006), p. 81; Orit Rosin, "Ha-Medinai, Ha-Orech Ve-Ha-Iton: Ben-Gurion, Shocken Ve-Iton Haaretz" [The Statesman, the Editor and the Newspaper: Ben-Gurion, Shocken and Haaretz], ibid., pp. 29–34.

12. Segev, *1967*, pp. 104, 119; Lammfromm, *Levi Eshkol*, pp. 462, 467; Rosenthal et al., eds, *Levi Eshkol*, p. 511.

13. *Maariv*, March 7, 9 and 10, 1967; Lammfromm, *Levi Eshkol*, p. 474.

14. Gluska, *Eshkol*, p. 77; Yaari, *Fatah*, p. 75.

15. Gluska, *Eshkol*, pp. 122, 131–136, 140–141; Rosenthal et al., eds, *Levi Eshkol*, p. 473.

16. *Davar*, July 29, 1966.

17. Gluska, *Eshkol*, pp. 144–148; Rosenthal, *Yitzhak Rabin*, pp. 410–413.

18. Nimrod, *Ha-Neshek*, pp. 37–41; Gluska, *Eshkol*, pp. 152–153; Rosenthal, *Yitzhak Rabin*, pp. 414–415.

19. *Davar*, October 14, 1966; Gad Croizer, "Hakamat Gder Ha-Tsafon Ba-Mered Ha-Aravi Ve-She'elat Kishlona: Bchina Mechudeshet" [Constructing the Northern Wall: Did It Fail? A Reappraisal], *Katedra*, No. 120 (2006); "Palestine: Tegart's Wall," *Time*, June 20, 1938; Seth J. Frantzman, "Tegart's Shadow," *Jerusalem Post*, October 21, 2011; Haber, *Hayom*, p. 56.

20. Gluska, *Eshkol*, p. 162; Haber, *Hayom*, p. 107.

21. Rubin, *The Limits of the Land*, pp. 211–213; Gluska, *Eshkol*, p. 137; Rosenthal, *Yitzhak Rabin*, p. 391.

22. Haber, *Hayom*, p. 107; Rubin, *The Limits of the Land*, pp. 234, 240.

23. Haber, *Hayom*, p. 107; *Maariv*, July 20 and October 21, 1966; *Davar*, November 3, 1966.

24. Gluska, *Eshkol*, p. 154, 162–164; Haber, *Hayom*, pp. 107–109; Rubin, *The Limits*, p. 242.

25. Gluska, *Eshkol*, pp. 123, 164; Haber, *Hayom*, p. 109.

26. Gilboa, *Shesh Shanim*, p. 75; Gavish, *Sadin*, pp. 96–97.

27. Docs No. 332, 334, 343, Vol. 18, FRUS, 1964–1968; *New York Times*, December 18, 1966.

28. Segev, *1967*, pp. 168–169; Shlaim, *Lion*, p. 227; *Maariv*, December 27, 1966; Lammfromm, *Levi Eshkol*, pp. 467–471.

29. Paul Staniland, "Defeating Transnational Insurgencies: The Best Offense Is a Good Fence," *Washington Quarterly*, Vol. 29, No. 1 (Winter 2005–06), p. 32; Edward J. Drea,

McNamara, Clifford and the Burdens of Vietnam, 1965–1969 (Washington, DC: Historical Office of the Secretary of Defense, 2011), pp. 127–130; Uri Avnery, *Optimi* (Tel Aviv: Yediot Ahronot, 2016), Vol. 2, p. 88; Minutes of a General Staff Meeting, January 23, 1967, file 8\120\2009, IDFA.

30. Avnery, *Optimi*, p. 88; Minutes of a General Staff Meeting, January 23, 1967, file 8\120\2009, IDFA.
31. *New York Times*, November 21, 1966. This cabinet meeting's minutes, as well as many others, are still under lock and key in the Israeli State Archives, after being reclassified in the early 1990s. A month earlier Eshkol did tell the government that he had instructed the military to put more resources into preventive measures, and added that $3,000 had been allotted to train dogs. See: Government Minutes, October 9, 1966, ISA; Doc. No. 345, Vol. 18, FRUS, 1964–1968; *Davar*, November 6, 1966.
32. *Maariv*, January 28, 1966; *New York Times*, December 1, 1966; Seymour J. Deitchman, "The 'Electronic Battlefield' in the Vietnam War," *Journal of Military History*, Vol. 72 (July 2008); for corroborating evidence see Docs No. 337, 343, 344, Vol. 18, FRUS, 1964–1968.
33. General Staff Minutes, December 5, 1966, File 3\120\2009, IDFA.
34. General Staff meeting, December 12 and 13, 1966, File 3\120\2009, IDFA.
35. General Staff Minutes, December 13, 1966, File 3\120\2009, IDFA; General Staff Minutes, January 23, 1967, File 8\120\2009, IDFA.
36. *Maariv*, December 4, 1966; Deitchman, "The 'Electronic Battlefield,' " p. 885.
37. Doc. No. 388, Vol. 18, FRUS, 1964–1968.
38. Gluska, *Eshkol*, p. 177; Segev, *1967*, p. 227.
39. Gluska, *Eshkol*, pp. 176–178.
40. Minutes of a General Staff Meeting, January 23, 1967, File 8\120\2009, IDFA.
41. Rosenthal, *Yitzhak Rabin*, pp. 431–433.
42. Rosenthal, *Yitzhak Rabin*, pp. 430–431, 434; *Maariv*, May 12, 1967; Gilboa, *Mar Modiin*, *passim*; Geoffrey Wawro, *Quicksand: America's Pursuit of Power in the Middle East* (New York: Penguin Press, 2010), p. 255.
43. Gluska, *Eshkol*, pp. 184–185; Haber, *Hayom*, pp. 141–142; *Maariv*, March 12, 1967.
44. Gluska, *Eshkol*, pp. 190–194; Bartov, *Daddo*, pp. 135–136; Haber, *Hayom*, pp. 142–144; *Maariv*, April 9, 1967.
45. Gluska, *Eshkol*, pp. 192–196; Bartov, *Daddo*, p. 136; *Maariv*, April 9, 1967; Ezer Weizman, *Leha Shmayim, Leha Ha-Aretz* [He Who Owns the Sky Shall Have the Land] (Tel Aviv: Maariv, 1975), p. 241.
46. Gluska, *Eshkol*, pp. 198–199, 212; General Staff Minutes, April 24, 1967, File 8/120/2009, IDFA; *New York Times*, May 8, 1967; *Davar*, May 9, 1967; *Maariv*, May 9, 1967.
47. Gilboa, *Mar Modiin*, p. 230.

Chapter 12: Rabin's Schlieffen Plan

1. Irving L. Janis, "Groupthink," *Psychology Today* (November 1971), pp. 84–90.
2. Uri Bar Yoseph, *The Watchman Fell Asleep: The Surprise of Yom Kippur and Its Sources* (Albany, NY: SUNY Press, 2005).
3. Guy Laron, " 'Logic Dictates That They May Attack When They Feel They Can Win': The Egyptian Army, the 1955 Czech–Egyptian Arms Deal and the Israeli Intelligence," *Middle East Journal*, Vol. 63, No. 1 (Winter 2009), pp. 69–84.
4. Yigal Sheffi, *Hatra'a Be-Mivhan: Prashat Rotem Ve-Tfisat Ha-Bitahon shel Yisrael, 1957–1960* [The Rotem Affair and Israel's Security Concept] (Tel Aviv: Maarahot, 2008).
5. Gilboa, *Mar Modiin*, p. 107.
6. Ibid., pp. 126, 131, 134.
7. General Staff Minutes, December 12, 1966, File 3\120\2009, IDFA; General Staff Minutes, April 24, 1967, File 8\120\2009, ibid. Gluska, *Eshkol*, p. 186; Gilboa, *Mar Modiin*, p. 216.
8. Gilboa, *Mar Modiin*, pp. 192–193, 244–245; Gluska, *Eshkol*, pp. 252–254; Eban, *Autobiography*, p. 332.
9. Gavish, *Sadin*, p. 119; Rabin, *Pinkas*, pp. 144–145.

10. Historians have clashed mightily over the interpretation of the Schlieffen Plan. The latest word on the topic is: Annika Mombauer, "Of War Plans and War Guilt: The Debate surrounding the Schlieffen Plan," *Journal of Strategic Studies*, Vol. 28, No. 5 (2005).

11. Rosenthal, *Yitzhak Rabin*, pp. 444–445; Gluska, *Eshkol*, pp. 223–226; Matitiahu Mayzel, *Ha-Maaracha al Ha-Golan, Yuni 1967* [The Golan Heights Campaign, June 1967] (Tel Aviv: Maarahot, 2001), p. 32.

12. Gluska, *Eshkol*, pp. 226–227; Uzi Narkiss, *Ahat Yerushalaym* [United Jerusalem] (Tel Aviv: Am Oved, 1975), p. 59.

13. Rosenthal, *Yitzhak Rabin*, pp. 456–458; Segev, *1967*, pp. 260–261; Haber, *Hayom*, pp. 166–170.

14. Yehezkel Ha-Meiri, *Me-Shney Evrey Ha-Rama* (Tel Aviv: Levin-Epstein, 1970), p. 40; Bartov, *Daddo*, pp. 139–140; Rosenthal, *Yitzhak Rabin*, pp. 454–455; Mayzel, *Ha-Maaracha*, pp. 108–123.

15. Gavish, *Sadin*, pp. 11–12, 89–90.

16. Gavish, *Sadin*, pp. 90–92, 102–106; El-Gamasy, *The October War*, pp. 36–37; Gluska, *Eshkol*, p. 158.

17. Gavish, *Sadin*, pp. 105–110; Gluska, *Eshkol*, pp. 260–265; Avnery, *Optimi*, Vol. 2, pp. 84–85.

18. Gavish, *Sadin*, p. 113.

19. Rosenthal, *Yitzhak Rabin*, pp. 449–450; Gavish, *Sadin*, p. 119.

20. Narkiss, *Ahat*, pp. 23–53; Tamari, *Ha-Uma*, p. 369; Weizman, *Leha*, p. 261; *Haaretz*, June 5, 2016.

21. Narkiss, *Ahat*, pp. 51, 64.

22. Weizman, *Leha*, pp. 172–173, 183, 208, 244; General Staff Minutes, March 27, 1967, file 8\120\2009, IDFA.

23. Dani Shalom, *Ke-Raam Be-Yom Bahir: Kach Hushmedu Cheylot Ha-Avir Ha-Arviyim Be-Milchemet Sheshet Ha-Yamim* [Like a Bolt from the Blue: This is How Arab Air Forces were Destroyed in the Six Day War] (Rishon Le-Tzion: Ba-Avir, 2002), pp. 13–14, 20–21; Tamari, *Ha-Uma*, pp. 242–246.

24. Shalom, *Ke-Raam*, pp. 23–27, 39, 59, 61–62, 134; Weizman, *Leha*, pp. 198, 205–206, 210. The Israeli assessment of the Egyptian Air Force is corroborated by Egyptian sources. See Mahmud al-Jawadi, *Fi Aaqab al-Nakasa, Mudhakrat Qadat al-Askariya al-Misriyah* [The Origins of Defeat: The Recollections of Egyptian Officers] (Cairo: Dar al-Khiyal, 2001), p. 134.

25. Haber, *Hayom*, p. 56; Weizman, *Leha*, pp. 173–178, 196–198, 228; Shalom, *Ke-Raam*, pp. 38, 43; Yitzhak Greenberg, *Heshbon ve-Otzma: Taktziv Ha-Bitahon mi-Milhama le-Milhama, 1957–1967* [Budgets and Power: The Growth of the Defense Budget from War to War] (Tel Aviv: Misrad Ha-Bitachon, 1997), Table 17.

26. Weizman, *Leha*, pp. 226–228; Zach Levey, "The United States Skyhawk Sale to Israel, 1966," *Diplomatic History*, Vol. 28, No. 2 (April 2004), p. 270. See also David Tal, "Symbol Not Substance? Israel's Campaign to Acquire Hawk Missiles, 1960–1962," *International History Review*, Vol. 22, No. 2 (June 2000).

27. Weizman, *Leha*, pp. 233–239, 245; Shalom, *Ke-Raam*, pp. 68–69; Rabin, *Pinkas*, p. 114.

28. Rosenthal, *Yitzhak Rabin*, pp. 454–455; Rabin, *Pinkas*, pp. 152–153, 156; Gluska, *Eshkol*, pp. 268–269; Haber, *Hayom*, pp. 164–165, 171–172.

29. Rabin, *Pinkas*, p. 156; Gluska, *Eshkol*, pp. 274–275; Haber, *Hayom*, pp. 173–174.

30. Rabbi Shlomo Goren, *Be-Oz Ve-Taatzumut* [With Might and Strength] (Tel Aviv: Yediot Ahronot, 2013), pp. 264–267.

31. Rabin, *Pinkas*, pp. 147–151; Moshe Dayan, *Avnei-Derech* [Milestones] (Jerusalem: Idanim, 1976), pp. 399–400.

32. Rabin, *Pinkas*, p. 158; Gluska, *Eshkol*, p. 275.

33. Rabin, *Pinkas*, pp. 16, 159.

34. Eban, *Autobiography*, p. 333; Shalom, *Diplomatya*, p. 242; Segev, *1967*, p. 292; Weizman, *Leha*, pp. 258–259; Goldstein, *Rabin*, pp. 151–152.

35. Eban, *Autobiography*, pp. 332–334; Gilboa, *Mar Modiin*, p. 262; Gluska, *Eshkol*, p. 491; Gavish, *Sadin*, p. 123; Moshe Bitan, *Yoman Medini, 1967–1970* [Political Diary] (Tel Aviv: Olam Chadash, 2014), p. 42.

36. Haber, *Hayom*, pp. 175–176; Goldstein, *Eshkol*, pp. 548–549; Gilboa, *Mar Modiin*, pp. 263–264; Segev, *1967*, p. 264.
37. Weizman, *Leha*, p. 259; Gluska, *Eshkol*, p. 489; Segev, *1967*, p. 265; Gavish, *Sadin*, pp. 124–125.

Chapter 13: From Yemen to Texas

1. Bar-Zohar, *Hayav*, pp. 217–221, 252–253.
2. Ibid., pp. 218–219; Asher Orkaby, "The 1964 Israeli Airlift to Yemen and the Expansion of Weapons Diplomacy," *Diplomacy & Statecraft*, Vol. 26. No. 4 (2015), pp. 663–664.
3. Eugene Rogan and Tewfik Aclimandos, "The Yemen War and Egypt's War Preparedness," in Louis and Shlaim, eds, *The 1967 Arab–Israeli War*, p. 159; William Taylor Finn III, *Toll Gates and Barbicans of Empire: The United States, Great Britain and the Persian Gulf, 1950–1968* (PhD dissertation, University of Virginia, 2002), pp. 339–340.
4. Bar-Zohar, *Hayav*, pp. 218–219; Orkaby, "The 1964 Israeli Airlift," pp. 663–664; Yogev Elbaz, "Oyev Oyvi Ho Yedidi: Meuravut Yisrael Be-Milhemet Ha-Ezrahim Be-Teyman Ke-Helek Me-Ha-Milhama Ha-Kara beyn Yisrael U-Mitzrayim" [The Enemy of my Enemy is my Friend: Israeli Involvement in the Civil War in Yemen and the Israeli–Egyptian Cold War], *Hayo-Haya*, Vol. 10 (2004), pp. 83–84.
5. Elbaz, "Oyev," pp. 84–86; Orkaby, "The 1964 Israeli Airlift," pp. 666–667; Amit, *Rosh Be-Rosh*, pp. 215–219.
6. Elbaz, "Oyev," pp. 86–87.
7. Zach Levey, "Israel's Involvement in the Congo, 1958–68: Civilian and Military Dimensions," *Civil Wars*, Vol. 6, No. 4 (Winter 2003), pp. 26–28.
8. Ephraim Evron to Moshe Bitan, "A Conversation with Rostow," March 31, 1967, File 7938\10, ISA; letter from Avraham Harman to Abba Eban, March 31, 1967, ibid.
9. Top Secret, unsigned, undated memo (it does mention that McLean was going back to Riyadh on February 26), File 7437/1, ISA. I am grateful to Yogev Elbaz for sharing this document with me.
10. Letter from Avraham Harman to Abba Eban, March 31, 1967, File 7938\10, ISA; letter from Avraham Harman to Moshe Bitan, March 31, 1967, ibid.
11. Yogev, "Oyev," p. 87; Gluska, *Eshkol*, p. 205; Trita Parsi, *Treacherous Alliance: The Secret Dealings of Israel, Iran, and the United States* (New Haven, CT: Yale University Press, 2008), pp. 19–38.
12. Parsi, *Treacherous Alliance*, pp. 39–48.
13. Gluska, *Eshkol*, pp. 205–206.
14. Walt W. Rostow, "Notes on a New Approach to US Economic Foreign Policy," *World Politics*, Vol. 5, No. 3 (April 1953); Lloyd C. Gardner, *Pay Any Price: Lyndon Johnson and the Wars for Vietnam* (Chicago: Ivan R. Dee, 1997), pp. 28–29; David Milne, *America's Rasputin: Walt Rostow and the Vietnam War* (New York: Hill & Wang, 2008), pp. 64–67.
15. Gardner, *Pay Any Price*, pp. 32–33; Milne, *America's Rasputin*, pp. 57–58; Matthew Connelly, *A Diplomatic Revolution: Algeria's Fight for Independence and the Origins of the Post-Cold War Era* (New York: Oxford University Press), pp. 144–145.
16. Finn III, *Toll Gates and Barbicans*, p. 330.
17. Jeffry Frieden, "Sectoral Conflicts and Foreign Economic Policy, 1914–1940," *International Organization*, Vol. 42, No. 1 (Winter 1998); Bruce Cumings, *The Origins of the Korean War* (Princeton, NJ: Princeton University Press, 1990), Vol. 2, pp. 35–78; See Figure 1 in Gregory Hooks and Leonard E. Bloomquist, "The Legacy of World War II for Regional Growth and Decline: The Cumulative Effects of Wartime Investments on US Manufacturing, 1947–1972," *Social Forces*, Vol. 71. No. 2 (December 1992). This was the reason why organized labor, specifically the AFL-CIO, and some companies lobbied for foreign aid. See James M. Hagen and Vernon W. Ruttan, "Development Policy under Eisenhower and Kennedy," *Journal of Developing Areas*, Vol. 23, No. 1 (October 1988), pp. 12–15.
18. David Milne, *America's Rasputin*, p. 70; Gardner, *Pay Any Price*, p. 34; Amy Elizabeth Davis, *Politics of Prosperity: The Kennedy Presidency and Economic Policy* (PhD dissertation, Columbia University, 1988), pp. 32–33; William S. Borden, "Defending Hegemony: American Foreign Economic Policy," in Thomas G. Paterson, ed., *Kennedy's Quest for*

Victory: American Foreign Policy, 1961–1963 (New York: Oxford University Press, 1989), p. 60; Frieden, *Global Capitalism*, p. 340.

19. Gardner, *Pay Any Price*, p. 35; Davis, *Politics of Prosperity*, p. 33; Borden, "Defending Hegemony," p. 59.

20. Stephen McGlichey, "Building a Client State: American Arms Policies Towards Iran, 1950–1963," *Central European Journal of International and Security Studies*, Vol. 6, No. 2 (2012), pp. 25–33; April R. Summitt, "For a White Revolution: John F. Kennedy and the Shah of Iran," *Middle East Journal*, Vol. 58, No. 4 (Autumn 2004); Paul Kingston, "Rationalizing Patrimonialism: Wasfi al-Tal and Economic Reform in Jordan, 1962–1967," in Tariq Tell, ed., *The Resilience of the Hashemite Rule: Politics and the State in Jordan, 1946–67* (Beirut: Les Cahiers du CERMOC, 2001); Parker T. Hart, *Saudi-Arabia and the U.S.: The Birth of a Security Partnership* (Bloomington, IN: Indiana University Press, 1998), pp. 113–135; Douglas Little, "From Even-Handed to Empty-Handed: Seeking Order in the Middle East," in Paterson, ed., *Kennedy's Quest*, p. 168.

21. Douglas Little, "The New Frontier on the Nile: JFK, Nasser, and Arab Nationalism," *Journal of American History*, Vol. 75, No. 2 (September 1988); Hagen and Ruttan, "Development Policy," pp. 8–9.

22. "Statement by President John F. Kennedy at a Press Conference, May 8, 1963," in "Middle East Crisis, Volume 2," National Security File, Box 196, Lyndon B. Johnson Library.

23. Cohen, *Israel and the Bomb*, pp. 115–136; Zaki Shalom, *Beyn Dimona Le-Washington: Hamaavak al Pituh Ha-Optzia Ha-Garinit Shel Yisrael* [Between Dimona and Washington: The Development of Israel's Nuclear Option] (Beersheba: Ben-Gurion University Press, 2004), pp. 70–85. See also Warren Bass, *Support Any Friend: Kennedy's Middle East and the Making of the US–Israel Alliance* (New York: Oxford University Press, 2004).

24. Hagen and Ruttan, "Development Policy," p. 10; Robert David Johnson, *Congress and the Cold War* (New York: Cambridge University Press, 2006), pp. 92–101; Robert David Johnson, "Constitutionalism Abroad and at Home: The United States Senate and the Alliance for Progress, 1961–1967," *International History Review*, Vol. 21, No. 2 (1999); Andrew David and Michael Holm, "The Kennedy Administration and the Battle over Foreign Aid: The Untold Story of the Clay Committee," *Diplomacy & Statecraft*, Vol. 27, No. 1 (2016).

25. Roland Popp, "An Application of Modernization Theory during the Cold War? The Case of Pahlavi Iran," *International History Review*, Vol. 30, No. 1 (2008), p. 96.

26. Matthew Jones, "U.S. Relations with Indonesia, the Kennedy–Johnson Transition, and the Vietnam Connection, 1963–1965," *Diplomatic History*, Vol. 26, No. 2 (Spring 2002), p. 258; "Memo of Conversation," November 19, 1963, Doc. No. 253, Vol. 21, FRUS, 1961–1963; Johnson, *Congress*, p. 100; Ethan Nadelmann, "Setting the Stage: American Policy toward the Middle East, 1961–1966," *International Journal of Middle East Studies*, Vol. 14, No. 4 (November 1982), p. 445.

27. Gardner, *Pay Any Price*, pp. 5–9; Dean Rusk, *As I Saw It* (New York: Penguin, 1990), p. 335.

28. Gardner, *Pay Any Price*, pp. 9, 194.

29. Gardner, *Pay Any Price*, p. 10.

30. Gardner, *Pay Any Price*, p. 8.

31. Gardner, *Pay Any Price*, pp. 12–13; Figure 1 in Hooks and Bloomquist, "The Legacy of World War II for Regional Growth."

32. Gardner, *Pay Any Price*, pp. 13–15; Bruce J. Schulman, *From Cotton Belt to Sunbelt: Federal Policy, Economic Development, and the Transformation of the South, 1938–1980* (New York: Oxford University Press, 1991), pp. 88–111; Ann Markusen et al., *The Rise of the Gunbelt: The Military Remapping of Industrial America* (New York: Oxford University Press, 1991), pp. 8–50; Kari Frederickson, *Cold War Dixie: Militarization and Modernization in the American South* (Athens, GA: University of Georgia Press, 2013). For a useful discussion of the connections between American foreign policy and US economic geography, see Peter Trubowitz, *Defining the National Interest:*

Conflict and Change in American Foreign Policy (Chicago, IL: University of Chicago Press, 1998).

33. Mitchell Lerner, "'A Big Tree of Peace and Justice': The Vice Presidential Travels of Lyndon Johnson," *Diplomatic History*, Vol. 34, No. 2 (April 2010), pp. 357–360; William I. Kaufman, "Foreign Aid and the Balance-of-Payments Problem: Vietnam and Johnson's Foreign Economic Policies," in Robert A. Devine, ed., *The Johnson Years: Vietnam, the Environment and Science* (Lawrence, KS: University Press of Kansas, 1987), p. 80.

34. Douglas Little, "Nasser Delenda Est: Lyndon Johnson, the Arabs, and the 1967 Six-Day War," in H.W. Brands, ed., *The Foreign Policies of Lyndon Johnson* (College Station, TX: Texas A&M University Press, 1999), p. 149.

35. Lerner, "'A Big Tree,'" p. 359; Olivia Sohns, *Lyndon Baines Johnson and the Arab–Israeli Conflict* (PhD dissertation, University of Cambridge, 2014), pp. 35–73; Jones, "U.S. Relations with Indonesia," p. 260; "Memo of Conversation," August 31, 1963, Vol. 4, FRUS, 1961–1963.

36. Gardner, *Pay Any Price*, 90.

Chapter 14: A Short Tether

1. Matthew Jones, "A Decision Delayed: Britain's Withdrawal from South East Asia Reconsidered, 1961–68," *English Historical Review*, Vol. 117, No. 472 (June 2002), p. 576.

2. Finn III, *Toll Gates and Barbicans*, p. 339; Matthew Jones, "Creating Malaysia: Singapore Security, the Borneo Territories, and the Contours of British Policy, 1961–63," *Journal of Imperial and Commonwealth History*, Vol. 28, No. 2 (May 2000), pp. 85–87.

3. Finn III, *Toll Gates and Barbicans*, pp. 339–340; Jones, "Creating Malaysia."

4. Finn III, *Toll Gates and Barbicans*, pp. 240–309; Jones, "U.S. Relations with Indonesia," pp. 252–258; Rakove, *Kennedy, Johnson*, pp. 148–149.

5. Moya Ann Ball, "Revisiting the Gulf of Tonkin Crisis: An Analysis of the Private Communication of President Johnson and his Advisers," *Discourse & Society*, Vol. 2, No. 3 (1991), p. 283; Jones, "A Decision Delayed," p. 579; Finn III, *Toll Gates and Barbicans*, p. 319.

6. Finn III, *Toll Gates and Barbicans*, p. 314; John Dumbrell, "The Johnson Administration and the British Labour Government: Vietnam, the Pound and East of Suez," *Journal of American Studies*, Vol. 30, No. 2, Part 2 (August 1996); Scott Newton, "The Two Sterling Crises of 1964 and the Decision Not to Devalue," *Economic History Review*, Vol. 62, No. 1 (February 2009); Michael J. Oliver, "The Management of Sterling, 1964–1967," *English Historical Review*, Vol. 126, No. 520 (June 2011); Kevin Boyle, "The Price of Peace: Vietnam, the Pound, and the Crisis of the American Empire," *Diplomatic History*, Vol. 27, No. 1 (January 2003), p. 43; Tore T. Petersen, *The Decline of the Anglo-American Middle East, 1961–1969: A Willing Retreat* (Brighton: Sussex Academic Press, 2006), p. 71.

7. Jones, "U.S. Relations with Indonesia," pp. 262–263.

8. Rusk, *As I Saw It*, p. 337.

9. Douglas Little, "Choosing Sides: Lyndon Johnson and the Middle East," in Robert A. Divine, ed., *The Johnson Years: LBJ at Home and Abroad* (Lawrence, KS: University Press of Kansas, 1994), pp. 156–157; Ferris, *Nasser's Gamble*, pp. 134–135; William J. Burns, *Economic Aid and American Foreign Policy toward Egypt, 1955–1981* (Albany, NY: SUNY Press, 1985), p. 153; Petersen, *The Decline*, p. 53.

10. Jones, "U.S. Relations with Indonesia," pp. 277–278; Jones, "A Decision Delayed," p. 579; Rakove, *Kennedy, Johnson*, p. 150.

11. David N. Gibbs, *The Political Economy of Third World Intervention: Mines, Money, and US Policy in the Congo Crisis* (Chicago, IL: Chicago University Press, 1991).

12. Pijero Gleijeses, "'Flee, the White Giants are Coming!' The United States, the Mercenaries, and the Congo, 1964–1965," *Diplomatic History*, Vol. 18, No. 2 (1994), pp. 215–219.

13. Terrence Lyons, "Keeping Africa off the Agenda," in Warren I. Cohen and Nancy Tucker, eds, *Lyndon Johnson Confronts the World: American Foreign Policy, 1963–1968* (New York: Cambridge University Press, 1994), pp. 256–259.

14. See American and West German reports of the incident and its aftermath in: Docs No. 110–111, Vol. 18, FRUS, 1964–1968; Cairo (Federer) to Bonn, November 28, 1963, Bestand B36, Band 73, PAAA; Cairo (Federer) to Bonn, December 3, 1963, ibid.; Burns, *Economic Aid*, p. 158.
15. Pamela Sodhy, "Malaysian–American Relations during Indonesia's Confrontation against Malaysia, 1963–66," *Journal of Southeast Asian Studies*, Vol. 19, No. 1 (March 1988), p. 131.
16. Burns, *Economic Aid*, pp. 158–159.
17. Ibid., pp. 160–161.
18. Ibid., p. 163; Doc. No. 151, Vol. 18, FRUS, 1964–1968.
19. Ball, "Revisiting the Gulf of Tonkin Crisis"; Gardner, *Pay Any Price*, p. 138; Robert Dallek, *A Flawed Giant: Lyndon Johnson and His Times, 1961–1973* (New York: Oxford University Press, 1998), pp. 262–268; Alan McPherson, "Misled by Himself: What the Johnson Tapes Reveal about the Dominican Intervention of 1965," *Latin American Research Review*, Vol. 38, No. 2 (2003).
20. Kaufman, "Foreign Aid," pp. 89–100; Johnson, "Constitutionalism Abroad," pp. 434–437.
21. Nick Cullather, "LBJ's Third War: The War on Hunger," in Francis J. Gavin and Mark Atwood Lawrence, eds, *Beyond the Cold War: Lyndon Johnson and the New Global Challenges of the 1960s* (New York: Oxford University Press, 2014), p. 123.
22. Kristin L. Ahlberg, *Transplanting the Great Society: Lyndon Johnson and Food for Peace* (Columbia, MO: University of Missouri Press, 2008), pp. 106–146.
23. Doc. No. 213, Vol. 25, FRUS, 1964–1968; Lyndon Johnson, *The Vantage Point: Perspectives on the Presidency, 1963–1969* (New York: Popular Library, 1971), pp. 222–231.
24. Rakove, *Kennedy, Johnson*, pp. 229–230; Doc. No. 208, Vol. 18, FRUS, 1964–1968; Burns, *Economic Aid*, p. 164; Cairo to DOS, June 24, 1965, Doc. No. CK3100179176, DDRS; Cairo to DOS, June 26, 1965, Doc. No. CK3100195515, DDRS; Cairo to DOS, August 5, 1965, Doc. No. CK3100191451, DDRS. Nasser's report to the Americans on his talks with Enlai was identical to the one he gave to the Soviets. See: memo of conversation between the Soviet ambassador to Cairo, Yerofeev, and UAR PM Ali Sabri, April 8, 1965, in Naumkin et al., eds, *Bliznovostochnyi Konflikt*, Vol. 2, pp. 464–467.
25. Burns, *Economic Aid*, pp. 163–166; Rakove, *Kennedy, Johnson*, pp. 198–200; Nadelmann, "Setting the Stage," p. 448.
26. Burns, *Economic Aid*, pp. 166–167; Rakove, *Kennedy, Johnson*, pp. 199–201; Docs No. 282, 290, 302, Vol. 18, FRUS, 1964–1968.
27. William B. Quandt, "Lyndon Johnson and the June 1967 War: What Color Was the Light?" *Middle East Journal*, Vol. 46, No. 2 (Spring 1992), p. 200; Doc. No. 42, Vol. 19, FRUS, 1964–1968.

Chapter 15: Arming the Middle East

1. Milne, *America's Rasputin*, pp. 98–100.
2. Ibid., pp. 153–154.
3. Gardner, *Pay Any Price*, p. 189.
4. "Conversation at Lunch with W. W. Rostow," letter from Avraham Harman to Moshe Bitan, April 12, 1965, File MFA 4301\4, ISA.
5. "Conversation with Rostow," letter from Ephraim Evron to Moshe Bitan, March 31, 1967, File A 7938\10, ISA.
6. A memo from Harry McPherson to Lyndon Johnson, dated May 19, 1966, which found its way to File A 7939\2, ISA; Zach Levey, "United States Arms Policy toward Jordan, 1963–68," *Journal of Contemporary History*, Vol. 41, No. 3 (July 2006), pp. 536–539; on military aid to Asian allies, see Sodhy, "American–Malaysian Relations."
7. Little, "Choosing Sides," pp. 168–169; Petersen, *The Decline*, p. 70.
8. Claudia Castiglioni, "No Longer a Client, Not Yet a Partner: The US–Iranian Alliance in the Johnson Years," *Cold War History*, Vol. 15, No. 4 (2015), p. 10; Little, "Choosing Sides," pp. 169–170; Stephen McGlinchey, "Lyndon B. Johnson and Arms Credit Sales to Iran, 1964–1968," *Middle East Journal*, Vol. 67, No. 2 (Spring 2013).

9. Kaufman, "Foreign Aid," p. 101; Harman to Moshe Bitan, April 21, 1967, File A 7938\10, ISA.
10. Castiglioni, "No Longer a Client," p. 15.
11. On US–Jordanian relations at the time see: Douglas Little, "A Puppet in Search of a Puppeteer? The United States, King Hussein, and Jordan, 1953–1970," *International History Review*, Vol. 17, No. 3 (August 1995); Levey, "United States Arms Policy"; Kristi N. Barnwell, "'Caught Between His Friends and His Enemies': The Evolution of American–Jordanian Collaboration in the 1960s," *Diplomacy & Statecraft*, Vol. 22, No. 2 (2011).
12. Zach Levy, "The United States' Skyhawk Sale to Israel, 1966: Strategic Exigencies of an Arms Deal," *Diplomatic History*, Vol. 28, No. 2 (April 2004).
13. Top Secret, unsigned, undated memo, File 7437\1, ISA.
14. Andrew L. Jones, "The Johnson Administration, the Shah of Iran, and the Changing Pattern of U.S.–Iranian Relations, 1965–1967," *Journal of Cold War Studies*, Vol. 9, No. 2 (Spring 2007), pp. 89–90; Castiglioni, "No Longer a Client," pp. 12–13.
15. Jones, "The Johnson Administration," p. 79; Castiglioni, "No Longer a Client," p. 10.
16. Ahlberg, *Transplanting the Great Society*, pp. 147–206.
17. Letter from Avraham Harman to Moshe Bitan, April 26, 1966, File MFA 3975\13, ISA.
18. Sohns, *Lyndon Baines Johnson*, pp. 35–54.

Chapter 16: Secret Liaisons

1. Zaki Shalom, *Beyn*, p. 163; Cohen, *Israel and the Bomb*, pp. 202–205.
2. Shalom, *Beyn*, p. 131.
3. Rubin, *The Limits of the Land*, pp. 169–170; Moshe Gat, "The Great Powers and the Water Dispute in the Middle East: A Prelude to the Six Day War," *Middle Eastern Studies*, Vol. 41, No. 6 (November 2005), p. 927; Rabin, *Pinkas*, p. 124. Just two months earlier Komer held the opposite view: Letter from M. Gazit (counsel in DC) to Y. Herzog, January 6, 1965, File A 7979/1, ISA.
4. Segev, *1967*, p. 169.
5. Shalom, *Diplomatya*, p. 162; Oren, *Six Days*, p. 45; Harman to Abba Eban, March 31, 1967, File 7938\10, ISA; Harman to Bitan, March 31, 1967, ibid.
6. Minutes of General Staff Meeting, April 10, 1967, file 206/117/1970, IDFA; Doc. No. 7, Vol. 19, FRUS, 1964–1968.
7. Peter L. Hahn, "The View from Jerusalem: Revelations about U.S. Diplomacy from the Archives of Israel," *Diplomatic History*, Vol. 22, No. 4 (Fall 1998).
8. John B. Judis, *Genesis: Truman, American Jews, and the Origins of the Arab/Israeli Conflict* (New York: Farrar, Straus & Giroux, 2014).
9. Little, *Choosing Sides*, p. 152; Arlene Lazarowitz, "Different Approaches to a Regional Search for Balance: The Johnson Administration, the State Department, and the Middle East, 1964–1967," *Diplomatic History*, Vol. 32, No. 1 (January 2008), p. 30.
10. Letter from Ephraim Evron to Moshe Bitan, March 7, 1966, File MFA 3975\15, ISA.
11. Harman to Bitan, April 21, 1967, File A 7938\10, ISA; Bitan to Harman, April 30, 1967, File MFA 3977\ 22, ISA.
12. Lazarowitz, "Different Approaches," p. 33.
13. Doc. No. 389, Vol. 18, FRUS, 1964–1968; Evron to Bitan, March 17, 1967, File A 7938/10.
14. Ephraim Evron to Moshe Bitan, April 20, 1967, File 7938\10, ISA; Avraham Harman to Moshe Bitan, April 21, 1967, ibid.; Doc. No. 405, Vol. 18, FRUS, 1964–1968.
15. Cohen, *Israel and the Bomb*, pp. 195–205.
16. Raz, *Ha-Maavak*, pp. 131, 144–147, 165; Michaeli, *Hatum*, pp. 42–43.
17. Raz, *Ha-Maavak*, pp. 362, 470; Shalom, *Beyn*, p. 121; Doc. No. 391 (fn. 2), Vol. 18, FRUS, 1964–1968.
18. Cohen, *Israel and the Bomb*, pp. 205–207; Raz, *Ha-Maavak*, p. 408.
19. Cohen, *Israel and the Bomb*, pp. 175–194; Raz, *Ha-Maavak*, pp. 308–309.
20. Evron to Bitan, May 16, 1967, File A 7938\10, ISA; Segev, *1967*, p. 273; Drea, *McNamara, Clifford*, p. 429.

Chapter 17: Abba Eban's Tin Ear

1. Bitan, *Yoman Medini*, pp. 40–42; Rabin, *Pinkas*, p. 155.
2. Rosenthal, *Yitzhak Rabin*, pp. 456–458; Segev, *1967*, pp. 260–261; Haber, *Hayom*, pp. 166–170.
3. Rabin, *Pinkas*, pp. 152–153; Haber, *Hayom*, pp. 164–165; Bitan, *Yoman Medini*, pp. 35–37; Docs No. 36, 50, Vol. 19, FRUS, 1964–1968.
4. Saul Bronfeld, "The 'Chieftain Tank Affair': Realpolitik, Perfidy and the Genesis of the *Merkava*," *Contemporary British History*, Vol. 29, No. 3 (2015); Greenberg, *Heshbon Ve-Otzma*, Table 23.
5. Sylvia K. Crosbie, *A Tacit Alliance: France and Israel from Suez to the Six Day War* (Princeton, NJ: Princeton University Press, 1974); Edward A. Kolodziej, "France and the Arms Trade," *International Affairs*, Vol. 56, No. 1 (January 1980) pp. 55–58; Howard M. Sachar, *Israel and Europe* (New York: Vintage, 1998), pp. 77–97, 108–116; Jurgen Brauer and Hubert Van Tuyll, *Castles, Battles, and Bombs: How Economics Explains Military History* (Chicago, IL: University of Chicago Press, 2008), pp. 244–257; Raz, *Ha-Maavak*, pp. 229–248; Segev, *1967*, p. 229.
6. Raz, *Ha-Maavak*, pp. 360–363.
7. Haber, *Hayom*, pp. 107–108; Rosenthal, *Yitzhak Rabin*, pp. 456–458.
8. Zach Levey, "Israel's Strategy in Africa 1961–67," *International Journal of Middle East Studies*, Vol. 36, No. 1 (February 2004), pp. 72, 80–82; Shalom, *Diplomatya*, pp. 291–292.
9. Segev, *1967*, p. 256; Gluska, *Eshkol*, p. 247; Shalom, *Diplomatya*, p. 241; Shalom, *Ke-Esh*, p. 191.
10. Zach Levey, "Israel's Quest for a Security Guarantee from the United States, 1954–1956," *British Journal of Middle Eastern Studies*, Vol. 22, No. 1–2 (1995); Douglas Little, "The Making of a Special Relationship: The United States and Israel, 1957–68," *International Journal of Middle East Studies*, Vol. 25, No. 4 (November 1993), p. 569; Shalom, *Beyn*, pp. 109–110.
11. Rabin, *Pinkas*, pp. 127–128; Levey, "The United States Skyhawk Sale," pp. 262–263; Cohen, *Israel and the Bomb*, p. 207; Doc. No. 28, Vol. 19, FRUS, 1964–1968.
12. Doc. No. 13, Vol. 19, FRUS, 1964–1968; Shalom, *Diplomatya*, p. 259; Rosenthal, *Yitzhak Rabin*, p. 302; Heimann, *Sofa*, pp. 152–157; Jean-Pierre Filiu, "France and the June 1967 War," in Louis and Shlaim, eds, *The 1967 Arab-Israeli War*, p. 251.
13. Gilboa, *Mar Modiin*, p. 265; Gluska, *Eshkol*, p. 282.
14. Gluska, *Eshkol*, p. 286; Rabin, *Pinkas*, pp. 160–161.
15. Rabin, *Pinkas*, p. 161; Gluska, *Eshkol*, pp. 283–284; Segev, *1967*, pp. 275–276.
16. Gilboa, *Mar Modiin*, pp. 193–193, 227, 267; Shalom, *Ke-Raam*, p. 85.
17. Gluska, *Eshkol*, p. 287.
18. Shalom, *Ke-Raam*, pp. 142–144; Weizman, *Leha*, pp. 177, 205, 210.
19. Rabin, *Pinkas*, pp. 163–164; Gilboa, *Mar Modiin*, pp. 268–269; Gluska, *Eshkol*, pp. 287–288; Segev, *1967*, p. 277.
20. Evron to Bitan, March 17, 1967, File A 7938\10, ISA; Gluska, *Eshkol*, p. 491 (fn. 30); Joshua Michael Zeitz, " 'If I Am Not For Myself . . .': The American Jewish Establishment in the Aftermath of the Six Day War," *American Jewish History*, Vol. 88, No. 2 (June 2000), p. 259.
21. Doc. No. 54, Vol. 19, FRUS, 1964–1968.
22. Robert S. McNamara, *In Retrospect: The Tragedy and Lessons of Vietnam* (New York: Times Books, 1995), pp. 244–247, 264–266.
23. Docs No. 53, 58, 68, Vol. 19, FRUS, 1964–1968; Robert McNamara, "Britain, Nasser and the Outbreak of the Six Day War," *Journal of Contemporary History*, Vol. 35, No. 4 (2000), pp. 627–628; Moshe Gat, " Britain on the Eve of the Six Day War: The British Effort to End the Egyptian Blockade on the Straits of Tiran," *Review of International Affairs*, Vol. 3, No. 3 (Spring 2004), pp. 402–403; Drea, *McNamara, Clifford*, p. 430.
24. Zaki Shalom, "Israel's Foreign Minister Eban Meets President de Gaulle and Prime Minister Wilson on the Eve of the Six Day War," *Israel Affairs*, Vol. 14, No. 2 (2008); Sachar, *Israel and Europe*, p. 181.

25. Docs No. 64, 69, 71, 76, Vol. 19, FRUS, 1964–1968; Eban, *Autobiography*, p. 352.
26. Eban, *Autobiography*, p. 352.
27. Segev, *1967*, pp. 279–280; Melman and Raviv, *Shutafim*, pp. 113–120; Gluska, *Eshkol*, p. 296; Rabin, *Pinkas*, p. 167.
28. Segev, *1967*, p. 283; Gluska, *Eshkol*, p. 304.
29. Gilboa, *Mar Modiin*, p. 274.
30. Gluska, *Eshkol*, pp. 300–301; Shalom, *Ke-Raam*, p. 156.
31. Eban, *Autobiography*, pp. 351–353; Segev, *1967*, p. 123; Oren, *Six Days*, p. 113.
32. Michael Brecher with Benjamin Geist, *Decisions in Crisis: Israel, 1967 and 1973* (Berkeley, CA: University of California Press, 1980), pp. 136–137; Shalom, *Diplomatya*, pp. 366–367.
33. Doc. No. 71, Vol. 19, FRUS, 1964–1968.
34. Eban, *Autobiography*, pp. 354–355; Nick Kotz, *Judgment Days: Lyndon Baines Johnson, Martin Luther King Jr., and the Laws That Changed America* (New York: Houghton and Mifflin, 2004), pp. 34–35.
35. Eban, *Autobiography*, p. 354; Doc. No. 77, Vol. 19, FRUS, 1964–1968.
36. Zaki Shalom, "Lyndon Johnson's Meeting with Abba Eban, May 26, 1967: [Introduction and Protocol]," *Israel Studies*, Vol. 4, No. 2 (Fall 1999), p. 235; Segev, *1967*, p. 286.
37. Oren, *Six Days*, p. 115; Eban, *Autobiography*, p. 359; Quandt, "Lyndon Johnson and the June 1967 War," p. 214.
38. Eban, *Autobiography*, pp. 360–361; oral history interview with Arthur Goldberg, August 23, 1983, Lyndon B. Johnson Library, available at: www.lbjlib.utexas.edu/johnson/archives.hom/oralhistory.hom/GoldbergA/Goldberg.PDF (accessed August 25, 2016); Evron to Bitan, May 27, 1967, File A 7919/2, ISA.
39. Segev, *1967*, pp. 292–295; Oren, *Six Days*, pp. 121–123; Gluska, *Eshkol*, pp. 313, 316.
40. Eban, *Autobiography*, pp. 365–367; Gluska, *Eshkol*, p. 316; Oren, *Six Days*, p. 122.
41. Segev, *1967*, p. 295; Gluska, *Eshkol*, p. 320; Oren, *Six Days*, p. 123; Rabin, *Pinkas*, p. 170; Michaeli, *Hatum*, p. 138.
42. Gilboa, *Mar Modiin*, pp. 276–277.

Chapter 18: One Soviet Foreign Policy or Two?

1. The story is based on a telephone conversation between the author and Avraham Ben-Tzur which took place in the summer of 2007 and a subsequent telephone conversation with his son, Asa Ben-Tzur, in August 2016.
2. Ben-Tzur, *Gormim Sovyetiyim*, p. 90.
3. Alec Nova, *An Economic History of the USSR (1917–1991)* (London: Penguin, 1992), pp. 331–377; Philip Hanson, *The Rise and Fall of the Soviet Economy* (London: Longman, 2003), pp. 48–97.
4. Oscar Sanchez-Sibony, *Red Globalization: The Political Economy of the Soviet Cold War from Stalin to Khrushchev* (Cambridge: Cambridge University Press, 2014), pp. 91–172.
5. Y.V. Bystrova, *Sovetski Voino-Promishlini Komplex: Problemi Stanovlenia i Razvitia* [The Soviet Military-Industrial Complex] (Moscow: Institut Rosiskoy Istoria, 2006), pp. 470–472.
6. Some of these points are covered in William Taubman, *Khrushchev: The Man and his Era* (New York: Norton, 2003).
7. William J. Tompson, "The Fall of Nikita Khrushchev," *Soviet Studies*, Vol. 43, No. 6 (1991).
8. Discussion of the Brezhnev–Kosygin struggle is based on: Protocols of meetings between Czechoslovak Party Chairman and Antonin Novotny and Brezhnev, January 19–21, 1966 and February 4–6, 1967, Box 198, fond Antonin Novotny, NA; Moscow to Foreign Ministry, "Report on the Tasks of the Soviet Communist Party," January 12, 1967, TO-T, SSSR, 1965–69, Box 12, Folder 8 (311), A MZV; "Report on a conversation with a representative of the international department of the Soviet Communist Party, Comrade Kuskov, on the international Communist and workers' movements which took place in the Moscow Embassy on February 2, 1967," TO-T, SSSR, 1965–69, Box 12, Folder 8 (311), A MZV; "Policy and Politics in the CPSU Politburo: October 1964 to

September 1967," CIA, Directorate of Intelligence (Caesar XXX), August 31, 1967, available at: www.faqs.org/cia/docs/69/0000969857/POLICY-AND-POLITICS-IN-THE-CPSU-POLITBURO:-OCTOBER-1964-TO-SEPTEMBER-1967.html (accessed April 2, 2009); Richard D. Anderson, Jr., *Public Politics in an Authoritarian State, Making Foreign Policy During the Brezhnev Years* (Ithaca, NY: Cornell University Press, 1993). See also Vladislav M. Zubok, *A Failed Empire: The Soviet Union in the Cold War From Stalin to Gorbachev* (Chapel Hill, NC: University of North Carolina Press, 2007), pp. 192–207.

9. "Annual Politico-Economic Assessment", Moscow (D. E. Boster) to State Dept., Airgram A–965, December 17, 1965, CPF, 1964–1966, POL-2-3 Politico-Economic Reports USSR, Box 2883, RG 59, NARA.

10. Steven E. Hanson, "The Brezhnev Era," in Ronald Grigor Suny, ed., *The Cambridge History of Russia* (Cambridge: Cambridge University Press, 2006), Vol. 3.

11. "Report on NATO's Current Situation and the Main Facets of Our Work against that Organization," memo submitted by the KGB to the Czechoslovak secret services, January 25, 1967, Box 19, fond Antonin Novotny, NA; "Report on the Meeting of Warsaw Pact's Foreign Ministers which dealt with the German problem and the Question of European Security," appendix III to Politburo discussion which took place on April 8, 1967, Box 24, fond Antonin Novotny, NA.

12. "The Foreign Policy of the Soviet Union and the Effort of the CSPU to Unite the Global Communist Movement," December 12, 1966, f. 2, op. 3, delo 45, ll. 42, RGANI.

13. Ibid., ll. 16–24.

14. John Dumbrell and Sylvia Ellis, "British Involvement in Vietnam Peace Initiatives, 1966–1967: Marigolds, Sunflowers and "'Kosygin Week'," *Diplomatic History*, Vol. 27, No. 1 (January 2003); "Policy and Politics in the CPSU Politburo," p. 44.

15. Sergey Mazov, *A Distant Front in the Cold War: The USSR in West Africa and the Congo, 1956–1964* (Washington, DC and Stanford, CA: Woodrow Wilson Center Press and Stanford University Press, 2010), p. 183.

16. "Soviet Aid to Underdeveloped Countries," S. Borisov to A.N. Mukhitadinov, August 21, 1961, f. 5, op. 30, d. 371, ll. 227–236, RGANI; Elizabeth Kridl Valkenier, "New Trends in Soviet Economic Relations with the Third World," *World Politics*, Vol. 22, No. 3 (April 1970).

17. Westad, *The Global Cold War*, pp. 159, 168–169.

18. Paul Du Quenoy, "The Role of Foreign Affairs in the Fall of Nikita Khrushchev in October 1964," *International History Review*, Vol. 25, No. 2 (2003), pp. 348–349.

19. Anatoly Dobrynin, *In Confidence: Moscow's Ambassador to America's Six Cold War Presidents* (New York: Random House/Times Books, 1995), pp. 140–141.

20. Untitled letter from Gaforov to Brezhnev, March 12, 1966, f. 5, op. 30, d. 489, ll. 147–153, RGANI.

21. "Memo of Conversation between Gomułka, Brezhnev and Kosygin at the Kremlin," October 14, 1966, in Andrzej Paczkowski, ed., *Tajne Dokumenty Biura Politycznego: PRL–ZSSR 1956–1970* (London: Aneks, 1998), p. 416.

22. "Consultation between the Czechoslovak Foreign Ministry and the Soviet Foreign Ministry," May 22–26, 1966, in fond Antonin Novotny, Box 3, NA.

23. Anderson, *Public Politics*, p. 153; Franklyn D. Holzman, "Soviet Trade and Aid Policies," *Proceedings of the Academy of Political Science*, Vol. 29, No. 3 (Mar. 1969), p. 110.

24. Dobrynin, *In Confidence*, p. 651. See also Quintin V.S. Bach, *Soviet Aid to the Third World: The Facts and Figures* (Sussex: The Book Guild, 2003), p. 63.

25. Dobrynin, *In Confidence*, pp. 649–651; Ilya V. Gaiduk, *The Soviet Union and the Vietnam War* (Chicago, IL: Ivan R. Dee, 1996), pp. 59–62.

Chapter 19: Restraining Damascus, Disciplining Cairo

1. "Nasir's Reaction to Khrushchev's Ouster," October 16, 1964, Doc. No. CK 31007714892, DDRS; Memo of conversation between the East German ambassador and the Soviet Ambassador to Egypt, April 6, 1964, file DY 30\IV A2\20\894, SAPMO, BA. See also: Heikal, *1967*, pp. 77–84; Alexei Vassiliev, *Russian Policy in the Middle East: From Messianism to Pragmatism* (Reading: Ithaca Press, 1993), p. 63.

2. Anderson, *Public Politics*, pp. 153–154; "About the Visit of Egypt's President Nasser to the USSR (27.8-1.9.1965)," Moscow to Berlin, September 9, 1965, File A 001159, MFAA, PAAA.

3. Mohrez Mahmoud El Hussini, *Soviet–Egyptian Relations, 1945–85* (London: Macmillan, 1987), pp. 143–145, 148–150, 160–161.

4. El Hussini, *Soviet–Egyptian Relations*, pp. 162–167, 174; Nasr, *Mudhakirat Salah Nasr* (Cairo: Dar al-Khiyal, 1999), Vol. 3, p. 181; Mikhail Monakov, "The Soviet Naval Presence in the Mediterranean at the Time of the Six-Day War," in Ro'i and Morzov, eds, *The Soviet Union and the June 1967 Six Day War*, pp. 148–160.

5. Memo of conversation, September 23, 1963, File A 7936/1, ISA; Angelika Timm, *Hammer Zirkel Davidstern: Das gestörte Verhältnis der DDR zu Zionismus und Staat Israel* (Bonn: Bouvier, 1997), p. 178.

6. "Elaboration of the policy of PR Bulgaria toward Israel in the light of Bulgarian–Arab relations," submitted by Ivan Bashev [circa 1965], fond 1–B, op. 6, a.e. 5896, ll. 2–3, 23–29, 43–44, CDA.

7. Rajan Menon, "The Soviet Union, the Arms Trade and the Third World," *Soviet Studies*, Vol. 34, No. 3 (July 1982), p. 383; Joshua Wynfred and Stephen P. Gilbert, *Arms for the Third World: Soviet Military Aid Diplomacy* (Baltimore, MD: Johns Hopkins University Press, 1969), p. 23 (Table 2–1); Jon Glassman, *Arms for the Arabs: The Soviet Union and War in the Middle East* (Baltimore, MD: Johns Hopkins University Press, 1975), p. 34; "On the examination of opportunities for export of armaments for countries from Asia and Africa. Presented by Comrade T. Zhivkov," May 12, 1960, fond 1–B, op. 64, D. 268, CDA; Klaus Storkmann, *Geheime Solidarität: Militärbeziehungen und Militärhilfen der DDR in die "Dritte Welt"* [Secret Solidarity: East Germany's Military Aid and Relations in the "Third World"] (Berlin: Cristoph Links, 2012), pp. 107–110, 184–187.

8. M. Gazit to Harman, "The Arms Race in the Middle East," December 28, 1963, File MFA 4301/4, ISA; "A Conversation with the Senior Counselor in the Soviet Embassy in Washington, Alexander I. Zinchuk," M. Gazit (Washington) to A. Doron, head East European desk, December 28, 1963, File MFA 3573/24, ISA; Washington (Evron) to Foreign Ministry, October 17, 1965, File MFA 3573/22, ISA.

9. "Report by Sh. Mikonis and Moshe Seneh on their Talks with Suslov and Ponemarev," February 2, 1966, File A 7935/9, ISA.

10. Heller, *Yisrael*, p. 495.

11. "Memo by D. S. Chuvachin to the Minister of Foreign Affairs A. A. Gromyko," March 21, 1966, in Naumkin et al., eds, *Blizhnevostochnyi Konflikt*, Vol. 2, pp. 491–499.

12. "Memo of Conversation between Counselor at Soviet Foreign Ministry's Middle East Department, F. N. Fedatov, with the First Secretary of the UAR Embassy in the USSR, Y[usuf] Sharara," March 7, 1966, in Naumkin et al., eds, *Blizhnevostochnyi Konflikt*, Vol. 2, pp. 489–490; "Memo Written by A.D. Shchiborin, Head of the Middle East Department in the Soviet Foreign Ministry regarding the Speech of the Soviet Ambassador in Israel," March 19, 1966, ibid., pp. 490–491.

13. "Brief Prepared by the Middle Eastern Department at the Soviet Foreign Ministry regarding Israeli Intentions to Obtain Nuclear Weapons," February 23, 1966, in Naumkin et al., eds, *Blizhnevostochnyi Konflikt*, Vol. 2, pp. 487–489; see also untitled and unidentified document, March 30, 1966, File A 7935/9–A, ISA. Cf. Isabella Ginor and Gideon Remez, *Foxbats over Dimona: The Soviets' Nuclear Gamble in the Six-Day War* (New Haven, CT: Yale University Press, 2007), pp. 36–48.

14. See, for instance, "Chuvakhin-Eshkol Conversation," October 11, 1966, File A 7935/9, ISA.

15. "The Syrian Arab Socialist Renaissance Party," April 20, 1966, fond 5, op. 30, delo 489, ll. 216–219, RGANI.

16. Damascus (Mangold) to Bonn, September 7, 1964, Bestand B36, Band 126, PAAA; Ben-Tzur, *Gormim*, p. 64.

17. Ben-Tzur, *Gormim*, pp. 99–100.

18. Ibid., pp. 90–91; "An Analysis of the Joint Soviet–Syrian Communiqué," *Al-Munadil*, June 1966.

19. Ben-Tzur, *Gormim*, pp. 98–99; "An Analysis of the Joint Soviet–Syrian Communiqué," *Al-Munadil*, June 1966.
20. "An Analysis of the Joint Soviet–Syrian Communiqué," *Al-Munadil*, June 1966.
21. Ben-Tzur, *Gormim*, p. 106.
22. "Telegram from the Ambassador in Syria A. A. Barkovski to Soviet Foreign Ministry," May 11, 1966, in Naumkin et al., eds, *Blizhnevostochnyi Konflikt*, Vol. 2, pp. 503–504.
23. "Telegram from the Soviet Foreign Ministry to the Embassy in Jordan," May 24, 1967, in Naumkin et al., eds, *Blizhnevostochnyi Konflikt*, Vol. 2, pp. 505–506; "Memo of Conversation between Deputy Minister for Foreign Affairs, V. S. Semyonov, and Israeli Ambassador in Moscow, K. Kats," May 25, 1966, ibid., pp. 506–508; "Memo of Conversation between the Soviet Ambassador in Jordan, P. K. Slyusarenko, and King Hussein," May 28, 1966, ibid., pp. 508–512; "Soviet Telegram which was Delivered to Ambassador Katriel Katz on 25.5.1966," File A 7935/9, ISA; *al-Hayat*, May 28 and 31, 1966.
24. Washington (Nisim Yai'sh) to Foreign Ministry, "Soviet Arms Shipments to Arab Countries," August 25, 1966, File 4054/9, RG FM, ISA.
25. Bonn (N. Hadas) to Foreign Ministry, September 1, 1966, File MFA 4049/7, ISA; Paris (Y. Hadas) to Foreign Ministry, "The Soviet Union and the Middle East," December 7, 1966, File 4049/7, ISA; Ben-Tzur, *Gormim*, pp. 94–95.
26. "On the visit of a government delegation headed by Com. A.N. Kosygin to the United Arab Republic (May 10–18, 1966)," in Archiwum Akt Nowych, Warsaw, KC PZPR 2632, pp. 239–246.
27. Paris (Y. Hadas) to Foreign Ministry, June 6, 1966, File MFA 4049/5, ISA.
28. "Memo of Conversation between Gomulka, Brezhnev and Kosygin at the Kremlin", October 14, 1966, in Andrzej Paczkowski, ed., *Tajne Dokumenty Biura Politycznego: PRL–ZSSR 1956–1970*, pp. 402–403; "A Conversation with Donald Bergus, Head of the Egyptian Desk," November 30, 1966, File MFA 7305/7, ISA; "Borrowing from the Capitalists," *Time*, February 12, 1965.
29. "Soviet Arms Shipments to Arab Countries," Washington (Nisim Yai'sh) to Foreign Ministry, August 25, 1966, File MFA 4054/9, ISA.
30. Paris (G. Fadon) to Foreign Ministry, October 12, 1966, File MFA 4049/7, ISA.
31. "Memo of Conversation between the Soviet ambassador in the UAR, D. P. Pozhedaev, and First Vice-President of the UAR, Marshal Amer," May 19, 1967, in V.V. Naumkin et al., eds, *Blizhnevostochnyi Konflikt*, Vol. 2, pp. 557–560.
32. "Consultation between the Czechoslovak Foreign Ministry and the Soviet Foreign Ministry," May 22–26, 1966, Box 3, fond Antonin Novotny, NA; Paris (Y. Hadas) to Foreign Ministry, June 6, 1966, File MFA 4049/5, ISA; "Soviet and Chinese Objectives and Activities in the UAR," Memo by Donald C. Bergus, March 21, 1967, Lot File 71D469, Box 3, Folder "POL 1-22 Political Relations UAR/USSR," RG 59, NARA.
33. "Telegram of the Soviet ambassador in Israel D.S. Chuvachin, to Soviet Foreign Ministry," October 11, 1966, in Naumkin et al., eds, *Blizhnevostochnyi Konflikt*, Vol. 2, pp. 515–517.
34. Ibid.; "Telegram from the Soviet Foreign Ministry to the Soviet ambassador in Israel," October 11, 1966, ibid., p. 518; "Telegram from the Soviet Foreign Ministry to the Soviet ambassador in the UAR," October 11, 1966, ibid., pp. 518–519; "Telegram from the Soviet Foreign Ministry to the Soviet ambassador in Syria," October 13, 1966, ibid., pp. 521–522.
35. *al-Hayat*, October 11, 1966.
36. Gluska, *Eshkol*, p. 155.
37. "Report of the Soviet Foreign Minister, A. A. Gromyko, to the Central Committee of the Soviet Communist Party," November 1966 [exact date unknown], in Naumkin et al., eds, *Blizhnevostochnyi Konflikt*, Vol. 2, pp. 529–530.
38. Yitzhak Shichor, *The Middle East in China's Foreign Policy, 1949–1977* (Cambridge: Cambridge University Press, 1979), pp. 106–144.
39. James G. Hershberg, "Peace Probes and the Bombing Pause: Hungarian and Polish Diplomacy during the Vietnam War, December 1965–January 1966," *Journal of Cold War*

Studies, Vol. 5, No. 2 (2003), p. 66; Lorenz M. Luthi, "Twenty-Four Soviet-Bloc Documents on Vietnam and the Sino–Soviet Split, 1964–1966," *CWIHP Bulletin*, 16 (2008); Hanoi to Foreign Ministry, Telegram 9312, September 22, 1966, RG incoming telegrams, A MZV; Hanoi to Foreign Ministry, Telegram 162, January 6, 1967, ibid.; Hanoi to Foreign Ministry, Telegram 2700, March 14, 1967, ibid.

40. Damascus (M. Korselt) to Foreign Ministry, "Chinese activity in Syria, Political Report no. 4\67," February 18, 1967, Syrie, 1965–69, Box 2, Folder 13 (116\311), RG TO–T, A MZV.

41. Dobrynin, *In Confidence*, p. 651.

42. Cairo to Foreign Ministry, Arriving Telegram 10541, October 15, 1966, A MZV.

43. El-Hussini, *Soviet–Egyptian Relations*, p. 174.

44. Mohamed Hassanein Heikal, *The Sphinx and the Commissar: The Rise and Fall of Soviet Intelligence in the Middle East* (London: Collins, 1978), p. 168; Salah Nasr, *Mudhakirat Salah Nasr*, Vol. 3, pp. 181–184; "Letter, Fleet Admiral Sergei Goroshkov to Chief of General Staff, Marshal of the Soviet Union, Matvei Zakharov, January 3, 1967," in Ro'i and Morozov, eds, *The Soviet Union*, p. 282; "Memo of Conversation between the Soviet ambassador in the UAR, D. P. Pozhedaev, and First Vice-President of the UAR, Marshal Amer," May 19, 1967, in Naumkin et al., eds, *Blizhnevostochnyi Konflikt*, Vol. 2, p. 559; Moscow (Guthrie) to Secretary of State, Cable No. 2466, January 1, 1966, CPF, 1964–1966, POL 7 UAR, Box 2762, RG 59, NARA; translation from the Lebanese daily *al-Jadid*, February 24, 1967, File MFA 4049/7, ISA.

45. Damascus (M. Korselt) to Foreign Ministry, "The Visit of the Ba'th delegation in the USSR, Political Report no. 3," February 16, 1967, Syrie, 1965–69, Box 2, Folder 13 (116\311), RG TO–T, A MZV.

46. Ibid.; Jundi's quote taken from Damascus (Smythe) to State Dept., "New Evidence of SARG–Soviet Disillusion," February 20, 1967, Airgram A–367, CPF, 1967–1969, POL 17 SYR–US, Box 2511, RG 59, NARA.

47. Aharon Nuemark, *Mishtar Ha-Neo-Baath Be-Surya: Politika U-Mediniyut, 1966–1970* [The Neo-Baath Regime in Syria: Politics and Policy] (PhD dissertation, Bar-Ilan University, 2002), p. 108.

48. Avigdor Dagan, *Moscow and Jerusalem* (New York: Abelard-Schuman, 1970), p. 20; "Conversation with Shchiborin (reported by Gideon Refael)," April 27, 1967, File MFA 4048/30, ISA.

49. Cairo (Nes) to Secretary of State, April 26, 1967, Cable No. 6728, CPF, 1967–1969, POL 7 USSR, Box 2678, RG 59, NARA.

50. *al-Hayat*, March 29, 1967, p. 2; *al-Hayat*, March 30, 1967, p. 2; *al-Hayat*, April 2, 1967, p. 2.

51. "About the visit of Egypt's President Nasser to the USSR (27.8–1.9.1965)," Moscow to Berlin, September 9, 1966, File A 001159 MFAA, PAAA; "On the visit of a government delegation headed by Com. A.N. Kosygin to the United Arab Republic (May 10–18, 1966)," in AAN, KC PZPR 2632, pp. 239–246; Paris (Y. Hadas) to Foreign Ministry, June 6, 1966, File MFA 4049/5, ISA; translation from the Lebanese daily *al-Jadid*, February 24, 1967, File MFA 4049/7, ISA; Foreign Ministry, research department (G. Ben Ami), to Paris (Y. Hadas), "The Soviet Policy in Yemen," May 1, 1966, File MFA 4048/20, ISA; Cairo (Battle) to Secretary of State, "Soviet Attitude towards the UAR," June 10, 1966, Airgram A–1050, in NARA, RG 59, CPF, 1964–1966, Folder "Political Affairs & Rel. UAR–USSR," Box 2769.

52. Jesse Ferris, "Soviet Support for Egypt's Intervention in Yemen, 1962–1963," *Journal of Cold War Studies*, Vol. 10, No. 4 (Fall 2008), pp. 5–36; Viktor Andrianov, *Kosygin* (Moscow: Molodaya Gvardia, 2004), pp. 169–170.

53. James G. Blight and Philip Brenner, *Sad and Luminous Days: Cuba's Struggle with the Superpowers after the Missile Crisis* (Lanham, MD: Rowman & Littlefield, 2002), pp. 35, 122, 132; Karel Kaplan, *Kozheny Cheskoslovensko Reformy 1968* (Brno: Doplenek, 2000), pp. 108–112.

54. Paris (Y. Hadas) to Foreign Ministry, "The UAR and Aden," March 8, 1967, File MFA 4041/5, ISA.

55. *al-Hayat*, March 29 and 30, 1967.
56. Heikal, *1967*, pp. 416-418; Heikal, *The Sphinx and the Commissar*, pp. 169-170. For diplomatic reports that support Heikal's depiction of this meeting see: Bonn (Nitzan Hadas) to Foreign Ministry, "Gromyko's Visit to Cairo," April 11, 1967, File MFA 4049/7, ISA; Cairo (Nes) to Secretary of State, Cable No. 6728, April 26, 1967, NARA, RG 59, CPF, 1967-1969, POL 7 USSR, Box 2678; Cairo to Foreign Ministry, Arriving Telegram 4467, April 26, 1967, A MZV.
57. Moscow (Thompson) to US Department of State, "UAR Diplomat on Soviet Middle East Policies," April 25, 1967, Airgram A-1564, CPF, 1967-1969, POL UAR-USSR, Box 2557, RG 59, NARA.

Chapter 20: A Soviet Hall of Mirrors

1. Heikal, *1967*, pp. 611-612.
2. Research department to Foreign Ministry, May 24, 1967, ibid.
3. Paris to Foreign Ministry, May 23, 1967, File A 7920/3, ISA.
4. Richard B. Parker, ed., *The Six Day War: A Retrospective* (Gainesville, FL: University Press of Florida, 1996), p. 51; Morozov, "The Outbreak of the June 1967 War," p. 47; Cairo to Foreign Ministry, May 22, 1967, Arriving Telegram 5388, A MZV; Paris to DOS, May 23, 1967, CPF, 1967-1969, Folder POLITICAL AFFAIRS & REL ARAB-ISR, RG 59, NARA.
5. Ghaleb, *Maa Abd al-Nasser*, p. 121.
6. Heikal, *1967*, pp. 563-567.
7. al-Shukeiri, *al-Hazima*, pp. 109-113; Doc. No. 78, Vol. 18, FRUS, 1964-1968.
8. Doc. No. 65, Vol. 19, FRUS, 1964-1968; Murtagi, *Al-Fariq Murtagi Yurawi*, pp. 79-80; Fawzi, *Harb*, pp. 113-114, 123-124.
9. Fawzi, *Harb*, p. 124; Heikal, *1967*, pp. 573-574. My depiction of the events of May 27 is different from the one that appears in Oren, *Six Days*, pp. 119-121. Oren relies on an interview with the commander of the air force, Sidqi Mahmud (Suliman Mathhar, *Itirafat Qadat Harb Yunyu* (Cairo: Kitab al-Hurrya, 1990), p. 142), who was incarcerated after the war for alleged negligence. Other than Mahmud, there is no senior figure – neither Heikal nor the chief of staff, Fawzi – who acknowledges the sequence of events as Mahmud tells it.
10. Hadidi, *Shahid*, pp. 25-27; Interview with Shams Badran, *al-Hawadith*, September 2, 1977; "Memo of Conversation between the Soviet ambassador in the UAR, D.P. Pozhedaev, and First Vice-President of the UAR, Marshal Amer," May 19, 1967 in Naumkin et al., eds, *Blizhnivostochnyi Konflikt*, Vol. 2, pp. 557-560.
11. Interview with Shams Badran, *al-Hawadith*, September 2, 1977, p. 21. It is unclear, though, to whom the offer was made.
12. Hussini, *Soviet-Egyptian Relations*, pp. 148-150, 164-165.
13. Quoted in Parker, *Politics of Miscalculation*, p. 29.
14. Heikal, *1967*, pp. 614-616; Glassman, *Arms for the Arabs*, pp. 34-36; Ginor and Remez, *Foxbats*, p. 69; Hussini, *Soviet-Egyptian Relations*, pp. 160-161.
15. Heikal, *1967*, pp. 616-618; Ginor and Remez, *Foxbats*, p. 79.
16. "Protocol of the Meeting between Mister Alexei Kosygin, Soviet Prime Minister, and Shams Badran, Minister of War (26/5/1967)," in Amin Hewedi, *50 Aman min al-Awasif* (Cairo: Markaz al-Aharam, 2002), pp. 408-424.
17. Ibid.
18. Ibid.
19. Ibid.
20. Heikal, *1967*, p. 623.
21. Heikal, *1967*, p. 623; *al-Hawadith*, September 2, 1977, p. 21.
22. "Protocol of the Second Meeting between Mister Shams Badran, Minister of War, and the Soviet Prime Minister (27/5)," in Hewedi, *50 Aman min al-Awasif*, pp. 426-435.
23. Gluska, *Eshkol*, pp. 311-312; Segev, *1967*, p. 287.
24. Heikal, *1967*, pp. 577-578.

25. Doc. No. 84, Vol. 19, FRUS, 1964–1968; Telegram from Gromyko to Soviet ambassadors in satellite countries including Cuba, North Korea, Mongolia, and North Vietnam, May 28, 1967, in Naumkin et al., eds, *Blizhnivostochnyi Konflikt*, Vol. 2, pp. 568–569.
26. "Protocol of the Second Meeting between Mister Shams Badran, Minister of War, and the Soviet Prime Minister (27/5)," in Hewedi, *50 Aman min al-Awasif*, pp. 426–435.
27. Ibid.
28. Ibid.
29. Nasr, *Mudhakirat Salah Nasr*, Vol. 3, pp. 219–220; Richard B. Parker, ed., *The Six Day War: A Retrospective* (Gainesville, FL: University Press of Florida, 1996), p. 44. See also: *al-Hawadith*, September 2, 1977, p. 21.
30. "Policy and Politics in the CPSU Politburo," p. 36. See also Anderson, *Public Politics*, pp. 126–146.
31. Heikal, *1967*, p. 625; *al-Hawadith*, September 2, 1977, p. 21; Ginor and Remez, *Foxbats*, p. 237 (fn. 13).
32. "Draft Letter, Deputy Foreign Minister Valdimir Semyonov to the USSR Ambassadors in Cairo and Damascus, May 24, 1967" and "Draft Letter, CSPU General Secretary Brezhnev to UAR President Nasser, May 24, 1967," in Ro'i and Morozov, eds, *The Soviet Union*, pp. 285–287; Ben-Tzur, *Gormim*, p. 188.
33. Parker, ed., *The Six Day War*, p. 44; Fawzi, *Harb*, p. 95; Abd al-Latif Baghdadi, *Mudhakirat Abd al-Latif Baghdadi* (Cairo: al-Maktab al-Misri al-Hadith, 1977), pp. 273–275; Gluska, *Eshkol*, pp. 314–315.
34. See for instance memo of conversation between Nasser and Pozhedaev, June 1, 1967 in Naumkin et al., eds, *Blizhnivostochnyi Konflikt*, Vol. 2, pp. 572–574.
35. Doc. No. 86, Vol. 19, FRUS, 1964–1968.
36. Gluska, *Eshkol*, pp. 320–324; Segev, *1967*, pp. 308–310.

Chapter 21: A Very Israeli Putsch?

1. Haber, *Hayom*, pp. 157–158.
2. Mordechai Bar-On, *Moshe Dayan: Korot Hayav, 1915–1981* (Tel Aviv: Am Oved, 2014), p. 188.
3. Motti Golani, *Tihyeh Milhama Ba-Kayets* [There Will Be a War in the Summer] (Tel Aviv: Misrad Habitachon, 1997), Vol. 2.
4. Bar-On, *Moshe Dayan*, pp. 198–199.
5. Ibid., pp. 173, 188; Yael Dayan, *My Father, His Daughter* (Jerusalem: Steimatzky, 1985), pp. 97–99; Avneri, *Optimi*, Vol. 1, pp. 460–461.
6. Ibid., pp. 208–209; Shabtai Teveth, *Moshe Dayan* (London: Quartet, 1974), pp. 347–348, 354–363.
7. Bar-On, *Moshe Dayan*, pp. 211–212; Teveth, *Moshe Dayan*, p. 364.
8. Dayan, *Avnei-Derech*, p. 401; Yael Dayan, *My Father*, pp. 170–171.
9. Haber, *Hayom*, pp. 157–158.
10. Gilboa, *Shesh Shanim*, pp. 66–67.
11. *Maariv*, March 31, 1966; Government Minutes, July 3, 1966, ISA.
12. Dayan, *Avnei-Derech*, pp. 400, 402, 408; Haber, *Hayom*, p. 158; Gavish, *Sadin*, p. 133.
13. Dayan, *Avnei-Derech*, pp. 413, 415.
14. Sh. Daniel, ed., *Ha-Sar Haim Moshe Shapira* [Minister Haim Moshe Shapira] (Tel Aviv: Don, 1980), pp. 248–286; Eliezer Don-Yihiya, "Manhigut U-Mediniyut Ba-Tziyunut Ha-Datit: Haim Moshe Shapira, Ha-Mafdal U-Milchemet Sheshet Ha-Yamim" [Leadership and Policy of Religious Zionism: Haim Moshe Shapira, the Mafdal and the Six-Day War] in Yisrael Harel, ed., *Hatziyunut Ha-Datit: Idan Hatmurut* [Religious Zionism in an Era of Change] (Jerusalem: Byalik Institure, 2003), pp. 135–153.
15. *Maariv*, August 10 and December 1, 1965, January 4, July 26, October 21, and December 8 and 15, 1966; see the contribution of Minister Mordechai Bentov to government discussion on May 31, 1967, in ISA.

16. Nakdimon, *Likrat*, pp. 62–69, 98–100.
17. Gluska, *Eshkol*, pp. 489, 503; Nakdimon, *Likrat*, pp. 78–79; Meir Hazan, "Meoravoto shel Iton Haaretz Ba-Maaraha Ha-Politit Be-Tkofat Ha-Hamatna" [The Involvement of the *Haaretz* Newspaper during the Waiting Period], *Yisrael*, Vol. 10 (2006), p. 93.
18. Amnon Rubinstein, "Iton Haaretz Ve-Memshelet Eshkol" [*Haaretz* Newspaper and the Eshkol Government] in Susser, ed., *Shisha Yamim*, pp. 232–233.
19. Eban, *Autobiography*, p. 390.
20. Gluska, *Eshkol*, p. 489; Hazan, "Meoravoto," p. 90.
21. Yossi Goldstein, *Golda: Biographia* (Beersheba: Ben-Gurion University Press, 2012), pp. 468–471.
22. Ibid., pp. 389, 405, 441; Nakdimon, *Likrat*, pp. 96–97; Segev, *1967*, p. 329.
23. Nakdimon, *Likrat*, pp. 98, 112; Segev, *1967*, pp. 275, 292; Gluska, *Eshkol*, p. 329.
24. Nakdimon, *Likrat*, pp. 113–114; Shlomo Nakdimon, "Ben Gurion and Begin: A Love–Hate Relationship," *Haaretz*, January 12, 2013; Suzi Eben, *Zihronot* [Recollections] (Or Yehuda: Kineret, 2009), p. 269.
25. Nakdimon, *Likrat*, pp. 114–117.
26. Gluska, *Eshkol*, pp. 319, 501.
27. Nakdimon, *Likrat*, pp. 128–130.
28. Segev, *1967*, pp. 310–311; Gluska, *Eshkol*, p. 331; Michaeli, *Hatum*, p. 132; Gilboa, *Mar Modiin*, p. 279; Nakdimon, *Likrat*, p. 131.
29. Rabin, *Pinkas*, p. 172; Weizman, *Leha*, p. 237.
30. Segev, *1967*, p. 311; Michaeli, *Hatum*, p. 132.
31. Haber, *Hayom*, pp. 194–197; Rabin, *Pinkas*, p. 174; Segev, *1967*, p. 314.
32. Haber, *Hayom*, p. 197.
33. Ibid., p. 197.
34. Ibid., pp. 197–198; Rabin, *Pinkas*, p. 174.
35. Segev, *1967*, p. 325; Hazan, "Meoravoto," p. 98.
36. Oren, *Six Days*, p. 37.
37. Shlaim, *Lion*, p. 240.
38. Peters and Moore, "Beyond Boom and Bust," pp. 264–272.
39. Tariq Morawid Tell, *The Social and Economic Origins of Monarchy in Jordan* (New York: Palgrave, 2013), pp. 104–108.
40. Tell, *Social and Economic Origins*, pp. 107–108; Samir A. Mutawi, *Jordan in the 1967 War* (Cambridge: Cambridge University Press, 1987), p. 101.
41. Mutawi, *Jordan*, p. 101.
42. Tell, *Social and Economic Origins*, p. 108; Rubin, *The Limits of the Land*, pp. 243–244; Ashton, *King Hussein*, p. 110.
43. Memo of conversation between Ali Sabri and Dr. Scholz, May 31, 1967, File DY 30 J IV 2\2J\1968, SAPMO, BA; Mutawi, *Jordan*, p. 102.
44. Oren, *Six Days*, p. 128; Heikal, *1967*, pp. 656–661.
45. Heikal, *1967*, p. 661.
46. Nakdimon, *Likrat*, pp. 153–159.
47. Ibid., pp. 162–163.
48. Shulamit Levi and Elihu Katz, "Daat Ha-Kahak U-Matzav Ha-Ruch Be-Milhemet Sheshet Ha-Yamim" [Public Opinion and Mood in the Six-Day War] in Susser, ed., *Shisha Yamim*, pp. 246–247.
49. Nakdimon, *Likrat*, p. 186; Hazan, "Meoravoto," p. 107.
50. Nakdimon, *Likrat*, pp. 168–171; Segev, *1967*, p. 331.
51. Docs No. 99, 101, Vol. 19, FRUS, 1964–1968; Dayan, *Avnei-Derech*, p. 415.
52. Gideon Rephael to Jerusalem, May 30, 1967, File A 7919\2, ISA; Epie Evron to Jerusalem, May 30, 1967, ibid.; Evron to Jerusalem, May 31, 1967, ibid.
53. Rabin, *Pinkas*, pp. 177–178; Gilboa, *Mar Modiin*, p. 290; Gluska, *Eshkol*, p. 506.
54. Segev, *1967*, pp. 327, 337.
55. Gluska, *Eshkol*, p. 41.
56. Gilboa, *Mar Modiin*, p. 291; Government Minutes, June 1, 1967, ISA.

Chapter 22: Last Days

1. Fawzi, *Harb*, pp. 124–125; "A Report on the Consultations between the Chairmen of the Communist Parties of the European Socialist Countries in Moscow, 9 June [1967]," Box 65, fond Antonin Novotny, NA. Nasser also talked on the same day with Bob Anderson, an American businessman, and promised him he would not attack Israel. See Doc. No. 129, Vol. 19, FRUS, 1964–1968.
2. Merle Miller, *Lyndon: An Oral Biography* (New York: G.P. Putnam's Sons, 1980), p. 480; Nigel Ashton, "For King and Country: Jack O'Connell, the CIA, and the Arab-Israeli Conflict, 1963–71," *Diplomatic History*, Vol. 36, No. 5 (November 2012), pp. 889–890.
3. Bitan, *Yoman*, p. 45; Gilboa, *Mar Modiin*, p. 291; Ashton, "For King and Country," p. 892.
4. Gilboa, *Mar Modiin*, pp. 282–283.
5. Docs No. 124, 132, Vol. 19, FRUS, 1964–1968; Memorandum to the President from Richard Helms, June 2, 1967, available at: http://nsarchive.gwu.edu/NSAEBB/NSAEBB265/19670602.pdf (accessed September 19, 2016).
6. Doc. No. 124, Vol. 19, FRUS, 1964–1968.
7. Memorandum to the President from Richard Helms, June 2, 1967, available at: http://nsarchive.gwu.edu/NSAEBB/NSAEBB265/19670602.pdf (accessed September 19, 2016).
8. Fawzi, *Harb*, pp. 126–129; "Letter from Marshal Amer to Egyptian Armed Forces" in Hagai Golan and Shaul Shai, eds, *Nahshonim, 40 Shana Le-Milihemet Sheshet Ha-Yamim* [The Forty Year Anniversary of the Six-Day War] (Tel Aviv: Maarachot, 2007), pp. 513–514.
9. Segev, *1967*, pp. 343–347; Gluska, *Eshkol*, pp. 359–366.
10. Dayan, *Avnei-Derech*, pp. 421–422; Yaacov Erez and Ilan Kfir, *Sihot im Moshe Dayan* [Conversations with Moshe Dayan] (Tel Aviv: Messada, 1981), p. 47; Segev, *1967*, p. 347.
11. Gluska, *Eshkol*, pp. 372–373.
12. Ibid., pp. 362–363; Gilad Sharon, *Sharon: Hayav shel Manhig* [Sharon: The Life of a Leader] (Tel Aviv: Matar, 2011), pp. 126–129.
13. Gavish, *Sadin*, p. 155; Shalom, *Ke-Raam*, pp. 162–163.
14. Gavish, *Sadin*, p. 155; Erez and Kfir, *Sihot*, p. 53.
15. Segev, *1967*, pp. 353–354; Gluska, *Eshkol*, pp. 389–390.
16. Doc. No. 139, Vol. 19, FRUS, 1964–1968; Segev, *1967*, pp. 355–358; Gluska, *Eshkol*, pp. 390–400.

Conclusion: Six Days and After

1. Melubani, *Mi-Tzafon Tipatach*, p. 245; Stephen Biddle and Robert Zirkle, "Technology, Civil–Military Relations, and Warfare in the Developing World," *Journal of Strategic Studies*, Vol. 19, No. 2 (1996); Risa Brooks, "An Autocracy at War: Explaining Egypt's Military Effectiveness, 1967 and 1973," *Security Studies*, Vol. 15, No. 3 (2006).
2. For the influence of party affiliation on the appointment of officers during the 1950s, see Yoram Peri, *Between Battles and Ballots: Israeli Military in Politics* (Cambridge: Cambridge University Press, 1983), pp. 61–64, 78–80.
3. Based on an official investigation by the Egyptian Air Force into the causes of its defeat. A complete copy can be found in Heikal, *1967*, pp. 1041–1050.
4. Yoash Tzidon, *Ba-Yom, Ba-Layla, Ba-Arafel* [At Daytime, At Night time, In the Fog] (Or Yehuda: Maariv, 1995), pp. 313–314, 322–323.
5. "The Visit of the Czechoslovak President's Special Envoy, V. Koucki, in the UAR," June 26, 1967, Box 93, fond Antonin Novotny, NA; Shalom, *Ke-Raam*, pp. 215–220.
6. Weizman, *Leha*, p. 269; Kenneth M. Pollack, "Air Power in the Six-Day War," *Journal of Strategic Studies*, Vol. 28, No. 3 (June 2005).
7. Amira Shahar, "Ha-Honaa Be-Milhemet Sheshet Ha-Yamim" [Deception in the Six-Day War], in Golan and Shay, eds, *Nahshonim*, pp. 125–128.

8. Murtagi, *Al-Fariq Murtagi Yurawi*, pp. 79–93; Fawzi, *Harb*, pp. 109–112.
9. Ibid. Murtagi and Fawzi.
10. Gadi Bloom and Nir Hefetz, *Haroe: Sipor Hayav shel Ariel Sharon* [The Shepherd: A Biography of Ariel Sharon] (Tel Aviv: Yediot Ahronot, 2005), pp. 166–168; Yael Dayan, *Israel Journal: June 1967* (New York: McGraw-Hill, 1967), pp. 43, 51.
11. Dayan, *Journal*, p. 60; Bloom and Hefetz, *Haroe*, pp. 174–177.
12. Oren, *Six Days*, p. 214; Mark Harrison and John Barber, "Patriotic War, 1941 to 1945," in Ronald Grigor Suny, ed., *The Cambridge History of Russia*, Vol. 3 (Cambridge: Cambridge University Press, 2006).
13. Oren, *Six Days*, p. 181; Shalom, *Ke-Raam*, p. 136; Owen L. Sirrs, *The Egyptian Intelligence Service: A History of the Mukhabarat, 1910–2009* (New York: Routledge, 2010), pp. 94–102; Gilboa, *Mar Modiin*, p. 124; Shur, *Hotze*, pp. 187, 199, 207, 222, 263.
14. Wolfgang Lutz, *Shlihot Be-Kahir* [A Mission in Cairo] (Tel Aviv: Maariv, 1970), p. 83.
15. Oren, *Six Days*, p. 250.
16. Melubani, *Mi-Tzafon Tipatach*, p. 236.
17. Gavish, *Sadin*, pp. 199, 209–210, 218.
18. Segev, *1967*, pp. 291, 396–398; Dayan, *Journal*, p. 75.
19. Gavish, *Sadin*, p. 8; Segev, *1967*, p. 397.
20. Oren, *Six Days*, p. 135; Benny Michaelson, "Ha-Milhama Ba-Zira Ha-Yardenit" [Fighting on the Jordanian Front], in Efi Meltzer, ed., *Milchemet Sheshet Ha-Yamim* [The Six Day War] (Reut: Efie Meltzer, 1996), p. 167.
21. Oren, *Six Days*, pp. 185, 190.
22. Ibid., pp. 224–225.
23. Ibid., p. 231; Segev, *1967*, pp. 376–377.
24. Oren, *Six Days,* p. 246; Segev, *1967*, pp. 390–391.
25. Melubani, *Mi-Tzafon Tipatach*, p. 252.
26. Oren, *Six Days*, p. 230; Ha-Meiri, *Me-Shney*, pp. 84–94.
27. Bartov, *Daddo*, pp. 141, 147–149.
28. Mayzel, *Ha-Maaracha*, p. 278; Oren, *Six Days*, p. 276.
29. Mayzel, *Ha-Maaracha*, pp. 268–269; Gilboa, *Mar Modiin*, p. 323.
30. Mayzel, *Ha-Maaracha*, pp. 270–272; Gilboa, *Mar Modiin*, pp. 322–323.
31. Bartov, *Daddo*, pp. 152–153; Ha-Meiri, *Me-Shney*, p. 34; Erez and Kfir, *Sihot*, p. 51.
32. Ha-Meiri, *Me-Shney*, pp. 21–24; Mayzel, *Ha-Maaracha*, p. 286; Melubani, *Mi-Tzafon Tipatach*, p. 226.
33. Mayzel, *Ha-Maaracha*, p. 282.
34. Ha-Meiri, *Me-Shney*, pp. 24–25, 70; Nuemark, *Mishtar*, pp. 141–142; Melubani, *Mi-Tzafon Tipatach*, p. 247.
35. Melubani, *Mi-Tzafon Tipatach*, p. 238; Nuemark, *Mishtar*, p. 141.
36. Melubani, *Mi-Tzafon Tipatach*, pp. 237–238.
37. Ibid., pp. 256-257; Nuemark, *Mishtar*, p. 141.
38. Mayzel, *Ha-Maaracha*, pp. 287, 319; Melubani, *Mi-Tzafon Tipatach*, pp. 239–240; Oren, *Six Days*, p. 284.
39. Melubani, *Mi-Tzafon Tipatach*, pp. 234–235; Nuemark, *Mishtar*, p. 142.
40. Gilboa, *Mar Modiin*, p. 326; Mayzel, *Ha-Maaracha*, pp. 332–333; Melubani, *Mi-Tzafon Tipatach*, p. 231.
41. Mayzel, *Ha-Maaracha*, pp. 338–339.
42. Mayzel, *Ha-Maaracha*, pp. 340–341; Melubani, *Mi-Tzafon Tipatach*, p. 270; "On the Visit of a Delegation Headed by Vaclav Pleskot," 25–28 June 1967, Box 220, fond Antonin Novotny, NA.
43. Ginor and Remez, *Foxbats*, p. 172.
44. Compare Ginor and Remez, *Foxbats*, pp. 172–174, to Mikhail Monakov, "The Soviet Naval Presence," in Ro'i and Morzov, eds, *The Soviet Union*, pp. 164–166.
45. Segev, *1967*, p. 352; Doc. No. 144, Vol. 19, FRUS, 1964–1968.
46. Laron, *Origins of the Suez Crisis*, p. 176.
47. Oren, *Six Days*, p. 225.
48. Ibid., pp. 231, 262.

49. Ibid., pp. 235–237.
50. Ibid., pp. 262–271.
51. Ibid., p. 235.
52. Yoram Peri, "Political–Military Partnership in Israel," *International Political Science Review*, Vol. 2, No. 3 (1981).
53. Reuven Pedhazur, *Nitzchon Hamevucha: Mediniyut Memshelet Eshkol Ba-Shtachim Leachar Milchemet Sheshet Hayamim* (Tel Aviv: Bitan/Yad Tevenkin, 1996); Gershom Gorenberg, *The Accidental Empire: Israel and the Birth of the Settlements* (New York: Times Books, 2006).
54. Yossi Beilin, *Mehiro shel Ihud: Mifleget Ha-Avoda ad Milhemet Yom Ha-Kippurim* [The Price of Unity: The Labor Party up to the Yom Kippur War] (Ramat Gan: Revivim, 1985), pp. 42–43.
55. Rosenthal, *Eshkol*, p. 510; Grinberg, *Ha-Histadrut*, pp. 189–190.
56. Grinberg, *Ha-Histadrut*, pp. 189, 196–201.
57. Avi Raz, "The Generous Peace Offer That Was Never Offered: The Israeli Cabinet Resolution of June 19, 1967," *Diplomatic History*, Vol. 37, No. 1 (2013).
58. Avraham Ben Zvi, *Lyndon B. Johnson and the Politics of Arms Sales to Israel: In the Shadow of the Hawk* (London: Routledge, 2004), pp. 111–124; David Rodman, "Phantom Fracas: The 1968 American Sale of F-4 Aircraft to Israel," *Middle Eastern Studies*, Vol. 40, No. 6 (2004); Charles D. Smith, "The United States and the 1967 War," in Louis and Shlaim, eds, *The 1967 Arab-Israeli War*.
59. Bowen, *Six Days*, p. 292; Cairo to State Dept., "Live, Caesar, Live! – Nasser Stages Support Demonstrations," June 15, 1967, POL 15-1 UAR, CPF, 1967–1969, RG 59, NARA; Murtagi, *Al-Fariq Murtagi Yurawi*, pp. 196–197.
60. Bowen, *Six Days*, pp. 292, 318–322; Murtagi, *Al-Fariq Murtagi Yurawi*, pp. 196–202; Heikal, *1967*, pp. 1081–1089; Abd al-Magid Farid, *Nasser: The Final Years* (Reading: Ithaca Press, 1994).
61. Malcolm H. Kerr, "Hafiz Asad and the Changing Patterns of Syrian Politics," *International Journal*, Vol. 28, No. 4 (Autumn 1973).
62. Ginor and Remez, *Foxbats*, p. 212; Memo of conversation between Amin Hewedi, Egyptian Minister of Defense and Marshal Grechko, Soviet Minister of Defense, November 10, 1967, in Hewedi, *50 Aman min al-Awasif*, pp. 454–465.
63. See for instance, "Polish Record of Meeting of Soviet-bloc leaders (and Tito) in Budapest," July 11, 1967, KC PZPR, XI A/13, AAN, History and Public Policy Program Digital Archive, available at: http://digitalarchive.wilsoncenter.org/document/113622 (accessed October 2, 2016).
64. William T. Lee and Richard F. Staar, *Soviet Military Policy Since World War II* (Stanford, CA: Hoover Institution Press, 1986), pp. 66–70; Central Committee Meeting of the CPSU, June 6, 1967, f. 2, op. 3, delo 63, ll. 28–29, RGANI.
65. "The Aggression Committed by Israel Against the Arab Countries and the American Global Strategy," August 30, 1967, MfS, ZAIG 4624, BStU.
66. "On the Status of the Bulgarian Armed Forces in Light of Events in the Middle East," October 17, 1967, in Vojtech Mastny and Malcolm Byrne, eds, *A Cardboard Castle? An Inside History of the Warsaw Pact, 1955–1991* (Budapest: Central European University Press, 2005), pp. 245–248.
67. Yaacov Ro'i, "The Soviet Jewish Reaction to the Six Day War," in Ro'i and Morozov, eds, *The Soviet Union*.
68. Oren, *Six Days*, p. 297.
69. Oren, *Six Days*, pp. 305–306; *Atlas Karta Le-Tolodot Medint Yisrael: Asor Sheni* [An Atlas of Israeli History: The Second Decade] (Tel Aviv: Karta Ve-Misrad Ha-Bitachon, 1980), pp. 117–123, 151–165.
70. Government Minutes, October 15, 1967, ISA; Greenberg, *Cheshbon ve-Otzma*, Table 14; Yitzchak Greenberg, "Hitpathut Taktziv Ha-Bitachon Ve-Ha-Rehesh Ba-Shanim 1967–1973" [The Development of the Defense Budget in the Years, 1967–1973] in Hagai Golan and Shaul Shai, eds, *Milhama Ha-Yom: Hikrey Milhemet Yom Ha-Kippurim* [War Today: Studies of the Yom Kippur War] (Tel Aviv: Maarachot, 2003); Steven L. Spiegel,

Mark A. Heller and Jacob Goldberg, eds, *The Soviet-American Competition in the Middle East* (Lexington, MA: Lexington Books, 1988), Table 2-7.

71. Yaniv, *Deterrence Without the Bomb*, pp. 138–140, 148–149.

72. Emanuel Sakal, *Soldier in the Sinai: A General's Account of the Yom Kippur War* (Lexington, KY: University Press of Kentucky, 2014).

SELECT BIBLIOGRAPHY

Primary Sources

Unpublished

Bulgaria, Sofia:
Central State Archives (CDA)

Czech Republic, Prague:
Foreign Ministry Archive [A MZV – Arkhiv Ministerstvo Zharanichni Vechi]
National Archive [NA – Narodni Archiv]

Germany, Berlin:
Foreign Ministry Archive, Record Group of the West-German Foreign Ministry [PAAA – Politischen Archiv des Auswärtigen Amts] and Record Group of the East-German Foreign Ministry [MFAA – Ministerium für Auswärtige Angelegenheiten der Deutschen Demokratischen Republik]
National Archives [BA – Bundesarchiv], Record Group of Parties and Mass Organisations of the GDR [SAPMO – Stiftung Archiv der Parteien und Massenorganisationen]
Stasi Archive [BStU – Bundesbeauftragte für die Unterlagen des Staatssicherheitsdienstes der ehemaligen Deutschen Demokratischen Republik]

Israel, Jerusalem:
Israel Defense Forces Archive, Ramat Efal [IDFA]
Israeli State Archives [ISA], Record Groups of the Ministry of Foreign Affairs [MFA] and the Prime Minister's Office [A]

Russia, Moscow:
Russian State Archive of Recent History [RGANI – Rossiiskii Gosudarstvennnyi Arkhiv Noveishei Istorii]

United Kingdom, Kew, London:
British National Archives [BNA]

United States, College Park, Maryland:
National Archives and Records Administration [NARA], RG 59

Published

Declassified Documents Record System [DDRS]
Foreign Relations of the United States [FRUS]
Naumkin, V.V. et al., eds, *Blizhnevostochnyi Konflikt, 1957–1967: Iz Dokumentov Arkhiva Vneshnei Politiki Rossiskoi Federatsi* (Moscow: Mezhdunarodnyi Fond Demokratiya, 2003)
Paczkowski, Andrzej, ed., *Tajne Dokumenty Biura Politycznego: PRL-ZSSR 1956–1970* (London: Aneks, 1998)
Rosenthal, Yemima, *Yitzhak Rabin, Rosh Memshelet Yisrael: Mivhar Teudot* (Jerusalem: Israeli State Archive, 2005)
Rosenthal, Yemima et al., eds, *Levi Eshkol, Rosh Ha-Memeshala Ha-Shlishi: Mivhar Teudut Me-Pirkey Hayav* (Jerusalem: Israeli State Archive, 2002)

Newspapers

Davar
Haaretz
al-Hayat
Maariv
New York Times

Arab memoirs

Fawzi, Muhammed, *Harb al-Thlath Sawat, 1967–1970* (Beirut: Dar al-Wahda, 1983)
El-Gamasy, Mohamed Abdel Ghani, *The October War* (Cairo: American University in Cairo Press, 1989)
Ghaleb, Murad, *Maa Abd al-Nasser Wa-al-Sadat* (Cairo: Markaz al-Aharam, 2001)
Hamrush, Ahmed, *Qisat Thawrat Yuliyu: Kharif Abd al-Nasser*, Vol. 5 (Beirut: al-Mua'sasa al-Arabia lil-Dirasat wa-al-Nasher, 1978)
Heikal, Mohamed Hassanein, *1967: al-Infijar* (Cairo: Markaz al-Aharam, 1990)
Hewedi, Amin, *50 Aman min al-Awasif* (Cairo: Markaz al-Aharam, 2002)
Murtagi, Abd al-Muhsen, *Al-Fariq Murtagi Yurawi al-Haqaiq* (Cairo: Dar al-Watan al-Arabi, 1976)

Israeli memoirs

Amit, Meir, *Rosh Be-Rosh: Mabat Ishi al Aeyroim Gdolim U-Parshiyut Alumot* (Or Yehuda: Head Artzi, 1999)
Bitan, Moshe, *Yoman Medini, 1967–1970* (Tel Aviv: Olam Chadash, 2014)
Eban, Abba, *An Autobiography* (New York: Random House, 1977)
Dayan, Moshe, *Avnei-Derech* (Jerusalem: Idanim, 1976)
Gavish, Yeshayahu, *Sadin Adom: Sipur Hayay Me-Ha-Palmah Ve-Ad Beyt Ha-Palmah* (Or Yehuda: Zabam, 2016)
Haber, Eytan, *Hayom Tifrots Milchama: Zichronotav shel Tat-Aluf Yisrael Lior, Hamazkir Ha-Tsvai shel Rashey Ha-Memshala Levi Eshkol Ve-Golda Meir* (Tel Aviv: Idanim, 1987)
Narkiss, Uzi, *Ahat Yerushalaym* (Tel Aviv: Am Oved, 1975)
Rabin, Yitzhak, *Pinkas Sherut* (Tel Aviv: Maariv, 1979)
Sharett, Moshe, *Yoman Ishi* (Tel Aviv: Maariv, 1978)
Weizman, Ezer, *Leha Shmayim, Leha Ha-Aretz* (Tel Aviv: Maariv, 1975)

Secondary Literature

Ahlberg, Kristin L., *Transplanting the Great Society: Lyndon Johnson and Food for Peace* (Columbia, MO: University of Missouri Press, 2008)
Ashton, Nigel, "For King and Country: Jack O'Connell, the CIA, and the Arab-Israeli Conflict, 1963–71," *Diplomatic History*, Vol. 36, No. 5 (November 2012)
Anderson, Jr., Richard D. *Public Politics in an Authoritarian State: Making Foreign Policy During the Brezhnev Years* (Ithaca, NY: Cornell University Press, 1993)

BIBLIOGRAPHY 353

Bar-On, Mordechai, *Moshe Dayan: Korot Hayav, 1915–1981* (Tel Aviv: Am Oved, 2014)

Bar-Siman-Tov, Yaacov, *Linkage Politics in the Middle East: Syria between Domestic and External Conflict, 1961–1970* (Boulder, CO: Westview Press, 1983)

Bartov, Chanoch, *Daddo: 48 Shana Ve-Od 20 Yom* (Or Yehuda: Dvir, 2002)

Bar-Zohar, Michael, *Hayav U-Moto shel Nasich Yehudi: Dr Yaacov Herzof, Ha-Biografia* (Tel Aviv: Yediot Ahronot, 2003)

Ben-Tzur, Avraham, *Gormim Sovyetyim Ve-Milchemet Sheshet Ha-Yamim: Maavakim Ba-Kremel Ve-Hashpaatam Be-Ezurenu* (Tel Aviv: Sifriyat Hapoalim, 1975)

Beattie, Kirk J., *Egypt During the Nasser Years: Ideology, Politics, and Civil Society* (Boulder, CO: Westview Press, 1994)

Burns, William J., *Economic Aid and American Foreign Policy toward Egypt, 1955–1981* (Albany, NY: SUNY Press, 1985)

Cohen, Avi, *Ha-Hagana Al Mekorot Ha-Maym: Medinyut Hafalt Chayl Ha-Avir Le-Tkifa Bi-Gvol Yisrael-Surya, 1956–1967* (Tel Aviv: Misrad Ha-Bitahon, 1992)

Cohen, Avner, *Israel and the Bomb* (New York: Columbia University Press, 1998)

Castiglioni, Claudia, "No Longer a Client, Not Yet a Partner: The US–Iranian Alliance In the Johnson Years," *Cold War History*, Vol. 15, No. 4 (2015)

Dobrynin, Anatoly, *In Confidence: Moscow's Ambassador to America's Six Cold War Presidents* (New York: Random House/Times Books, 1995)

Elbaz, Yogev, "Oyev Oyvi Ho Yedidi: Meravut Yisrael Be-Milchemet Ha-Ezrachom Be-Teyman Ke-Chelek Me-Ha-Milchama Ha-Kara beyn Yisrael U-Mitzrayim," *Hayo-Haya*, Vol. 10 (2004)

Ferris, Jesse, *Nasser's Gamble: How Intervention in Yemen Caused the Six-Day War and the Decline of Egyptian Power* (Princeton, NJ: Princeton University Press, 2013)

Finn III, William Taylor, *Toll Gates and Barbicans of Empire: The United States, Great Britain and the Persian Gulf, 1950–1968* (PhD dissertation, University of Virginia, 2002)

Gardner, Lloyd C., *Pay Any Price: Lyndon Johnson and the Wars for Vietnam* (Chicago: Ivan R. Dee, 1997)

Gilboa, Amos, *Mar Modiin, Ahrale Yariv* (Tel Aviv: Yidiot Ahronot, 2013)

Gilboa, Moshe, *Shesh Shanim, Shisha Yamim: Mekoroteyah Vw-Korotyeh Shel Milchemet Sheshet Ha-Yamim* (Tel Aviv: Am Oved, 1969)

Ginor, Isabella and Gideon Remez, *Foxbats over Dimona: The Soviets' Nuclear Gamble in the Six-Day War* (New Haven, CT: Yale University Press, 2007)

Gluska, Ami, *Eshkol, Ten Pkuda!* (Tel Aviv: Maarachot, 2004)

Ha-Meiri, Yehezkel, *Me-Shney Evrey Ha-Rama* (Tel Aviv: Levin-Epstein, 1970)

Hazan, Meir, "Meoravoto shel Iton Haaretz Ba-Maaraha Ha-Politit Be-Tkofat Ha-Hamatna," *Yisrael*, Vol. 10 (2006)

Heydemann, Steven, *Authoritarianism in Syria: Institutions and Social Conflict* (Ithaca, NY: Cornell University Press, 1999)

Hinnebusch, Raymond A., *Authoritarian Power and State Formation in Ba'thist Syria: Army, Party and Peasant* (Boulder, CO: Westview Press, 1990)

Hooks, Gregory and Leonard E. Bloomquist, "The Legacy of World War II for Regional Growth and Decline: The Cumulative Effects of Wartime Investments on U.S. Manufacturing, 1947–1972," *Social Forces*, Vol. 71, No. 2 (December 1992)

Jones, Andrew L., "The Johnson Administration, the Shah of Iran, and the Changing Pattern of U.S.–Iranian Relations, 1965–1967," *Journal of Cold War Studies*, Vol. 9, No. 2 (Spring 2007)

Jones, Matthew, "U.S. Relations with Indonesia, the Kennedy–Johnson Transition, and the Vietnam Connection, 1963–1965," *Diplomatic History*, Vol. 26, No. 2 (Spring 2002)

Kaufman, William I., "Foreign Aid and the Balance-of-Payments Problem: Vietnam and Johnson's Foreign Economic Policies," in Robert A. Devine, ed., *The Johnson Years: Vietnam, the Environment and Science* (Lawrence, KS: University Press of Kansas, 1987)

Lerner, Mitchell, "'A Big Tree of Peace and Justice': The Vice Presidential Travels of Lyndon Johnson," *Diplomatic History*, Vol. 34, No. 2 (April 2010)

Levey, Zach, "United States Arms Policy toward Jordan, 1963–68," *Journal of Contemporary History*, Vol. 41, No. 3 (July 2006)

Little, Douglas, "Choosing Sides: Lyndon Johnson and the Middle East," in Robert A. Divine, ed., *The Johnson Years: LBJ at Home and Abroad* (Lawrence, KS: University Press of Kansas, 1994)

Louis, Wm. Roger and Avi Shlaim, eds, *The 1967 Arab-Israeli War: Origins and Consequences* (Cambridge: Cambridge University Press, 2012)

Mayzal, Matitiahu, *Ha-Maaracha al Ha-Golan, Yuni 1967* (Tel Aviv: Maarachot, 2001)

Melubani, Pesach, *Mi-Tzafon Tipatach Ha-Raa: Tzva Surya, Alilotav Ve-Milchamotav, Mabat Mi-Damesek* (Tel Aviv: Contento de Semrik, 2014)

Michaeli, Rachel, *Hatum al Ha-Shtar: Moshe Zanbar, Kalkelan Be-Olam Politi* (Tel Aviv: Yediot Ahronot, 2010)

Milne, David, *America's Rasputin: Walt Rostow and the Vietnam War* (New York: Hill & Wang, 2008)

Mufti, Malik, *Sovereign Creations, Pan-Arabism and Political Order in Syria and Iraq* (Ithaca, NY: Cornell University Press, 1996)

Nakdimon, Shlomo, *Likrat Shat Ha-Efes* (Tel Aviv: Ramador, 1968)

Nuemark, Aharon, *Mishtar Ha-Neo-Baath Be-Surya: Politika U-Mediniyut, 1966–1970* (PhD dissertation, Bar-Ilan University, 2002)

Oren, Michael B., *Six Days of War: June 1967 and the Making of the Modern Middle East* (New York: Ballantine Books, 2002)

Parker, Richard B., *The Politics of Miscalculation in the Middle East* (Bloomington, IN: Indiana University Press, 1993)

Parsi, Trita, *Treacherous Alliance: The Secret Dealings of Israel, Iran, and the United States* (New Haven, CT: Yale University Press, 2008)

Peters, Anne Mariel and Pete W. Moore, "Beyond Boom and Bust: External Rents, Durable Authoritarianism, and Institutional Adaptation in the Hashemite Kingdom of Jordan," *Studies in Comparative International Development*, Vol. 44, No. 3 (September 2009)

Petersen, Tore T., *The Decline of the Anglo-American Middle East, 1961–1969: A Willing Retreat* (Brighton: Sussex Academic Press, 2006)

Rabinovich, Itamar, *Syria under the Ba'th, 1963–66: The Army–Party Symbiosis* (Jerusalem: Israel Universities Press, 1972)

Rakove, Robert B., *Kennedy, Johnson, and the Nonaligned World* (New York: Cambridge University Press, 2012)

Ro'i, Yaacov and Boris Morozov, eds, *The Soviet Union and the June 1967 Six Day War* (Washington, DC and Stanford, CA: Woodrow Wilson Center Press and Stanford University Press, 2008)

Rubin, Avshalom, *The Limits of the Land: Israel, Jordan, the United States, and the Fate of the West Bank* (PhD dissertation, University of Chicago, 2010)

Segev, Tom, *1967: Ve-Ha-Aretz Shinta Panyeh* (Jerusalem: Keter, 2005)

Shalom, Dani, *Ke-Raam Be-Yom Bahir: Kach Hushmedu Cheylot Ha-Avir Ha-Arviyim Be-Milchemet Sheshet Ha-Yamim* (Rishon Le-Tzion: Ba-Avir, 2002)

Shalom, Zaki, *Beyn Dimona Le-Washington: Hamaavak al Pituh Ha-Optzia Ha-Garinit Shel Yisrael* (Beersheba: Ben Gurion University Press, 2004)

Shalom, Zaki, *Ke-Esh Be-Atzmotav: Ben Gurion Ve-Hamaavak al Dmut Ha-Hmedina, 1963–1967* (Beersheba: Ben Gurion University Press, 2004)

Sohns, Olivia, *Lyndon Baines Johnson and the Arab-Israeli Conflict* (PhD dissertation, University of Cambridge, 2014)

Susser, Asher, ed., *Shisha Yamim, Shloshim Shana: Mabat Chdash al Milchemet Sheshet Ha-Yamim* (Tel Aviv: Am Oved, 1999)

Van Dam, Nikolaos, *The Struggle for Power in Syria: Politics and Society under Asad and the Ba'th Party* (London: I.B. Tauris, 1996)

ILLUSTRATION CREDITS

INDEX